THE LIBRARY OF LITERATURE

UNDER THE GENERAL EDITORSHIP OF
JOHN HENRY RALEIGH
AND IAN WATT

An Anthology of Greek Tragedy

THE LIBRARY OF LITERATURE

AN ANTHOLOGY OF
Greek Tragedy

EDITED BY

ALBERT COOK

AND

EDWIN DOLIN

The Bobbs-Merrill Company, Inc.

INDIANAPOLIS & NEW YORK

The Bobbs-Merrill Company, Inc.
Indianapolis and New York

Designed by Joseph P. Ascherl

Library of Congress Catalog Card Number 75–173227
Printed in the United States of America
First Printing

To our wives Carol and Jan

CONTENTS

EURIPIDES

Preface

The Greek tragedies in this book have been translated with the aim of creating actable plays which are still as much as possible line-by-line versions of the original. This is a difficult undertaking. In the theater the best hope of success may lie with loose adaptation, as in the case of Robert Lowell's *Prometheus*. But close translations have their place also, both for reading and for performance. Four of the plays in this book have already been produced.

Of course, both translations and adaptations are necessary and the more of both the better. Interest in the literature, art and thought of ancient Greece continues to grow. Interpretive works to meet this interest have never been so good as now. But no matter how excellent the interpretive material, in the end the decisive factor in contemporary response to classical culture will be the quality of the translations and adaptations available.

The eight tragedies presented here are intended to be read and performed as plays without recourse to background information. However, for those interested in what is known of the history of classical tragedy, an Introduction provides basic material, while a Bibliography suggests further reading.

All stage directions are suggestions of the translators. No stage directions have survived from the original productions in antiquity.

We wish to express our gratitude to Prof. T. B. L. Webster, who read the archaeology section of the Introduction; to professors Ian Watt and Roger de Laix, who read the whole Introduction; and to several anonymous readers of the translations. Their comments and suggestions have been of great help. None of these readers is responsible for the defects that remain.

THE EDITORS

February 1971

Introduction

I. THE NATURE OF GREEK TRAGEDY

A Greek tragedy could have many plots, themes and moods. Some told of hopeless disasters. Others had happy, even joyful endings. Some were intricate, others simple.

We can follow Aeschylus from grandiose, if conventional, ideas of ambition and disaster in the *Persians,* through the theme of relentless curse in the *Agamemnon,* to the almost reckless power and wit with which he handles theological issues in the *Prometheus Bound.* Sophocles' plays tend to seem alike in having a strong, trapped hero, but the importance of the other characters is so plain and the plot development so various that each play makes an impression of uniqueness. Euripides offers astonishing diversity: romantic adventures on distant shores (*Helen, Iphigeneia in Tauris*); terrifying denunciations of militarism (*The Trojan Women*); exquisite investigations of the young contending with a world beyond their control or even understanding (*Hippolytus, Iphigeneia in Aulis, The Bacchae*).

Amid so much variety of story and treatment, only one common element appears, the assumption by both playwright and public that the characters and their dangerous situations are to be taken seriously.

About the external characteristics of tragedy more generalizations are possible. In form, tragedies were verse plays with music and dance; that is, the spoken scenes were separated from each other by choreographed songs closely connected with the plot. In terms of time and place of performance, tragedy was limited during the fifth century B.C., except for unusual cases, to only one city, Athens, and to the festivals of only one god, Dionysus. The performers consisted normally of a chorus of Athenian citizens and two or three professional actors. Both chorus and actors were disguised by costumes and masks. Performances were competitive and victory was decided by the typical Athenian method of interweaving chance with the judgment of the average man.

Thus, throughout the fifth century, the word "tragedy" referred, on the whole, not to an internationally practiced art form, as do the words "film" and "opera" today, but rather to a local event confined to certain days of the year and to certain conditions of performance. Furthermore, during this century, tragedy, as a well-known component of Athenian state holidays, could hardly be separated in the minds of foreigners and citizens from the idea of Athens as the ruler of an empire possessing hundreds of subject cities, a fleet which controlled the Mediterranean and a treasury of formidable resources.

Tragedy continued for hundreds of years after the fifth century and the defeat of Athenian democracy in the Peloponnesian War. It spread beyond Athens to almost every city in the Greek world, where theaters were constructed as a matter of course. But it was no longer the same. The intricate involvement of chorus with action, already loosened at the end of the fifth century, gradually dissolved altogether. The chorus continued to be present and to sing, but its songs often had such general subject matter that they could be transferred from one play to another and inserted at any point in the action. Meanwhile the once exclusive link between tragedy and the festivals of Dionysus was broken. Tragedy remained associated with Dionysus and his holidays, but it was also performed at festivals of the Muses, Apollo, Hera, and Sarapis.

Thus the form of tragedy long outlived the spirit which had created it during the archaic age and which sustained it during the lives of Aeschylus, Sophocles, and Euripides. To be complete, therefore, a definition of tragedy would have to take account of the centuries-long change in the chorus's function and in the geographic and temporal circumstances of performance. What we normally mean by Greek tragedy is a serious play in verse which has choral portions related to the plot and was composed for performance at an Athenian festival of Dionysus between 500 and 400 B.C.

It should be added that, because only Athenian plays of the fifth century have survived, we associate tragedy with a strong religious sense, whether it appears essentially unbroken as in Aeschylus and Sophocles, or deeply troubled and probing as in Euripides. This religious sense, closely connected with Athenian patriotism and with pan-Hellenic values, probably had more to do with the power of tragedy than we realize.

II. EARLY TRAGEDY

1. ARCHAEOLOGICAL EVIDENCE

In the previous section we were interested in a practical, working definition of Greek tragedy based on relatively uncontroversial data and ignoring completely the question of origin. Now, however, it is time to take up this fascinating problem. Of course, in view of the many times the material has been presented, it might be questioned whether any reasonable purpose is served by doing so again. The answer is that new evidence and argument have appeared which are not yet easily accessible to the non-specialist. This is particularly so in the case of archaeology, and so it is appropriate to begin there.

So far as our purpose is concerned, the first important fact established by archaeology is that there was theater in many areas of Greece before there was tragedy. By theater is meant here a spectacle in which the performers assume identities other than their own. Once it is established that pre-tragic theater existed, there is no avoiding reflection on its potential relevance to subsequent developments. This is especially the case when it is remarked that early sixth century theater and classical tragedy had peculiar features in common: both were performed as part of fertility cult, and both involved transvestite costumes. These traits are distinctive enough to suggest that tragedy was originally one of many costume dances which flourished in archaic cult.

Substantial evidence about these archaic cult performances came to light during excavation of the temple of Artemis Orthia in

Sparta. Found at the pre–550 level were dedicatory masks proving that Greek tradition had been right in reporting that Spartan men had a custom of wearing ugly female masks and women's clothes at religious celebrations. Also found were grinning masks with animal ears and red faces, which lent plausibility to another written tradition, this one about satyr dances near Sparta. Since Artemis, as worshipped at this temple, was a fertility goddess, neither transvestite nor satyr dances in her honor are surprising. Both have widely known connections with fertility.

Excavations elsewhere showed that in the vicinity of Thebes and also in Ionia, across the Aegean Sea, satyr costume performances took place which were contemporary with those in Sparta. In these areas the religious connection was with Dionysus, not Artemis. The Ionian example is particularly interesting. A fragmentary painting dated about 550 shows men carrying a boat-shaped float on which other men ride in satyr costume. There is later evidence of similar floats in Athens. They carried not merely satyrs but Dionysus also—whether represented by a statue or masked man is uncertain.

Although satyr costume such as we found in Sparta, Thebes, and Ionia cannot yet be proved conclusively for Athens in the mid-sixth century, there is every probability that it *was* used there at that time for the same purposes as elsewhere in Greece. Our other category of disguise, transvestite dress such as that in Sparta, has been definitely proved for Athens. Two Athenian vases from about 550 show a chorus of men in women's clothes. The only issue is what circumstances occasioned the wearing of so peculiar a costume. Analogy with Sparta makes a fertility cult performance likely. In Athens the god appropriate to such an activity was Dionysus. And, in fact, a costume detail in one of the pictures indicates that the chorus is imitating nymphs (or perhaps maenads) who were imagined as regularly accompanying that god.

(Dionysus and Artemis are the only Greek divinities normally accompanied by a cortège, which consisted of nymphs in the case of Artemis, and of satyrs, nymphs, maenads and, probably, "fat dancers" in the case of Dionysus. These "fat dancers" were popular subjects of vase painting in Athens and elsewhere between 600 and 550. Their stomachs and buttocks appear to have been enlarged by padding. A mixing bowl for wine commonly figures in the scene, which suggests a connection with Dionysus. Some scholars think they were a variety of the satyr, but their actual Greek name is not known.)

In short, it was common at fertility festivals to imitate the imaginary attendants of the god who was being honored. All the essentials of theater were present, especially the most important of all, impersonation. The significance of impersonation dances for the history of Greek drama is obvious. Masks, transvestite costume, the worship of Dionysus, dancing and singing, which are all found together in early fertility cult, turn up again later in Athenian comedy and tragedy. Now, a line of development from mummery and high-jinks to comedy is easy to imagine. But moving from an erotic and probably drunken atmosphere of this sort to classical tragedy is another matter.

On the other hand, it is important to remember that there could have been two sides to fertility cult performance, just as there were two sides to Dionysus. One side of this god appears in his desire to be surrounded by a happy *komos* of nymphs and satyrs. A different side appears in his affection for another type of follower, the maenad. This word means "crazy" in the sense of "raving" and refers to actual or imagined women, who in a state of *ecstacy* (being beside oneself, as in a trance) go into the mountains (*oreibasia*), wear animal skins, carry sticks topped with leaves (*thyrsoi*), dance, capture wild animals, tear them limb from limb (*sparagmos*) and eat them raw (*omophagia*). The extent to which this rite occurred in Greece is disputed, but maenadism existed, although it appears to have taken place as a rule under official supervision with little opportunity for the spontaneous emotions depicted by vase painting, myths, and such plays as Euripides' *Bacchae*.

There is no doubt that maenads make quite a different impression from the dancers we considered earlier. The latter were men who, costumed as nymphs or satyrs, danced in an alcoholic, erotic, and relaxed atmosphere, as implied by the word *komos*. But maenads were women who danced without masks in a non-erotic, non-alcoholic atmosphere centered on the *sparagmos,* whether it was actually performed or only remembered.

Is it possible that the young men who loved to imitate the male and female members of Dionysus' *komos* also imitated that contrasting Dionysian type, the maenad? There is reason to think so.

First, we have seen that dressing and dancing as a woman was a well-established custom in Athens as in Sparta, so that adoption of the maenad costume would merely have extended a mode of impersonation already in use.

Second, indications are that such a costume was actually adopted for Dionysian performances in Athens in the 530s. The evidence for this is a change in the content of vase paintings which take Dionysian themes as subject matter. Between 600 and the 530s, Athenian paintings show us the feminine members of Dionysus' *komos* as sexual and drinking companions of the satyrs. Often the occasion for their unrestrained celebrations is a happy event in Dionysus' career: for instance, his marriage with Ariadne or his success in bringing Hephaistos back to Olympus with the help of wine. Now, there is little reason to doubt, in spite of skepticism, that paintings of the Dionysian *komos* reflect in an idealizing manner the tone and scenario of cult theater where masked and costumed young men delighted in the vigorous dancing required to represent the wild force of the satyrs and the divine energy of their female companions. Therefore when maenads, with their leaf-topped staffs, limb-torn animals, and violent resistance to sexual approaches from the satyrs, suddenly appear in Dionysian paintings, it is reasonable to assume that a new type of performance has been devised, one in which the activities of "crazed women" are imitated by the men who acted in fertility cult performances. The atmosphere of maenad imitations would, of course, have been quite different from that of the *komos*. The myths associated with maenads did not relate such joyous events as Dionysus' marriage or his diplomatic success with the help of wine. On the contrary, the maenad myths told how legendary kings, like Pentheus and Lycurgus, tried to repress maenads along with their god and, after initial success, were punished. In Pentheus' case, the punishment was *sparagmos*.

If the portrayal of maenads and their stories during the 530s was a decisive step in the development of tragedy, then traces of the event can be seen in the Athenian tradition that this was the decade when tragic drama first received official recognition. It was also the

time when Thespis was said to have produced a *Pentheus,* and
when the Pentheus myth began to be a subject of vase painting.
Once maenads became a popular part of the fertility cult spectacle
in Athens, it would not be surprising if the performers sought to
extend their range in this emotional sphere by portraying other
conflicts between legendary heroes and the gods. There were stories
of this type in abundance. In fact, the first two preserved plays of
Aeschylus, the *Persians* and the *Seven Against Thebes,* and the
first preserved play of Sophocles, the *Ajax,* have this type of plot
in which a hero encounters the enmity of the gods and suffers.

Thus, a line of impersonations can be posited which extends
from satyrs, nymphs, fat dancers, Dionysus, Ariadne, and Hephaistos, through maenads, Pentheus, and Lycurgus, to Xerxes in
the *Persians* and Eteocles in the *Seven Against Thebes,* all within
the context of cult performances in honor of Dionysus.

It would be possible to make a more confident judgment about
the origin of tragedy if only we were better informed about the
decades extending from 530 to the production in 472 of our first
preserved tragedy, the *Persians.* We do know that only one actor
was used until Aeschylus added a second sometime after 500. We
also have a few names, such as Choirilus, Pratinas and Phrynichus,
and the subjects of some of their plays. The impression they make
is that the tone and style of tragedy were essentially established by
the 490s. But before that time we are forced back to masks, pictures and a few traditions.

The preceding outline of how tragedy could have been born is
one approach among several. However, it has advantages. First, it
makes maximum use of archaeological data, which, it needs to be
emphasized, is the only reliable evidence available which was contemporary with the events. Second, this archaeologically based outline, although more detailed, is in harmony with Aristotle's history
of tragedy in the *Poetics,* the only ancient treatment of the subject
of any extent which is still extant.

2. WRITTEN EVIDENCE

The Greeks were as curious as our own age about the origin of
tragedy and wrote many books bearing on the subject. Unfortu-

nately, only a few fragments and a brief treatment in Aristotle's *Poetics* have survived. What to make of this small amount of evidence frankly baffles scholars, although they have done their best to build from it—much like paleontologists from a dinosaur bone—a satisfying and impressive structure. We will look briefly at their results, but our first requirement is a summary of the ancient evidence. It can be divided into three groups, pro-Dorian, pro-Athenian, and Aristotelian.

Our knowledge of the pro-Dorian view is based on a passage in Herodotus, who wrote during the second half of the fifth century. Herodotus remarks, while discussing another issue, that "tragic choruses" had been known in the partly Dorian city of Sicyon in the Peloponnesus shortly after 600. These choruses, according to Herodotus, had at one time been performed in honor of a "hero" (meaning a legendary figure whose tomb received public honors), but were later transferred to Dionysus. There are a few other references to Sicyon, as well as to another Dorian city in the Peloponnesus, Corinth, as the original site of tragedy, but they are so late—generally Byzantine—and so lacking in detail that one hardly knows what to do with them. We can be certain, at any rate, from a remark in Aristotle, that some Dorians, probably from Sicyon and Corinth, did claim to have invented tragedy, and this is substantially all that can be said with confidence about the ancient Dorian theory of the origin of tragedy.

We have more information about the pro-Athenian view, which is first discernible in some detail in an inscription of about 265 B.C., although it must have been in existence for a long time before then. (There is a complex dispute about this among scholars.) The inscription says that the poet Thespis first produced a play at the festival of Dionysus in Athens in the 530s and that a *tragos* (male goat) was connected with the performance, probably as a prize. Later, during the third century, two poems state quite plainly that Thespis invented tragedy for his fellow villagers and that tragedy was at the beginning "games in the country woods and celebrations" (*paignia* and *komoi*). Another third-century poem may be relevant. It referred to the Attic village of Icaria as the place where "first they danced around the *tragos*," which suggests that the author of the poem thought *tragoidia* originated in Icaria, a village sometimes called the home of Thespis.

The pro-Athenian theory to be inferred from the preceding citations is that *tragoidia* received this name because it was performed in competition for a goat prize (or perhaps in connection with a goat sacrifice which followed the prize); secondly, that Thespis was the first significant producer of this goat-song performance; and, thirdly, that his creative activity occurred in the Athenian countryside before being transferred to the city itself.

Unfortunately, although we have many more details of this view than of the pro-Dorian, we lack a piece of information crucial for making its outline understandable. How did this view explain tragedy's remarkable transition from "games in the country woods and celebrations" to the the the seriousness of classical tragedy?

We turn now to the Aristotelian account, which is known almost exclusively from one page in the *Poetics* written during the third quarter of the fourth century. The *Poetics* statements about early tragedy can be summarized as follows: tragedy began as a form of dithyramb and went through a "satyric" phase, when it was oriented toward the dance and its language was humorous or amusing; it became serious only late in its development; only one actor was available until Aeschylus introduced a second.

The first question usually asked about this account is whether, in Aristotle's mind, the dithyrambic and satyric phases coincided. They probably did. Two archaic references to the dithyramb indicate that it was accompanied by intoxication, which fits satyrs well. Moreover, a classical vase painting has been found which shows aging satyrs singing at a festival where the only choral performance we know of was the dithyramb. This suggests that satyr costume and dithyramb were compatible and perhaps an old custom.

The second question which arises from Aristotle's account concerns the mysterious and crucial transition from satyresque to serious. How did he explain so basic a change? Unfortunately, we do not know, so that both the Aristotelian and pro-Athenian theories, as they now exist, leave us ignorant and puzzled just when we expect them to be most informative.

There is one further piece of information about Aristotle's view which should be included because of its usefulness in most attempts to reconstruct a plausible outline of early tragedy. An orator of the fourth century A.D., citing Aristotle as authority, says that the tragic chorus originally sang to the gods by itself, but then Thespis invented prologues and speeches. If this is an authentic quotation from a lost work of Aristotle, we can fill in part of the pre-Aeschylean gap in the *Poetics* with at least one name, Thespis, and an additional event, the invention of the first speaking actor.

When we turn from the ancient written evidence to modern theories, we find that, on the whole, they follow one or the other of the ancient views and thus fall into roughly the same three categories. For example, the Dorian view, based on tragic choruses in a hero cult at Sicyon, can be taken as a typical case of how serious drama may have developed. The chorus and perhaps an actor or two lamented the hero at his tomb and, according to this hypothesis, put on a play representing his sufferings; this practice was then presumably absorbed by Dionysian cult and grew in Attica into tragic drama. This would account well enough for the role of heroic legend in classical tragedy; on the other hand, there is little or no supporting evidence, while such testimony as does exist about the origin of tragedy apparently points in a different direction.

Other modern scholars are attracted by the pro-Athenian account and the idea of tragedy's having begun as rudimentary theater in Attica with Thespis as a leading personality. Some scholars of this persuasion envisage a solemn, even frightening, animal sacrifice as the occasion for a masked play. The notable role of sacrificial death in classical tragedy would go back to this origin. There are also pro-Athenian scholars who argue for the opposite, a secular non-religious origin. They suggest that brilliant, creative artists thought of the idea of putting epic poetry, such as the *Iliad,* into dramatic form, with the emphasis on the actor from the beginning, while the chorus was only secondary. Other scholars accept the tradition of a simple, rural theater in the Attic countryside, which gradually grew more sophisticated, particularly with the help of Dorian music.

Those moderns who follow the third of the ancient theories, Aristotle's, have the advantage of the more impressive evidence in quantity, and perhaps, although this point is arguable, in quality also. On the other hand, they face the problem of how a satyr kind of performance could have transformed itself into serious classical tragedy. The most common explanation is to suppose that, somehow, there was a gradual expansion of the scope of performance until one powerful personality, perhaps Aeschylus, firmly established the heroic legends, such as those about Oedipus or Herakles, as the only proper subject matter of tragedy.

In conclusion, mention must be made of another type of modern theory which is only loosely connected with any of the ancient evidence. Centered on the idea of a "year god" (*eniautos daimon*) or "dying god," it suggests that tragedy grew from a ritual which represented the sufferings and triumph of Dionysus as a symbol of the cycle of seasons from decline and death in winter to rebirth in spring. This view has wide popularity except among specialists, who object to the lack of ancient evidence and the difficulty of finding the proposed ritual scheme in the surviving plays. But the "dying god" idea is not without some scholarly supporters and may be due for a renewal of its own, now that the name "Dionysus" has been found on Mycenaean inscriptions and a similarity has been observed between dancing women in Minoan-Mycenaean art and the maenads of classical Greece. It could be that a Minoan-Mycenaean ritual concerning Dionysus as a year god survived into the archaic age in a modified form.

One problem which all the modern theories have to face is the meaning of the word "tragedy." Aristotle says nothing about it at all. The Athenian-Thespis view seems to have assumed, as we noticed, that the word means "song for a goat prize," and this interpretation, or the similar "song at a goat sacrifice," is the most likely to be correct in terms of Greek linguistics. But there was a minority view in antiquity which suggested that *tragoidia* meant "song of goats" in the sense "song of men costumed as goats." This interpretation has been accepted by many modern scholars, in particular by a group who have adopted the Aristotelian approach. They assume that tragedy began as a costume chorus of goat singers in the Peloponnesus, where Pan, the goat god, had his home. This type of chorus was supposedly then borrowed by the Athenians, who kept the Peloponnesian name, but changed the costume to the satyr type with which they were familiar. Thus, it is assumed, tragedy began as a goat chorus but was performed in Athens by a satyr chorus until it became serious.

The only new light which we may reasonably expect on these questions is from archaeology. Every so often a vase or other object turns up which adds to or modifies our picture of choral and theater performances in the archaic period. We have seen in the section on archaeology something of what this picture is like at the moment. It indicates that there was no lack of theater in Greece at the time tragedy came into being. It also indicates a way in which a tragic drama could have developed in the cult of Dionysus—a progression from satyrs and nymphs through maenads and Pentheus to plays about legendary heroes in danger. This amplification of the Aristotelian view can be used as a working hypothesis without following those modern pro-Aristotelians who interpret tragedy as a "song of men in goat costume" and say it was borrowed from the Peloponnesus by Athenians. The most probable meaning of *tragoidia* fits perfectly well into the Aristotelian scheme, if we suppose that a fertility cult chorus received its name from the male goat which was sacrificed to Dionysus after being awarded to the singers as a prize. This type of sacrifice and chorus probably occurred all over Greece, so that many areas, including Sicyon and Corinth, could have claimed the origin of goat-song. On the other hand, the Athenians, having moved farthest from the original cult dances, could claim that what tragedy finally became was theirs only.

III. TRAGEDY IN THE CLASSIC PERIOD

1. THE DRAMATIC FESTIVALS

Athenian tragedies were performed during several holiday periods in honor of the god Dionysus. The chief Dionysiac holiday during which tragedy was performed was called "the Dionysia in the City" or "the Great Dionysia." This religious festival took place in the early spring. It was an important event and lasted about five days. Ordinary business was suspended and many officials and private citizens from other cities were in Athens for the occasion. Before the festival began, a statue of Dionysus, kept in an old temple near the theater, was taken outside the city to another temple in an olive grove called the Academy. On one of the evenings before the festival, the statue was brought to the theater in procession, and kept there during the performances. The main participants in the procession were the young men of the city, who sang songs in honor of the god and carried torches.

a. The Procession

The first day of the festival began with an elaborate procession (*pompē*) culminating in a sacrifice (*thysia*). One of the animals killed was a bull offered by the young men mentioned above. Probably first in the procession was an unmarried girl of prominent family who carried a golden basket of items to be offered in the sacrifice. Many other persons, both men and women, participated officially, all of them dressed as splendidly as possible.

One aspect of the Dionysia procession was the display of a representation of the phallus. Part of the evidence for this custom is a passage in a play of Aristophanes which describes the type of procession occurring during the "Rural Dionysia," a festival like the City Dionysia, but held in midwinter in the country districts of Attica. In the play the chief character tells his daughter to walk ahead and carry a special basket for the occasion. Next come two slaves whom he orders to hold the image of the phallus upright. Finally comes the head of the family, who sings and tells his wife to watch from the roof.

Other evidence for the presence of the phallus in the Dionysia procession is a mid-fifth century inscription indicating that the colonies of Athens sent phalli to the Great Dionysia as a mark of respect to their founding city. An idea of the normality of this aspect of Greek religious life is given by a remark of Heraclitus, who lived in Ionia about 500: "If it were not Dionysus in whose

honor they were marching in procession and singing the song for
the phallus, what they were doing would be disgraceful."

b. *Dithyramb*

It is uncertain when the competition took place among the choruses singing dithyrambs. Each of the ten Attic tribes (*phylai*)
probably entered two choruses of fifty members each, one of boys
and one of men, making a total of 1,000 persons. The competition
may have been distributed over two different days, perhaps one
day for men and one for boys.

As was also customary with tragedy and comedy, the expense
for the equipment and training of each chorus was undertaken by
a wealthy citizen called the *chorēgus*. This expense could be large.
In one example from the fifth century, a *chorēgus* spent 2,000
drachmas for a dithyrambic men's chorus and 1,500 for a boys'
chorus. What these sums mean in our terms can be calculated by
the fact that a drachma was an ordinary day's wage in ancient
Athens.

The site of the dithyrambic competition is uncertain. It may
have been the theater of Dionysus. It may have been the *agora*
(the city square or marketplace).

c. *Comedy*

During normal times there were five comedies, each of them by
a different author. However, during part of the Peloponnesian
War (431–405), only three comedies were offered. It is uncertain
when the comic performances were given. When there were only
three comedies, one was probably performed on the afternoons of
days assigned to tragedy. When there were five comedies, two may
have been presented on separate days in combination with groups
of dithyrambs, while each of the three remaining comedies followed a set of tragedies.

Attic comedy of the fifth century was a unique sort of theater.
It was similar to tragedy in some ways, alternation of spoken dialogue with choral songs and use of the same basic meters. But it
differed from tragedy in important respects. The plots seem to
have been loose, more like an idea on which to string a set of

situations. And the situations, unlike an episode in the usually stricter plots of tragedy, allowed the use of numerous minor characters who came and went in quick succession. Comedy's language was full of words not used in polite conversation and of mockery of the solemn diction of tragedy. The central character was usually an average man of contemporary times, quite different from tragedy's heroes of the distant past. The chorus consisted of twenty-four *choreutae,* as contrasted with tragedy's earlier twelve and later fifteen. The costumes of the comic chorus varied greatly, ranging from representations of animals and birds to old men and women. The actors, on the other hand, seem to have had a standard costume with padding around the midriff and a leather phallus.

d. *Tragedy*

Tragedy occupied three days of the festival. Each poet whose plays had been accepted by the city administration had a day to himself and presented three tragedies and one satyr-play. The playwright was called *poietes* ("maker"), also *didaskalos* ("teacher"). The name *didaskalos* reflects his manifold function. He composed the plot, dialogue, and words for the songs. He wrote the music, devised the dance steps, and directed the production. In addition, during the early years of the fifth century, the *didaskalos* acted the chief role of the play himself. Today, in a musical comedy (which, structurally, is our closest art form to Attic tragedy), these functions are carried out by diverse individuals: the writers of the "book," dialogue, lyrics, music, and musical arrangement; the producer; the choreographer; and the director.

Greek playwrights had the help of a scene painter, although the exact nature of their sets is unclear. In the early fifth century scene painting must have been elementary. Toward midcentury, however, drawing which gave the effect of perspective was introduced. But the outdoor character of Greek theaters makes it unlikely that anything similar to a realistic set was attempted.

Further technical help for the playwright came from musicians and maskmakers. The accompaniment for the sung portions of tragedy was chiefly provided by what is customarily referred to as the flutist, *aulētēs* in Greek. (The word "flute" is misleading, because the instrument was a reed.) The *aulētēs* could be important to success in all three festival performances—dithyramb, comedy, and tragedy. Sometimes a *kitharistēs* was needed. He played a stringed instrument, the *kithara.*

The maskmakers had much to do before a dramatic festival, since all members of the cast wore masks. The evidence available from vase paintings suggests that fifth century masks did not present the grotesque, strained expression and the high-piled triangle of hair in front which are familiar to us from tragic masks of the Roman era. Attic masks of the classical period were moderately naturalistic, although stylized in some ways. For instance, it is probable that masks representing women were white, contrasting with a darker shade used for male masks.

Besides masks, chorus and actors wore clothing expressive of their roles. We know little about this, but some probabilities are suggested by vase paintings. A long, elaborately embroidered gown with sleeves down to the wrists, something quite different from ordinary Greek clothing, was used for some roles. This gown presumably indicated wealth and high position. A great variety of other costumes is probable. As to footgear, neither the actors nor the chorus wore boots with thick soles. Boots of this type came into use at some time after the classical period. The vase paintings suggest that during the classical age soft boots without thick soles, but with tops reaching halfway up the calf, were worn for some parts, particularly female ones.

There was originally one actor. Aeschylus is said to have added the second and Sophocles the third. In any event, three actors seem to have been standard from about 460 onward. (A fourth actor might have been necessary for some plays.) Of course, each actor normally played several roles in the same play.

The use of the terms *protagonist, deuteragonist,* and *tritagonist* for the first, second, and third actors respectively is current in discussion of Greek theater. These terms, meaning "first competitor," "second competitor," "third competitor," were probably used in Athens to describe actors as well as other types of contestants, but the ordinary word in Greek for actor was *hypokritēs.* Precisely why this word, which meant "answerer" or "interpreter," came to acquire the almost exclusive meaning "actor" is not clear. The *hypokritai* were professionals and consequently different from members of the chorus, who were ordinary Athenian citizens or, perhaps sometimes, resident aliens called metics who were an important part of Athenian society.

Although some argument can be made for the existence of an original tragic chorus of fifty, the weight of the evidence suggests that the number was twelve during the first part of the fifth century and then was raised to fifteen. The satyr plays apparently had only twelve *choreutae* throughout. One group of twelve or fifteen *choreutae* may have acted through the sequence consisting of three tragedies and one satyr play which was given at each day's presentation.

The poet could thus rely on experienced professionals for his main roles. What latitude he enjoyed in selecting the chorus of amateur singers and dancers, we cannot say, but he knew he would be able to rehearse the twelve or fifteen *choreutae* over a period of time. The musicians (*aulētēs* and *kitharistēs*) were professionals. The Athenian state paid a salary to the chief actor and probably to the other actors and professionals as well, including the poet. But for the expense of the chorus and costumes, the playwright depended on the *chorēgus,* who was officially appointed from a list of wealthy citizens, one *chorēgus* to each *didaskalos.* Besides the cost of costumes, which was considerable in a time when clothing was much more expensive than today, production costs included a room for the chorus to practice in and, apparently, all or a portion of their living expenses during the rehearsal period. A *chorēgus* might spend as much as 3,000 drachmas to produce a set of three tragedies and a satyr play.

Prizes for the various competitions have been mentioned. How was it decided who would get them? Certain references suggest the following procedure. A list of judges was drawn up by each Athenian tribe. Before the performances began, a group of ten judges, one from each tribe, was chosen by lot from these lists. After the performances the verdicts of the ten judges were placed in a jar and five were drawn by lot. The prizes were awarded on the basis of the five verdicts actually drawn. The remaining five did not count.

e. *Aesthetic Aspects of Tragedy*

The plots of tragedy were almost all taken from the large body of legend surrounding certain princely families of the distant past. These legends (*mythoi*) were accepted as basically factual by nearly everybody, although it was understood that details of the stories could vary widely. In fact, no myth had a fixed form. As a consequence, the playwrights had wide latitude in plot development. Moreover, they were quite willing to invent variations of their own, when convenient.

The practice of retelling legends about the heroes had been developed in choral poetry to a point of narrative sophistication. The dithyrambs sung during the Dionysia are an example of this choral narrative. Tragedy, while part of the broad tradition of narrative music, differed from it in that, instead of narrating the story from start to finish as the dithyramb singers did, the chorus in a tragedy pretended to be caught in a dangerous crisis whose outcome they did not know. Consequently their choral songs, no longer having the function of narrating the story, assumed other forms, such as descriptions of the present state of affairs, prayers to the gods, suggestions to another character, or reflective efforts to understand and grapple with the crisis at hand by means of maxims embodying the stored experience and wisdom of the people. Of course, the chorus could narrate some relevant event of the past, as in the description of the sacrifice of Iphigeneia in the *Agamemnon*. And they might also narrate a myth as an exemplary event useful for understanding the present, but narrative was no longer their main subject.

Conventional terms for various choral songs are mentioned as early as Aristotle's *Poetics:*

parodos ("going by" or "going in") first song of the chorus
exodos ("going out") last song of the chorus
stasimon ("stationary thing") any song between the *parodos* and *exodos* sung by the chorus alone

kommos ("beating" of head in lamentation) duet between the
   chorus and an actor with mournful theme
monody ("song of one") a song by one actor alone

Most choral songs were strophic (one stanza composed on the
same metrical pattern as a following stanza). Songs not composed
with strophic responses were called *astropha*. The metrical patterns involved are fairly well understood, but do not provide a
sure guide as to the nature of the dance movements and musical
accompaniment. In fact, just what a choral performance looked
and sounded like has been lost.

The delight in formal order evident in these strophic songs appears also in the spoken sections (*episodes*) which were dominated
by the actors. For example, some dialogue was composed of alter-
nating one-line or two-line units (*stichomythia*). Another type
of dialogue, used to indicate excitement, involved a change of
speaker in midline (*antilabē*). The long, uninterrupted speech,
called *rhesis,* was also carefully constructed to satisfy the Greek
love of formal oratory. These speeches were not felt to be long-
winded, awkward ways to communicate offstage events that would
have been better presented to the audience as scenes in themselves.
On the contrary, the *rhesis* was a cherished piece of bravura performance, savored in every detail by an audience quite content
with the "artificial" conventions of its theater.

The obvious sharp differentiation of one part of the play from
the other was emphasized by linguistic peculiarities. In the choral
parts many words were pronounced in the manner of the Dorians,
whose dialect differed markedly from that of the Athenians. (Use
of Dorian pronunciation and forms was customary in choral music,
whether dramatic or not.) On the other hand, in the spoken parts,
the language was close to, but not identical with, colloquial Attic.

Overall the language of tragedy shows two characteristics: first,
pervasive echoes of the old epic language used by Homer and
Hesiod; second, a vocabulary of amazing richness. With respect
to richness of language, Attic tragedy is very close to Shakespeare
and the whole Elizabethan cultural atmosphere, while it is corre-
spondingly far from the taste of Racine and French classicism.

Unfortunately, the variety and richness of language is almost impossible to retain in translation.

f. *Satyr Play*

Each day's performance of three tragedies was normally concluded by a satyr play (*satyroi*) by the same poet. These were relaxed, humorous parodies of tragic situations and style, shorter than a tragedy in length and with a chorus of men dressed as satyrs. Their mask was snub-nosed, with animal ears and a beard. The rest of the costume consisted of a pair of tights equipped with a phallus and horsetail, as well as whatever other clothing the circumstances called for. Surviving plays and fragments show that the men of the chorus were referred to as "beasts," or "wild animals." But this did not mean they were fierce and savage like Homeric lions. Rather, their part called for them to be cowardly, lazy, and treacherous, ever ready to get drunk, unrestrainedly erotic, and indifferent to the ordinary values of Greek society. Usually they were led by an older, white-haired satyr called Silēnos or Papposilēnos.

Into this anarchic, hedonistic atmosphere the playwrights brought conventional epic heroes such as Herakles or Odysseus and then exploited the possibilities for comic contrast and parody. The plots were often adapted from the same legends used in the day's tragedies. In form, the satyr play was like a tragedy: scenes of dialogue alternated with choral song and dance. The number of *choreutae* was apparently twelve, with two actors. Occasionally, instead of a *satyroi,* the day's performance concluded with a short, light tragedy with a happy ending.

g. *Tetralogy, Trilogy*

A series of three tragedies and satyr play is sometimes called a "tetralogy" and three tragedies without a satyr play a "trilogy." These terms are convenient, but may be misleading, if they are taken to mean that a trilogy or tetralogy always had a common subject matter throughout. In fact, the connected trilogy or tetralogy with all three or four plays on the same subject was the exception, not the rule. Very few closely connected trilogies were written, except by Aeschylus (whose *Oresteia* is the only surviving example of the type). Aeschylus himself did not always use this form. In general, a Greek tragedy was a separate, independent, and rather short play, having little or no connection in subject matter with the other plays performed together with it on the one day's bill.

h. *Dramatic Festivals Other than the City Dionysia*

So far this discussion has been centered on the City Dionysia, because this is the most important festival for the history of tragedy. But tragedies and comedies were also presented at two other Attic festivals of Dionysus called the Lenaea and the Rural Dionysia.

The Lenaea occurred two months before the City Dionysia in a month corresponding to January/February. Little is known about the details of this festival, but something can be said about the dramatic part of it. Normally only two tragic poets competed, each with two tragedies and no satyr play. There were five comedies, the same number as at the City Dionysia. (During part of the Peloponnesian War the number was reduced to three, as at the City Dionysia.) A prize was awarded to the best tragic actor and to the best comic actor from the time the dramatic competition was established on official lines, about 442 for comedy and during the 430s for tragedy. Tragedies and comedies were evidently presented every year at the Lenaea until after 200 B.C. In early days the site of the performance was probably the *agora;* a change to the Theater of Dionysus is likely, although at what date the change occurred is not clear.

As the figures for the numbers of plays suggest (four tragedies and five comedies as opposed to the City Dionysia's nine tragedies, three satyr plays, and five comedies), the Lenaea was more significant for comedy than for tragedy. Aristophanes, the famous comic poet, often presented plays at the Lenaea, whereas the famous tragic poets seem rarely to have entered this festival.

The Rural Dionysia was an ancient festival celebrated locally in the towns, small and large, outside Athens in the Attic peninsula. Its date seems generally to have been December. Theaters of some sort existed in the rural towns, although only a few remains have been found. We know from literature that a large theater existed in the port of Athens, the Peiraeus, and that this town, large enough to have been a polis by itself, celebrated the Rural Dionysia on a scale comparable to the City Dionysia or the Lenaea.

How many tragedies and comedies were offered at the various Rural Dionysia, and how often they were repetitions of plays which had already been presented at the City Dionysia or Lenaea, is not known. But there is evidence that these townships were serious about their local festivals. Pride in local drama is shown by inscriptions and other evidence from Eleusis, Salamis, Icaria, Aixone, and Collutus, besides the Peiraeus.

The preceding survey of the three dramatic festivals has been designed to show how deeply rooted in Attic life of the fifth century was the performance and experience of tragedy, as well as of music and dance in general. Each year choruses of amateurs acted in at least thirteen tragedies, three satyr plays, and ten comedies at the City Dionysia and Lenaea alone; other choruses were active in the Attic countryside. It is plain that the Athenians found intense satisfaction in the execution of dramatic and lyric works; that many, if not most, had personally participated in such performances; and that they were experienced judges. What we read when we take up a Greek play is not something composed for the few, but popular art. It is sometimes easy, sometimes hard, to understand why tragedy had this appeal. But we can be reasonably sure that it did, that it had an intense hold on the mind and emotions of an audience which was composed, in effect, of the whole people gathered for a national celebration.

2. The Theater of Dionysus in Athens

Precision about the theater in which the plays of Aeschylus, Sophocles, and Euripides were produced is impossible, because almost nothing of what exists today in the theater area goes back to the fifth century. But the following details are probable.

The orchestra was sixty-six feet in diameter and apparently circular; its surface may have been hard-packed dirt or clay; a stone altar presumably stood in the center.

On the downhill side of the orchestra, away from the spectators, was space for a temporary building apparently constructed of wood for each year's performance. This building, the *skēnē* ("shelter"), had a large central door and perhaps two side doors as well. The roof was firm enough to support several actors and properties.

The *skēnē* was not a stage in our sense of the word, but a wooden building whose interior could serve as an "offstage" area and dressing room, while one of its walls functioned as a backdrop for proceedings in the orchestra. This wall, the one facing the audience, could be decorated to represent a palace, a cliff, or any scene desired. It also acted as a sounding board of apparently extraordinary efficiency.

During the classical period, the chorus and actors probably performed on the same level, that of the orchestra. But it is possible that a series of two or three wide steps, on which the actors could stand, led from the orchestra level up to a low platform running along the *skēnē* wall. A stage of the high platform type, sharply differentiated from the orchestra, did not come into existence until long after the classical period of Aeschylus, Sophocles, and Euripides. When a high stage of this type was built in Athens, it was probably called a *logeion*.

The spectators (*theatai*) sat on wooden benches on the hillside overlooking and surrounding the orchestra in a half circle. The word *theatron* was used for both the seating area and the entire theater complex, including orchestra and *skēnē*.

Near the middle of the fifth century, a rebuilding of the theater was begun. This work, associated by archaeologists with the statesman Pericles, was not completed until after he died in 429. A rectangular stone foundation was laid where it would be useful in setting up the wooden *skēnē* building. Behind the *skēnē* area a large stone building, more than 200 feet long, was constructed. This building and the *skēnē* area were connected by a short flight of steps, apparently to facilitate passage between the two during performances. Actors could dress and wait in the long building and then make their appearance before the audience either by going up the flight of steps into the *skēnē* and out through the central doors or by walking around the building and coming in through the *parodos*.

Toward the end of the fourth century, the Athenians rebuilt the whole theater in stone. This new theater is associated with Lycurgus, a statesman of the time. The seating capacity of the Lycurgan theater has been estimated at between 14,000 and 17,000. The lower figure is more likely for the theater of the classical period.

At least two mechanical devices for special effects may have been used in the fifth century. One, the *eccyclēma,* seems to have been used to roll out actors and stage properties into view of the spectators. Another device, the crane (*geranos*), seems required in order to handle the appearance of heroes and gods flying through the air.

3. ARISTOTLE'S ANALYSIS OF TRAGEDY IN THE *Poetics*

In the *Poetics* Aristotle attempts to be as specific as possible about what differentiates the best tragedy from the rest. First, he says, the outstanding tragedy must have a tight plot. Each event should follow from the other in a probable or necessary manner and there should be no superfluous incidents. Second, the dramatic situation should go through a transformation into the opposite of what it had been. This transformation should, if possible, be connected with a discovery by one or more of the characters about the true identity of one or more of the other characters in the play. Discovery can also consist of the realization that someone has or has not actually carried out a crucial act, or else in the identification of a significant object.

An example, given by Aristotle, of the change of a dramatic situation into its opposite (*peripeteia*) accompanied by discovery of identity (*anagnōrisis*) is provided by Euripides' *Iphigeneia in Tauris*. Orestes has come to the Crimea by divine command. Captured by the inhabitants, he is about to be sacrificed according to custom by the priestess in charge, who happens to be his sister. The two have been separated since childhood and do not recognize each other until, by a probable but surprising development, Orestes comes to understand that the priestess is his sister Iphigeneia. The situation, which seemed headed toward inevitable disaster, is transformed into its opposite. Brother and sister unite and escape.

Plots with happy endings, such as the *Iphigeneia in Tauris,* are specifically praised by Aristotle. But he is just as definite in recommending tragedies with unhappy endings. In this case, too, the plot must be tight and include a change of situation into its opposite accompanied by a recognition. Aristotle also recommends, in a famous passage, that the unhappy situation be the result of a serious mistake (*hamartia*), a misunderstanding of the facts, on the part of one or more of the chief characters. An example, which Aristotle cites, of a tragedy with unhappy ending combining all three features, *peripeteia, anagnōrisis* and *hamartia,* is Sophocles' *Oedipus the King.* Oedipus, before the opening of the play, had, without knowing who they were, killed his father and married his mother (*hamartia*). During the play he learns the identity of the man he killed and the woman he married (*anagnōrisis*), and, as a consequence, both his own situation and that of his family changes from one of great good fortune into the opposite (*peripeteia*).

Aristotle further claims that the tragic effect is best realized when there is surprise, when events occur contrary to expectation, while continuing to be either probable or necessary. The question arises: contrary to whose expectation, that of the characters in the play or that of the audience? The audience at *Oedipus the King* could hardly have been surprised when Oedipus discovered he was an incestuous parricide. The story was well known. Even the moment when the revelation is made is unlikely to have been unexpected, so that in this play the *peripeteia* occurs contrary to the expectation of the characters, but not that of the audience. On the other hand, there are some scenes in extant tragedy which probably surprised the audience—for instance, the return of the bow to Philoctetes in the Sophoclean play of that name. Still, the majority of tragedies known to us contain very few surprises for the spectators, but many indeed for the characters, and this is what Aristotle most probably had in mind when he advocated the occurrence of events contrary to expectation. The audience knows the priestess is Iphigeneia, but Orestes is astonished when he learns her identity. The same applies to *Oedipus the King.* Jocasta, the first to understand what is happening, is so overwhelmed that she leaves the stage. Everything has turned out contrary to her expectation. But the audience has known all the relationships from the beginning.

Besides "complex" tragedies which have both *peripeteia* and *anagnōrisis,* or at least one of the two, Aristotle's theory also recognizes "simple" tragedy, Aeschylus' *Prometheus* or Sophocles' *Ajax,* for example, which have neither discovery of identity nor complete reversal of Fortune. Aristotle granted that simple tragedies could be effective, if their plots followed a probable or necessary course of events, but he believed they were not so dramatically satisfying as plays with *peripeteia* and *anagnōrisis.*

We have been considering the aspect of tragedy Aristotle stressed most, the plot, and we have described two examples of what are, from his point of view, ideal examples of plotting, *Oedipus the King* and *Iphigeneia in Tauris.* We might now ask why Aristotle placed so high a value on tragedy's having tight, naturalistic, plotting, as well as *hamartia, anagnōrisis* and *peripeteia.*

His demand for naturalistic plots was not limited to tragedy. It was part of a theory covering all fiction. According to him the virtue of imagination, as opposed to history, is that imagined events can be shaped by the mind in such a way as to make the structure of their mutual dependence clear and understandable, whereas what has actually happened is too multifarious and diffuse to be grasped and understood as a unified whole. Fiction, Aristotle says, because it exhibits a logical structure, is more "scientific" and serious than history. ("Scientific" is the best translation of the Greek word "philosophic" which Aristotle uses here.) Moreover, fictions, he says, are instructive. One learns from them, as from any form of *mimesis* ("imitation") through comparing representation with original. This idea of the instructive power of models is one of the major problems in Aristotle's theory of art.

Exactly what does one learn by comparing the model with the reality? Whatever be the answer to that question, it seems clear that the more tightly logical the imaginary structure, the more it satisfies Aristotle's ideal of an object that is like life, but life as coherence, not confusion.

While the idea of an ideal plot reflects Aristotle's general theory of mental structures, his interest in *hamartia* is closely involved with the special case of tragic plot. According to Aristotle, the purpose of tragedy is to arouse the emotions of fear and pity. We fear, he says, a misfortune which occurs to persons like ourselves, since it might occur to us, too, and we pity those whose imminent or actual misfortune is undeserved. The characters in a tragedy should thus be decent, sincere persons, no more at fault and so no more deserving of unhappiness than ourselves.

Now, a plot involving sympathetic characters of this kind could be designed so that their misfortunes are accidental. We would pity the characters, certainly, but the arbitrary nature of the disaster would conflict with the ideal of a logical sequence of events, and therefore would not receive Aristotle's full approval. The alternative plot seems to be for the misfortunes to follow logically from the actions of the characters. But what sort of action by decent, sincere people would lead logically to disaster? An action whose true nature was not understood at the time it was committed—in other words, a mistake arising from simple ignorance (*hamartia*).

The play may or may not include the moment of mistaken action, but it will certainly include the moment when the nature of the act becomes clear, the moment of *anagnōrisis*. Its dramatic value is evident. Surprise, astonishment and then despair if the error proves irretrievable, or wild joy if there is time to avoid the worst.

After discovery of the truth, the future of the characters is likely to be very different. The facts impose themselves. All may be lost and what were reasonable hopes, even confident expectations, a moment before, are annihilated. Or the near certainty of ruin is removed. The future becomes open and hopeful. In either eventuality, there is *peripeteia*.

The connection between Aristotle's first principles, logical plot producing fear and pity, and the results in practice, "ideal" tragedies of the *Oedipus the King* and *Iphigeneia in Tauris* type, is fairly clear. It can be summarized as follows: the best tragedy provides both a maximum of plot logic and a maximum of audience sympathy for the chief character or characters. To the extent that these characters are conscious, when they perform a harmful act, audience identification, supposedly, declines and the tragedy is less good.

But the bias of the author is evident. His ideal stresses innocence of action and the shock of sudden knowledge at the expense of the anguish of divided motivation, when the tragic consequences of the only decisions open are fairly clear and yet some decision must be taken. There is also the case of the basically sympathetic character who, under abnormal stress, commits a rash or even criminal act, like Medea, or Theseus in the *Hippolytus,* or Pentheus in the *Bacchae.*

We will return to this point, but it is time now to turn from how Aristotle defines the best tragedy to what he says about tragedy as a whole. All tragedy, he says, aims at giving pleasure by exercising the emotions of fear and pity. This effect can occur, though in a less satisfactory manner, without *anagnōrisis* and *peripeteia;* for example, characters who suffer helplessly, such as Medea's children, arouse these emotions. So does the fate of Ajax or Prometheus, although neither play has a discovery or reversal.

Second, all tragedy accomplishes a *katharsis* of the emotions of fear and pity. The word *katharsis* is not explained in the *Poetics,* and much effort has been expended in an effort to determine precisely what Aristotle meant. In ordinary Greek, *katharsis* means the act of bringing something into a state of cleanness. It was used in medicine to refer to purgation of the body and in religion to refer to the purification of the soul through mystery ritual. The question concerning the *Poetics* is, does *katharsis* of pity and fear mean that pity and fear are expelled from the mind like impurities from the body, or that these emotions are aroused in order to be, in some sense, purified themselves? The argument about this question continues.

Finally, all tragedy is composed of six elements: plot, characters, thought, diction, music, and spectacle. The last three refer to the play's sensory façade, what we see and hear. The first three, particularly plot, refer to the play's inner structure, the shaping force that is the real object of our attention. Aristotle's concern with structure led him to criticize what seems to have been a tendency in his time to encourage a display of the second element, character portrayal, at the expense of the first, plot logic. True to his idea that the playwright is a designer of imaginary actions, Aristotle has no patience with those who fail to keep first things first. The events are primary and call the tune to which the other elements should dance, each in its place. Character (*ēthē*) is a distant second in importance. Thought (*dianoia*) comes next. It refers to a character's capacity to articulate ideas, prove a point or describe a situation with force and clarity. Diction (*lexis*) is the whole verbal expression of the drama. Music (*melopoiia*) and spectacle (*opsis*) are barely mentioned in the *Poetics*. Aristotle is clearly not much interested in either, although he insists that the choral songs (*melopoiia*) be relevant to the plot and credits spectacle with great power over the spectators.

It has often been remarked that Aristotle does not discuss the religious aspect of Greek tragedy, whereas, in the fifth century, tragedy almost always concerned the relations between the gods and human beings. His emphasis is strongly humanistic and directed to the impact on decent people of misfortunes which they have incurred simply through unavoidable ignorance. But in the legends exploited by the great fifth century tragedians, there is a brooding concern with the mystery of evil. Are men responsible for their own destruction, do the gods will it for purposes of their own, is there some immensely complex interweaving of causes? The classical attitude of humble supplication and praise in the face of this mystery was certainly an important element in the emotional impact of classical tragedy, but it receives no attention at all in the *Poetics*.

Besides this omission, there are difficulties in applying Aristotle's scheme to the tragedies we know. For instance, few would question that the *Agamemnon* and *Antigone* are great tragedies, but neither seems to have *peripeteia* or *anagnōrisis,* at least in the sense in which Aristotle uses these terms in the *Poetics.*

Perhaps more serious, the application of the *hamartia* criterion with rigor would exclude stories of the Orestes type from the highest category because Orestes is not mistaken about the nature of his act. He knows he is killing his mother. And yet we probably feel great pity for him in spite of Aristotle. Figures such as Orestes and Medea actually can seem more tragic than those of the Oedipus type, who act in ignorance. Full consciousness and conflicting impulses combine to make their dramatic situation particularly affecting.

Aristotle's acute intelligence opened up important questions concerning aesthetics in general and drama in particular. But his strong preference for one limited kind of play interferes with a balanced approach to the actual variety of tragedies we have.

IV. TRAGEDY AFTER THE CLASSICAL PERIOD

Attic tragedy had begun to spread to other Greek cities during the classical period. This extension of tragedy beyond Attica continued during the fourth century and the Hellenistic age (323–30 B.C.). Side by side with it went the construction of theaters in almost every Greek city. In the meantime, tragedies of intrigue and family trouble had influenced the development of a new type of drama in Athens, which, in its turn, spread to the rest of the world. This was called New Comedy, whose chief practitioner was Menander (342–292).

Although our knowledge of the development of Greek tragedy after 400 is based on imperfect evidence, one point is clear: the actors became increasingly more important, while the chorus continued to decline. A prize for the best actor at the Dionysia and also at the Lenaea had been instituted during the fifth century. During the fourth century famous actors became important public figures and served as ambassadors between states on matters of vital importance. In the theater, their skill was crucial to the success of the hundreds of new tragedies which continued to be written. The actors also put on "old" tragedies, mainly those of Euripides, as vehicles for their skill. Concurrently, the playwrights of this period often made no attempt to write choral songs with subject matter closely connected with the plot of the play. Instead, the chorus might perform a song which could be inserted into any play at any point in the action. (Aristotle called such songs *embolima*).

A significant change in the physical design of the theater marks the fading of the chorus's connection with the plot and the supreme importance of the actor. The change was the appearance of the stage in the modern sense of the word: a high platform strictly separated from the orchestra level. We do not know exactly when the high stage was built in Athens; it was probably a little after 300. Elsewhere, a high stage appears to have become the rule by 200.

V. LIVES OF AESCHYLUS, SOPHOCLES, AND EURIPIDES

1. AESCHYLUS

Aeschylus was born about 525 to a land-owning family in Eleusis, an Attic town a few miles west of Athens, and died in Sicily about 456. During his life he participated in some of the most crucial events in Greek history. When he was a boy, the Athenians expelled the family which had ruled their city as autocrats for a generation. Then, as Athens was reorganizing herself as a democracy, serious problems of foreign policy involved her in wars with her neighbors, and an almost disastrous conflict with Persia.

Aeschylus was in his twenties when the cities of Ionia revolted against the Persian empire, which controlled the entire Middle East. Athens gave help to the Ionians and, in reprisal, was invaded in 490 by a Persian force, which was defeated at Marathon, a town on the eastern coast of Attica. Aeschylus fought in this battle, as did his brother, who was killed. Ten years later, when Aeschylus was about forty-five, he fought the Persians again, this time at the naval battle of Salamis, an island just outside the harbor of Athens. The king of Persia himself had led his forces to Greece. The defeat of the Persians and their king by predominantly Athenian sea power and a combination of infantry led by Sparta completely changed the political life of Greece. Athens emerged from the war as the leader of more than 200 Greek cities, large and small, in the islands and along the shore of the Aegean Sea.

What began as a free alliance was transformed during Aeschylus' later years into an Athenian empire, which lasted for the rest of the fifth century and came close to dominating all of Greece.

Only seven of Aeschylus' almost eighty plays have been preserved. He began dramatic competition shortly after 500, and was victorious for the first time in 484. His total of thirteen first prizes indicates that he was successful more than half the time.

Aeschylus made two trips to Sicily. During the first he stayed at the court of Hieron, tyrant of the great city of Syracuse, a patron of many poets. During the second trip, he lived in Gela. It is reasonable to suppose that this Sicilian experience influenced his thinking. His first trip preceded the composition of all the extant plays except the *Persians*. The *Prometheus Bound* may have been written during his second and final stay. The possible ways in which Sicily may have affected Aeschylus are a matter of dispute, but it is worth noting that Aeschylus was not a provincial playwright cut off from the significant intellectual events of his time. During this period southern Italy and Sicily produced the mystical-scientific school of Pythagoras and the powerful philosophical systems of Parmenides and Empedocles.

All seven preserved plays are from the last part of Aeschylus' life. In 472, when he was about fifty-three, he produced the *Persians,* part of an unconnected trilogy which won first prize. Four years later, he was defeated by Sophocles but triumphed in 467 with a connected trilogy on the Oedipus saga, of which the *Seven Against Thebes* is extant. The *Suppliants* was part of a winning trilogy about the fifty daughters of Danaus who, all but one, killed their husbands on the wedding night. It was produced sometime in the 460s. The *Oresteia* won first prize in 458, when Aeschylus was about sixty-seven. All three tragedies from this trilogy, but not the satyr play, are preserved. The date of the *Prometheus Bound* is not known, but seems to be from the poet's last years.

The serious themes of Aeschylus' preserved plays could be misleading as to the range of his talents. He was particularly famous in antiquity for his satyr plays, of which only small fragments are known today.

2. SOPHOCLES

Sophocles was born about 495 and died in 406. A member of a well-to-do family, he lived in Athens all his life and held numerous public offices: in 441 he was elected "general," a position more like our admiral; in 443–442 he was *Hellenotamias,* meaning treasurer of the Delian League, the group of cities which formed the Athenian empire; he also performed public religious functions connected with various gods of healing. He saw the height and the decline of Athenian power, but not its final defeat.

Sophocles composed about 125 plays, of which seven are preserved. His first victory came in 468, when he was a little over thirty years old. The total number of his victories is variously given, but seems to have been eighteen at the City Dionysia and six at the Lenaea. (Tragic competition at the Lenaea appears to have begun about 440.) His total number of victories makes Sophocles the most popular tragic poet of the fifth century, so far as we know.

His theatrical innovations included a third actor and the increase of the chorus from twelve to fifteen. Unlike Aeschylus, he composed few connected trilogies (perhaps only one). He favored the single, independent play. In this respect he may have been following the traditional practice.

We are less informed about the dates of Sophocles' plays than about those of Aeschylus. The *Ajax* is probably the first. The *Antigone* is put about 442. The *Trachiniae* may be from the 430s, but could be earlier. *Oedipus the King* is assigned to the 420s. The

Electra may be near the *Philoctetes,* which was produced in 409. The *Oedipus at Colonus* was presented in 401. These two dates are the only certain ones.

Sophocles' family home was in Colonus, a village just north of Athens, which he celebrated in his last play.

3. EURIPIDES

Euripides was born about 483 B.C. on the island of Salamis, a possession of Athens. Like the other two famous tragedians, he received an education typical of the well-to-do class in Athens. He was strongly influenced by the rationalistic and skeptical ideas of certain men whose thought became particularly important in the latter half of the fifth century. These were the sophists and pre-Socratic philosophers, who questioned most or all presuppositions, social, religious and intellectual, and advanced their own theories or techniques. Many touches and themes in Euripides' plays can be understood against the background of this movement.

Nothing is known about Euripides' participation in civic life. It seems to have been minimal. He produced twenty-two tetralogies—that is, at least sixty-six tragedies and twenty-two satyr plays, or the equivalent. An interesting example of this latter category, a substitute for a satyr play, is the *Alcestis,* which was the final piece in a tetralogy, but did not have a satyr chorus. The plot, while ultimately humorous, has moments of extreme pathos. Besides the *Alcestis,* which is difficult to classify, we have sixteen tragedies, a satyr play (the *Cyclops*), and a tragedy, the *Rhesus,* generally regarded as spurious. The total amounts to almost three times as many preserved plays as for either Aeschylus or Sophocles. (This abundance results partly from the popularity of Euripides in the centuries after his death.) His first production was in 455, when Aeschylus was dead and Sophocles had been competing for many years, but his first victory did not come until 441, when he was forty or more, and he won first prize only four times during his life, in marked contrast to Sophocles' eighteen or more victories and Aeschylus' thirteen. There may be some justification for the story that he left Athens for Macedonia during his last years because of annoyance at the reception given his plays in his native city. He died in Macedonia early in 406, after having lived there two years.

EDWIN DOLIN

February 1971

Bibliography

GENERAL

Arias, P., and Hirmer, M. *A History of 1000 Years of Greek Vase Painting*. New York, n.d.

Arnott, P. *An Introduction to the Greek Theatre*. New York, 1961.

Bieber, M. *The History of the Greek and Roman Theatre*. 2nd ed. Princeton, 1961.

Cook, A. *Enactment: Greek Tragedy*. Chicago, 1971.

Flickinger, R. *The Greek Theater and Its Drama*. 4th ed. Chicago, 1936.

Harsh, P. W. *A Handbook of Classical Drama*. Stanford, 1948.

Jaeger, W. *Paideia*. Translated by G. Highet. New York, 1945. Vol. 1.

Jones, J. *On Aristotle and Greek Tragedy*. New York, 1962.

Kitto, H. D. F. *Greek Tragedy*. 3rd ed. London, 1961.

Kranz, W. *Stasimon*. Berlin, 1933.

Lattimore, R. *The Poetry of Greek Tragedy*. Baltimore, 1958.

———. *Story Patterns in Greek Tragedy*. Ann Arbor, 1964.

Lesky, A. *Greek Tragedy*. New York, 1965.

———. *A History of Greek Literature*. New York, 1966.

———. *Die Tragische Dichtung der Hellenen*. 2nd ed. Goettingen, 1964.

Lucas, D. W. *The Greek Tragic Poets*. 2nd ed. London, 1959.

Lucas, F. L. *Tragedy: Serious Drama in Relation to Aristotle's "Poetics."* rev. ed. New York, 1962.

Pickard-Cambridge, A. *The Dramatic Festivals of Athens*. 2nd ed. Revised by J. Gould and D. M. Lewis. Oxford, 1968.

Pohlenz, M. *Die Griechische Tragoedie*. 2 vols. 2nd ed. Goettingen, 1954.

Rosenmeyer, T. *The Masks of Tragedy*. Austin, Tex., 1963.
Webster, T. B. L. *The Greek Chorus*. New York, 1970.
————. *Greek Theatre Production*. 2nd ed. London, 1970.

ORIGIN OF TRAGEDY

GENERAL

Bergk, T. *Griechische Literaturgeschichte*. Berlin, 1884. Vol. 3, pp. 3–13.
Burkert, W. "Greek Tragedy and Sacrificial Ritual." *Greek, Roman and Byzantine Studies* VII (1966):87–121.
Dieterich, A. "Die Entstehung der Tragoedie." *Archiv fuer Religionswissenschaft* II (1908):163–191.
Else, G. F. *The Origin and Early Form of Greek Tragedy*. Martin Classical Lectures. Cambridge, Mass., 1965.
Farnell, L. *The Cults of the Greek States*. Oxford, 1896–1909. Vol. V, pp. 234–237.
Guépin, J. P. *The Tragic Paradox*. Amsterdam, 1968.
Lesky, A. *A History of Greek Literature*. New York, 1966. pp. 223–232.
————. *Die Tragische Dichtung der Hellenen*. 2nd ed. Goettingen, 1964. pp. 11–49.
Mueller, K. O. *A History of the Literature of Ancient Greece*. London, 1858. Vol. I, pp. 381–387.
Murray, G. "Excursus on the Ritual Forms Preserved in Greek Tragedy." In *Themis*, by J. Harrison. Cambridge, 1913.
Nietzsche, F. *The Birth of Tragedy*.
Nilsson, M. *Geschichte der Griechischen Religion*. 2nd ed. Munich, 1955. Vol. I, pp. 162, 234–235, 571–572, 720–721.
Patzer, H. *Die Anfaenge der Griechischen Tragoedie*. Wiesbaden, 1962.
Pickard-Cambridge, A. *Dithyramb, Tragedy and Comedy*. Oxford, 1927. 2nd ed. Revised by T. B. L. Webster. Oxford, 1962.
Pohlenz, M. "Die Satyrspiele und Pratinas von Phleius." In *Kleine Schriften*. Hildesheim, 1965. Vol. II, pp. 473–496.

Reisch, E. "Zur Vorgeschichte der Attischen Tragoedie." In *Festschrift Theodor Gomperz*. Vienna, 1902. pp. 451–473.

Ridgeway, W. *The Origin of Tragedy*. Cambridge, 1910.

Trendall, A., and Webster, T. B. L. *Illustrations of Greek Drama,* forthcoming.

Webster, T. B. L. *Greek Art and Literature 700–530 B.C.* New York, 1959. pp. 55–77.

———. "Some Thoughts on the Pre-History of Greek Drama." *Bulletin of the Institute of Classical Studies* (University of London) 5 (1958):43–48.

Wilamowitz-Moellendorff, U. von. *Euripides Herakles*. Berlin, 1889. Vol. I, pp. 43–119.

Ziegler, K. "Trogoedia." In *Real-Encyclopaedie der Classischen Altertumswissenschaft,* edited by Pauly-Wissowa. Vol. VI, A2, pp. 1899ff.

Mask, Costume, and Fertility Cult in Sparta, Ionia, Boeotia, and Athens

Sparta:

Dickins, G. "The Sanctuary of Artemis Orthia at Sparta." *Journal of Hellenic Studies* Supplement V. Edited by R. M. Dawkins. (1929):plates LVI, 1; LXII, 1; LIV, 1 and 2; fig. 125; pp. 163ff.

Lane, E. A. "Laconian Vase Paintings." *Annual of the British School at Athens* XXXIV (1933–34):plate 39a, pp. 148, 160.

Nilsson, M. *Geschichte der Griechischen Religion*. 2nd ed. Vol. I, pp. 161–162, 499.

Pickard-Cambridge. *Dithyramb, Tragedy and Comedy*. 2nd ed. plate XIIa.

Webster. *Greek Theater Production*. plate 6a.

Ionia:

Boardman, J. "A Greek Vase from Egypt." *Journal of Hellenic Studies* 78 (1958):4–12.

Pickard-Cambridge. *Dithyramb, Tragedy and Comedy*. 2nd ed. fig. 4, p. 84.

Webster. *Greek Theatre Production*. plate 6b.

Boeotia:

Bielefeld, E. "Ein Boiotischer Tanzchor des 6. Jahrhunderts vor Christ." In *Festschrift fuer Friedrich Zucker zum 70. Geburtstage,* edited by W. Mueller. Berlin, 1954. pp. 27–35 with plate.

Athens:

Arias and Hirmer. *A History of 1000 Years of Greek Vase Painting.* Plate XXII, plates 206–211 with text pp. 372–375.

Beazley, J., and Caskey, L. *Attic Vase Paintings in the Museum of Fine Arts, Boston.* Part 2. London and Boston, 1954. Text for no. 99, pp. 55–61.

Pickard-Cambridge. *Dithyramb, Tragedy and Comedy.* Plates IV, Vb, VIa and b.

———. *Dramatic Festivals of Athens.* 2nd ed. Fig. 11–13, 17–23, 37.

Seeberg, Axel. "Padded Dancers." *Bulletin of the Institute of Classical Studies,* in press.

MAENADS

Arias and Hirmer. *A History of 1000 Years of Greek Vase Painting.* Fig. 94, 95, 99, 100.

Dodds, E. R. *The Greeks and the Irrational.* Berkeley, 1951. pp. 270–282.

Edwards, M. W. "Representations of Maenads on Archaic Red-Figure Vases." *Journal of Hellenic Studies* LXXX (1960):78–87.

ARISTOTLE'S POETICS

Bywater, I. *Aristotle on the Art of Poetry.* Oxford, 1909.

Else, G. F. *Aristotle "Poetics": Translated with an Introduction and Notes.* Ann Arbor, Mich., 1967.

———. *Aristotle's "Poetics": the Argument.* Harvard, 1957.

Golden, L., and Hardison, O. *Aristotle's "Poetics": A Translation and Commentary for Students of Literature.* Englewood Cliffs, N.J., 1968.

Grube, G. M. A. *Aristotle on Poetry and Style.* New York, 1958.
House, H. *Aristotle's "Poetics."* London, 1956.
Jones, J. *On Aristotle and Greek Tragedy.* London, 1962.
Lucas, D. W. *Aristotle "Poetics": Introduction, Commentary and Appendixes.* Oxford, 1968.
Lucas, F. L. *Tragedy: Serious Drama in Relation to Aristotle's "Poetics."* New York, 1962.
Schaper, E. *Prelude to Aesthetics.* London, 1968.

AESCHYLUS
(Besides sections in Harsh, Kitto, Lesky, and D. W. Lucas)

Dodds, E. R. *The Greeks and the Irrational.* Berkeley, 1951. Ch. II.
Finley, J. F. *Pindar and Aeschylus.* Harvard, 1955.
Golden, L. *In Praise of Prometheus.* Chapel Hill, N.C., 1966.
Havelock, E. A. *Prometheus with a Translation of Aeschylus' "Prometheus Bound."* Seattle and London, 1969.
Herington, C. J. *The Author of the "Prometheus Bound."* Austin, Tex., 1970.
Kitto, H. D. F. *Form and Meaning in Drama.* 2nd ed. London, 1960.
Kerenyi, C. *Prometheus.* New York, 1963.
Murray, G. *Aeschylus, the Creator of Tragedy.* Oxford, 1940.
Podlecki, A. *The Political Background of Aeschylean Tragedy.* Ann Arbor, 1966.
Reinhardt, K. *Aischylos als Regisseur und Theologe.* Bern, 1949.
Solmsen, F. *Hesiod and Aeschylus.* New York, 1949.
Thomson, G. *Aeschylus and Athens.* New York, 1949.
———. *Aeschylus: the "Prometheus Bound."* Cambridge, 1932.

SOPHOCLES
(Besides sections in Harsh, Kitto, Lesky, and D. W. Lucas)

Adams, S. *Sophocles the Playwright.* Toronto, 1957.
Bowra, C. *Sophoclean Tragedy.* Oxford, 1944.

Errandonea, I. *Sofocle*. Madrid, 1958.

Kirkwood, G. *A Study of Sophoclean Tragedy*. Cornell, 1958.

Kitto, H. D. F. *Sophocles, Dramatist and Philosopher*. London, 1958.

Knox, B. *The Heroic Temper*. Berkeley and Los Angeles, 1964.

———. *Oedipus at Thebes*. New Haven, 1957.

Reinhardt, K. *Sophokles,* 3rd ed. Frankfurt a. Main, 1947.

Waldock, A. J. A. *Sophocles the Dramatist*. Cambridge, 1951.

Webster, T. B. L. *Introduction to Sophocles*. Oxford, 1936.

Whitman, C. H. *Sophocles*. Harvard, 1951.

EURIPIDES

(Besides sections in Harsh, Kitto, Lesky, and D. W. Lucas) ·

Conacher, D. J. *Euripidean Drama*. Toronto, 1967.

Dodds, E. R. *Euripides: Bacchae*. 2nd ed. Oxford, 1960.

Grube, G. M. A. *The Drama of Euripides*. London, 1941. 2nd ed. New York, 1961.

Murray, G. *Euripides and His Age*. 2nd ed. London and New York, 1946.

Webster, T. B. L. *The Tragedies of Euripides*. London, 1967.

Winnington-Ingram, R. *Euripides and Dionysus*. Cambridge, 1948.

Zuntz, G. *The Political Plays of Euripides*. Manchester, 1955.

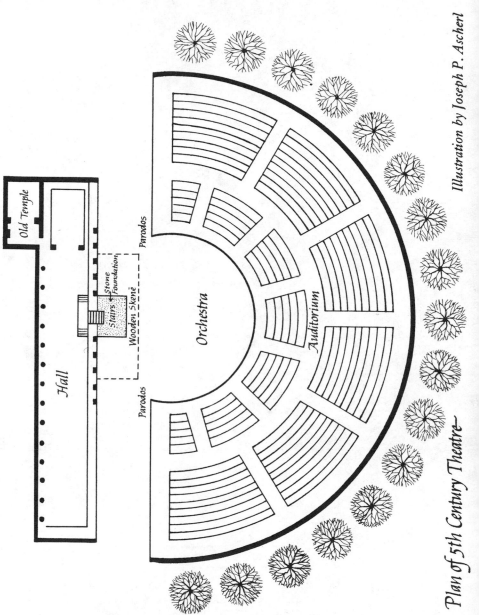

Old Temple

Hall

Parodos

Stone Foundation

Stairs

Wooden Skene

Parodos

Orchestra

Auditorium

Illustration by Joseph P. Ascherl

Plan of 5th Century Theatre—

An Anthology of Greek Tragedy

AESCHYLUS

Agamemnon

TRANSLATED BY
WILLIAM SYLVESTER

INTRODUCTORY NOTE

The *Agamemnon* is one of the most powerful plays ever written. Its structure has been often discussed. The very first scene sets the tone with its mixture of anxiety and joy. Then begins the brooding music of the chorus as it ponders the web of evil which binds the kingdom. Clytemnestra's mixture of daring and deliberation, the herald's alternate news of victory and disaster—to all this Agamemnon's brief, charged appearance seems the climax, but is followed by one of the great solo performances of literature, Kassandra's lonely vision and appeal.

The sources of the story in the *Agamemnon* are partly known to us, chiefly books 1, 3, 4, and 11 of the *Odyssey*. An interesting difference between the play and the *Odyssey* is that in Homer it is Aigisthos who kills Agamemnon. He invites the king to a banquet where twenty picked men, who have been placed in ambush, fight with Agamemnon and his retainers until all are dead except Aigisthos himself. The contrast between this version, with its emphasis on masculine violence, and that of the play indicates what importance Aeschylus placed on Clytemnestra and the theme of opposition between husband and wife, male and female.

The *Agamemnon* was produced in 458, when Athens was involved in serious wars both with its Greek neighbors and with Persia in Egypt. It won first prize as part of a trilogy called the *Oresteia,* which is the only extant trilogy by any Greek dramatist.

CHARACTERS

WATCHMAN

CHORUS of Argive Elders

CLYTEMNESTRA, wife of AGAMEMNON

HERALD

AGAMEMNON, king of Argos

KASSANDRA, daughter of Priam and slave of AGAMEMNON

AIGISTHOS, cousin of AGAMEMNON

Agamemnon

THE SCENE. *Palace of the Atreidae in Argos. The* WATCHMAN *is on the roof. Stage right, a shrine.*

WATCHMAN. I beg the gods to let me go from this job
  Of keeping watch, the whole year long, my bed
  The rooftop of the Atreidae, resting on
  My arms, like a dog; I've come to know the crowds
  Of stars at night that bring both winter and summer
  To mortal men, the shining leaders, standing
  Out in the sky, the stars, when they fade away . . .
        . . . and when they rise
  And now I keep a watch for the torch, the bright
  Light of the fire that brings the news from Troy,
  Report of its capture. This is the way we are governed:
  By the heart of a woman who sticks to her hopes like a man.
  When I get up and down at night from my bed,
  Wet with dew, no dream can come to me:
  Fear instead of Sleep is standing before me.
  I cannot shut my eyes tight in sleep.
  And if I want to sing or hum a tune
  An antidote to take the place of sleep
  I weep for the turn of fortune to this house,

  [*Light flashes, but* WATCHMAN *does not see it yet.*]

  Not as it was before, when jobs were done
  In the very best way, and thoroughly. Maybe

  [*sees the flashing*]

  Now I'll have good luck and leave this job:
  The fire appearing in the murk may bring good news.

[1–21]

Oh hail, flame in the night, making it bright
As day, you're bringing many songs and dances
To Greece, for the favor of this turn of fortune.
Ahoy! Ahoy!
I yell a clear signal to Agamemnon's queen
To get up from her bed, and quickly through the house
Sing a Hallelujah of good omen
For this light; If the city of Troy is really
Conquered, as the burning torch clearly proclaims;
And I, I will solemnly dance a prelude,
For when the king throws the dice, I think his luck
Is my luck too, and that torch has thrown the winning doubles.
If only I can grasp the well-beloved
Hand of the king in mine, when he comes home.
About the rest—I'm silent . . . A huge ox stands
On my tongue. If the house itself had a voice it would speak
Most clearly. I choose to make sense for those in the know;

[CHORUS *begins to enter.*]

For those who aren't, I choose to forget everything.
CHORUS. Ten years it's been since
    Priam's great enemy,
    Menelaos the king, and Agamemnon
    Two thrones, thanks to Zeus; two scepters
    Bound by honor; mighty; the partners, sons of Atreus
    Led a thousand ships from the
    Shores of Argos, a
    Battle force for the cause; they
    Loved to rage,
    They cried: "Oh god of war!"
    As vultures suffer for their children
    That are missing from the nest,
    Wheel high in the air and
    Drive their wings into the air like oars in the oarlocks,
    They've lost the care of nesting with the little birds.
    But some god on high,
    Apollo, Pan, or Zeus

Hears the cry of the vultures
(Immigrants in the god-owned sky)
Birds that shriek
For the Furies
To avenge the robbery.
More powerful Zeus, god of friends
Eventually sends the sons of Atreus
Against Paris.
Because of a woman who had many men,
Many will wrestle, limbs will grow weak,
Knees will go down into the dust,
Spears will break in the ritual of war
For Greek and Trojan alike.
That's the way it's fated to be, whatever may be right now.
No secret libations, no public tears
Will soften the rage: a sacred
Fire that was not lit.
But we are old, much too old for duty.
Left out of the general call to arms,
We stayed at home
Leaning on our canes, weak as children.
For the young, a marrow in the chest
Rages within, and

[*Enter* CLYTEMNESTRA *center doors. She stands there.*]

For old men too; the god of war is not here;
For the very old, the leaves are withered,
An old man makes his way on three feet.
No better than a child,
He wanders like a daydream.
But you, oh daughter of
Tyndareus, Queen Clytemnestra,

[CLYTEMNESTRA *moves toward the shrine. She stands before it,
arms outstretched palms down.*]

What has happened? What news? What do you understand?
What are the reports?

Why do the heralds announce a sacrifice?
For all the gods that guard the city,
These above, and those below the earth, the sky gods,
The gods of the marketplace
The altars are burning with gifts.
In this place, in that place, high as the sky
The flames go up
Fed by the sacred oil
That encourages, gently, and directly
The oil brought out from the royal house.
Tell me whatever you can,
Be willing to cure my worries.
At one moment, evil thoughts rise up
But you make the altars shine
And hope beats away unending grief,
A pain in my mind, destroying life.

1st Strophe

[*The light from the shrine flares up.*]

I can proclaim it: the command of good omen for fully
    grown men

[CHORUS *moves toward* CLYTEMNESTRA.]

Was at the road. Persuasion from the gods inspires
My song, and my age still gives me strength.
Hear how the command of the Greeks, double throned, leaders
    of youth
Single in purpose
Were sent as avengers to Troy,
Spears in their hands, inspired by fortune-telling birds:
Kingly birds appeared before the kings of the ships,
One bird black, the other with a white tail
Appearing on the right, the spear-throwing side, by the rooftop
    blackened by smoke
Placed for all to see,
The birds fed on a pregnant hare

Her course interrupted, not won.
Sing of agony, agony, but let the right win out.

[CHORUS *moves away from* CLYTEMNESTRA.]

1ST ANTISTROPHE

The army had a good fortune-teller who saw that the courage
of the
Sons of Atreus, the warriors, was two-fold and that the two
birds, eaters of unborn hares,
Were like the leaders of the army. The man deciphered it:
"They who get under way, someday they'll kill the town of Troy
All of the towers and walls,
And the cattle in front of the walls,
The rich town is fated to fall by force.
May the gods keep away the curse of darkness
Cutting the bridle for Troy before we become
An army; sacred Artemis, out of pity, hates those birds,
Hounds-with-wings her father sends to
Sacrifice the fearful hares and before they are born.
She hates the feast of the eagles."
Sing of agony, agony, but let the right win out.

EPODE

[*center*]

The Beautiful Goddess, who is kindly to
Young lions, fresh as the dew but fierce, untouchable,
Who takes delight in young animals
And in the sucking beasts of the field,
She begs that all of the signs work out,
The signs on the right side and also on the bad.
Apollo, the healer, keep her from sending
Winds against the Greeks,
From holding the ships a long time in the harbor,
From insisting upon another sacrifice, a lawless one, without
food
One that leads to war within families and fears no man

Until Anger himself, hideous and clever,
Will rise up to guard the house and remember to avenge a
    child.
That is what Chalcas proclaimed to the leader's house,
About the birds on the way, about what would happen, and
    about good things too,
And so, the proper sounds are:
Sing of agony, agony, but let what's right win out.

2ND STROPHE

[*to* CLYTEMNESTRA]

Zeus, whoever he is,
If he cares for the name
I invoke him by,
Mulling over everything
I cannot find any other
But Zeus if truly the senseless weight upon my mood
Is to be thrown away.

2ND ANTISTROPHE

[*away from* CLYTEMNESTRA]

Another god once was mighty,
Ready to burst out into fighting,
I shall not name him, as if he had never existed
Another god rose up and chanced upon
One who threw him down and now he's gone.
Whoever thinks first, then gives a victory cry of Zeus:
Reaches right thoughts about everything.

3RD STROPHE

[*toward* CLYTEMNESTRA]

He opens the path of right thinking to men,
He sets up an authoritative law
To learn by suffering.
And in sleep, the memory of work

Drips before the heart.
Right thinking comes like a thrust of a spear.
Good luck comes from sacred powers
In violence seated at the helm.

3RD ANTISTROPHE

[*away from* CLYTEMNESTRA]

The older leader
Of the Greek ships
Didn't find any fault with the fortune-teller
And was swept along by the winds against him.
Bad weather emptied the ship of its jugs of food
And tormented the Achaean host
In the region of Aulis, by the roaring shore,
Opposite Chalcas,

4TH STROPHE

[*toward* CLYTEMNESTRA]

The winds from Strymon brought
Unemployment, famine, and bad anchorage, so that
Men wandered
The ships and cables weren't spared.
A long stretch of time against them
Wore away and shredded the flower of Argos.
The fortune-teller, relying on Artemis,
Announced a way out for the leaders
That was a greater burden than the sharp weather,
And the sons of Atreus struck the ground with their poles
And couldn't keep back the tears.

4TH ANTISTROPHE

[*away from* CLYTEMNESTRA]

The older leader spoke out and said:
"An overwhelming fate, if I don't obey;
Overwhelming too,

If I hack down my child, delight of our house—
To defile a father's hands
With streams of virgin blood before an altar?
Which way is without evil?
How can I become deserter?
To commit a dreadful mistake against my fellows?
But to calm the winds by a sacrifice,
By a virgin's blood . . .
They'll think of it, passionately, very passionately
And they're right. Let the right win."

5TH STROPHE

[*toward* CLYTEMNESTRA]

But when he put on the strap of necessity
His mood shifted to a different direction and blew against
The sacred rules and laws
He was ready to break down everything.
Madness makes men bold
By evil advice, the first cause of disaster.
He endured the sacrificing of a daughter
To support a war,
To avenge a woman,
A ritual for the ships.

5TH ANTISTROPHE

[*away from* CLYTEMNESTRA]

Her screams, her cries to her father,
Her virgin's life meant nothing
To the comrades in arms.
After a prayer, her father told the attendants
To grasp her, to lift her
Like a goat, above the altar.
She strained forward, and fell out of her clothes.
On her pretty mouth
To keep back the shrieks
That would have cursed the house,

6TH STROPHE

[*toward* CLYTEMNESTRA]

There was a strong gag that made her silent.
As her yellow dress fell toward the ground
She struck with her eyes each
Sacrificer in turn, pleading for pity,
She stood out clearly, as if in a picture, wishing
To speak. Many times with
Her father, and the men at a good table,
She had sung beautifully, with the voice of a girl who'd never
    been rammed
She'd chant a hymn after the third libation
To show her love to her father.

6TH ANTISTROPHE

[*away from* CLYTEMNESTRA]

What happened next, I didn't see, and can't speak of.
Chalcas ability didn't fail.
Justice tilted toward those who learn
Through suffering. What is to be,
Is to be heard of when it happens.
There's no use to be sad in advance.
It will come with the rising morning light
And what is to be, may it work out well.
And that's the wish of the nearest defender, the only
Guard for the land of Apis.

[CHORUS, *stage left;* CLYTEMNESTRA, *stage right*]

I've come to worship your power, Clytemnestra:
It's right to honor a leader's wife
When the throne is desolate, without a man.
Perhaps you have good news, perhaps you don't.
Perhaps you have hopes and so make sacrifices.
I'd be happy to hear, but if you're silent, I won't be bitter.
CLYTEMNESTRA. The morning brings good news, as the saying goes:

Let Daylight be born from her mother, Night, "the kindly time."
You'll learn of a joy greater than you
Had hoped for: The Greeks have taken Priam's city.
CHORUS. What's that? Your saying escapes me, I can't believe it.
CLYTEMNESTRA. Troy belongs to the Greeks. Do I say it clearly?
CHORUS. Joy creeps through me, and calls forth tears.
CLYTEMNESTRA. Your eyes accuse you of having sound sense.
CHORUS. Why believe it? Is there some token as proof?
CLYTEMNESTRA. There is. And why not? Unless there's a trick
    by a god.
CHORUS. Perhaps you respect the persuasive shapes in a dream.
CLYTEMNESTRA. I wouldn't accept the report of a sleeping mind.
CHORUS. Perhaps you are fattened by an unfledged report.
CLYTEMNESTRA. You really berate me as if I'd the mind of a child.
CHORUS. Just how long ago was the city ravaged?
CLYTEMNESTRA. Last night, I say, "the kindly time," giving birth
    to this light.
CHORUS. Who could get here so quickly? What messenger?
CLYTEMNESTRA. Hephaistos, bright god of fire. From Mount Ida
    The runner fire, came here from beacon to beacon,
    Mount Ida sent it to the Hermean crag in Lemnos,
    And thirdly, from the island, the mighty torch
    Was taken at the peak of Athos, sacred to Zeus.
    Reaching over the sea, as if skimming it
    With joy and strength, the light was a traveller
    The resinous torch with golden beams, as bright
    As the sun brought new to the lookout at Makistos
    Who wasn't hesitant, or senseless, conquered
    By sleep. No—he passed on the messenger's portion
    The light of the distant beacon, over the rivers
    Of Euripus signalled, and came to the guards at Messapion.
    They made an answer of light that sent out the news.
    They took a heap of gray heather and set it on fire.
    The powerful light did not grow dark; it leaped
    Radiant as the moon over the plain
    Of Asopus to the crags of Cithaeron

And there woke up another runner of fire.
The light from a distance was not refused by the watch.
It burned more brightly than others I mentioned. It shot
Over the marshy lake that glittered like Gorgon's
Eyes and came to the mountain where goats were wandering
And stirred up the ancient practice of fire, a relay.
They thought of nothing else, but of lighting the fire
And sent a huge flame in the shape of a beard; it struck
Beyond the headland at the Saronic straits,
Far away. It darted down and reached the top
Of Arachne the watch post at the edge of the city.
It fell down here, at the house of Atreus.
This light had a grandfather, the fire from Mount Ida,
A succession I set up for the bearers of fire:
One after another followed fully the law,
First runner and last, both winners in a great act.
That is the sign, I say to you, the certain
Token sent to me by my husband from Troy.

CHORUS. I'll call to the gods later, my lady, but first
  I'd like to hear the whole story again, all of it.
  I wish to be astonished by your words.

CLYTEMNESTRA. The Greeks hold Troy today.
  I think a mixed cry stands out in the city:
  Pour vinegar and oil into a vessel
  Then speak to them: they are no friends:
  The conquered and the supreme are separate,
  The screams of two kinds of fortune can be heard
  One kind for those who fall upon the bodies
  Of brothers, of men; some children fall upon
  The father from which they sprang—a wailing out
  Through necks no longer free, wailing the ruin
  Of those they loved the most. Another kind
  For others, after the battle, their job of walking
  Around at night sets them, starving, at breakfast
  On whatever the city has. Not arranged
  By rank but, as they drew their chance, by lot,

Now they're living in captured Trojan houses.
They've passed from the dew and ice of the open air.
They have no watch to keep, lucky men
They're blessed and they will sleep throughout the night.
If they worship the gods that protect the city, the temples
Of the gods in the conquered land, then they,
The conquerors, won't be conquered there in turn.
I fear a rage may break upon the army
An overwhelming greed to grasp at things
That are taboo. They have to come home again safely
Around the turn and down the other half
Of the race. If the army returns without swerving from
The gods, if anything evil suddenly happens,
The pain of the dead might be staring at us still.
You've heard what I, a woman, have to say.
Let the right flourish, so it can be clearly seen
I grasp at the profit of many good things.
CHORUS. You speak like a man, my lady, wisely and well.
 Now that I've heard from you the certain proof
I'm ready to give my thanks and chant to the gods.
Good favor and honor has worked out from the pain.
O Zeus the king, and Night a friend
Who places one in many graces
Who threw upon the towers of Troy
A covering network—neither the fully grown
Nor the young could struggle above that
Fishnet of slavery, in justice ensnaring everyone—
I worship Zeus, god of hospitality,
Who did all of this long ago
Bending bow against Paris so that
The arrow wouldn't fall foolishly,
Either too low, or above the stars:

7TH STROPHE

[*toward* CLYTEMNESTRA]

They have to tell of the blow from Zeus,

It is present and can be traced.
He has done what he determined to do. Some say
The gods don't think that mortals are worthy of care.
By whom the grace of sacred things was trampled
People who say so are not reverent,
And now it is clear that a curse
Comes to grandchildren of insufferable men
Puffed up bigger than they should be,
In a house that's filled with too much,
Too much to be good. Let there be just enough
So as not to be harmful
To one who has a fair share of wisdom.
Common sense is a kind of luck.
There isn't any protection
For the man who is too rich
And who has kicked justice
Out of sight from its place of honor.

7TH ANTISTROPHE

[*away from* CLYTEMNESTRA]

He is driven by wretched Persuasion, child of
Unbearable Destruction who plans in advance
There isn't any cure. The harm isn't hidden.
It stands out in horrid bright light;
Brought to justice,
He becomes black, like bad brass
That is rubbed and worn:
A boy runs after a bird with wings
And brings unbearable suffering to his people
No god will listen to the prayers
But forces down an unjust man
Who gets wound up in such things,
Like Paris, who came into the
House of the Atreidae
And dirtied the hospitable table
By stealing the wife.

8TH STROPHE

[*toward* CLYTEMNESTRA]

She left her people:.those with shields
A confusion of military companies,
Sailors getting armed, preparing for war;
She took Destruction for her dowry to Troy;
She stepped lightly through the
Gates, daring the undarable. With many groans,
The poets of the house sang out:
"Oh oh, the house! the house! the chiefs!
Oh the bed, and those pathways that loved the man."
He is seen sitting alone, silent,
Dishonored, not believing it.
She is over the sea and he suffers.
A ghost seems to rule the house.
The man hates the grace
Of beautiful shapes. The statues
That are empty of eyes
And every Aphrodite limps away.

8TH ANTISTROPHE

[*away from* CLYTEMNESTRA]

His dreams show the welcome picture
Of someone who mourns
But it's all in vain.
It isn't true; a man sees what he wants to.
It slips from his arms
Out of sight, and then
It flies away with sleep.
That is the grief in his house and home,
And a greater grief surpasses it:
Mourning is clearly seen
In every house of those who left
The land of Greece together.
Hearts are burdened everywhere.

Many things go right to the liver.
They know whom they sent away,
But urns and ashes came
To each house, instead of men.

9TH STROPHE

[*toward* CLYTEMNESTRA]

Ares, who exchanges gold for bodies,
Who holds the scale in a battle of spears
Sends back to their relatives from Troy
Burned up dust, ashes, bitterly wept for
In neatly arranged urns, instead of men.
They praise and moan for each man:
This one knew how to fight;
Another was brave, and fell in the general murder
For another man's wife.
They growl in silence.
A jealous pain creeps over them,
Because of those plaintiffs, the Atreidae;
Others possess the Trojan earth,
And their beautiful bodies are
Covered by it, in tombs by the Trojan wall

9TH ANTISTROPHE

[*away from* CLYTEMNESTRA]

Angry, resentful people have a deep, bass voice
To call in a debt set up publicly as a curse.
A fear remains in my mind:
That I'll hear about something shrouded in night,
Because the gods don't look away
From those who kill many times. The black
Furies in time will change the luck
For a lucky but unjust man
And wear away his life
And make him dim, and when he can't be
Seen at all, nothing can be done about it.

It is dangerous to hear too many good things about himself:
For lightning strikes out from
The eyes of Zeus.
I want to have power but not envy,
Not enough power to destroy cities
May I never see my life as a captive of others.
The fire brought good news.
A report spread quickly through the
City. Who knows
If it's true, or it's a lie from the gods?
A fire passed the good news from one place to another
Enflamed our hearts, but who would be such a child,
Or senseless enough to become discouraged, if the story were
    different.
A woman is sudden: she will agree
That fortune has come before it really has.
Very persuasive, the word of a female crosses boundaries
And passes on quickly, but quickly dies
A report proclaimed by a woman dies.

CLYTEMNESTRA [angrily].

We'll learn soon enough about the bright signals that bring
Us light, about the fire and about the relays
Whether they're true, or whether the light that came
So cheerfully has cheated our minds like a dream.
I see a herald from the shore and he
Is in the shadow of olive branches; dust—
A thirsty sibling to clay—is a witness
And I am reassured. He won't be silent.
He won't remain unheard; he won't burn wood
In the mountain for signals made of smoke and fire
Instead, his words will be clear and bring good news.
(I shrink from the other kind of news)
May he come to add good to the good that has appeared.

CHORUS. If anyone in the city prays for anything else
    Let him harvest the mistake of his mind.

HERALD. Oh hail, land of my fathers, oh earth of the Greeks,
    I've come to you on the tenth day of this year

Many hopes have snapped, but one held firm. I never
Really believed that I would die in Greece
And have my share in the dearest rites of death.
Oh hail to the land and hail to the light of the sun,
Hail to Zeus, the highest god of the country,
Hail to Apollo the leader: oh may he never
Shoot any more arrows against us with his bow.
Your anger was with us enough at Scamander, but now
Deliver us, heal us, Apollo, the leader, and I speak
To all of the gods presiding over us.
I honor Hermes most, himself a herald
A precious herald who is worshipped by heralds.
And the lesser gods too who sent us upon our way
May they be kind to the remains of the army, after
So many spears: Oh home of kings, oh friendly
Roofs, and chairs of state, statues that face
The sun with glittering eyes, if ever before
And after so long a time, oh, welcome your king.
He comes to you, bringing light in "the kindly time"
For every single person here to share.
King Agamemnon clearly deserves warm welcome
He hacked down Troy with a pickaxe of Zeus the avenger.
He made an end of citizens, shrines, the statues
Of the gods; the soil, the seeds and sperm
Are utterly dead. That's what he tied around Troy.
Our leader, the older of the two, comes home.
He is rich, and now deserves to be honored the most
Of all men. Neither Paris nor his city
That shares the penalty can boast their
Drama was greater than their pathos. Convicted
Of assault and larceny the verdict went
Against him. He also lost in an action for
Repossession. His country and land is utterly
Ruined: His father's house cut down, destroyed.
Priam's sons paid double for their mistake.

CHORUS. Welcome, herald from the army of Greeks: be happy.

HERALD. I'm ready to die, if the gods are longing for me.

CHORUS. Did longing for your fatherland upset you?
HERALD. So much, my eyes are filled with tears of joy.
CHORUS. You're stricken then with a disease of merriment?
HERALD. How's that? Tell me so I can master your words.
CHORUS. You were struck by a longing for those who longed for you.
HERALD [*ambiguously*].
　You say the country yearned for the yearning army.
CHORUS. So much, that I've often groaned in a black mood.
HERALD. Something caused such a hateful fear for the army.
CHORUS. I have an old way of healing hurts—by silence.
HERALD. Did someone make you tremble, with the commanders
　　away?
CHORUS. So much, that death would be good, as you've put it.
HERALD. But if you take the long view, it's worked out well.
　You might say things go easily at times;
　Sometimes you have a complaint. Except for the gods,
　Who ever lives out his life without getting hurt?
　If I were to talk about the heavy work—
　The quarters were cramped, the beds were hard, the covers
　Bad. Was anything right? Everything made
　Us groan. On land, an ever more hateful thing
　Was added: our beds were close to the enemy walls;
　The dew drizzled down from the sky and up from the ground
　Of the meadows, a steady harm that filled the wool
　Of all our clothing with bugs. If I were to talk
　About winter that killed the birds or about the snow
　That came from Mount Ida and brought unbearable cold
　Or else about the heat and the fullness of noon
　At sea: the air was still, not a single wave
　A sudden sleep of death. What need is there
　To go through all of that again? The job
　Is over. It's over also for the dead.
　Never again will they think about getting up again.
　We who are the remains of the army from Greece
　We've won. Our gain is not pulled down
　By those who suffer. Why count out the dead
　With pebbles? Why should the living groan at bad luck?

I think that we who are in the light of the sun
Deserve to be happy, to let our boast rise over
The sea and land. "A band of Greeks grabbed hold
Of Troy. Here are the spoils they nailed to their houses.
An ancient splendor for the gods throughout
The land." When people hear this, they'll praise the city.
The generals will do honor to the favor
From Zeus who brought it about. You have my words.

CHORUS. I'm conquered by your words; I will not shy
 Away. When an old man learns his lesson well,
 He's young again, but probably Clytemnestra
 And the house are most concerned in this that makes me rich.

CLYTEMNESTRA. I shouted with joy a little while ago
 When the fire came, first messenger in the night
 Spelling the taking, the utter destruction of Troy.
 Some people spoke out against me: "Because of the signals
 You think that Troy is ruined now; how very much like a
   woman
 For her heart to rise up with hope."
 And so they spoke and made me seem distraught.
 I made the sacrifices anyway,
 And they, like women, shouted here and there
 In the city. They bayed out praise; their incense put
 The flames to sleep and made the incense smoke on the shrines.
 Do you need to tell me anything more right now?
 The leader himself will give me all the news
 And I must hurry to welcome back in the very
 Best way my honored man. What light ever flashes
 More sweetly for a woman than when she opens
 The gates for her husband, saved in a war by a god?
 Take that as a message back to my mate, and let
 The people's darling come back as fast as he can
 To find his wife as faithful as he left her
 A watchdog in the house, loyal to him
 Hostile to enemies, always the right reaction.
 No seal was ever torn, not once in the war.
 I've had no delight from another man; no scandal.

I've been hot metal thrust into water that's cold.
And what I say is loaded with truth; there's nothing
Disgraceful for a well-born woman to sing it out.
CHORUS. And now that she has spoken, her words'll be pretty
To you, if you have a clear interpreter.
It's your turn to speak, oh herald; I want to hear
About Menelaos, whether he's back with you,
And safely returning, dear ruler of this ground.
HERALD. I can not say that the false is pretty
After a long time I can not drop fruits for friends to pick up.
CHORUS. Say something, perhaps, that's true, but also good.
If truth is split from good, that's hard to hide.
HERALD. The man has vanished from the Grecian army
Both he and his ship, and what I say's not false.
CHORUS. Was he in sight when he sailed from Troy; or did
A storm upon the entire fleet select him?
HERALD. You've hit the target like an expert in archery;
The agony was long; your story was brief.
CHORUS. Is he presumed among the living or dead?
What do the other sailors say about him?
HERALD. No report is clear, and no one knows
Save Helios who makes things grow on earth.
CHORUS. Tell us about the storm that came upon
The fleet and finished its work through spiteful forces.
HERALD. To stain a clear bright day with evil words
Is surely not the way to honor the gods.
A herald has a hateful face, if he brings
To a city the abhorred disaster of an army slain
A wound for all the city and all the people slain,
The double scourge, disaster, loved by Ares
A hateful pain drives many men away
From many homes as if they were polluted.
A man who wears disaster on his back
Should clearly spell a ritual song to the Furies.
But if he comes to a city rejoicing in
Its happiness, with happy news about
A saving action . . . how can I mix with good

The bad, and speak of storms, the fury of
The gods against the Greeks? The former enemies,
Fire and sea, together swore a truce
And showed their faith to each other by killing the desperate
Band of Greeks. The evil waves rose in a stormy
Sea at night, ships blasted against each other
A Thracian force that butted like a horn.
The gale, the spray, the driving rains—as if
An evil shepherd whipped them—sank them out
Of sight. The bright light of the sun came up:
We saw the Aegean sea, blossoming with
Bodies of Greeks, and the wrecks of ships. Some god
Not a mortal grabbed the tiller, and either stole
Us away, or pleaded for us and our ship—its hull
Still pure, and Fortune was willing to sit on our ship:
It didn't get the force of waves at anchor;
It didn't run into the rocky earth.
We escaped from the watery hell, so later in
The whiteness of day, we didn't trust our luck
Our moods were grazing on the recent suffering
The evil pounding of our miserable fleet.
And now, if any of them are breathing still
They speak of us as dead. Why not? We think
The same about them. May it work out for the best.
And most of all, expect Menelaos to
Return, and expect that a ray of sun will find
Him still with sight and among the living. There's hope
That he'll come back to his house again, and by
The workings of Zeus, who doesn't wish to destroy
The race, know then that what you've heard is the truth.

1ST STROPHE

[*moving toward stage left*]

CHORUS. Who gave the name
   With such complete truth?
   Was it a being we cannot see

Someone who spoke accurately
Of things before they happened,
Named her Helen, clearly Hell-on
Ships, men and towns. Helen—
Her wedding had spears and fighting.
She sailed out of the
Richly threaded canopy
Zephyrs born of the earth, drove her by his blast
Many men, fighters with shields, hunters,
Followed the last tracks made by oars,
By those who had found a harbor
At the beach of Simois, where leaves grow.
Such was the will of Murderous Strife.

1st Antistrophe

[*to stage right*]

Rage that thinks things through.
Drove upon Troy
A marriage that's rightly called a "bond."
Much later, Revenge totaled up the bill
Due for disgracing both a table
And Zeus who shares the hearth.
Revenge gave it those who bellowed a song of nubility
And left the wedding song for the relatives to sing.
They had to learn a different hymn,
To groan out a great varied threnody
Priam's old city must now call
Paris the hideously married
Everywhere a varied threnody
Uttered for senseless
Suffering, the blood of a people.

2nd Strophe

[*to stage left*]

A lion's child
That loved the nipple but got no milk

Was reared in a man's house
A tame prelude
To its life
Delighting the adults
Loving children
In their arms,
Like a nursing baby
Looking happy, forced
By its belly to fawn
At their hands.

2ND ANTISTROPHE

[*to stage right*]

In time it displayed
The character of its parents
It returned the favor
To those who had reared it
(This uninvited guest)
By making a feast out of a mad
Slaughter of sheep.
The house was wet throughout with blood,
An agony to the household without a fight
A huge slaughtering,
By a god's will, it had been reared with others
To be a sacrificer for Revenge.

3RD STROPHE

[*to stage left*]

That is how a calm
Came to the city of Troy, no wind
Gentle ornaments of wealth
Eyes that glanced with gentleness,
A flower of desire ate into their hearts.
But she swerved away from all this
And made a bitter fulfillment of the marriage
An evil companion settled with

The sons of Priam.
Zeus, kind to strangers,
Sent and escorted a Fury
Who brings tears to brides.

3RD ANTISTROPHE

[*to stage right*]

A long time ago, mortal men first said
That when happiness is fully grown
It never dies without children,
That out of good fortune,
A misery blossoms that is never satisfied.
But I say impiety is the cause
(I'm alone in this thought,
Split off from the others).
Impiety breeds many more things
Of the very same kind.
The just house
Always has pretty progeny.

4TH STROPHE

[*to stage left*]

Old hybris likes to hatch young hybris
In evil mortals.
Sooner or later,
At an appointed day, hybris joins Atē
A force greater than battle and war
An unholy courage, a black Atē
For the smoke-blackened hearth,
A child like her parents.

4TH ANTISTROPHE

[*to stage right*]

Justice is bright
In smoke-filled houses

And honors the right sort of life
She looks the other way
And leaves, when hands are foul,
Even in gold-sprinkled houses

[*Enter* AGAMEMNON *followed by* KASSANDRA *et al.*]

Where men give a false distinction to wealth.
She comes to the reverent,
And brings everything to a good conclusion.

[CHORUS *turns far stage right by* CLYTEMNESTRA *and faces*
AGAMEMNON.]

Oh king, who destroyed the city of Troy
Son of Atreus,
Tell me how to speak to you, how to honor you
Neither too much, nor too little,
But with just the right courtesy.
Many mortals think more about seeming than being
And they miss a just proportion.
Everyone who is ready to groan
At another's pain, doesn't really
Feel the pain in his own liver
Any more than the joy, forced upon an unsmiling
Face for another's good fortune.
But if you can judge sheep,
You can't miss the look in a man's eye
Who seems to have honest thoughts,
But fawns with watery friendship.
I won't hide it from you. The picture
I once had of you was so ugly, no Muse would recognize it.
When you led the army for Helen's sake,
You had no grasp on the tiller of your soul,
You made a sacrifice,
To cure men who were dying.
But I'm not bitter now, not unfriendly.
The job has turned out well
You will ask questions and in time you'll find out

Those who were just, and those who weren't
Among the people who stayed in the city.
AGAMEMNON. First, it is right to address Argos and the gods
Of the region, who were in part the cause of my coming
Home—of my exacting justice from
Priam's city. The gods first heard the unspoken
Rival arguments, then dropped a stone
In a jar, explicitly voting for the death of Troy.
Destruction in one urn, the hope of a hand
Approached the other, but it wasn't filled up. The city
Is conquered, and still is distinguished by smoke. A fierce
Wind lives so the ashes that die with the city send forth
Rich, thick smoke. We should never forget to pay
The gods for this again and again. We
Got even for an arrogant robbery. A Grecian
Monster killed the city for a woman's sake.
A brood from a horse, a crowd of men bearing shields
Leaping up as the Pleiades were sinking
A lion jumped over the wall to eat raw flesh
To lick his fill with the blood of tyrants. I've stretched
This prelude out to the gods; but I've heard and held
In my mind your moods. I agree with them, and you
Have a supporter in me. Very few men
Really have it within them to respect—
Without being jealous—A friend who has good fortune.
Hostility is a poison that comes at the heart,
A double load for the owner of the disease,
His very own sorrows weigh him down and he groans
When he gazes upon the happiness of a stranger.
I know what conversations are: they're mirrors.
When people seem kind, the image is of a shadow.
Odysseus did not want to sail, the only
One, but he was easily led when once
In harness I speak of him, whether he's dead or alive.
For the rest, we will set up general meetings, and
Assembled, consider whatever concerns the city
And the gods, consider how to strengthen

Beautiful things and how to make them last.
We'll try to burn out, and graciously cut away
With wisdom, to turn a disease away and put it
To flight, for anything needing a medicine.

[*one step forward, half turning downstage as if speaking to the palace.*]

And now I'll go to my home, where the rafters are black
With smoke from the hearth, to shake hands first with the gods
Who sent me away and brought me back. And now
That victory's at my side, may it stay in place.
CLYTEMNESTRA. Men of the city!

[AGAMEMNON *looks at her directly for the first time.*]

Elders of Greece! I'm not
Ashamed of the kind of love I have for my husband.
I'll tell you about it: Fright is a thing that dies
For men, in time; something I have not learned
From others but from my life; I'll tell you about
The pain, as long as he was in front of Troy:
First, it's a striking evil for any woman
To stay at home alone, to be split away
From her husband. She keeps on hearing rumors:
One man screams throughout the house about a growing
Disaster; another man brings a worse disaster
To scream throughout the house. If he'd been drilled
With as many wounds as rumors that flooded the house
He'd be as full of holes as a net. If he
Had died as many times as people said,
He'd be a second Geryon, three bodies
Boasting that under a cloak of earth each shape—
(Plenty of earth above him, I do not speak
Of the amount below)—he died in every shape he took.
The rumors kept coming back, and so, many times,
They freed my neck from a noose by force.
That is why our son Orestes doesn't
Stand here as he should at our side a sign of our faith.

Don't be surprised by this, for he is protected by
Our friend with a spear, the Phocian
Strophius rears him and spoke, before it was
Announced to me, of a double disaster, your danger
In front of Troy, the shouts of people threatening
To tear down the councils, without a leader. Mortal
Men kick hard with their heels whoever is down.
They're like that. Those are the reasons without deceit.
My tears, a rapid fountain, have run dry,
Not a drop left. I went to bed late, my eyes
Hurt from mourning as no one paid attention
To the beacon stands. The delicate fluttering
Of a gnat resounded like a barking, to wake
Me, from my dreams where I saw more sufferings than could
Have happened in the time I was asleep. I endured
All that. My mood is now without pain. I'd name
That man the watchdog of the house, the first
And saving stay of a ship, a pillar that runs
From roof to the ground, a father's only child,
Land that wasn't hoped for, appearing to sailors
A flowing spring for a traveller, who is parched,
After a storm, the sight of a day that is fair.
It's sweet to escape from need. That's the way
He should be extolled. We want to envy; we held
Up against evils, and now my dearest of all
Step down from this chariot, but not on this earth leader
Of men, not with the foot that ruined Troy.
Slaves! Why hesitate? You have been told
To spread out carpets on the grounds, to make
A road of purple carpets right away
Let Justice, wide awake, escort him with care,
With the help of the gods to the home he never hoped
To see again. Let everything be as fated.
AGAMEMNON. Child of Leda, and guardian of my house,
    You rightly stretched your speech out, like my absence.
    Praise however should come from other people.
    Do not make me delicate, a kind

Of woman. Do not cringe upon the ground and cry out
Like some barbaric thing. Don't
Bring jealousy down, by decorating my path
To step upon woven, beautiful things is a way
To celebrate the gods and strikes me as fearful.
Let the procedures be without fear.
Honor me as a man, I say, not a god.
Fame will resound without embroidered footmats
Right thinking is the greatest gift from the gods
If a man completes his life and he's rich, why then
It's right to praise him. If I do, as I have done, I will be
    confident.

CLYTEMNESTRA. Do not say a word against my purpose.
AGAMEMNON. My purpose cannot be destroyed. Be sure of that.
CLYTEMNESTRA. You were terrified, and made a promise to
    the gods.
AGAMEMNON. I knew exactly what I meant, when I spoke.
CLYTEMNESTRA. What would Priam have done, if he'd won out?
AGAMEMNON. He would have walked on tapestries, all right.
CLYTEMNESTRA. Do not be afraid that men will blame you.
AGAMEMNON. But the people have a powerful voice.
CLYTEMNESTRA. No one competes with a man who isn't envied.
AGAMEMNON. It isn't womanly to long for a struggle.
CLYTEMNESTRA. To give way is splendid for a fortunate man.
AGAMEMNON. So that's what you want to win in this argument?
CLYTEMNESTRA. Obey me. Let me have my own power.
    If you willingly leave it to me—you are stronger.
AGAMEMNON. If that's the way it seems to you, let someone
    Quickly take these boots off, slaves for my feet
    To step on; when I tread down upon these purple

[He moves toward the purple carpet, but stops at the edge.]

Embroideries, of the gods,
Let no jealous eye from above strike me.
A shame holds me back, to ruin with my feet
Wealth of the house, weavings worth silver.
So much for that. Graciously escort

This foreign woman to the house
A god from above looks with favor
If we use power mildly.
Nobody willingly stoops to slavery.
She is a gift from the army, a flower
Picked for me alone from among many.
Since I listen to you, I am overruled,
And will go to the house, pressing my feet down on purple.
CLYTEMNESTRA. There is the sea and who will drain it? It breeds
A replenishing ooze of purple, rich as silver
For staining clothes. Thanks to the gods oh king
Our house has plenty of things like these. Our house
Does not know how to be in misery. If
An oracle had suggested it, when I
Was figuring ways of saving this man's life
I would have stepped on many rich clothes to keep
A vow for the house. A root remains, leaves flourish
Above the house and stretch out a shade against
The scorching Dog Star. So your coming back
To your home is like bringing warmth in winter.
When Zeus makes wine from unripe grapes, then
The house is cool while the master moves about.
Zeus, Zeus the fulfiller, fulfill my prayers;
And have a care for what you wish to fulfill.

[AGAMEMNON *treads on the purple carpet.*]

IST STROPHE

CHORUS. Why is this fright facing my
    Prophetic heart,
    So constantly fluttering?
    Not bidden, not paid for, a chant sings of the future.
    Why can't I spurn it
    Like a bad dream?
    Why doesn't an obedient courage

[*Exit* AGAMEMNON.]

Make a throne in my mood?

It's been a long, long time
Since the navy set out for Troy
Threw out the cables,
Threw up the sand.

1st Antistrophe

My own eyes tell me
They are coming home
I am my own witness
Without a lyre, but like a hymn
The threnody of the Furies within
My soul sings on, self-taught.
I have no hope, no dear courage.
The feelings of the viscera
Are not foolish.
The heart swirls against the mind
Where justice is known.
But I pray that I am wrong
That it doesn't come about.

2nd Strophe

There's such a thing as too much health
That can break through into disease.
Fate never swerves
But a man sails
Straight upon a hidden reef
And to keep the ship from drowning
The whole house from sinking
Filled to bulging with freight
Something must be thrown overboard,
Just the right amount.
But Zeus can spread out a gift.
The yearly tracing of furrows
Destroys famine.

2nd Antistrophe

But once a deadly blow is prematurely struck
A man's dark blood is on the ground.

Who can lift it up again by incantation?
Zeus didn't save from harm
That man who knew how
To raise up the dead.
It's in the order of things,
My lot, no other lot,
Keeps me from getting more from the gods,
My heart would pour this out,
Running faster than my tongue
Now it mutters in the dark,
Grieving with no hope
Of winding anything up.
My mind is on fire.

CLYTEMNESTRA. You too Kassandra, I say, go inside, since Zeus
Isn't angry, and lets you in our house to stand
By the altar with the slaves and share the ritual
Washings. Step down from the chariot; don't be proud.
Once Herakles was sold, they say, and had
To eat bread with slaves. But if the balance
Tips the wrong way, one's lucky to find a master
With well-established wealth. The newly rich
Are cruel to their slaves in everything but we
Are strict but fair. And now I've told you our customs.

CHORUS. She's spoken to you, and spoken clearly enough.
You're caught in a net, and that's your lot. You should
Obey her now but perhaps you won't.

CLYTEMNESTRA. Unless she is like a swallow, the one possessed
By unknown words that are barbaric, I may
Reach her mind, my words might well persuade her.

CHORUS. Follow her. She's told you things are best the way
They are. Obey. Come down from the seat on the wagon.

CLYTEMNESTRA. I don't have time to waste outside.
Inside the house, the sheep are at the altar,
Ready for sacrificing, a joy we hadn't
Hoped for. But you, if you're going to act, do it.
But if you're senseless, if my words cannot reach you
Don't talk. Gesture with your stranger's hand.

CHORUS. The stranger seems to need a clear interpreter

She's like a newly caught beast—that's her style.
CLYTEMNESTRA. She's mad, she listens to her evil mind
She comes here captured from a city. She doesn't
Know how to wear a bridle, until she has foamed
Her fierceness away in blood. I won't throw away
More words merely to be dishonored.
CHORUS. I'm sorry for her; I will not rage. Poor thing,
Come—let the chariot be empty, take on
The yoke of strange necessity, willingly.

1ST STROPHE

KASSANDRA. Oh agony, agony. The pain, the pain
Apollo, Destroyer
CHORUS. Why do you call on Apollo and wail?
He's not the right god for laments.

1ST ANTISTROPHE

KASSANDRA. No no no no. Never, never,
Apollo. Destroyer.
CHORUS. Again, she invokes the wrong god.
He's never present at lamentations.

2ND STROPHE

KASSANDRA. Apollo. Destroyer.
Apollo who guards the streets
Destroying me, utterly a second time.
CHORUS. She may prophesy, about her own evils.
A gift of the gods in the mind of a slave.

2ND ANTISTROPHE

KASSANDRA. Apollo, Destroyer.
Apollo who guards the streets, destroys me
Where oh where are you bringing me. To what house?
CHORUS. To the Atreidae's house. If you don't recognize it,
I'll tell you, and it's not false.

3RD STROPHE

KASSANDRA. Oh, oh
God-hater stood by and saw

The killing of kind, and the ropes,
A place to kill man, the ground is sprinkled
CHORUS. The stranger seems like a dog with a good nose
Searching for a murder she'll find one.

3RD ANTISTROPHE

KASSANDRA. Here is the evidence I believe in:
Infants, screaming as they are slaughtered
A father gnawing upon baked flesh.
CHORUS. We've heard about your glory as a prophet
But we aren't looking for one.

4TH STROPHE

KASSANDRA. Oh, never: What is she bringing about?
What new anguish?
She is going to do a great evil in the house
Unbearable, to her loved ones
Beyond help, there's no
Defense here at all.
CHORUS. What does this mean? I don't understand.
I know what you meant a moment ago: the city thunders
with it.

4TH ANTISTROPHE

KASSANDRA. Despicable woman: So that's your aim?
The man in your bed, your husband,
The bath, the water, he's clean and shining. But your purpose?
It will be quick, hand over hand, reaching out . . .
CHORUS. Still I do not understand. These riddles are like
Spots before my eyes, sayings of a god, undecipherable.

5TH STROPHE

KASSANDRA. Oh, never, never. What's this I see?
A net from hell
The net is the wife, an accomplice in murder.
Treachery, never satisfied, will warble and gloat
At a killing that calls for revenge by stoning.

CHORUS. What sort of Fury do you call
   To sing above the house. Your words aren't clean and shining.
   A drop, a purple stain speeds to my heart
   That stain, if a man's brought down by spear,
   Comes with the last rays of light.
   Disaster comes quickly.

5TH ANTISTROPHE

KASSANDRA. Oh, oh. Keep the cow away from the
   Bull. She's caught him in a garment,
   Black-horned devising, she strikes.
   He falls into the bath.
   I speak of a murderous trick in a caldron.
CHORUS. I can't brag. I don't know much about the sayings of gods.
   But this seems evil to me.
   Are the sayings of gods ever pretty
   For mortals? The long-winded ways of
   Prophets teach us to be afraid.

6TH STROPHE

KASSANDRA. Oh, oh, misery for an evil lot
   I pour my sufferings on top of his.
   I'm miserable. Why did you bring me here?
   To die with you? Is that it?
CHORUS. A mad mind, carried away by the gods,
   You wail for yourself,
   A tune without a tune, yellow and shrill
   You can't cry enough, a miserable mood, alas,
   The nightingale's "Itys, Itys," a double flourishing,
   Of agony for one's life.

6TH ANTISTROPHE

KASSANDRA. Oh, oh the warbling of the nightingale ends
   The gods covered her body with feathers, gave her
   A sweet stretch of time without cries.
   A double-edged spear will split me.
CHORUS. Which gods carry you away

In useless suffering
And make you come out with
Songs, senseless cries, loud sounds?
Who set the edges of that path toward
Prophecy of evil?

7TH STROPHE

KASSANDRA. Oh, the wedding. The wedding of Paris killed his
    family.
Oh Scamander, the river of my ancestors,
I grew up on your shores, long ago, oh misery,
Now it seems that I must sing my prophecies
Standing by the rivers of the dead.
CHORUS. What have you said? It's all too clear
A little child could get the point.
I'm struck by a killing sting
From the enormous pain of what's happened, you whimper
And I am shattered to hear it.

7TH ANTISTROPHE

KASSANDRA. Oh pain, pain, my city is cut to the ground
All of my father's sacrifices,
Killing again and again, beasts that were grazing
Nothing helped, nothing saved the walls,
Nothing stopped the suffering we were doomed for,
And my own hot blood will soon fall to the ground.
CHORUS. Your words are like those of a moment ago
An evil-minded power bears you down,
Makes you sound out lamentations of death
I don't discern the end of it.
KASSANDRA. The oracle's answer will now be clear and not
Behind a veil, a bride; a new, a bright
Arrival, like a wind at sunrise, it will seem.
A wave, a greater agony, will wash
Over and break to the rays of light. I won't
Use any more riddles. Watch me and go along
As I track after the smell of ancient ills.

Every chorus that leaves this house grunts
Together, ugly sound with an ugly message.
The house is drunk with courage by feeding on human
Blood. The Furies, party-makers, stay
In the house, disorderly crowd ill-bred like the others
And not to be driven out, they moan their chant
In the house. Of the first and ancient hatred, one
Following after another. They despise
A brother's bed, the one who trampled upon it.
(Doing what Thyestes did to Atreus' wife)
Am I an archer who has missed or hit?
Do I babble, knock on a door to tell you lies?
You can swear to it, under oath that I
Know about the ancient mistake of this house.

CHORUS. How could an oath, no matter how firm, be a cure?
    You astound me: brought up beyond the sea
    You speak a language that's strange, but what you say
    Is right, as if you'd been here all along.

KASSANDRA. Apollo, the prophet, employed me for this role.

CHORUS. You mean that he—a god—was struck with lust?

KASSANDRA. I was ashamed to speak about it, before.

CHORUS. One is delicate, when things go well.

KASSANDRA. His breath heaved favor upon me, he was a contender.

CHORUS. And you went through the making of children like others?

KASSANDRA. Apollo and I were one, and I betrayed him.

CHORUS. After you had the gift of telling the future?

KASSANDRA. After I told my people what they'd suffer.

CHORUS. Wasn't Apollo's anger crippling for you?

KASSANDRA. Afterwards, no one believed my words.

CHORUS. And yet your prophecies seem true to us.

KASSANDRA. Agony agony, evil evil!
    The dreadful pain of prophecy is upon
    Me, whirls me again in an anarchy of discordant
    Preludes. You see them. The young outside the house
    Children, unreal, the shape of dreams like those
    Killed by their kin with hands full of meat, food
    Of that house; they hold their entrails you can see it,

A pitiful burden, the hearts lungs liver kidneys
Their own father ate. I tell you a punishment
Is plotted here, staying at home, in
And out of bed, a coward, a lion waiting
For the return alas of the ruler. (And I
Must stoop to slavery.) The leader of the fleet,
Troy's ravager, doesn't know. Her tongue, the hateful
Bitch, has made a long speech. She's cheerful, radiant
But she will kill him secretly—when
She gets her chance for evil. Such is her darling
The female killer of the male. What
Can I call her? Unnatural serpent? Fore-and-aft sting?
Or Scylla who lives in the rocks that wreck a sailor?
A storming mother from Hades breathing war
Against her own kind? She never drinks a truce.
There isn't a thing she wouldn't dare to do.
She wailed as if ecstatic at the turn
Of war, so grateful for his safe return.
If I cannot persuade you, then . . . never mind:
What will be, will be. You'll see it soon:
Pity will make you call me a truthful prophet.
CHORUS. I know what you mean by the feast of Thyestes, the eating
Of children's flesh. I bristle, and I am full
Of fear because of the truth, not the images.
But when I hear the rest . . . I'm utterly lost.
KASSANDRA. Agamemnon's death! You'll see it, I tell you.
CHORUS. Poor woman! Lull your voice with proper words.
KASSANDRA. No healer presides, or cures what I have to say.
CHORUS. Not if it happens that way. May it not happen.
KASSANDRA. You pray against it, but they're concerned about killing.
CHORUS. What man is preparing to do this painful thing?
KASSANDRA. You've clearly missed the point of my prophecies.
CHORUS. Who will do this? Who are they? I don't understand.
KASSANDRA. And yet I understand Greek, only too well.
CHORUS. The oracles at Pytho are Greek, and yet they're hard to
understand.

KASSANDRA. No no! A fire comes over me. No no.
   Never never. Apollo, Lynceus, help me, help me.
   A lioness with two feet lies down with the wolf;
   The lion—nobly born—is away. She'll kill
   Me—help me—as if she made a medicine
   And mixed it with revenge as my reward.
   Boasting she sharpens a sword for a man; she says
   She'll kill; They brought me here, and that's her excuse.
   Why do I have these ornaments, this scepter,
   The beads that hang upon my neck, they mock me.
   Before I'm doomed, before my fate, I will
   Destroy you, go down to destruction and
   I will follow. Make someone else rich with destruction.
   Look! Apollo himself undoes my robes.
   He led me into mysteries, dressed in robes.
   People scorned me among my friends, hatefully, madly.
   They called me "beggar" as if I wandered about
   For alms, "miserable," "starve!"
   I see the future. The prophet Apollo kills me.
   A chopping block, and not my father's altar
   Is there, for me. I see my sacrifice
   Hot blood and slaughter. We shall not die dishonored
   By gods, for someone will come to avenge us, a son
   Who'll kill his mother, avenge his father. A stranger
   Returned to this land, an exile a wanderer,
   He'll settle destruction within his clan. The gods
   Have been sworn a great oath. His father unburied stretched out
   Will drive him. Why do I feel sorry? And why
   Do I groan aloud? I saw what happened to Troy
   The attackers were freed by the judgment of the gods,
   But I am going to suffer and to die.
   I call this door the gates of Hades, I pray
   The right sort of stroke, so I need to struggle in death.
   When the blood runs, may I close my eyes together.
CHORUS. Miserable miserable woman, but also wise.
   You have spoken at length. But if you know

The truth about your death, why are you not
Afraid, like an ox driven by a god
You tread so boldly to the altar?

KASSANDRA. Strangers, there's no way out and no more time.

CHORUS. But you would have the best of it, if you were last.

KASSANDRA. The day is here. I won't go far if I run.

CHORUS. You can endure, because you are courageous.

KASSANDRA. Happy people are never called courageous.

CHORUS. To die and be famous is a gift for mortals.

KASSANDRA. No! father, no! You—and your children.

CHORUS. What do you want? What fear makes you turn away?

KASSANDRA [utters a guttural sound].

CHORUS. Why do you retch? What horror is in your mood.

KASSANDRA. The house is breathing murder, and drips blood.

CHORUS. How's this? You smell the sacrifice at the hearth.

KASSANDRA. It stands out exactly like the smoke at a grave.

CHORUS. You're not speaking about a Syrian incense.

KASSANDRA. I'll go to the house and shriek about our fate,
Agamemnon's and mine. The life I've had
Will have to do. Oh strangers! I'm not a bird
In a shrub. I moan "oh me . . ." from fear. Remember
Me when I am dead. One woman dies
For another; another man falls for an ill-wedded man.
I am a suppliant about to die.

CHORUS. You suffer. I pity your death that a god foretold.

KASSANDRA. I've one more speech, perhaps a dirge, my own,
I lift my hands to the sun, that farthest light,
To pray that those who killed the two of us
May hatefully be killed. To kill a slave's
An easy conquest. Poor busy mortals! I pity
Success that can be turned by a shadow, but
I pity more the misfortune that a stroke
Of a sponge wipes out forever, no picture left.

CHORUS. Men die and are greedy for prosperity, They never
Have enough.
People may point their fingers at a rich house, but who
Shuts out prosperity

And clearly says, "Enough, don't enter!"? None. The blessed
Gods gave a gift
And let him take Priam's city. Let him return, honored
By gods. But suppose
Now he had to die, pay death for the deaths of those who
Died before.
Who among mortal men would brag that he was born
Never to be hurt if heard such news?

AGAMEMNON [*offstage*]. Oh me! I'm struck a deadly blow and deep.

CHORUS. Silence! Who screams that he's been hurt by a blow?

AGAMEMNON. Oh me! Another blow, I'm struck again.

CHORUS. I think the deed is done from the cries of the king.
We mustn't stumble but find a plan together.

1. I tell you what I think best to do: Let's have
The criers call the citizens to this house.

2. It seems to me, we should rush in at once
And while the sword is drawn, we'll have the proof.

3. I share the judgment of my partner. I vote
For doing something or other: and now's the time.

4. It's clear. This prelude is a sign that they
Are working a tyranny upon the city.

5. We're wasting time; they tread upon a decent
Delay; they'll act at once, no sleep in their hands.

6. I don't know how to set up any plan;
One cannot act unless one plans as well.

7. And I agree with you. I'm at a loss:
Words will never bring the dead to life.

8. Shall we stretch out our lives and be withdrawn
Before these ravagers who'll rule the house?

9. That is unbearable; it's a greater thing
To die, a more gentle end than tyranny.

10. But shall we take a prophecy as proof
Should we assume he's dead from just his groans?

11. We should have clear knowledge about this before we talk
And guessing is quite different from clear knowledge.

12. One thing about this overwhelms me clearly.
We must know what has happened to Agamemnon.

CLYTEMNESTRA. I've said many things appropriate to the moment
I'm not ashamed to say the opposite now.
What else but hate an enemy who seemed a friend?
Was I to fence them in so they couldn't leap out?
This feud had been in my mind for a long time.
The clash was put off, but finally it came.
I stand here, where I rushed upon him. I've done it.
I do not deny it. He could not run away
He could not avoid his death. I wind an endless
Net, like a fishnet around him, an evil rich robe.
I strike him twice. Right there. And twice he screams.
His limbs grow limp. A third stroke is my prayer
To Zeus who lives beneath the earth and protects
The dead. He lies there, and vomits out his own
Life. He gasps out killing spurts of blood and I
Am drenched by a dew, drizzling and black, and I
Am glad. The fields are sown, the sprouts come up,
A gift of the gods, and in birth, the flower buds
Are bright as metal ornaments upon
A dress. And now you have it, old men of Greece.
Be thankful if you care to. I am ecstatic.
We pour the right libation on the dead:
My curses are right, exactly right
He mixed accursed evils into a bowl
And then he drank it off when he came home.
CHORUS. We are astonished. You are so insolent:
To swagger with words like that about your husband.
CLYTEMNESTRA. You put me on trial as a giddy woman, but I
Don't tremble. You know the facts, so find
Some fault or other if you like, or approve
It's all the same. There he is. My Agamemnon.
My husband. A corpse. This right hand did
The job, and justly too. So there you have it.

1st Strophe

CHORUS. Woman, you've tasted
An evil thing, grown from the earth,

You've drunk poison from the flowing sea
To set up such a sacrifice. The people curse you:
You hurled him away, you cut down. You'll be an exile,
With the heavy hatred of the citizens.
CLYTEMNESTRA. You sentence me to exile from the city
To hatred from citizens, people's curses, but you
Did not bear up against the man lying there.
As if a beast were to die, some sheep from a big
And grazing flock, with no regard he killed
His daughter, my dearest, the one I suffered for
In childbirth—a spell against the Thracian winds.
Why didn't you exile him as a price for his
Pollution? But when you hear about my acts
You judge me roughly. I tell you: go ahead
And threaten. But be ready for the same.
The hand that conquers me, can also rule me.
If it's the other way about, through a god,
You will be taught, and you will learn but
Too late, how to be calm and prudent.

1st Antistrophe

CHORUS. You are ambitious
Your thoughts ring high and wide
Blood has dripped into your mind and made you mad.
The clot is clearly in your eyes
You have no friend and in return
Stroke for stroke you must pay.
CLYTEMNESTRA. Now hear me: my oath is strong because it's right
    and proper.
I did what I did for my child by Dike goddess
Of justice, Atē, Destruction, Erinys, the Furies.
I cut his throat for them. My hopes will never
Step into the halls of fear. Not so long
As Aigisthos, right-thinking, keeps my hearth fire lit.
His loyalty is outstanding. He is a shield.
He gives me enormous courage. But there lies
The ravager of a woman who fondled one Chryseis

After another at Troy, and the slave who saw signs
And slept with him, a faithful prophesying
Whore, the two of them wore out the benches
On the ship. They got what they deserved.
I've told you about him. She died like a swan, and sang
Her last in death. Those lovers lie there. The thought
Of her is a delicacy when I lie down.

2ND STROPHE

CHORUS. No no. If only we could find
　Unending sleep quickly, without agony,
　Without long suffering in bed
　Our protector was most kind
　But now he's tamed
　He endured much because of a woman,
　A woman cut off his life.

Oh insane Helen,
You and only you killed so many.
So many lives are at Troy.
You have a supreme adornment
An unforgettable one: the blood won't
Wash away. The house was strong against strife,
But strife was there, sharp agony for the husband.

2ND ANTISTROPHE

CLYTEMNESTRA. Don't pray for death
　In your grief.
　Don't turn your spite against Helen
　And call her a woman destroyer
　Of men, as if she had killed
　All of the Greeks at Troy,
　As if she alone caused a wound that won't close.
CHORUS. A force falls upon the house
　And two sons of Tantalus
　Atreus and Thyestes
　A force exerted through women

Who have that sort of mind
(My heart is born down)
A hateful raven
Perches on the body
And sings all out of key.

3RD STROPHE

CLYTEMNESTRA. And now good judgment
   Has straightened out your face:
   You called upon a power within this house,
   A power, fattened three times,
   Who raises a lust in the belly to lick blood
   A new, godlike juice, before the old pain wears off.
CHORUS. You praise an enormous power
   That bears a heavy anger against a house.
   Oh oh what an evil praise for an unending
   Greed for ruin.
   No, no! It's through Zeus.
   He caused it all did it all.
   Without Zeus, nothing is completed for men who die.
   A god ordered everything about this.
   Alas, alas, king, king!
   How can I weep for you?
   How can I put my loving mood into words?
   You lie there in this woven spider's web
   You breathe out your life in a blasphemous death.
   Oh me, oh me. To lie there like a slave,
   Married to death, because your wife's hand
   On a two-edged javelin brought you to a treacherous end.

3RD ANTISTROPHE

CLYTEMNESTRA. You talk loudly, as if I did it.
   But don't fool yourselves
   I am not Agamemnon's wife.
   It was the age-old, piercing power of revenge,
   Alastor, a fantasm, looking like that dead man's wife.
   He did it. He took that man, whose life had run its course

Who had eaten an ugly feast,
And made of him a supreme sacrifice for the young.
CHORUS. How can we testify that you were not
  The cause of this murder?
  How? How? But a spirit, Alastor.
  Born to avenge the father might have helped you.
  The god of killing, black Ares, forces his way
  Through kindred streams of blood. Wherever he moves
  He brings a justice for the cold, congealed
  Blood of the children, served up as meat.

  Oh no. Oh no. king, king!
  How can I weep for you?
  How can I put my loving mood into words?
  You lie there in this woman spider's web.
  You breathe out your life in a blasphemous death
  Oh me, oh me, to lie there like a slave,
  Married to death, because your wife's hand
  On a two-edged javelin brought you to a treacherous end.

4TH STROPHE

CLYTEMNESTRA. I don't think it was a slave's death
  Didn't he use deceit?
  Bring destruction upon the house, upon
  Iphigeneia, wept for, again and again,
  The child I bore from him? I raised her.
  He deserves to suffer for what he did not deserve to do.
  He's not to brag loudly in Hades.
  He's paid for what he has done
  By death with a sword.
CHORUS. I can't figure out which way to turn.
  My mind is robbed
  Of clever attention. The house is falling
  I am afraid
  That a rattling rain of blood will ruin the house, now
  The drizzling has stopped. The Fates, the Moirae,
  Are sharpening justice

On a new whetstone, for a new and damaging act.
Oh earth, earth. If only you
Had received me graciously, before I had seen him
Down in that bed on the ground
The silver-sided bath.
Who will bury him? Who will sing the funeral song? And you?
Are you bold enough to do it?
To mourn aloud for the man you killed?
A criminal completion
For the rites of his soul? A wretched tribute for his great acts?
What tears
Will shoot forth with praise at the tomb of this godlike man?
Who will do it with a truthful mind?

4TH ANTISTROPHE

CLYTEMNESTRA. You are not to trouble yourself with this loving care.
I made him fall down.
I killed him, and I will bury him,
Without wailings from the house
But a happy welcome, as is proper
From his daughter, Iphigeneia.
He will meet her at the rapid
River of pain.
She will throw her arms around her father,
And kiss him.
CHORUS. Reproach has met reproach.
It is hard to judge.
The ravager is ravaged; the killer pays the price;
That's the way it is, while Zeus remains on his throne.
One suffers for what one has done: that is the law.
Who can throw a generation of curses out of the house?
The tribe is glued together for destruction.

CLYTEMNESTRA. You have boarded this oracle with truth.
I have made an oath.
With the powers of the house of Pleisthenes
I am willing to endure what has been

Hard to endure; but for what remains
Let the power go to some other house
And wear them down with self-slaughter.
If I have a little bit of what I own,

[*Enter* AIGISTHOS *and* BODYGUARD.]

I have enough, if that takes away from our halls,
The madness of killing one another.
AIGISTHOS. Oh splendid light of day that brings revenge!
Now I can say that gods watch over the pains
Of earth and avenge the mortals. I've seen this man
In a cloth, woven by the Furies, lying
Unburied, I'm glad to say, paying for
The tricks by his father's hand. When this man's father
Atreus ruled the land, he banished his brother
Thyestes, my father, to put it clearly. He called
My father's sovereignty in doubt and drove
Him from his city and his home. Thyestes
Suffered and returned, begging for shelter,
And found a steady fate for himself, no killing
No letting of blood upon his father's ground.
As a welcome, Atreus, the godless father
Of that man—there!—with more ambition than kindness
Pretended to butcher for a feast, but served to
My father, a banquet of the children's flesh,
Cutting them up, all the way down to the feet
And out to the hands. Spaced at intervals
They sat at the table. Thyestes noticed nothing
But right away began to eat a meal
And as you see, he spread disaster for
The entire house. As soon as he recognized
His own unrighteousness, he screamed, and falling
Backwards, he vomited out the gobbets, and then
He called for unbearable death to the race of Pelops,
He kicked the table over: a sign of the curse:
"Die like that, you and the Pleisthenes."
You see the result. That man is trodden down.

I was just, when I stitched together this killing.
I was the thirteenth, forced into exile, a tiny
Thing in swaddling clothes, going with
My wretched father. I grew up, and Justice
Brought me back again. I was outside
The door, but in effect I grabbed that man:
I'd put the pieces of the deadly plan
Together, and so I'd find it lovely now
To die: I've seen that man in the snare of Justice.

CHORUS. Aigisthos, I don't respect your gloating over
Evil: You alone have killed that man?
You say you planned this pitiful murder? I say
In Justice, your head will not escape the curses
Hurled by people—and be sure of this—death by stoning.

AIGISTHOS. You sound like that? You, at the oars below?
The man topside is ruler. You'll be taught
A lesson, a heavy one to learn when you are old:
How to be temperate. But being tied in prison
And fasting are two eminent doctors, prophets
Who'll teach you, even when you're old. If you
Can see at all, you can see this: Don't dig
Your heel into an ox-goad: you'll suffer pain.

CHORUS. You woman! We have come from fighting
But you stayed home, defiling that man's bed,
The leader of the army: you plotted his death.

AIGISTHOS. That sort of thing is the start of weary wailing.
Your tongue is not at all like Orpheus:
His voice led everything to beneficence.
Your childish yappings are exasperating:
You'll be led away, controlled, and tamed.

CHORUS. As if you'd be sole ruler over Greeks
You? Who plotted that man's death but didn't
Have the courage to do the killing yourself?

AIGISTHOS. The deceitful part—that's clearly the woman's job.
He'd squint at me, his age-old enemy.
I'll try to use his money to rule the people.
I'll put the disobedient under a harness

A heavy one, no rope for a barley-fed filly.
Hateful hunger, shares quarters with the dark
But all the same will see him turn quite mild.
CHORUS. You with your evil soul, why didn't you
Destroy him yourself? Instead, a woman who
Pollutes the land, the gods of the land—she killed him.
And does Orestes look upon the light?
May he return, his fortune gentle-minded
So he can kill them both, and rule instead.
AIGISTHOS. Since that's the way you act and speak, you'll learn a
lesson quickly
Up with your swords! Friendly guards!

[*Enter* GUARDS *from center.*]

There's work to be done!
LEADER OF THE GUARDS. Up now with the swords! Grab them by
the hilts and be ready!

[*The* CHORUS *is cowed by the armed* GUARDS.]

AIGISTHOS [*advances beyond the* GUARDS *to threaten the* CHORUS
personally].
But I too have my sword, and I do not refuse to die.
CHORUS [*unarmed, but closing ranks*].
You speak of death, and we accept the omen, whatever may
happen.
CLYTEMNESTRA. Stop that! [*turns to* AIGISTHOS] My dearest one,
let us work evil no more:
Even the people here are many to reap, a scrawny harvest.
We have our sufferings now in swarms, so let us have no more
blood.
Old and honored men, go back to your homes before you cause
suffering.
Accept what is done, what had to happen, the way we had
to do it.
If our afflictions could only come to an end! We'd accept that
now.
The heavy hoof of power has struck us with misfortune.

There you have a woman's words, if you care to understand
  them.

AIGISTHOS. That they should select such words! To throw such idle
  words at me!
As if they're willing to let their power be tested by luck but you
Do not have an orderly mind or you wouldn't misjudge your
  master.

CHORUS. The Argives do not usually fawn upon an evil man.

AIGISTHOS. I'll be among you in the days to come to bring you
  vengeance.

CHORUS. Not if a power brings Orestes back and restores his rule.

AIGISTHOS. I know that men who flee the country are nourished
  with hope.

CHORUS. Go ahead and grow fat, and be a stain on justice! How
  very much like you!

AIGISTHOS. You'll pay me back for this stupidity at the proper time.

CHORUS. Brag and be bold, and be like the rooster next to his
  female!

CLYTEMNESTRA. Do not pay attention to these idle yappings. You
And I will rule the house, and we'll put everything in order.

AESCHYLUS
Prometheus Bound
TRANSLATED BY
EDWIN DOLIN AND ALFRED SUGG

INTRODUCTORY NOTE

The *Prometheus Bound* is famous both for its compelling theme, proud defiance of tyranny, and for its peculiarities as a play and mythological document.

The wide appeal of the theme requires no discussion. The name of Prometheus is synonymous with the idea of a desperate and selfless fight against arbitrary authority on behalf of human freedom and progress. Not so well known is that the most authoritative version of the Prometheus myth before Aeschylus' play contained an entirely different point. In that version, as told in Hesiod's *Theogony* and *Works and Days,* Prometheus was the cause of all of mankind's troubles. His partly successful attempts to outwit Zeus for the sake of human beings outraged the king of the gods, who sent Pandora and her jar. of troubles as punishment, whereupon the golden age came to an end and man was doomed to suffer in the world as we know it. Prometheus, whose name was understood to mean "forethought," turns out to be not forethoughtful enough, and the consequences are disastrous.

When Aeschylus used the story, he reversed its sense. In his version, Prometheus only came to mankind's aid when the miserable creatures were set to be annihilated by Zeus for unexplained reasons. There is no hint of a golden age lost. Instead the first humans live wretchedly like ants in dark caves until Prometheus shows them not merely fire, but all technology. Specifically mentioned are house building, astronomy, the alphabet, animal husbandry, ship construction, medicine, mantic, and mining. This role of savior and culture founder for Prometheus seems to have been invented either entirely or mainly by Aeschylus, whose innovations did not stop there. In Hesiod's poems Zeus, although not omniscient, is equipped with a prudent knowledge of the future because of the help of Earth, primeval mother of the gods. But in Aeschylus, Zeus is ignorant precisely of what is crucial to his survival; the identity of the female, whether goddess or mortal, with whom marriage would be fatal, since her son is destined to be greater than his father. Aeschylus has imported this motif into the Prometheus story without the slightest justification in previous tradition. Further, he has made Earth the ally, not of Zeus, as in Hesiod, but of Prometheus. In fact, contrary to all previous versions, he makes Earth Prometheus' mother, an astonishing innovation. Add to this, the portrait of Zeus, in the *Prometheus Bound,* as a despicable tyrant, quite unlike the revered, just god of Aeschylus' other plays, and one has an idea of the drastic revision of the traditional story which the playwright was willing to make.

Although surprising, this transformation of the Hesiodic myth is understandable as the consequence of a new vision of the relation between man and god, whether this vision was exclusive to Aeschylus or common to a group. But less understandable, till now at least, are some problems of dramaturgy. Many judicious critics consider this play low in dramatic, as opposed to ideological, interest, except for the first and last scenes, because, in their view, Prometheus' role appears to be confined to passive suffering instead of being one of struggle, while his speeches about past and future often seem to lack relevance to the central action. Moreover, at one point, Ocean, the father of the chorus, enters but makes no reference to his daughters, nor do they afterwards mention his visit. (A simple explanation here is to assume that during this episode the chorus is offstage, but the mechanism for this arrangement is obscure.)

One solution to the dramaturgical problem is to suppose that the play is not by Aeschylus, but by an intellectual, not talented for playwrighting, who was making propaganda for his idea of a self-sufficient human progress through technology. Few critics have accepted this view. Another solution is the hypothesis that Prometheus, far from simply enduring and complaining, is struggling with Zeus in every sentence he speaks. According to this view, Prometheus assumes that Zeus is attentive to events on stage and consequently takes every opportunity to threaten him with disaster unless he agrees to Prometheus' terms. The form of the threat is a gradual specification, through direct statement and allusion, of the prophecy about Zeus' potentially fatal marriage. The threat has a basis in the traditional importance of Earth, Prometheus' mother and the original source of prophecy, as a crucial force in the wars of the gods.

The *Prometheus Unbound* is only preserved in fragments, but this much is clear. Prometheus' imprisoned relatives, the Titans, have been released by Zeus. Prometheus himself is delivered from the eagle, who eats his liver, by Zeus' son, Herakles. Prometheus discloses the secret of the fatal bride and, whether before or after this disclosure, is freed from his chains. In honor of Prometheus humans wear garlands on their heads, a recompense for his bonds. Whether or not there was a third play making up a trilogy on the Prometheus theme is disputed. The *Prometheus* was probably one of Aeschylus' last plays. No information as to prizes awarded or not awarded has been preserved.

CHARACTERS

AUTHORITY

HEPHAISTOS

(silent) BRUTE FORCE

PROMETHEUS

CHORUS of Daughters of OCEAN

OCEAN

IO

HERMES

Prometheus Bound

THE SCENE. *A wild terrain, dominated by a crag that seems perched on the edge of the void. At first, the stage is empty, except for the whine of the winds, but soon four figures make their way up toward the face of the cliff.* AUTHORITY *points to the summit.* PROMETHEUS, *in the lead and in bonds, pauses, then continues upward, followed closely by* AUTHORITY *and further behind by* HEPHAISTOS *and* BRUTE FORCE. *When the two in the lead reach the level at the base of the crag,* AUTHORITY *unties the prisoner. The other two continue their climb.*

AUTHORITY. The edge of the earth, Scythia. What a place!
Some trek—for this forsaken, trackless waste!

[*to* HEPHAISTOS, *who has reached the top*]

We're here, Hephaistos: now it's up to you.
Well?—Your father told you, didn't he,
to give this renegade a taste of steel?
To let him feel the bit—the binds of chains
unbreakable, sunk into these high rocks?
That's the cliff.
    Did he not plunder what
was yours, Hephaistos? blazing fire? The key
to every kind of skill he gave to men—
You must agree a crime like that deserves
reprisal from the gods; you must agree
he should be taught to heed the rule of Zeus
and give up all this deep concern for men—
HEPHAISTOS. For you, Authority, and you, Brute Force—
the order Zeus gave you is carried out!

And you can go. But I must still find heart
to nail to a mountainside a god whose blood's
my own with nothing shielding him against
the wind and cold. And yet I have no choice.
My father told me to. And when Zeus speaks,
it cannot be put off—

[*He takes out the gear he needs.*]

                    Prometheus?
You're thinking. What? You're devious. And bold.
And way ahead of everybody else!
So different from your mother, Themis, who's
straightforward, open, clear—
                              Prometheus,
these bolts and clamps I've forged will not come loose!
I'm going to hang you on this distant crag
where you will never see a human face
nor hear a human voice! It doesn't matter
now what either of us wants: you'll hang
until your skin is broiled by the sun's
bright flames; until you long for night and stars
and then for day again to thaw the night's
cruel frost! You'll break, because the only way
to bear such suffering is hope of help—
and no one now alive can give you help.
Was it worth this, your "humanity?"
What you thought was so important—taking
up for worthless men—in the teeth of all
the other gods' resentment and of right—
was it worth your standing sleepless guard
at a wretched pile of rock—upright, your knees
unbent? Well, when you think your cries of pain
must surely make Zeus come to pity you,
you'll slowly realize how hard of heart
are those like Zeus, whose power is newly won.
AUTHORITY. Come on! What good is feeling sorry for
    him but to put off what you have to do?
    Anyway, of all the gods whose enemy

he is, you ought to hate him most, since he
betrayed you most by giving fire to men.
HEPHAISTOS. You forget. We're friends—and even family.
AUTHORITY. I don't forget. But orders from your father
outweigh everything! Or don't they?—Well?
HEPHAISTOS. As *always,* you are pitiless and cruel!
AUTHORITY. So tell me how it's going to cure his ills
to cry about him. You—don't waste your tears.
HEPHAISTOS [*picking up the chains*]. The hands that *can* do this—
what hate they earn!
AUTHORITY. Your hate is wasted, too, since—bluntly put—
skill's not to blame for what's the trouble now.
HEPHAISTOS. But still, I'd wish my skill on someone else.
AUTHORITY. Everything's hard except to rule the gods.
Can anyone do what he wants but Zeus?
HEPHAISTOS [*indicating the chains*]. No one. Why else would I be
here with these—
AUTHORITY. Then, quickly! Start to fasten him before
your father notices this long delay.

[HEPHAISTOS *fastens the clamps around the hands of*
PROMETHEUS.]

HEPHAISTOS. Then notice this! The bit is set in place.
AUTHORITY. The clamps around his arms: drive their spikes first!

[HEPHAISTOS *begins to nail* PROMETHEUS' *arms to the rock.*]

Put muscle into it! He'll hang on rock—
HEPHAISTOS. I'm doing it, I'm doing my job, I—
AUTHORITY. Hit harder! *If* the chains aren't tight—if there
is *any* play—he'll use it to get loose!
HEPHAISTOS. I'm sure he won't budge this hand anyway.
AUTHORITY. Now, pin the other one. Smart as he is,
he'll find he's only second best to Zeus!
HEPHAISTOS. But *he*—alone!—can say I'm doing wrong.
AUTHORITY. Now, pound the steel right through his chest! When
once
that stubborn spike bites down, he's pinned for good!
HEPHAISTOS. Aaeee! I'm sorry, Prometheus, for *you.*

AUTHORITY. Stalling again? This pity that you feel
  for one Zeus hates, you next may need yourself.
HEPHAISTOS. Then watch what only *you* could bear to see!

[*He drives the stake through* PROMETHEUS' *chest.*]

AUTHORITY. I only see him get his just deserts.
  Now, hurry: put the chains around his ribs—
HEPHAISTOS. Don't tell me what to do! Though *do,* I must—
AUTHORITY. Not only will I tell you what to do,
  I'll *hound* you. There! Down low! Force *in* his legs!
HEPHAISTOS. It's done, and didn't take so long to do.
AUTHORITY. Again! Hit hard the shackle's bolts, since he
  who'll check your work won't understand mistakes!
HEPHAISTOS. Your words sound just the way you look: they're
    both—
AUTHORITY. And you? Who cares if someone soft like you
  complains that I am obstinate and hard—
HEPHAISTOS. Let's go. He's netted—hand and foot—in chains.
AUTHORITY [*to* PROMETHEUS]. Try acting high and mighty now—
    out here!
  Keep right on stealing from the gods their rights
  and handing them to worthless human beings.
  Perhaps your human friends can ease your pain!
  You think they can, Prometheus? *I* don't!
  The name the gods have given you is wrong:
  would one whose name means "forethought" be where you
  are now? You'll need to "think ahead," I'd say,
  to wriggle out of *this,* Prometheus!

[*Exit* AUTHORITY, BRUTE FORCE, HEPHAISTOS.]

PROMETHEUS. You, sky, divine—hear me! And winds—
  winged and swift—I call on you; and you,
  rivers, running; and you, waves, laughing
  endlessly over the sea; and you, earth—
  mother of all; and you, sun, whose eye
  this circle is, that misses nothing—see:
  all of you! See what I—a god—endure
  at the hands of gods; see what they've done to me!

[*He looks in all directions, expectantly.*]

Yes, see me waste myself in struggling with
a brutal wrong whose torture yet will last
for years on countless thousand years; all just
because it's what the blessed ones' new chief
devised. For *me!* Alas, I think of what
I suffer now and what is still to come.
How will it end? When will its limit dawn?

[*His tone changes.*]

But wait! I know exactly what's in store—
each small detail! There's no surprise; no suffering I can't anticipate. And since
I know, as well, that struggling will not change
necessity, I must put up as best
I can with fate—with all that must still be.
I cannot talk about it, but I can't
refrain from talking either. Caught! I'm strapped
beneath this yoke because of what I showed
to men: the way to power. I am he
who stalks the secret source of fire and he
who hid it, smouldering, inside a reed.
And fire will teach men—now—all kinds of skills
and schemes! Yes, *that* is what I did and what
I'm paying for: chained up—exposed and raw!

[*Suddenly he hears a whirring sound.*]

What's that? That sound?

[*He sniffs the air.*]

                    And suddenly I smell
around me—what? I can't make out. It's strange:
the smell of mortals? Or of gods? Or both?

[*The sound stops;* PROMETHEUS *cranes his neck, but does not
discover the sound's source.*]

Who comes? Who watches? Who would brave the world's

steep edge to see me suffering? Who's there?
What can he want? You, all of you, look here
at me, a *god,* held wretched prisoner.

[*His tone changes.*]

Zeus hates me; so, of course, they all do, too!
Those toadies who—near *him*—on tiptoe tread!
And why? Because I championed men too much.
That eerie whine again! And close! Could birds
with beating wings so fill the void with noise?
Whatever's coming towards me frightens me—

1st Strophe

chorus. Shhhhh! Don't be afraid. We came to help.
Together—each one in the place arranged
for her. We came by means of wings that strove
for speed to get us here—to this high peak.
You should have heard how hard we talked to make
our father let us come. But fast winds drove.

[PROMETHEUS *continues to try to catch a glimpse of who is talking, but doesn't succeed.*]

You see: way deep inside our cave I heard
a thunderous crash. Of *steel.* And stunned from fear
and shock, we found our normal modesty
quite gone. I knew I had to hurry, so
I came still barefoot. But our cars have wings.
prometheus. Ah! Ah! You, of burgeoning Tethys born,
and daughters, too, of Ocean—he whose currents
roll relentlessly around the whole
of earth—come see how I've been nailed above
this mountain's gorge to keep a bitter watch!

1st Antistrophe

chorus. I see, Prometheus, but mistily,
because my eyes are full of tears. And fear-
fully because I saw your chains are made
of steel. Your flesh will rot here on the rocks!

And on Olympos brand new gods command.
Zeus makes new laws, or changes them, and now
there's nothing clear except that those who once
were powerful he shuts up in the dark.
PROMETHEUS. Ah, *if* he'd only put me under earth!
Or lower still, in endless Tartarus,
beneath the place where human corpses lie;
if only he had put me *there;* though bound
with chains unbreakable as these, at least
no god nor anybody else could gloat.
But as it is, I know my enemies
are laughing as I flap here in the breeze!

2ND STROPHE

CHORUS. Laughing? Who? What god has heart for that?
Not *one* feels anything but sorrow for
your plight—except for Zeus! But *he,* still set
on vengeance for the past, keeps pressing down
the sons of heaven, and will not change until
he's either had enough or—what can't be!—
somehow, someone, with cunning, takes his throne.
PROMETHEUS. It's *coming!* Yes! I tell you that the time
will come—and I am certain of it!—when
the king of gods will see that he needs *me,*
his wronged and tortured prisoner. For there's
a plan—a new one!—aimed at Zeus, to rob
him of his puffed-up prominence and power!
And nothing he may try will work. He can't
persuade me; even though he finds words sweet
enough to cast a spell, I won't respond. Nor will
I shrink from threats, however fierce.
I will not tell him what I know until
he turns me loose and pays me for this wrong.

2ND ANTISTROPHE

CHORUS. Your suffering, that might well counsel you
to take more care, makes you instead thus careless: speaking out whatever's on your mind

without considering the consequences!
I'm afraid! Just thinking of your fate,
fear grips my heart! How can you know your pain
will end when well you know how hard of heart
the son of Kronos is? He can't be touched!
PROMETHEUS. He's merciless, I know. And I know, too,
that he alone, according to his whim,
decides what justice is. And yet, one day,
when he's hit hard—the way I've just described—
he'll soften up. You'll see; the day will come
when Zeus, his wrath collapsed, will form with *me*
a firm alliance that will help us both.

CHORUS. Explain it all. Tell everything. Like why
Zeus robs you of your honored place, and why
he tortures you? What reason does he have
for such brutality? Unless you think
it's dangerous to speak out, tell us. Why?
PROMETHEUS. It hurts to talk about it; yet, to keep
it in hurts, too. Since both are bad, why not?
When first the gods got mad and chose up sides,
the ones who wanted Kronos out were all
for making Zeus the king—that's what they said!
The others, though, said just the opposite:
that Zeus—if they held sway—would never rule!
These last were Titans, as was Kronos, too.
Well, I could see at once just what to do.
I told the Titans my idea, and tried
to talk them into it. But they—strong sons
of earth and sky—would have no part of my
advice to win by schemes and skill. Their pride—
or stubbornness!—would not allow a thought
except that force would keep, and easily,
their rule secure. But I had heard, and not
just once, my mother prophesy—my mother, Themis—
Earth!—one form with many names: she told
me how the future is to be decided.

"*Not* by force nor yet by doggedness
should those who gain the upper hand maintain
authority and rule, but rather guile
and wiles." And while I told them this in some
detail, they didn't think it worth their while
to even entertain the point my words
were making *over-all!* And so I thought
it best, considering the way things stood—
back then, I mean—to switch to Zeus' side;
my mother with me. *He* accepted help
as willingly as I had offered it.
The scheme was mine by which the sight of Kronos—
old, indeed, but Titan still—and sight as well
of all the ones who took his side, is now
covered by darkness, deep in Tartarus.
Zeus took that kind of help from me—and here
you see what *he* thinks up to pay me back!
There is a sickness tyrants always seem
to catch: they cannot ever trust their friends.
But you, I think, asked *why* Zeus tortures me;
and now's the time, I think, to make it clear:
when he was seated on his father's throne,
immediately and by himself, Zeus set
about arranging everything into
a system meshed as closely as a net!
It all fit perfectly—except for men.
Those suffering human beings he ignored.
And if he could have just removed that race
and shut it up in darkness—*all* of it!—
he longed to plant a new one in its place.
And but for me, nobody said him nay.
But I had nerve and I contrived a way
to rescue mortals from the certainty
of death that hovered over them. That's *why*
I'm humbled here by suffering—why pain's
my lot, and pity, too, from those who have
to look at me. It was from pity that

I made my move for mortals. Yet, it seems
I'm not thought worthy of the same myself.
Instead, this lesson in obedience,
you see—in discipline!—was forced on me,
a spectacle that should bring shame on Zeus!
CHORUS. The heart that does not feel for what you bear,
   Prometheus, is made of iron or rock.
   My own heart aches at seeing this: a sight
   that—heaven knows—I'd never ask to see.
PROMETHEUS. My *friends* are moved to help by what they see.
CHORUS. You're sure you did no more than what you said?
PROMETHEUS. The thought of death obsessed mankind till I—
CHORUS. Did what? How could you cure a fault like that?
PROMETHEUS. I gave them the illusion they weren't doomed.
CHORUS. Yes, men would benefit from such a gift.
PROMETHEUS. And don't forget I also gave them fire.
CHORUS. Oh, yes—you gave those worthless men bright fire.
PROMETHEUS. The fire by which they'll learn both skills and
      schemes.
CHORUS. And this is *all* the reason that Zeus has—
PROMETHEUS. For torturing me? Yes! Without surcease.
CHORUS. You mean no *limit* for your struggle's set?
PROMETHEUS. No, none! Though *he* can stop it, when he chooses—
CHORUS. When he chooses! What's the chance of that
   when *you* were in the wrong? Or don't you see—?
   I take no pleasure saying this, and since
   you clearly don't like hearing it, let's say
   no more. You should be trying to get loose!
PROMETHEUS. How easy—when your hands are clean—to give
   advice; to tell someone who's stuck knee-deep
   in trouble how he's wrong. But I, of course,
   knew all of this. And did it anyway—
   without a qualm. I'm saying, yes, that *I*,
   of my free will and eagerly, did wrong!
   You're right. Nor did these hands that helped men out
   of trouble manage to stay clean themselves!
   But I could not have guessed that *this*

would be the price I'd have to pay: to waste
my strength; to shrivel up, on windblown rocks—
alone! atop a crag, with *no one* else
nearby. But wait! What I am suffering now—
don't cry for that. Come down; down on the ground.
And I will tell you, then, what's yet to happen—
everything!—right to and through the end.
I ask you: come and share my misery.
It's true that now it's I who's suffering,
but don't forget, such trouble has a way
of passing on and touching *all* in turn.
CHORUS. Your words, Prometheus, don't strike deaf ears.
    And it is easy now to leave this winged
    car—to leave the sacred sky whose pure,
    unsullied air is path for birds—and come
    to jagged earth—

[*The* CHORUS *appears in a sweep.*]

                We want to hear it *all:*
    the story of your struggles; to the end—!

[*They hear the sound of* OCEAN's *swift approach and scatter off
as quickly as they came.* OCEAN *appears flying through the air
on a horse with wings.*]

OCEAN. I've travelled far, Prometheus, to see
    you; but, I'm here. I had no bit with which
    to guide this streaking bird—but will. And brain.
    As you must know, I feel the pain of your
    misfortune, too. Of course, our kinship's cause
    enough to urge my coming here, but fam-
    ily aside, there's none whose place or whose
    prestige I'd see set higher than your own.
    That's true; you'll see. I'm not the sort to say
    what someone else would like to hear without
    good reasons. Tell me what to do to help,
    and you shall never say you have a friend
    who's more dependable than Ocean. None.

PROMETHEUS. Ha! What's this? Have *you* come, too? To see
    my torture for yourself—up close? Where did
    you find the guts to leave that stream that's named
    for you? or yet your caves whose roofs are solid
    rock? and breach the earth, that mothers iron?
    Are you thus far outside your element
    to gape? Or grieve? Well, look at me! See here
    the friend of Zeus: who helped him found
    his tyranny and whom he humbles now!
OCEAN. Yes, *I* can see, Prometheus. And though
    I know you're very clever—subtle!—still
    I want to give you this advice—the best:
    be realistic! Know yourself for what
    you are, and you will see you're out of step.
    A *new* king rules, you know, and one who may—
    however high above us is his throne—
    be listening as you hurl, like sharpened spears,
    these wild, relentless words. And if he heard,
    you then would find this present wrath, compared
    with what's to come, is merely fun and games.
    You've suffered much, my friend; you're overwrought;
    you ought to check your gall and seek thereby
    to stop this torture, too. Prometheus,
    what I am going to say may seem to you
    an old cliché, but: "High-and-mighty talk
    does not go long unanswered," mark my words!
    But you have yet to learn humility.
    Instead of yielding in adversity,
    you seem to seek more trouble for yourself;
    though surely you don't need to go to school
    to *me* to learn that riding with the punch
    is wiser far than sticking out your chin
    when your opponent's in a class all by
    himself—and savage!—*and* makes up the rules!
    I'm going to go right now to see what I
    can do to get you out of this. So you
    sit tight, and don't make matters worse. And try,
    at least, to hold that reckless tongue of yours.

With a mind like a steel trap, you ought to know
the penalty for sounding off is stiff!
PROMETHEUS. Let me congratulate you on the way
you've managed to exonerate yourself
in this. It *was* you, wasn't it, who boldly
shared with me in everything I did?
But that is hardly to the point, right now.
Forget it. Why be bothered trying to
persuade him since you haven't got a chance?
Persuasion's *not* for him! Besides, you might—
in doing what you do—get hurt yourself!
OCEAN. Oh, yes, you're better far at talking sense
to others than in talking to yourself.
And I speak now from my experience,
not what I've heard. Don't hold me back when I'm
all set and eager; don't! I'm confident
that Zeus will grant me what I ask, and with
no strings attached; I *feel* he'll turn you loose.
PROMETHEUS. Your offer's very generous; nor shall
I soon forget how you have lacked for nothing
in your zeal to help. But don't trouble
yourself. It won't do any good for *me,*
so you'll end up with nothing for your trouble—
if, indeed, you really take the trouble—
So, since you find yourself well out of it,
sit tight. *I'm* not one who, just because
he's miserable, wants all the company
that he can get to suffer, too. Not *me.*
For I am sad my brother Atlas must—
in lands far west of here—stand holding on
his shoulders pillars separating heaven
and earth. I pitied, too, that son of Earth,
whose home was Cilician caves, the time
I saw him—all his hundred heads and raging
monster's strength—subdued by sheer brute force.
Fierce Typhon—yes!—who stood defying *all*
the gods, with Gorgon-lightning flashing from
his eyes and hissing horribly from grisly

jaws, as though he'd topple Zeus' rule.
But Zeus' thunderbolt, that never sleeps
and breathes a fiery flame itself, got to
him; stunned him from his high-and-mighty boasts,
and pierced on through until it hit his heart.
He glowed as embers glow, his strength destroyed.
Right now he lies stretched out and helpless by
a sea-strait, pressed beneath Mount Aetna, on
whose top Hephaistos sits and works his forge;
exactly where, one day, the mountain will
explode, and streams of fire will boil out
and eat with savage jaws the plowed-smooth farms
of Sicily. Just so will Typhon's rage
spew forth a driving rain of scalding fire,
though now he's but an ashy cinder left
by Zeus' thunderbolt. But why tell you
all this? You know it; well! You have no need
to go to school to *me*. So, play it safe,
as only you know how. And let me drain
my woe, till Zeus' pride has spent its wrath.
OCEAN. But when the malady is wrath, you know,
the remedy, Prometheus, is words.
PROMETHEUS. Yes, words applied in time might make him soft,
but—anger swollen to the limit? No!
OCEAN. I'll *go* to school to you: what harm is there
in zeal and readiness to take a risk?
PROMETHEUS. If all your effort's futile—and naive!
OCEAN. Yes, *let* that be what's wrong with me! It's best,
if you know what's good for you, to play the fool.
PROMETHEUS. Then *I* will be the one who'll seem a fool!
OCEAN. I see. You're telling me to go back home.
PROMETHEUS. Lest cries of mine earn *you* an enemy.
OCEAN. You mean the one whose power is newly won?
PROMETHEUS. Be careful. If distress should turn to wrath—!
OCEAN. My teacher is *your* plight, Prometheus.
PROMETHEUS. Then, go! Set out! And hold your new resolve!
OCEAN. You shout to me to do what I've begun
already. See: the wings of this four-legged

bird are tapping on the smooth sky's path.
He'd gladly bend his knees at home, and rest!

[*Exit* OCEAN. *The* CHORUS *come back onstage.*]

1ST STROPHE

CHORUS. My sorrow for your fate, Prometheus,
is such I cried: my tears a warm stream
flowing down my cheeks, that still are wet.
It's terrible for Zeus to hold his power
thus—dictating laws to suit himself,
and nakedly display before the gods
of old his haughty, insolent command.

1ST ANTISTROPHE

Already all the earth cries out its grief.
The men of Europe, westward, mourn the passing
of the ancient grandeur, grandeur that
belonged to *you* and to your brothers, too.
In sacred Asia, eastward, mortals feel
your suffering and, heartsick, weep out loud.

2ND STROPHE

And Amazons, fearless women of war,
who dwell in that part of the earth called Colchis;
and Scythians here at the world's edge,
and those who dwell beside the strait of Maeotia.

2ND ANTISTROPHE

And Chalybes: born for fight; their city
high up on a peak near Caucasus,
dreadful in battle—a thundering roar
from a horde of sharp spear-points.

ASTROPHA[1]

Only one other god up till now have I seen

1. The metrical form of this part of the Chorus is not clear. It is possible that the original words have become disordered.

thus hopelessly, helplessly bound: Atlas!
who holds up the wheel of the sky,
and groans, for all his great strength.

And the sea-waves shout their support as they crash;
and the depths of the sea can be heard to stir;
and dark Hades, deep within the earth, rumbles;
and the waters of the pure, quick-running rivers grieve,
in pity, for such suffering.

PROMETHEUS. Don't think I'm keeping quiet because I'm who
I am nor yet because I'm obstinate.
I brood. I think how I'm mistreated. Who
but I, indeed, established for the gods
the limits of their present offices?
But I won't speak of that; because I'd just
be telling you what you already know.
I *will* speak, though, of what I did for men:
of how I found them helpless babes, and made
them use their power of reason, made them think!
I do not mean to say that humans do
me wrong—I don't blame *them!* Yet I must tell
you in detail how heartfelt was my help.
It's true, they *did* have eyes, before—but didn't
see. And ears—but didn't hear. Instead,
they spent their dragged-out time as in a dream—
disordered, purposeless. They didn't live,
for instance, in the sun, in houses made
of brick or wood, but dug deep sunless caves
into the ground, like ants! Nor could they read
the seasons' signs—not so as to be *sure,*
at least—of winter's coming on, or spring's
new buds, or summer's heat that ripens crops.
Everything they did was hit-or-miss
until I taught them, finally, about
the stars: the way they rise and, *much* more difficult to understand, just how they fall!

I then revealed to them their minds' unique
capacity for numbers; found for them
the alphabet, the Muses' mother; means
for culture *and* remembering everything!
I was the first to bring big beasts beneath
the yoke, to make their bodies into slaves by means
of yoke-straps, thus relieving mortals of
their hardest work. With bit and bridle I
had horses drawing gorgeous chariots,
the rich man's glorious show of wealth. And ships?
No one but I invented linen wings
for boats to drive them swiftly through the seas.
Yes, I did all of this, the more fool I:
that finding schemes to solve man's plight have yet
no clever plan to help myself shake off
the suffering that I endure here now.

CHORUS. How terrible and strange! Your mind lost
its way and failed. And like bad doctors who
themselves have fallen sick, you now despair
of finding medicine to cure yourself.

PROMETHEUS. But hear the rest and you'll be more amazed!
The ways and means I've thought of to get out
of hopeless situations, chief of which
was this: when anyone fell sick, there was
no remedy—not potable, nor herb,
nor salve—and so they'd waste away, till *I*
disclosed the way to mix up soothing drugs,
with which they fight off every kind of ill.
And as for knowing what the future holds:
I set in order all the many ways
of telling what will come. I was the first
who could interpret dreams: which ones would turn
out true; which not. And portents, too,
that hide in spoken words—a matter of
no little difficulty—I explained
to them; and omens meant for travelers.
Precise rules I set down about the birds of prey:

just how they fly when what they augur's good
and when it's not; and what the pattern is
of each one's life—their friendships and their feuds,
and get-togethers. Prophecy by means
of animals I rationalized: the smoothness
of the entrails and what hue they'd have
to have to please the gods; the subtle and
deceptive shape of gall and liver-lobe.
And when I set on fire the leg bones wrapped
in fat—the great spine, too—I showed the way
toward mastering a skill most difficult
to understand. I bared the shrouded meaning
in the flames, as though I healed blind eyes.
I did all this, and more: those hidden ones,
beneath the earth, that *would* help men and *will:*
the metals, bronze and iron, and gold and silver,
too. Who'd say that he discovered them
ahead of me would just be blurting air.
Yes, in a word, I'll tell you everything—
and that one word's my name—"Prometheus!"
which means, you know, to think ahead,
by which to every skill are mortals led.
CHORUS. Oh, since you *shouldn't,* give off helping men!
Since now you're in such trouble, help yourself!
My hopes are high that from these chains you'll yet
get loose and find you're no less strong than Zeus.
PROMETHEUS. But Fate, that brings all things when it's their time,
has not decreed for that to happen—yet.
I *will* escape these chains, but only when
I've been thus mangled by a thousand pains:
by *far* less strong is skill than what must be!
CHORUS. But who, then, has control of what must be?
PROMETHEUS. Three fates; and vengeance-fiends—who don't forget!
CHORUS. So Zeus, then, *has* less strength than someone else?
PROMETHEUS. In wrestling fate, at least, he won't succeed!
CHORUS. But isn't fate, for Zeus, just endless power?
PROMETHEUS. I cannot tell you—now. Don't ask again!

CHORUS. It must be awesome since you hide it so.
PROMETHEUS. Change the subject! This is not the time
   to speak of that. So far as possible,
   it must be kept concealed, since *by* so keeping
   it, shall I succeed in getting loose
   from this disgraceful bondage and from pain.

1ST STROPHE

CHORUS. Oh, Zeus! who rules all: may his sovereignty never
   be pitted against what *I* want! Nor may I
   ever stand aloof from the gods at their festivals, holy
   occasions when cattle are slaughtered beside the unquench-
   able stream of my father's resources, Ocean. Never
   may I allow any blasphemy past my lips;
   but remember *this,* keeping it always in mind.

1ST ANTISTROPHE

It's sweet to live life without fear of the future,
content every day with friendship's sustenance.
And my heart is chilled when I look at you wasting away,
all alone, and disfigured by thousands of pains just because
you insist upon doing what *you* want, without being fearful
of Zeus. In honoring mortals, you *have* your way;
but, Prometheus, *by* such, you go way too far.

2ND STROPHE

What's a favor that doesn't earn a favor?
Can you inform me, my friend, what help can come—
if any—from benighted man? You still
don't see that fatal feebleness that keeps
the human race in chains or, rather, in
a dream. And *never* will their scheming to
disturb the harmony of Zeus succeed!

2ND ANTISTROPHE

That's the lesson I've learned, Prometheus,
from seeing your ruinous fate. And suddenly,

I hear two songs, but, oh, how different
they are: the one, I sing; the other, that
I sang when you were at your wedding bath—
your bride, Hesionē, my sister, whom
you wooed with gifts, and then took home, your wife.

[*Suddenly, a shriek is heard offstage. The* CHORUS *and* PROME-
THEUS *start, but cannot see.* IO, *human-heifer, bursts onto the
stage. The* CHORUS *shrink back.*]

IO. Where on earth is this? Who lives here. Who
is this I see thus hobbled by a harness made
of stone, exposed to whirling winds and cold?
Was what you did so wrong that you must be
destroyed for punishment? Please, *tell* me, where
on earth I've wandered to—
                    Aaee! Aaeee!
Again! The sting caresses me!
The ghost of earth-born Argos! Keep him off! Oh, god,
I'm scared. I see him watching me. He's there!
The herdsman with the thousand eyes. No, there!
He's coming! Everywhere! Those eyes! They fool
me. Yes, I know he's dead and buried, but
the earth won't keep him covered up. He leaves
his grave and hunts me down; I run and run!
in sand beside the salt sea; hungry—!

[*the sound of oboes*]

The reed-pipes answer me. Clearly. Strong.
This music that lulls to sleep. Oh, Oh!
I've come so far. Where will this wandering lead?
Oh, son of Kronos, tell me: *why?* What have
I done so wrong that you would yoke me with
this misery? Oh, god, the sting that drives
me! Frightened, broken—yes, insane with fear!
Or is that what you want, to drive me mad?
I can't stand it! Set me aflame with fire;
or cover me with earth; to sea-beasts feed

me—*any*thing! But answer, Lord, my prayer.
By now the painful rigors of my wanderings
have taught me well: I've learned! And still
I cannot find the way to stop. But do
you hear me speak? The girl with heifer's horns?
PROMETHEUS [*from behind her*]. Of course! It's Inachos' daughter
    that I hear:
the girl spun onward by the stinging goad,
who fires the heart of Zeus himself with love
and—hated by his wife, by Hera—now
is cruelly forced—for discipline, of course—
to run a course whose laps are limitless!
IO. How is it that *you* know my father's name?
    Who are you? Clearly, you're in agony;
but tell me how you know precisely who
I am and name the very sickness that
afflicts me, sickness sent by god to wear
me out; that goads me when I think it's gone
to still more wandering.
               Aeeeee! Aeeeee!
A torture that won't even let me eat!
I've raced about—I lurch and buck—defenseless
in the grip of some well-thought-out plan
of vengeance! Unlucky ones, we're cursed;
but none as miserably as I. But you,
perhaps, can tell me what remains for me
to suffer. *Can* you? Clearly? *Is* there some
device to cure my malady? Please, tell
me, if you know. I've searched far; so far—
PROMETHUS. I'll tell you, clearly, *all* you want to know;
    not weaving riddles but straightforwardly,
the way one should when talking to one's friends.
I am Prometheus, who gave men fire.
IO. Prometheus! What mortal doesn't know
    the good you've done? Why's *this* befallen you?
PROMETHEUS. I *was* lamenting my sad plight. No more!
IO. Then—could you do one favor for me? Please—

PROMETHEUS. Just ask me. I can tell you anything.
IO. Who hung you, hobbled so, on this high cliff?
PROMETHEUS. Hephaistos did—but Zeus devised the plan!

[IO *whirls, then backs away.*]

IO. To be thus punished, what did you do *wrong?*
PROMETHEUS. What I've said's enough! *You* ought to know.

[IO *indicates silently that she does.*]

IO. Then to the point: how will my wandering *end?*
　　And when? Have I much longer yet to wait?
PROMETHEUS. Not knowing's better for you than to know.
IO. Don't, please; don't keep my fate from me—
PROMETHEUS. I haven't said I *wouldn't* answer you.
IO. Then, tell me. Everything! You're stalling: why?
PROMETHEUS. I'm slow because—I know you'll be upset!
IO. Please, don't protect me when I long to know.
PROMETHEUS. Since you're so set on hearing it, I'll tell—
CHORUS. No, wait! Let *us* have what we long for, too.
　　We'd like to find out, first, about the ills
　　she's had to bear, if *she* can bring herself
　　to talk about her many wanderings.
　　And then she'll hear about what's left from you.
PROMETHEUS. It's up to Io. Would you grant them what
　　they ask? They are your father's sisters. And
　　it's worth your while to let yourself spill out
　　your bitterness when you are *sure* your aud-
　　ience will pay you back with sympathy.
IO. I don't see how I can refuse.

[*to the* CHORUS]

　　　　　　　　What's more,
　　I'll tell you *all* you want to know in such
　　a way there'll be no doubt it's true. And yet
　　I'm so ashamed to speak of it—the storm
　　the gods unleashed—and of my looks and why
　　their monstrousness was clapped on me—poor me—

It all happened so fast, I—. Every night,
bright visions breached my bedroom, luring me
with velvet words: "You're such a lucky girl;
why drag through life a virgin when it's possible to make the greatest match of all?
Zeus longs for you; his heart's on fire;
he wants to join with you to share in love's
delights. Can you just kick aside a god's desire?
Come out," they'd say, "to Lerna's meadows, deep—
near where your father keeps his sheep and cows;
come out, that Zeus, desire discharged, may rest."
I couldn't sleep. These dreams beset me every
night, until, at last, I had to tell
my father, who sent many messengers
to Delphoi and Dodōna, asking of
their oracles what he should do or say
that most would please the gods. Returning, they
reported only riddles: dark, ambig-
uous and difficult to understand.
But finally an oracle *did* come
that told my father, Inachos, just what
he had to do—without a doubt! It said,
unless he wanted Zeus's fiery thunderbolt to shut away in darkness his
entire race, that he should banish *me*—
from home, from country; rid his flock of me,
who, free, would range as far as earth extends.
The oracle was from Apollo. So, he did:
he sent me out and shut the doors behind
me, though it wasn't something either of
us wanted. But, he had to do it, forced
by Zeus as by a bit that cut his mouth!
At once my mind and body were distorted
by these horns you see adorning me!
And prodded by the sting-mouthed cattle-fly,
I raced, with frenzied leaps, to Kerkhnē's sweet,
fresh stream and Lerna's spring. And all the while,

the eyes of earthborn Argos, herd for cows—
and therefore at his best!—were with me, watching
every step I took until—despite
his thousand eyes—his death sneaked up on him.
But *I,* through country after country, still
am driven, stroked by a god-sent scourge, the fly!
[*to* PROMETHEUS] I've finished telling what was done to me.
Now, tell me, if you can, what I must still
go through. And tell the truth. Don't tell me, out
of pity, what will comfort me; don't lie!
Of all the plagues that can deform us, that
to be ashamed of most is playing false!

CHORUS. What's that you're saying? What? Oh, no. No!
Never! I mean, I never thought that words
so ordinary still could sound so foreign
to my ears. Nor yet that anything
so hard to handle as this double edge
of sheer repulsiveness and fearfulness
was going to drain my marrow so of warmth.
O Life, O Fate, is *this* how it will be?
I shudder seeing Io's destiny.

PROMETHEUS. Yet it's too soon to feel afraid and sad.
Hold back your grief, until you hear the rest.

CHORUS. Go on, then; tell it—all! When one is sick,
it helps to know, for sure, what pain's still left.

PROMETHEUS [*to the* CHORUS]. What you requested, you received:
to grant
it was for me an easy thing: that is, that
she herself would tell you the details
of her misfortune. *Now* the rest: what this
poor girl, from Hera, still must bear.
[*to* IO] And *you,* whose father's Inachos, mark well my words:
I'll tell you what your journey's *end* will be.
First, when leaving here, turn east across
the virgin, unplowed fields of Scythia,
whose nomads live high off the ground in fast,
wheeled carts, concealed by woven coverings.

They're long-range bowmen; don't go near, but keep
hard by the surf-marked shore, though rocky, till
that country's well behind you. Toward your left,
then, live the savage Chalybes, whose skill
is working steel. Outsiders don't, without
regret, come near. Keep on until you reach
the river called, for good cause, "Arrogance":
don't cross it, since it's hard to cross, until
you see its source, the very highest mountain
of the Caucasus, whose top blurts out
the braggart stream. As you surmount those peaks
among the stars, go south, until you reach
the Amazons, who husbands hate, and who—
in time—will settle in Themiskūra, around
Thermōdon, there where Salmydessos lies,
a cruel, rock-toothed jaw beside the sea—
the bane of ocean visitors and cruel
step-mother to their ships. To guide
a girl will Amazons be more than glad,
and you will come upon Cimmeria—
a band of land that makes a great lake's narrow gate. Here, summon up your courage; leave
the land behind and cross the strait that's called
"Maeotia" now, but which for all time men
will call, in memory of what you did,
the "Bosporus" or "where the cow once found
her way." Leave Europe, then, and Asia greet.

[*to the* CHORUS *in particular*]

Do any of you think that this is other
than abuse of power? Is not the king
of gods in this—and all else, too—revealed
a tyrant? Causing her, a mortal, just
because she pricked his lust, to wander so?
[*to* IO] You'll see what little joy your lover gives,
my girl; for all I've said, "pre"-prologue is.
IO. Oh, no! Still more! Ah, Aeeee—!

PROMETHEUS. You snort and roar? I can't imagine what
  you'll do when you've found out what's still in store—
CHORUS. It cannot be that she must bear still more—
PROMETHEUS. Disaster! Like a hurricane at sea!
IO. Why should I go on living then? Why don't
  I throw myself—at once—from this brute cliff!
  When I have hit the ground, I will be rid
  of all my sufferings. To finish it—
  to die!—beats dragging through one's days so hurt.
PROMETHEUS. What would you do, if you were me, whom fate
  will not let die. Death *would* have been a way
  to rid myself of suffering, but as
  it is: no limit for my struggle's set
  till Zeus is banished from his tyrant throne.
IO. Zeus banished from his throne? You can't mean that!
PROMETHEUS. I'd guess that you'd be glad to see it happen—
IO. *Glad?* How else should one he's hurt so feel?
PROMETHEUS. Then take it for a fact. I'm *sure* of it!
IO. But who will seize his power. It's absolute!
PROMETHEUS. His own stupidity: *he*'ll manage it.
IO. But how? Would it endanger you to tell?
PROMETHEUS. He's going to make a marriage he'll regret!
IO. With mortal or with god or can't you say?
PROMETHEUS. A girl? A goddess? No, I cannot tell you—
IO. Will his *wife,* though, make him lose his throne?
PROMETHEUS. Her child, born greater than his father, will.
IO. Is there no means by which Zeus may escape?
PROMETHEUS. No, none! Except for *me*—if I were loose.
IO. Who's going to turn you loose if Zeus forbids?
PROMETHEUS. There's someone: one of your descendants, Io—
IO. What? A child of mine will set you free?
PROMETHEUS. Yes, yours: three generations after ten.
IO. This you predict, it's dark—not like before.
PROMETHEUS. Both this and what's in store for *you* are dark—
IO. You said you'd tell me! Don't deprive me now!
PROMETHEUS. I'll make a gift of *one* of them, not both.
IO. Not both? I have to choose? What were they, then?

PROMETHEUS. To hear, in full, what's still to come, for *you;*
    or else, to know the one who'll rescue *me.*
CHORUS. Do *her* one favor, and the other one—
    do that for me. Oh, please! Go on and tell
    her where she's still to wander. Then tell *me*
    who's going to set you free. I want to know!
PROMETHEUS. Well, since you're *all* so eager, I will not
    refuse to tell you—everything you ask.
    [*to* Io] First, Io: write down on the tablet of
    your memory your journey's frantic course:
    when you have crossed the channel that divides
    two continents, go toward the sun whose flames
    you'll see arising from the rolling sea,
    until you reach, at last, the Gorgon plains—
    Kisthēnē—where the Phorkids live: three girls
    who long have lived unwed. They look like swans
    and share—all three!—a single eye and tooth.
    On them the sun's rays never look by day
    nor moon by night. Their sisters are nearby:
    the winged Gorgons, three, with snakes for hair,
    abhorred by mortals since no human being
    can look on them and keep on drawing breath—
    though why that kind of guard should be is worth
    attending to. But there is still another
    startlingly repulsive sight: I mean
    the Griffons—Zeus' savage, sharp-tongued dogs:
    beware of them! And watch for, too, the horde
    of one-eyed Arimaspian horsemen living
    near the river, Affluence, a golden
    flow of wealth: you keep away from them!
    At last you'll reach the wide world's other edge—
    a land of blacks who live beside the sun's
    dark source, a spring, where there's a stream called Aeth-
    iope: pursue its banks until you find
    the final cataract, from whose huge pal-
    isade, called Byblos, is ejected streaming
    waters—sweet and fresh—of holy Nile.

To that three-cornered land between its legs,
Nilōtis, will the river guide you on
your way. And that's the place where Fate decrees
that Io found a distant colony,
which Io's children shall perpetuate.
If parts of this seem muffled—hard to get:
repeat them to be sure you've got it right.
I have more leisure than I'd choose to have.
CHORUS. If you have anything to tell her still,
about her stormy wanderings; or if
you didn't mention something—add it, please!
But if you've told her everything, it's our
turn now. Remember? What you promised us?
PROMETHEUS. She knows the whole point of her journeys now.
But so she knows she hasn't heard in vain,
I'll speak about her struggles in the past,
before she came here: words that by themselves
will prove that what I prophesy is true.
I won't tell all: why bore you with a mass
of small details when *one* will do the trick?
The high-point!
[*to* IO]   which was when you reached
Dodōna—steep-backed height, supported by
Molossian earth—where both Thesprotian Zeus'
throned oracle is found and those
incredible, mysterious trees as well:
the oaks that speak aloud to people, oaks
that spoke to *you,* with dazzling clarity
and *not* in riddles, hard to understand
and dark. They said, "You'll be the famous wife
of Zeus." I see you might agree with what I say.
But then, the cattle-fly attacked! And, leaping
crazily, you rushed along the shore:
at first toward Rhea's womblike gulf; then in-
land, forced back here, whirled wildly by the wind.
That gulf, believe me, will in time by all
mankind be called "The Sea of Io," proof

to all posterity that you passed by.
This should be evidence enough my mind
sees somewhat more than just what's here and now.

[*to the* CHORUS]

To tell the rest to all of you, and *her*, as well:
I'll pick my story up where I broke off.
There is a city called Kanōbos, built
right at the silt-encrusted mouth of Nile—
right at the outmost edge of land! and that's
the place where Zeus, with just a touch, will give
you back your sanity. A hand, which *then*
will bear no trace of fear, will brush you, whereupon you'll bear by Zeus a dark-skinned son,
whose name, Epaphos, means "a gentle touch"
to signify the way he was conceived.
And he will harvest crops from all the earth
the waters of the broad Nile irrigate.
Five generations after him will fifty
females come again to Argos, not
because they want to, but because they do
not want to marry their first cousins, who,
insane with male desire, like hawks near doves,
will closely chase unchaste fulfillment, which
can *not* be caught because a god will keep
the bodies of their brides inviolate.
Oh, they'll be welcomed by the Argive land,
all right: by murder! at the hands of females
who, at night, will watch and wait their chance.
Yes! Every wife—her bloody two-edged sword
blade wet with a love I pray be sent to those
I hate—will rob each husband of his life.
But *one!* Desire for children will so blunt
the edge of one girl's purposeful resolve
that she will fail to kill the man beside
her, choosing rather to be called a coward
than a murderess. And it is *she*

who will beget the race of Argive kings.
Just how's a story that's too long to tell:
The *point* is that from her seed there shall grow
a man both brave and famous for his bow—
a man because of whom will *I* be free!
My mother told this oracle to me—
in great detail—my *Titan* mother, old,
and wise. "But, how?" you ask. The story's long
and wouldn't be of any use to *you*.

[*Suddenly* 10 *screams.*]

10. Aeeeee! Aeeeee! Again! It begins again!
The flashing pain! My head is hot; my heart's
on fire! I'm going mad. I feel the fly's
mouth on me, like a lance-point, even if
it wasn't forged in fire. In fear, my heart
is kicking at my breast; with spinning eyes,
I can't control my legs or what I say.
I feel stark madness welling up. My words
come out all wrong—they're tossed about, like muddy
wrack, on blind, inexorable waves. Aeeeee! [*Exit* 10.]

1st Strophe

CHORUS. I see how carefully thought out, and wise,
and true, is the injunction that it's better
far to marry someone like yourself
than long for marriage with the spoiled rich;
or, if you're poor and humble, those whose pride
is all puffed up because they're nobly born.

1st Antistrophe

O, goddess, Moira—Fate: I pray that you
will not see me in Zeus' bed; nor near,
as brides are near, to any husband who
from heaven's come. I'm frightened. *That* young girl,
who only seeks to stay a virgin, still
is driven, cruelly, by Hera's wrath.

EPODE

I'm not afraid of marriage, not as long
as those who marry are on equal terms.
But otherwise, I dread it! May no god,
with longing, lock his lovesick eye on me!
In such a hopeless war, I'd helpless be.
For how could *I* escape from Zeus' plan?

PROMETHEUS. No matter how stubborn Zeus is,
    I tell you he'll be humbled yet! Because
    the marriage he is getting ready for
    himself will throw him out! will banish him
    from throne and tyranny, and shut him up
    in darkness. Then, and only then, will be
    fulfilled his father's curse—the curse old Kronos
    breathed when *he* was banished from the throne
    he'd held so long. That's what the future bodes!
    And not a single god—for sure!—can help
    him get around it saving *me,* who knows
    both end and means. And I don't give a damn.
    Just let him try, with any confidence,
    to sit up there behind his airy claps
    of thunder! Let him shake his lightning all
    he wants! What help can such things be against
    his own unbearable undoing and
    his own disgrace? Because he has *himself*
    handpicked the fierce opponent who'll confront
    him—picked a fighter! who's unbeatable;
    who'll find a flame more fulminous than light-
    ning and a crash out-thundering thunder's roar,
    and who will melt that three-pronged fork with which
    Poseidon shakes the earth until she's sick!
    And Zeus will *know,* when he has stumbled on
    his nemesis, how great the difference is
    between the master's life and slavery!
CHORUS. You're calling what you wish for, "Zeus' fate"!

PROMETHEUS. It happens what I'd like is happening.

CHORUS. We should expect someone to flatten Zeus?

PROMETHEUS. And worse than mine's the fix he'll find he's in.

CHORUS. You're not afraid to hurl such reckless taunts?

PROMETHEUS. Why should one be afraid who cannot die?

CHORUS. He might find torture for you worse than this.

PROMETHEUS. Then let him! Nothing's coming *I* don't see.

CHORUS. The wise are careful not to speak like that.

PROMETHEUS. Go on: say prayers! Yes, bow and scrape before
   whoever's in authority. But Zeus,
   to *me*, means less than nothing! Let
   him, for his little while, do what he wants.
   He won't be king of gods for long—
   Who's this? [HERMES *enters, hurriedly*.]
            Is Zeus' emissary *here*?
   It must be something's happened that the new
   king's flunky comes to tell us all about.

HERMES [*to* PROMETHEUS]. You there! Smart one! I mean *you*,
   show-off!
   You *are* the one who wronged the gods by stealing
   fire? And more, by finding means to make
   the worthless mortals more important, kept
   it up? My *father* orders you to say—
   and say exactly!—what the marriage is
   you're boasting of that is to banish him
   from his authority. And he insists
   that you not speak in riddles, but explain
   it point by point! Prometheus, don't make
   me have to come here twice! You *must* see Zeus
   will not give in to just a lot of talk!

PROMETHEUS. Well, now: the way you speak your piece, thus proud
   and arrogant, befits a godly "errand
   boy." You're young yet, *all* of you! Your power
   is newly won. And so, of course, you all
   suppose that life in heaven is trouble-free.
   But *I*'ve seen others banished from such height.
   And I'll be first in line to see the third one fall:

the *present* ruler, who will be expelled
most shamefully of all. And quickest, too!
You're thinking—what? Why there's no sign in me
of craven cringing vis-a-vis these up-
start gods? But nothing could be further from
the fact, you see. So, run on back the way
you came. You won't get what you want from me!
HERMES. You got yourself into this bind by being—
once before!—as obstinate as now.
PROMETHEUS. But can't you see that I would rather bear
my agony than be a slave, like you?
HERMES. To be a slave to *rock* is better, I've
no doubt, than being Zeus' trusted aide.
PROMETHEUS. That arrogant remark just suits its source!
HERMES. You're in your glory in this fix—
PROMETHEUS. My glory? Yes! A glory that I wish were crowning
all my enemies—including you!
HERMES. You don't think *I'm* to blame in any way?
PROMETHEUS. I do. My enemies are all the gods
who profited, then paid me back with pain!
HERMES. You've gone insane; you're *sick,* just like they say—
PROMETHEUS. If hating enemies is "sick," I'm sick!
HERMES. If you had *won,* you'd be unbearable—

[PROMETHEUS *groans.*]

What's that? Zeus doesn't understand that word.
PROMETHEUS. He'll *learn* it—well! In time. And all else, too.
HERMES. And *you?* You still don't understand restraint.
PROMETHEUS. You're right. I still let lackeys talk to me.
HERMES. You *won't* explain what father wants to know?
PROMETHEUS. I could pay back the favor he's done me.
HERMES. A child might play these games of yours; not *me!*
PROMETHEUS. A child? Aren't *you* a child? A baby's more
intelligent than you if you expect
that I am going to tell you anything!
There is no scheme, no torture, Zeus can use
to get me to reveal it; none! *Except*

undoing these humiliating chains.
So—what? Let flames and smoke be hurled! Let him,
with blinding snow and thunder in the earth,
shake everything into confusion! *I*
cannot be broken! *I* won't tell him—ever!—
who, from tyranny, will banish him.
HERMES. Of course! You look to *that* to help you. Right?
PROMETHEUS. I looked some time ago. And made my plans.
HERMES. You've lost your mind. You're scared to face the facts
   your painful plight at present makes quite plain.
PHOMETHEUS. And you've lost *yours!* to think that by
   this badgering you'll make me change my mind.
   You're talking to the wind! Don't ever think,
   from fear of Zeus, that I'll turn womanish
   and *beg* him—like a woman, hands turned up—
   to let me out of bondage. No! I'm far
   from doing that: I'll never *beg* him; no!
HERMES. What sense is there to try more words when nothing
   I say, either—and I've begged!—provokes
   a hint you're weakening. Like some unbroken
   filly, still you bite the bit and strain
   and fight the reins! But all this fuss must come
   to nothing since your scheme has nothing back
   of it. But obstinance! which—by itself,
   without a power base—is next to nothing.
   If I can't persuade you, do you have
   an inkling of the storm that threatens you—?
   A huge and final wave of suffering
   that will engulf and crush you utterly!
   Just listen: first, my father's thunder and
   his lightning flash will tear apart this jagged
   crag and hide you underneath the stone's
   rock-hard embrace. When you've dragged through an age
   of time and come back into light, then Zeus'
   dog—the eagle, red, with wings outspread—
   will cut your flesh to bits like some great rag!
   a guest who uninvited comes to dine
   and eats all day—yes, chews your liver till

it's black with blood. You're thinking this won't happen,
but it will! Nor will it end until
some god accepts as his your suffering
and readily agrees to leave the sun's
bright light for Hades and go down into
the gloom of Tartarus. Think all you want.
But don't forget I haven't made this up!
Nor is it just a boast. It's true. For Zeus
can't lie. Whatever *he* predicts will fall
out so; his every word! So, watch out for
your*self!* Just think it over. Surely good
advice is better than sheer stubbornness!

CHORUS. What Hermes says makes sense to us. To seek
wise counsel's all he's telling you to do—
and drop this stubbornness. Oh, do that. Please!
The wise may not, without disgrace, be wrong.

PROMETHEUS. You surely cannot think that anything
this "aide" announced surprises *me!* And where's
"disgrace" in pain that enemies inflict?
So let it happen. *Let* the frizzly, two-edged
fire be flung at me! Yes, *let* the sky
swell up with thunder, stabbed by flashing pains
from savage winds! Let cyclones shake the earth's
foundations to the roots! And let a sea
wave, roaring savagely, slam up against
the stars and wipe their paths from heaven; *let*
it lift my body high and headlong hurl
it down to blackest Tartarus, awhirl
with all the force of brute necessity—!
But still, he cannot kill me. There's no way!

HERMES. So, that's your plan? Though if you hadn't lost
your mind, you couldn't make a speech like that.
His attitude's no different from a lunatic's! So must he not be still insane?
But *you,* who only sympathize with what
he suffers—you, at least, must move. And fast!
Away from here! The brutal bellowing
of thunderclaps may make you stupid, too.

CHORUS. To think I'll listen to that kind of talk
  is your mistake. You're not confusing me.
  Because I know that *that's* one thing I can
  not bear! Stop telling me to like what's wrong.
  With *him*, I'm ready now to suffer what
  I must. I've learned to hate a traitor to
  his own. Betrayal is a sickness that
  disgusts me more than any other kind.
HERMES. But what about what *I'm* predicting? Don't
  complain about your blind and hopeless ruin,
  if you're caught; nor ever say Zeus forced
  on you a fate you couldn't help. It isn't
  so! You made the choice, *know*ing what
  you're doing. Nothing secret will have been
  the cause if you discover that you're woven
  deep within an endless net of ruin;
  no! The cause will be your foolishness.

  [*Exit* HERMES. *The earth shakes. Thunder and lightning.*]

PROMETHEUS. Ah, there! It's happening! In *fact;* not words!
  The earth is rolling! Really! From the depths
  the thunder bellows back. And lightning's fire,
  in zig-zag flashes, blazes out above.
  The dust is swirled by whirling winds that leap
  and fight each other, openly at war.
  Because of *me* does Zeus' brute and frightening force move openly, where all can see!

  [*The ultimate blast rocks the stage; the* CHORUS *scream and scatter; the rock that holds* PROMETHEUS *encloses him, as he calls.*]

  You, mother, blessed and honored, see!
  And *you,* sky, that swiftly rolls your light
  around for all to share, you, see—see *me!*
  And what I suffer here! Unjustly.

  [*The cataclysm subsides. The stage is empty.*]

SOPHOCLES

Oedipus the King

TRANSLATED BY
ALBERT COOK

INTRODUCTORY NOTE

Surely the most famous of Greek plays, *Oedipus the King,* has fascinated far more than professional scholars. Its story provided the model for Sigmund Freud's theory of the sexual relationships between child and parents, a crucial doctrine in contemporary psychology, which has affected the whole modern view of the family. Aristotle's citation of *Oedipus the King* as a model tragedy, complete with *hamartia* (error), *anagnorisis* (recognition of the identity of a relative), and *peripeteia* (change of situation into its opposite), has made it an object of perennial analysis by literary and dramatic critics. The notion of the king who pollutes his own land and can only save it by being driven into exile appeals to students of comparative religion and anthropology.

Whether or not these views and uses of the tragedy are justified, no one disputes that as a play, apart from ideological relevance, it is a fascinating creation. Most obviously, there is its display of "dramatic irony." Hardly a sentence goes by which does not compel the audience's attention to Oedipus' ignorance of reality, his energetic, unconscious progress toward disaster. A corollary to this element is the sense of direct involvement of the gods, particularly of Apollo. As Oedipus himself proclaims, it was Apollo who arranged his sufferings, and, when he says these words, so artfully has the dramatic development been handled, the original audience must have shivered with an uncanny sense of the god's presence there among them. All classical Greek tragedy was religious, at least to some extent, but none more so than this one.

Neither the other plays of its tetralogy nor the date of the *Oedipus the King* are known. Scholars generally place it in the 420s. It was not part of a tetralogy which won first prize.

CHARACTERS

OEDIPUS, king of Thebes
A PRIEST
CREON, brother-in-law of OEDIPUS
CHORUS of Theban elders
TEIRESIAS, a prophet
JOCASTA, sister of CREON, wife of OEDIPUS
MESSENGER
SERVANT of Laius, OEDIPUS' father
SECOND MESSENGER
(silent) ANTIGONE and ISMENE, daughters of OEDIPUS

Oedipus the King

THE SCENE. *Before the palace of Oedipus at Thebes. In front of the large central doors, an altar; and an altar near each of the two side doors. On the altar steps are seated supplicants—old men, youths, and young boys—dressed in white tunics and cloaks, their hair bound with white fillets. They have laid on the altars olive branches wreathed with wool fillets.*

The old PRIEST OF ZEUS *stands alone facing the central doors of the palace. The doors open, and* OEDIPUS, *followed by two attendants who stand at either door, enters and looks about.*

OEDIPUS. O children, last born stock of ancient Cadmus,
    What petitions are these you bring to me
    With garlands on your suppliant olive branches?
    The whole city teems with incense fumes,
    Teems with prayers for healing and with groans.
    Thinking it best, children, to hear all this
    Not from some messenger, I came myself,
    The world renowned and glorious Oedipus.
    But tell me, aged priest, since you are fit
    To speak before these men, how stand you here,
    In fear or want? Tell me, as I desire
    To do my all; hard hearted I would be
    To feel no sympathy for such a prayer.
PRIEST. O Oedipus, ruler of my land, you see
    How old we are who stand in supplication
    Before your altars here, some not yet strong
    For lengthy flight, some heavy with age,

This translation has appeared in a previous collection edited by Albert Cook, *Oedipus Rex: A Mirror for Greek Drama* (Wadsworth, 1963).

[1–17]

Priests, as I of Zeus, and choice young men.
The rest of the tribe sits with wreathed branches,
In marketplaces, at Pallas' two temples,
And at prophetic embers by the river.
The city, as you see, now shakes too greatly
And cannot raise her head out of the depths
Above the gory swell. She wastes in blight,
Blight on earth's fruitful blooms and grazing flocks,
And on the barren birth pangs of the women.
The fever god has fallen on the city,
And drives it, a most hated pestilence
Through whom the home of Cadmus is made empty.
Black Hades is enriched with wails and groans.
Not that we think you equal to the gods
These boys and I sit suppliant at your hearth,
But judging you first of men in the trials of life,
And in the human intercourse with spirits:—
You are the one who came to Cadmus' city
And freed us from the tribute which we paid
To the harsh-singing Sphinx. And that you did
Knowing nothing else, unschooled by us.
But people say and think it was some god
That helped you to set our life upright.
Now Oedipus, most powerful of all,
We all are turned here toward you, we beseech you,
Find us some strength, whether from one of the gods
You hear an omen, or know one from a man.
For the experienced I see will best
Make good plans grow from evil circumstance.
Come, best of mortal men, raise up the state.
Come, prove your fame, since now this land of ours
Calls you savior for your previous zeal.
O never let our memory of your reign
Be that we first stood straight and later fell,
But to security raise up this state.
With favoring omen once you gave us luck;
Be now as good again; for if henceforth

You rule as now, you will be this country's king,
Better it is to rule men than a desert,
Since nothing is either ship or fortress tower
Bare of men who together dwell within.

OEDIPUS. O piteous children, I am not ignorant
Of what you come desiring. Well I know
You are all sick, and in your sickness none
There is among you as sick as I,
For your pain comes to one man alone,
To him and to none other, but my soul
Groans for the state, for myself, and for you.
You do not wake a man who is sunk in sleep;
Know that already I have shed many tears,
And travelled many wandering roads of thought.
Well have I sought, and found one remedy;
And this I did: the son of Menoeceus,
Creon, my brother-in-law, I sent away
Unto Apollo's Pythian halls to find
What I might do or say to save the state.
The days are measured out that he is gone;
It troubles me how he fares. Longer than usual
He has been away, more than the fitting time.
But when he comes, then evil I shall be,
If all the god reveals I fail to do.

PRIEST. You speak at the right time. These men just now
Signal to me that Creon is approaching.

OEDIPUS. O Lord Apollo, grant that he may come
In saving fortune shining as in eye.

PRIEST. Glad news he brings, it seems, or else his head
Would not be crowned with leafy, berried bay.

OEDIPUS. We will soon know. He is close enough to hear.—
Prince, my kinsman, son of Menoeceus,
What oracle do you bring us from the god?

CREON. A good one. For I say that even burdens
If they chance to turn out right, will all be well.

OEDIPUS. Yet what is the oracle? Your present word
Makes me neither bold nor apprehensive.

CREON. If you wish to hear in front of this crowd
  I am ready to speak, or we can go within.
OEDIPUS. Speak forth to all. The sorrow that I bear
  Is greater for these men than for my life.
CREON. May I tell you what I heard from the god?
  Lord Phoebus clearly bids us to drive out,
  And not to leave uncured within this country,
  A pollution we have nourished in our land.
OEDIPUS. With what purgation? What kind of misfortune?
CREON. Banish the man, or quit slaughter with slaughter
  In cleansing, since this blood rains on the state.
OEDIPUS. Who is this man whose fate the god reveals?
CREON. Laius, my lord, was formerly the guide
  Of this our land before you steered this city.
OEDIPUS. I know him by hearsay, but I never saw him.
CREON. Since he was slain, the god now plainly bids us
  To punish his murderers, whoever they may be.
OEDIPUS. Where are they on the earth? How shall we find
  This indiscernible track of ancient guilt?
CREON. In this land, said Apollo. What is sought
  Can be apprehended; the unobserved escapes.
OEDIPUS. Did Laius fall at home on this bloody end?
  Or in the fields, or in some foreign land?
CREON. As a pilgrim, the god said, he left his tribe
  And once away from home, returned no more.
OEDIPUS. Was there no messenger, no fellow wayfarer
  Who saw, from whom an inquirer might get aid?
CREON. They are all dead, save one, who fled in fear
  And he knows only one thing sure to tell.
OEDIPUS. What is that? We may learn many facts from one
  If we might take for hope a short beginning.
CREON. Robbers, Apollo said, met there and killed him
  Not by the strength of one, but many hands.
OEDIPUS. How did the robber, unless something from here
  Was at work with silver, reach this point of daring?
CREON. These facts are all conjecture. Laius dead,
  There rose in evils no avenger for him.
OEDIPUS. But when the king had fallen slain, what trouble

Prevented you from finding all this out?
CREON. The subtle-singing Sphinx made us let go
    What was unclear to search at our own feet.
OEDIPUS. Well then, I will make this clear afresh
    From the start. Phoebus was right, you were right
    To take this present interest in the dead.
    Justly it is you see me as your ally
    Avenging alike this country and the god.
    Not for the sake of some distant friends,
    But for myself I will disperse this filth.
    Whoever it was who killed that man
    With the same hand may wish to do vengeance on me.
    And so assisting Laius I aid myself.
    But hurry quickly, children, stand up now
    From the altar steps, raising these suppliant boughs.
    Let someone gather Cadmus' people here
    To learn that I will do all, whether at last
    With Phoebus' help we are shown saved or fallen.
PRIEST. Come, children, let us stand. We came here
    First for the sake of what this man proclaims.
    Phoebus it was who sent these prophecies
    And he will come to save us from the plague.

1st STROPHE

CHORUS. O sweet-tongued voice of Zeus, in what spirit do you come
    From Pytho rich in gold
    To glorious Thebes? I am torn on the rack, dread shakes my
      fearful mind,
    Apollo of Delos, hail!
    As I stand in awe of you, what need, either new
    Do you bring to the full for me, or old in the turning times
      of the year?
    Tell me, O child of golden Hope, undying Voice!

1st ANTISTROPHE

First on you do I call, daughter of Zeus, undying Athene
    And your sister who guards our land,
    Artemis, seated upon the throne renowned of our circled Place,

And Phoebus who darts afar;
Shine forth to me, thrice warder-off of death;
If ever in time before when ruin rushed upon the state,
The flame of sorrow you drove beyond our bounds, come also
    now.

2ND STROPHE

O woe! Unnumbered that I bear
The sorrows are! My whole host is sick, nor is there a sword
    of thought
To ward off pain. The growing fruits
Of glorious earth wax not, nor women
Withstand in childbirth shrieking pangs.
Life on life you may see, which, like the well-winged bird,
Faster than stubborn fire, speed
To the strand of the evening god.

2ND ANTISTROPHE

Unnumbered of the city die.
Unpitied babies bearing death lie unmoaned on the ground.
Grey-haired mothers and young wives
From all sides at the altar's edge
Lift up a wail beseeching, for their mournful woes.
The prayer for healing shines blent with a grieving cry;
Wherefore, O golden daughter of Zeus,
Send us your succor with its beaming face.

3RD STROPHE

Grant that fiery Ares, who now with no brazen shield
Flames round me in shouting attack
May turn his back in running flight from our land,
May be borne with fair wind
To Amphitrite's great chamber
Or to the hostile port
Of the Thracian surge.
For even if night leaves any ill undone
It is brought to pass and comes to be in the day.

O Zeus who bear the fire
And rule the lightning's might,
Strike him beneath your thunderbolt with death!

3RD ANTISTROPHE

O lord Apollo, would that you might come and scatter forth
Untamed darts from your twirling golden bow;
Bring succor from the plague; may the flashing
Beams come of Artemis,
With which she glances through the Lycian hills.
Also on him I call whose hair is held in gold,
Who gives a name to this land,
Bacchus of winy face, whom maidens hail!
Draw near with your flaming maenad band
And the aid of your gladsome torch
Against the plague, dishonored among the gods.

OEDIPUS. You pray; if for what you pray you would be willing
To hear and take my words, to nurse the plague,
You may get succor and relief from evils.
A stranger to this tale I now speak forth,
A stranger to the deed, for not alone
Could I have tracked it far without some clue,
But now that I am enrolled a citizen
Latest among the citizens of Thebes
To all you sons of Cadmus I proclaim
Whoever of you knows at what man's hand
Laius, the son of Labdacus, met his death,
I order him to tell me all, and even
If he fears, to clear the charge and he will suffer
No injury, but leave the land unharmed.
If someone knows the murderer to be an alien
From foreign soil, let him not be silent;
I will give him a reward, my thanks besides.
But if you stay in silence and from fear
For self or friend thrust aside my command,
Hear now from me what I shall do for this;
I charge that none who dwell within this land

Whereof I hold the power and the throne
Give this man shelter whoever he may be,
Or speak to him, or share with him in prayer
Or sacrifice, or serve him lustral rites,
But drive him, all, out of your homes, for he
Is this pollution on us, as Apollo
Revealed to me just now in oracle.
I am therefore the ally of the god
And of the murdered man. And now I pray
That the murderer, whether he hides alone
Or with his partners, may, evil coward,
Wear out in luckless ills his wretched life.
I further pray, that, if at my own hearth
He dwells known to me in my own home,
I may suffer myself the curse I just now uttered.
And you I charge to bring all this to pass
For me, and for the god, and for our land
Which now lies fruitless, godless, and corrupt.
Even if Phoebus had not urged this affair,
Not rightly did you let it go unpurged
When one both noble and a king was murdered!
You should have sought it out. Since now I reign
Holding the power which he had held before me,
Having the selfsame wife and marriage bed—
And if his seed had not met barren fortune
We should be linked by offspring from one mother;
But as it was, fate leapt upon his head.
Therefore in this, as if for my own father
I fight for him, and shall attempt all
Searching to seize the hand which shed that blood,
For Labdacus' son, before him Polydorus,
And ancient Cadmus, and Agenor of old.
And those who fail to do this, I pray the gods
May give them neither harvest from the earth
Nor children from their wives, but may they be
Destroyed by a fate like this one, or a worse.
You other Thebans, who cherish these commands,

May Justice, the ally of a righteous cause,
And all the gods be always on your side.

CHORUS. By the oath you laid on me, my king, I speak.
I killed not Laius, nor can show who killed him.
Phoebus it was who sent this question to us,
And he should answer who has done the deed.

OEDIPUS. Your words are just, but to compel the gods
In what they do not wish, no man can do.

CHORUS. I would tell what seems to me our second course.

OEDIPUS. If there is a third, fail not to tell it too.

CHORUS. Lord Teiresias I know, who sees this best
Like lord Apollo; in surveying this,
One might, my lord, find out from him most clearly.

OEDIPUS. Even this I did not neglect; I have done it already.
At Creon's word I twice sent messengers.
It is a wonder he has been gone so long.

CHORUS. And also there are rumors, faint and old.

OEDIPUS. What are they? I must search out every tale.

CHORUS. They say there were some travellers who killed him.

OEDIPUS. So I have heard, but no one sees a witness.

CHORUS. If his mind knows a particle of fear
He will not long withstand such curse as yours.   .

OEDIPUS. He fears no speech who fears not such a deed.

CHORUS. But here is the man who will convict the guilty.
Here are these men leading the divine prophet
In whom alone of men the truth is born.

OEDIPUS. O you who ponder all, Teiresias,
Both what is taught and what cannot be spoken,
What is of heaven and what trod on the earth,
Even if you are blind, you know what plague
Clings to the state, and, master, you alone
We find as her protector and her savior.
Apollo, if the messengers have not told you,
Answered our question, that release would come
From this disease only if we make sure
Of Laius' slayers and slay them in return
Or drive them out as exiles from the land.

But you now, grudge us neither voice of birds
Nor any way you have of prophecy.
Save yourself and the state; save me as well.
Save everything polluted by the dead.
We are in your hands; it is the noblest task
To help a man with all your means and powers.

TEIRESIAS. Alas! Alas! How terrible to be wise,
Where it does the seer no good. Too well I know
And have forgot this, or would not have come here.

OEDIPUS. What is this? How fainthearted you have come!

TEIRESIAS. Let me go home; it is best for you to bear
Your burden, and I mine, if you will heed me.

OEDIPUS. You speak what is lawless, and hateful to the state
Which raised you, when you deprive her of your answer.

TEIRESIAS. And I see that your speech does not proceed
In season; I shall not undergo the same.

OEDIPUS. Don't by the gods turn back when you are wise,
When all we suppliants lie prostrate before you.

TEIRESIAS. And all unwise; I never shall reveal
My evils, so that I may not tell yours.

OEDIPUS. What do you say? You know, but will not speak?
Would you betray us and destroy the state?

TEIRESIAS. I will not hurt you or me. Why in vain
Do you probe this? You will not find out from me.

OEDIPUS. Worst of evil men, you would enrage
A stone itself. Will you never speak,
But stay so untouched and so inconclusive?

TEIRESIAS. You blame my anger and do not see that
With which you live in common, but upbraid me.

OEDIPUS. Who would not be enraged to hear these words
By which you now dishonor this our city?

TEIRESIAS. Of itself this will come, though I hide it in silence.

OEDIPUS. Then you should tell me what it is will come.

TEIRESIAS. I shall speak no more. If further you desire,
Rage on in wildest anger of your soul.

OEDIPUS. I shall omit nothing I understand
I am so angry. Know that you seem to me

Creator of the deed and worker too
In all short of the slaughter; if you were not blind,
I would say this crime was your work alone.
TEIRESIAS. Really? Abide yourself by the decree
You just proclaimed, I tell you! From this day
Henceforth address neither these men nor me.
You are the godless defiler of this land.
OEDIPUS. You push so bold and taunting in your speech;
And how do you think to get away with this?
TEIRESIAS. I have got away. I nurse my strength in truth.
OEDIPUS. Who taught you this? Not from your art you got it.
TEIRESIAS. From you. You had me speak against my will.
OEDIPUS. What word? Say again, so I may better learn.
TEIRESIAS. Didn't you get it before? Or do you bait me?
OEDIPUS. I don't remember it. Speak forth again.
TEIRESIAS. You are the slayer whom you seek, I say.
OEDIPUS. Not twice you speak such bitter words unpunished.
TEIRESIAS. Shall I speak more to make you angrier still?
OEDIPUS. Do what you will, your words will be in vain.
TEIRESIAS. I say you have forgot that you are joined
With those most dear to you in deepest shame
And do not see where you are in sin.
OEDIPUS. Do you think you will always say such things in joy?
TEIRESIAS. Surely, if strength abides in what is true.
OEDIPUS. It does, for all but you, this not for you
Because your ears and mind and eyes are blind.
TEIRESIAS. Wretched you are to make such taunts, for soon
All men will cast the selfsame taunts on you.
OEDIPUS. You live in entire night, could do no harm
To me or any man who sees the day.
TEIRESIAS. Not at your hands will it be my fate to fall.[1]
Apollo suffices, whose concern it is to do this.

1. This reading is based on the interpretation of the papyrus text by
Bernard Knox in *Oedipus at Thebes* (New Haven: Yale University Press,
1957), pp. 198–199. The usual reading is "Not at my hands will be your fate
to fall."

OEDIPUS. Are these devices yours, or are they Creon's?
TEIRESIAS. Creon is not your trouble; you are yourself.
OEDIPUS. O riches, empire, skill surpassing skill
  In all the numerous rivalries of life,
  How great a grudge there is stored up against you
  If for this kingship, which the city gave,
  Their gift, not my request, into my hands—
  For this, the trusted Creon, my friend from the start
  Desires to creep by stealth and cast me out
  Taking a seer like this, a weaver of wiles,
  A crooked swindler who has got his eyes
  On gain alone, but in his art is blind.
  Come, tell us, in what clearly are you a prophet?
  How is it, when the weave-songed bitch was here
  You uttered no salvation for these people?
  Surely the riddle then could not be solved
  By some chance comer; it needed prophecy.
  You did not clarify that with birds
  Or knowledge from a god; but when I came,
  The ignorant Oedipus, I silenced her,
  Not taught by birds, but winning by my wits,
  Whom you are now attempting to depose,
  Thinking to minister near Creon's throne.
  I think that to your woe you and that plotter
  Will purge the land, and if you were not old
  Punishment would teach you what you plot.
CHORUS. It seems to us, O Oedipus our king,
  Both this man's words and yours were said in anger.
  Such is not our need, but to find out
  How best we shall discharge Apollo's orders.
TEIRESIAS. Even if you are king, the right to answer
  Should be free to all; of that I too am king.
  I live not as your slave, but as Apollo's.
  And not with Creon's wards shall I be counted.
  I say, since you have taunted even my blindness,
  You have eyes, but see not where in evil you are
  Nor where you dwell, nor whom you are living with.

Do you know from whom you spring? And you forget
You are an enemy to your own kin
Both those beneath and those above the earth.
Your mother's and father's curse, with double goad
And dreaded foot shall drive you from this land.
You who now see straight shall then be blind,
And there shall be no harbor for your cry
With which all Mount Cithaeron soon shall ring,
When you have learned the wedding where you sailed
At home, into no port, by voyage fair.
A throng of other ills you do not know
Shall equal you to yourself and to your children.
Throw mud on this, on Creon, on my voice—
Yet there shall never be a mortal man
Eradicated more wretchedly than you.

OEDIPUS. Shall these unbearable words be heard from him?
Go to perdition! Hurry! Off, away,
Turn back again and from this house depart.

TEIRESIAS. If you had not called me, I should not have come.

OEDIPUS. I did not know that you would speak such folly
Or I would not soon have brought you to my house.

TEIRESIAS. And such a fool I am, as it seems to you.
But to the parents who bore you I seem wise.

OEDIPUS. What parents? Wait! What mortals gave me birth?

TEIRESIAS. This day shall be your birth and your destruction.

OEDIPUS. All things you say in riddles and unclear.

TEIRESIAS. Are you not he who best can search this out?

OEDIPUS. Mock, if you wish, the skill that made me great.

TEIRESIAS. This is the very fortune that destroyed you.

OEDIPUS. Well, if I saved the city, I do not care.

TEIRESIAS. I am going now. You, boy, be my guide.

OEDIPUS. Yes, let him guide you. Here you are in the way.
When you are gone you will give no more trouble.

TEIRESIAS. I go when I have said what I came to say
Without fear of your frown; you cannot destroy me.
I say, the very man whom you long seek
With threats and announcements about Laius' murder—

This man is here. He seems an alien stranger,
But soon he shall be revealed of Theban birth,
Nor at this circumstance shall he be pleased.
He shall be blind who sees, shall be a beggar
Who now is rich, shall make his way abroad
Feeling the ground before him with a staff.
He shall be revealed at once as brother
And father to his own children, husband and son
To his mother, his father's kin and murderer.
Go in and ponder that. If I am wrong,
Say then that I know nothing of prophecy.

1st Strophe

CHORUS. Who is the man the Delphic rock said with oracular voice
　　Unspeakable crimes performed with his gory hands?
　　It is time for him now to speed
　　His foot in flight, more strong
　　Than horses swift as the storm.
　　For girt in arms upon him springs,
　　With fire and lightning, Zeus' son
　　And behind him, terrible,
　　Come the unerring Fates.

1st Antistrophe

From snowy Parnassus just now the word flashed clear
To track the obscure man by every way,
For he wanders under the wild
Forest, and into caves
And cliff rocks, like a bull,
Reft on his way, with care on care
Trying to shun the prophecy
Come from the earth's mid-navel,
But about him flutters the everliving doom.

2nd Strophe

Terrible, terrible things the wise bird-augur stirs.
I neither approve nor deny, at a loss for what to say,

I flutter in hopes and fears, see neither here nor ahead;
For what strife has lain
On Labdacus' sons or Polybus' that I have found ever before
Or now, whereby I may run for the sons of Labdacus
In sure proof against Oedipus' public fame
As avenger for dark death?

2ND ANTISTROPHE

Zeus and Apollo surely understand and know
The affairs of mortal men, but that a mortal seer
Knows more than I, there is no proof. Though a man
May surpass a man in knowledge,
Never shall I agree, till I see the word true, when men blame
    Oedipus,
For there came upon him once clear the winged maiden
And wise he was seen, by sure test sweet for the state.
So never shall my mind judge him evil guilt.

CREON. Men of our city, I have heard dread words
    That Oedipus our king accuses me.
    I am here indignant. If in the present troubles
    He thinks that he has suffered at my hands
    One word or deed tending to injury
    I do not crave the long-spanned age of life
    To bear this rumor, for it is no simple wrong
    The damage of this accusation brings me;
    It brings the greatest, if I am called a traitor
    To you and my friends, a traitor to the state.
CHORUS. Come now, for this reproach perhaps was forced
    By anger, rather than considered thought.
CREON. And was the idea voiced that my advice
    Persuaded the prophet to give false accounts?
CHORUS. Such was said. I know not to what intent.
CREON. Was this accusation laid against me
    From straightforward eyes and straightforward mind?
CHORUS. I do not know. I see not what my masters do;
    But here he is now, coming from the house.

OEDIPUS. How dare you come here? Do you own a face
So bold that you can come before my house
When you are clearly the murderer of this man
And manifestly pirate of my throne?
Come, say before the gods, did you see in me
A coward or a fool, that you plotted this?
Or did you think I would not see your wiles
Creeping upon me, or knowing, would not ward off?
Surely your machination is absurd
Without a crowd of friends to hunt a throne
Which is captured only by wealth and many men.
CREON. Do you know what you do? Hear answer to your charges
On the other side. Judge only what you know.
OEDIPUS. Your speech is clever, but I learn it ill
Since I have found you harsh and grievous toward me.
CREON. This very matter hear me first explain.
OEDIPUS. Tell me not this one thing: you are not false.
CREON. If you think stubbornness a good possession
Apart from judgment, you do not think right.
OEDIPUS. If you think you can do a kinsman evil
Without the penalty, you have no sense.
CREON. I agree with you. What you have said is just.
Tell me what you say you have suffered from me.
OEDIPUS. Did you, or did you not, advise my need
Was summoning that prophet person here?
CREON. And still is. I hold still the same opinion.
OEDIPUS. How long a time now has it been since Laius—
CREON. Performed what deed? I do not understand.
OEDIPUS. —Disappeared to his ruin at deadly hands.
CREON. Far in the past the count of years would run.
OEDIPUS. Was this same seer at that time practicing?
CREON. As wise as now, and equally respected.
OEDIPUS. At that time did he ever mention me?
CREON. Never when I stood near enough to hear.
OEDIPUS. But did you not make inquiry of the murder?
CREON. We did, of course, and got no information.
OEDIPUS. How is it that this seer did not utter this then?

CREON. When I don't know, as now, I would keep still.
OEDIPUS. This much you know full well, and so should speak—
CREON. What is that? If I know, I will not refuse.
OEDIPUS. This: If he had not first conferred with you
   He never would have said that I killed Laius.
CREON. If he says this, you know yourself, I think;
   I learn as much from you as you from me.
OEDIPUS. Learn then: I never shall be found a slayer.
CREON. What then, are you the husband of my sister?
OEDIPUS. What you have asked is plain beyond denial.
CREON. Do you rule this land with her in equal sway?
OEDIPUS. All she desires she obtains from me.
CREON. Am I with you two not an equal third?
OEDIPUS. In just that do you prove a treacherous friend.
CREON. No, if, like me, you reason with yourself.
   Consider this fact first: would any man
   Choose, do you think, to have his rule in fear
   Rather than doze unharmed with the same power?
   For my part I have never been desirous
   Of being king instead of acting king.
   Nor any other man has, wise and prudent.
   For now I obtain all from you without fear.
   If I were king, I would do much unwilling.
   How then could kingship sweeter be for me
   Than rule and power devoid of any pain?
   I am not yet so much deceived to want
   Goods besides those I profitably enjoy.
   Now I am hailed and gladdened by all men.
   Now those who want from you speak out to me,
   Since all their chances' outcome dwells therein.
   How then would I relinquish what I have
   To get those gains? My mind runs not so bad.
   I am prudent yet, no lover of such plots,
   Nor would I ever endure others' treason.
   And first as proof of this go on to Pytho;
   See if I told you truly the oracle.
   Next proof: see if I plotted with the seer;

If you find so at all, put me to death
With my vote for my guilt as well as yours.
Do not convict me just on unclear conjecture.
It is not right to think capriciously
The good are bad, nor that the bad are good.
It is the same to cast out a noble friend,
I say, as one's own life, which best he loves.
The facts, though, you will safely know in time,
Since time alone can show the just man just,
But you can know a criminal in one day.

CHORUS. A cautious man would say he has spoken well.
O king, the quick to think are never sure.

OEDIPUS. When the plotter, swift, approaches me in stealth
I too in counterplot must be as swift.
If I wait in repose, the plotter's ends
Are brought to pass and mine will then have erred.

CREON. What do you want then? To cast me from the land?

OEDIPUS. Least of all that. My wish is you should die,
Not flee to exemplify what envy is.

CREON. Do you say this? Will you neither trust nor yield?

OEDIPUS. [No, for I think that you deserve no trust.]

CREON. You seem not wise to me

OEDIPUS.   I am for me.

CREON. You should be for me too.

OEDIPUS.   No, you are evil.

CREON. Yes, if you understand nothing.

OEDIPUS.   Yet I must rule.

CREON. Not when you rule badly.

OEDIPUS.   O city, city!

CREON. It is my city too, not yours alone.

CHORUS. Stop, princes. I see Jocasta coming
Out of the house at the right time for you.
With her you must settle the dispute at hand.

JOCASTA. O wretched men, what unconsidered feud
Of tongues have you aroused? Are you not ashamed,
The state so sick, to stir up private ills?
Are you not going home? And you as well?

Will you turn a small pain into a great?

CREON. My blood sister, Oedipus your husband
   Claims he will judge against me two dread ills:
   Thrust me from the fatherland or take and kill me.

OEDIPUS. I will, my wife; I caught him in the act
   Doing evil to my person with evil skill.

CREON. Now may I not rejoice but die accursed
   If ever I did any of what you accuse me.

JOCASTA. O, by the gods, believe him, Oedipus.
   First, in reverence for his oath to the gods,
   Next, for my sake and theirs who stand before you.

CHORUS. Hear my entreaty, lord. Consider and consent.

OEDIPUS. What wish should I then grant?

CHORUS. Respect the man, no fool before, who now in oath is strong.

OEDIPUS. You know what you desire?

CHORUS.   I know.

OEDIPUS.   Say what you mean.

CHORUS. Your friend who has sworn do not dishonor
   By casting guilt for dark report.

OEDIPUS. Know well that when you ask this grant from me,
   You ask my death or exile from the land.

CHORUS. No, by the god foremost among the gods,
   The Sun, may I perish by the utmost doom
   Godless and friendless, if I have this in mind.
   But ah, the withering earth wears down
   My wretched soul, if to these ills
   Of old are added ills from both of you.

OEDIPUS. Then let him go, though surely I must die
   Or be thrust dishonored from this land by force.
   Your grievous voice I pity, not that man's;
   Wherever he may be, he will be hated.

CREON. Sullen you are to yield, as you are heavy
   When you exceed in wrath. Natures like these
   Are justly sorest for themselves to bear.

OEDIPUS. Will you not go and leave me?

CREON.   I am on my way.
   You know me not, but these men see me just.

CHORUS. O queen, why do you delay to bring this man indoors?

JOCASTA. I want to learn what happened here.

CHORUS. Unknown suspicion rose from talk, and the unjust
    devours.

JOCASTA. In both of them?

CHORUS.   Just so.

JOCASTA.   What was the talk?

CHORUS. Enough, enough! When the land is pained
    It seems to me at this point we should stop.

OEDIPUS. Do you see where you have come? Though your intent
    Is good, you slacken off and blunt my heart.

CHORUS. O lord, I have said not once alone,
    Know that I clearly would be mad
    And wandering in mind, to turn away
    You who steered along the right,
    When she was torn with trouble, our beloved state.
    O may you now become in health her guide.

JOCASTA. By the gods, lord, tell me on what account
    You have set yourself in so great an anger.

OEDIPUS. I shall tell you, wife; I respect you more than these men.
    Because of Creon, since he has plotted against me.

JOCASTA. Say clearly, if you can; how started the quarrel?

OEDIPUS. He says that I stand as the murderer of Laius.

JOCASTA. He knows himself, or learned from someone else?

OEDIPUS. No, but he sent a rascal prophet here.
    He keeps his own mouth clean in what concerns him.

JOCASTA. Now free yourself of what you said, and listen.
    Learn from me, no mortal man exists
    Who knows prophetic art for your affairs,
    And I shall briefly show you proof of this:
    An oracle came once to Laius. I do not say
    From Phoebus himself, but from his ministers
    That his fate would be at his son's hand to die—
    A child, who would be born from him and me.
    And yet, as the rumor says, they were strangers,
    Robbers who killed him where three highways meet.
    But three days had not passed from the child's birth

When Laius pierced and tied together his ankles,
And cast him by others' hands on a pathless mountain.
Therein Apollo did not bring to pass
That the child murder his father, nor for Laius
The dread he feared, to die at his son's hand.
Such did prophetic oracles determine.
Pay no attention to them. For the god
Will easily make clear the need he seeks.

OEDIPUS. What wandering of soul, what stirring of mind
Holds me, my wife, in what I have just heard!

JOCASTA. What care has turned you back that you say this?

OEDIPUS. I thought I heard you mention this, that Laius
Was slaughtered at the place where three highways meet.

JOCASTA. That was the talk. The rumor has not ceased.

OEDIPUS. Where is this place where such a sorrow was?

JOCASTA. The country's name is Phocis. A split road
Leads to one place from Delphi and Daulia.

OEDIPUS. And how much time has passed since these events?

JOCASTA. The news was heralded in the city scarcely
A little while before you came to rule.

OEDIPUS. O Zeus, what have you planned to do to me?

JOCASTA. What passion is this in you, Oedipus?

OEDIPUS. Don't ask me that yet. Tell me about Laius.
What did he look like? How old was he when murdered?

JOCASTA. A tall man, with his hair just brushed with white.
His shape and form differed not far from yours.

OEDIPUS. Alas! Alas! I think unwittingly
I have just laid dread curses on my head.

JOCASTA. What are you saying? I shrink to behold you, lord.

OEDIPUS. I am terribly afraid the seer can see.
That will be clearer if you say one thing more.

JOCASTA. Though I shrink, if I know what you ask, I will answer.

OEDIPUS. Did he set forth with few attendants then,
Or many soldiers, since he was a king?

JOCASTA. They were five altogether among them.
One was a herald. One chariot bore Laius.

OEDIPUS. Alas! All this is clear now. Tell me, my wife,

Who was the man who told these stories to you?
JOCASTA. One servant, who alone escaped, returned.
OEDIPUS. Is he by chance now present in our house?
JOCASTA. Not now. Right from the time when he returned
    To see you ruling and Laius dead,
    Touching my hand in suppliance, he implored me
    To send him to fields and to pastures of sheep
    That he might be farthest from the sight of this city.
    So I sent him away, since he was worthy
    For a slave, to bear a greater grant than this.
OEDIPUS. How then could he return to us with speed?
JOCASTA. It can be done. But why would you order this?
OEDIPUS. O lady, I fear I have said too much.
    On this account I now desire to see him.
JOCASTA. Then he shall come. But I myself deserve
    To learn what it is that troubles you, my lord.
OEDIPUS. And you shall not be prevented, since my fears
    Have come to such a point. For who is closer
    That I may speak to in this fate than you?
    Polybus of Corinth was my father,
    My mother, Dorian Merope. I was held there
    Chief citizen of all, till such a fate
    Befell me—as it is, worthy of wonder,
    But surely not deserving my excitement.
    A man at a banquet overdrunk with wine
    Said in drink I was a false son to my father.
    The weight I held that day I scarcely bore,
    But on the next day I went home and asked
    My father and mother of it. In bitter anger
    They took the reproach from him who had let it fly.
    I was pleased at their actions; nevertheless
    The rumor always rankled; and spread abroad.
    In secret from mother and father I set out
    Toward Delphi. Phoebus sent me away ungraced
    In what I came for, but other wretched things
    Terrible and grievous, he revealed in answer;
    That I must wed my mother and produce

An unendurable race for men to see,
That I should kill the father who begot me.
When I heard this response, Corinth I fled
Henceforth to measure her land by stars alone.
I went where I should never see the disgrace
Of my evil oracles be brought to pass,
And on my journey to that place I came
At which you say this king had met his death.
My wife, I shall speak the truth to you. My way
Led to a place close by the triple road.
There a herald met me, and a man
Seated on colt-drawn chariot, as you said.
There both the guide and the old man himself
Thrust me with driving force out of the path.
And I in anger struck the one who pushed me,
The driver. Then the old man, when he saw me,
Watched when I passed, and from his chariot
Struck me full on the head with double goad.
I paid him back and more. From this very hand
A swift blow of my staff rolled him right out
Of the middle of his seat onto his back.
I killed them all. But if relationship
Existed between this stranger and Laius,
What man now is wretcheder than I?
What man is cursed by a more evil fate?
No stranger or citizen could now receive me
Within his home, or even speak to me,
But thrust me out; and no one but myself
Brought down these curses on my head.
The bed of the slain man I now defile
With hands that killed him. Am I evil by birth?
Am I not utterly vile if I must flee
And cannot see my family in my flight
Nor tread my homeland soil, or else be joined
In marriage to my mother, kill my father,
Polybus, who sired me and brought me up?
Would not a man judge right to say of me

That this was sent on me by some cruel spirit?
O never, holy reverence of the gods,
May I behold that day, but may I go
Away from mortal men, before I see
Such a stain of circumstance come to me.

CHORUS. My lord, for us these facts are full of dread.
Until you hear the witness, stay in hope.

OEDIPUS. And just so much is all I have of hope,
Only to wait until the shepherd comes.

JOCASTA. What, then, do you desire to hear him speak?

OEDIPUS. I will tell you, if his story is found to be
The same as yours, I would escape the sorrow.

JOCASTA. What unusual word did you hear from me?

OEDIPUS. You said he said that they were highway robbers
Who murdered him. Now, if he still says
The selfsame number, I could not have killed him,
Since one man does not equal many men.
But if he speaks of a single lonely traveller,
The scale of guilt now clearly falls to me.

JOCASTA. However, know the word was set forth thus
And it is not in him now to take it back;
This tale the city heard, not I alone.
But if he diverges from his previous story,
Even then, my lord, he could not show Laius' murder
To have been fulfilled properly. Apollo
Said he would die at the hands of my own son.
Surely that wretched child could not have killed him,
But he himself met death some time before.
Therefore, in any prophecy henceforth
I would not look to this side or to that.

OEDIPUS. Your thoughts ring true, but still let someone go
To summon the peasant. Do not neglect this.

JOCASTA. I shall send without delay. But let us enter.
I would do nothing that did not please you.

1st Strophe

CHORUS. May fate come on me as I bear
Holy pureness in all word and deed,

For which the lofty striding laws were set down,
Born through the heavenly air
Whereof the Olympian sky alone the father was;
No mortal spawn of mankind gave them birth,
Nor may oblivion ever lull them down;
Mighty in them the god is, and he does not age.

1st Antistrophe

Pride breeds the tyrant.
Pride, once overfilled with many things in vain,
Neither in season nor fit for man,
Scaling the sheerest height
Hurls to a dire fate
Where no foothold is found.
I pray the god may never stop the rivalry
That works well for the state.
The god as my protector I shall never cease to hold.

2nd Strophe

But if a man goes forth haughty in word or deed
With no fear of the Right
Nor pious to the spirits' shrines,
May evil doom seize him
For his ill-fated pride,
If he does not fairly win his gain
Or works unholy deeds,
Or, in bold folly lays on the sacred profane hands.
For when such acts occur, what man may boast
Ever to ward off from his life darts of the gods?
If practices like these are in respect,
Why then must I dance the sacred dance?

2nd Antistrophe

Never again in worship shall I go
To Delphi, holy navel of the earth,
Nor to the temple at Abae
Nor to Olympia,

If these prophecies do not become
Examples for all men.
O Zeus, our king, if so you are rightly called,
Ruler of all things, may then not escape
You and your forever deathless power.
Men now hold light the fading oracles
Told about Laius long ago
And nowhere is Apollo clearly honored;
Things divine are going down to ruin.

JOCASTA. Lords of this land, the thought has come to me
    To visit the spirits' shrines, bearing in hand
    These suppliant boughs and offerings of incense.
    For Oedipus raises his soul too high
    With all distresses; nor, as a sane man should,
    Does he confirm the new by things of old,
    But stands at the speaker's will if he speaks terrors.
    And so, because my advice can do no more,
    To you, Lycian Apollo—for you are nearest—
    A suppliant, I have come here with these prayers,
    That you may find some pure deliverance for us:
    We all now shrink to see him struck in fear,
    That man who is the pilot of our ship.
MESSENGER. Strangers, could I learn from one of you
    Where is the house of Oedipus the king?
    Or best, if you know, say where he is himself.
CHORUS. This is his house, stranger; he dwells inside;
    This woman is the mother of his children.
MESSENGER. May she be always blessed among the blest,
    Since she is the fruitful wife of Oedipus.
JOCASTA. So may you, stranger, also be. You deserve
    As much for your graceful greeting. But tell me
    What you have come to search for or to show.
MESSENGER. Good news for your house and your husband, lady.
JOCASTA. What is it then? And from whom have you come?
MESSENGER. From Corinth. And the message I will tell
    Will surely gladden you—and vex you, perhaps.

JOCASTA. What is it? What is this double force it holds?
MESSENGER. The men who dwell in the Isthmian country
   Have spoken to establish him their king.
JOCASTA. What is that? Is not old Polybus still ruling?
MESSENGER. Not he. For death now holds him in the tomb.
JOCASTA. What do you say, old man? Is Polybus dead?
MESSENGER. If I speak not the truth, I am ready to die.
JOCASTA. O handmaid, go right away and tell your master
   The news. Where are you, prophecies of the gods?
   For this man Oedipus has trembled long,
   And shunned him lest he kill him. Now the man
   Is killed by fate and not by Oedipus.
OEDIPUS. O Jocasta, my most beloved wife,
   Why have you sent for me within the house?
JOCASTA. Listen to this man, and while you hear him, think
   To what have come Apollo's holy prophecies.
OEDIPUS. Who is this man? Why would he speak to me?
JOCASTA. From Corinth he has come, to announce that your father
   Polybus no longer lives, but is dead.
OEDIPUS. What do you say, stranger? Tell me this yourself.
MESSENGER. If I must first announce my message clearly,
   Know surely that the man is dead and gone.
OEDIPUS. Did he die by treachery or chance disease?
MESSENGER. A slight scale tilt can lull the old to rest.
OEDIPUS. The poor man, it seems, died by disease.
MESSENGER. And by the full measure of lengthy time.
OEDIPUS. Alas, alas! Why then do any seek
   Pytho's prophetic art, my wife, or hear
   The shrieking birds on high, by whose report
   I was to slay my father? Now he lies
   Dead beneath the earth, and here am I
   Who have not touched the blade. Unless in longing
   For me he died, and in this sense was killed by me.
   Polybus has packed away these oracles
   In his rest in Hades. They are now worth nothing.
JOCASTA. Did I not tell you that some time ago?
OEDIPUS. You did, but I was led astray by fear.

JOCASTA. Henceforth put nothing of this on your heart.
OEDIPUS. Why must I not still shrink from my mother's bed?
JOCASTA. What should man fear, whose life is ruled by fate,
    For whom there is clear foreknowledge of nothing?
    It is best to live by chance, however you can.
    Be not afraid of marriage with your mother;
    Already many mortals in their dreams
    Have shared their mother's bed. But he who counts
    This dream as nothing, easiest bears his life.
OEDIPUS. All that you say would be indeed propitious,
    If my mother were not alive. But since she is,
    I still must shrink, however well you speak.
JOCASTA. And yet your father's tomb is a great eye.
OEDIPUS. A great eye indeed. But I fear her who lives.
MESSENGER. Who is this woman that you are afraid of?
OEDIPUS. Merope, old man, with whom Polybus lived.
MESSENGER. What is it in her that moves you to fear?
OEDIPUS. A dread oracle, stranger, sent by the god.
MESSENGER. Can it be told, or must no other know?
OEDIPUS. It surely can. Apollo told me once
    That I must join in intercourse with my mother
    And shed with my own hands my father's blood.
    Because of this, long since I have kept far
    Away from Corinth—and happily—but yet
    It would be most sweet to see my parents' faces.
MESSENGER. Was this your fear in shunning your own city?
OEDIPUS. I wished, too, old man, not to slay my father.
MESSENGER. Why then have I not freed you from this fear,
    Since I have come with friendly mind, my lord?
OEDIPUS. Yes, and take thanks from me, which you deserve.
MESSENGER. And this is just the thing for which I came,
    That when you got back home I might fare well.
OEDIPUS. Never shall I go where my parents are.
MESSENGER. My son, you clearly know not what you do—
OEDIPUS. How is that, old man? By the gods, let me know—
MESSENGER. If for these tales you shrink from going home.
OEDIPUS. I tremble lest what Phoebus said comes true.

MESSENGER. Lest you incur pollution from your parents?
OEDIPUS. That is the thing, old man, that always haunts me.
MESSENGER. Well, do you know that surely you fear nothing?
OEDIPUS. How so? If I am the son of those who bore me.
MESSENGER. Since Polybus was no relation to you.
OEDIPUS. What do you say? Was Polybus not my father?
MESSENGER. No more than this man here but just so much.
OEDIPUS. How does he who begot me equal nothing?
MESSENGER. That man was not your father, any more than I am.
OEDIPUS. Well then, why was it he called me his son?
MESSENGER. Long ago he got you as a gift from me.
OEDIPUS. Though from another's hand, yet so much he loved me!
MESSENGER. His previous childlessness led him to that.
OEDIPUS. Had you bought or found me when you gave me to him?
MESSENGER. I found you in Cithaeron's folds and glens.
OEDIPUS. Why were you travelling in those regions?
MESSENGER. I guarded there a flock of mountain sheep.
OEDIPUS. Were you a shepherd, wandering for pay?
MESSENGER. Yes, and your savior too, child, at that time.
OEDIPUS. What pain gripped me, that you took me in your arms?
MESSENGER. The ankles of your feet will tell you that.
OEDIPUS. Alas, why do you mention that old trouble?
MESSENGER. I freed you when your ankles were pierced together.
OEDIPUS. A terrible shame from my swaddling clothes I got.
MESSENGER. Your very name you got from this misfortune.
OEDIPUS. By the gods, did my mother or father do it? Speak.
MESSENGER. I know not. He who gave you knows better than I.
OEDIPUS. You didn't find me, but took me from another?
MESSENGER. That's right. Another shepherd gave you to me.
OEDIPUS. Who was he? Can you tell me who he was?
MESSENGER. Surely. He belonged to the household of Laius.
OEDIPUS. The man who ruled this land once long ago?
MESSENGER. Just so. He was a herd in that man's service.
OEDIPUS. Is this man still alive, so I could see him?
MESSENGER. You dwellers in this country should know best.
OEDIPUS. Is there any one of you who stand before me
    Who knows the shepherd of whom this man speaks?

If you have seen him in the fields or here,
Speak forth; the time has come to find this out.

CHORUS. I think the man you seek is no one else
Than the shepherd you were so eager to see before.
Jocasta here might best inform us that.

OEDIPUS. My wife, do you know the man we just ordered
To come here? Is it of him that this man speaks?

JOCASTA. Why ask of whom he spoke? Think nothing of it.
Brood not in vain on what has just been said.

OEDIPUS. It could not be that when I have got such clues,
I should not shed clear light upon my birth.

JOCASTA. Don't, by the gods, investigate this more
If you care for your own life. I am sick enough.

OEDIPUS. Take courage. Even if I am found a slave
For three generations, your birth will not be base.

JOCASTA. Still, I beseech you, hear me. Don't do this.

OEDIPUS. I will hear of nothing but finding out the truth.

JOCASTA. I know full well and tell you what is best.

OEDIPUS. Well, then, this best, for some time now, has given me
    pain.

JOCASTA. O ill-fated man, may you never know who you are.

OEDIPUS. Will someone bring the shepherd to me here?
And let this lady rejoice in her opulent birth.

JOCASTA. Alas, alas, hapless man. I have this alone
To tell you, and nothing else forevermore.

CHORUS. O Oedipus, where has the woman gone
In the rush of her wild grief? I am afraid
Evil will break forth out of this silence.

OEDIPUS. Let whatever will break forth. I plan to see
The seed of my descent, however small.
My wife, perhaps, because a noblewoman
Looks down with shame upon my lowly birth.
I would not be dishonored to call myself
The Son of Fortune, giver of the good.
She is my mother. The years, her other children,
Have marked me sometimes small and sometimes great.

Such was I born! I shall prove no other man,
Nor shall I cease to search out my descent.

STROPHE

CHORUS. If I am a prophet and can know in mind,
Cithaeron, by tomorrow's full moon
You shall not fail, by Mount Olympus,
To find that Oedipus, as a native of your land,
Shall honor you for nurse and mother.
And to you we dance in choral song because you bring
Fair gifts to him our king.
Hail, Phoebus, may all this please you.

ANTISTROPHE

Who, child, who bore you in the lengthy span of years?
One close to Pan who roams the mountain woods,
One of Apollo's bedfellows?
For all wild pastures in mountain glens to him are dear.
Was Hermes your father, who Cyllene sways,
Or did Bacchus, dwelling on the mountain peaks,
Take you a foundling from some nymph
Of those by springs of Helicon, with whom he sports the most?

OEDIPUS. If I may guess, although I never met him,
I think, elders, I see that shepherd coming
Whom we have long sought, as in the measure
Of lengthy age he accords with him we wait for.
Besides, the men who lead him I recognize
As servants of my house. You may perhaps
Know better than I if you have seen him before.
CHORUS. Be assured, I know him as a shepherd
As trusted as any other in Laius' service.
OEDIPUS. Stranger from Corinth, I will ask you first,
Is this the man you said?
MESSENGER.   You are looking at him.
OEDIPUS. You there, old man, look here and answer me

What I shall ask you. Were you ever with Laius?
SERVANT. I was a slave, not bought but reared at home.
OEDIPUS. What work concerned you? What was your way of life?
SERVANT. Most of my life I spent among the flocks.
OEDIPUS. In what place most of all was your usual pasture?
SERVANT. Sometimes Cithaeron, or the ground nearby.
OEDIPUS. Do you know this man before you here at all?
SERVANT. Doing what? And of what man do you speak?
OEDIPUS. The one before you. Have you ever had congress with
  him?
SERVANT. Not to say so at once from memory.
MESSENGER. That is no wonder, master, but I shall remind him,
  Clearly, who knows me not; yet well I know
  That he knew once the region of Cithaeron.
  He with a double flock and I with one
  Dwelt there in company for three whole years
  During the six months' time from spring to fall.
  When winter came, I drove into my fold
  My flock, and he drove his to Laius' pens.
  Do I speak right, or did it not happen so?
SERVANT. You speak the truth, though it was long ago.
MESSENGER. Come now, do you recall you gave me then
  A child for me to rear as my own son?
SERVANT. What is that? Why do you ask me this?
MESSENGER. This is the man, my friend, who then was young.
SERVANT. Go to destruction! Will you not be quiet?
OEDIPUS. Come, scold him not, old man. These words of yours
  Deserve a scolding more than this man's do.
SERVANT. In what, most noble master, do I wrong?
OEDIPUS. Not to tell of the child he asks about.
SERVANT. He speaks in ignorance, he toils in vain.
OEDIPUS. If you will not speak freely, you will under torture.
SERVANT. Don't, by the gods, outrage an old man like me.
OEDIPUS. Will someone quickly twist back this fellow's arms?
SERVANT. Alas, what for? What do you want to know?
OEDIPUS. Did you give this man the child of whom he asks?
SERVANT. I did. Would I had perished on that day!

OEDIPUS. You will come to that unless you tell the truth.
SERVANT. I come to far greater ruin if I speak.
OEDIPUS. This man, it seems, is trying to delay.
SERVANT. Not I. I said before I gave it to him.
OEDIPUS. Where did you get it? At home or from someone else?
SERVANT. It was not mine. I got him from a man.
OEDIPUS. Which of these citizens? Where did he live?
SERVANT. O master, by the gods, ask me no more.
OEDIPUS. You are done for if I ask you this again.
SERVANT. Well then, he was born of the house of Laius.
OEDIPUS. One of his slaves, or born of his own race?
SERVANT. Alas, to speak I am on the brink of horror.
OEDIPUS. And I to hear. But still it must be heard.
SERVANT. Well, then, they say it was his child. Your wife
   Who dwells within could best say how this stands.
OEDIPUS. Was it she who gave him to you?
SERVANT.   Yes, my lord.
OEDIPUS. For what intent?
SERVANT.   So I could put it away.
OEDIPUS. When she bore him, the wretch.
SERVANT.   She feared bad oracles.
OEDIPUS. What were they?
SERVANT.   They said he should kill his father.
OEDIPUS. Why did you give him up to this old man?
SERVANT. I pitied him, master, and thought he would take him
   away
   To another land, the one from which he came.
   But he saved him for greatest woe. If you are he
   Whom this man speaks of, you were born curst by fate.
OEDIPUS. Alas, alas! All things are now come true.
   O light, for the last time now I look upon you;
   I am shown to be born from those I ought not to have been.
   I married the woman I should not have married,
   I killed the man whom I should not have killed.

IST STROPHE

CHORUS. Alas, generations of mortal men!

How equal to nothing do I number you in life!
Who, O who, is the man
Who bears more of bliss
Than just the seeming so,
And then, like a waning sun, to fall away?
When I know your example,
Your guiding spirit, yours, wretched Oedipus,
I call no mortal blest.

1ST ANTISTROPHE

He is the one, O Zeus,
Who peerless shot his bow and won well-fated bliss,
Who destroyed the hook-clawed maiden,
The oracle-singing Sphinx,
And stood a tower for our land from death;
For this you are called our king,
Oedipus, are highest-honored here,
And over great Thebes hold sway.

2ND STROPHE

And now who is more wretched for men to hear,
Who so lives in wild plagues, who dwells in pains,
In utter change of life?
Alas for glorious Oedipus!
The selfsame port of rest
Was gained by bridegroom father and his son,
How, O how did your father's furrows ever bear you, suffering
    man?
How have they endured silence for so long?

2ND ANTISTROPHE

You are found out, unwilling, by all-seeing Time.
It judges your unmarried marriage where for long
Begetter and begot have been the same.
Alas, child of Laius,
Would I had never seen you.
As one who pours from his mouth a dirge I wail,

To speak the truth, through you I breathed new life,
And now through you I lulled my eye to sleep.

SECOND MESSENGER. O men most honored always of this land
What deeds you shall hear, what shall you behold!
What grief shall stir you up, if by your kinship
You are still concerned for the house of Labdacus!
I think neither Danube nor any other river
Could wash this palace clean, so many ills
Lie hidden there which now will come to light.
They were done by will, not fate; and sorrows hurt
The most when we ourselves appear to choose them.
CHORUS. What we heard before causes no little sorrow.
What can you say which adds to that a burden?
SECOND MESSENGER. This is the fastest way to tell the tale;
Hear it: Jocasta, your divine queen, is dead.
CHORUS. O sorrowful woman! From what cause did she die?
SECOND MESSENGER. By her own hand. The most painful of the
action
Occurred away, not for your eyes to see.
But still, so far as I have memory
You shall learn the sufferings of that wretched woman:
How she passed on through the door enraged
And rushed straight forward to her nuptial bed,
Clutching her hair's ends with both her hands.
Once inside the doors she shut herself in
And called on Laius, who has long been dead,
Having remembrance of their seed of old
By which he died himself and left her a mother
To bear an evil brood to his own son.
She moaned the bed on which by double curse
She bore husband to husband, children to child.
How thereafter she perished I do not know,
For Oedipus burst in on her with a shriek,
And because of him we could not see her woe.
We looked on him alone as he rushed around.
Pacing about, he asked us to give him a sword,

Asked where he might find the wife no wife,
A mother whose plowfield bore him and his children.
Some spirit was guiding him in his frenzy,
For none of the men who are close at hand did so.
With a horrible shout, as if led on by someone,
He leapt on the double doors, from their sockets
Broke hollow bolts aside, and dashed within.
There we beheld his wife hung by her neck
From twisted cords, swinging to and fro.
When he saw her, wretched man, he terribly groaned
And slackened the hanging noose. When the poor woman
Lay on the ground, what happened was dread to see.
He tore the golden brooch pins from her clothes,
And raised them up, and struck his own eyeballs,
Shouting such words as these: "No more shall you
Behold the evils I have suffered and done.
Be dark from now on, since you saw before
What you should not, and knew not what you should."
Moaning such cries, not once but many times
He raised and struck his eyes. The bloody pupils
Bedewed his beard. The gore oozed not in drops,
But poured in a black shower, a hail of blood.
From both of them these woes have broken out,
Not for just one, but man and wife together.
The bliss of old that formerly prevailed
Was bliss indeed, but now upon this day
Lamentation, madness, death, and shame—
No evil that can be named is not at hand.

CHORUS. Is the wretched man in any rest now from pain?
SECOND MESSENGER. He shouts for someone to open up the doors
    And show to all Cadmeans his father's slayer,
    His mother's—I should not speak the unholy word.
    He says he will hurl himself from the land, no more
    To dwell cursed in the house by his own curse.
    Yet he needs strength and someone who will guide him.
    His sickness is too great to bear. He will show it to you
    For the fastenings of the doors are opening up,
    And such a spectacle you will soon behold

As would make even one who abhors it take pity.

CHORUS. O terrible suffering for men to see,
　Most terrible of all that I
　Have ever come upon. O wretched man,
　What madness overcame you, what springing daimon
　Greater than the greatest for men
　Has caused your evil-daimoned fate?
　Alas, alas, grievous one,
　But I cannot bear to behold you, though I desire
　To ask you much, much to find out,
　Much to see,
　You make me shudder so!

OEDIPUS. Alas, alas, I am grieved!
　Where on earth, so wretched, shall I go?
　Where does my voice fly through the air,
　O Fate, where have you bounded?

CHORUS. To dreadful end, not to be heard or seen.

1st Strophe

OEDIPUS. O cloud of dark
　That shrouds me off, has come to pass, unspeakable,
　Invincible, that blows no favoring blast.
　Woe,
　O woe again, the goad that pierces me,
　Of the sting of evil now, and memory of before.

CHORUS. No wonder it is that among so many pains
　You should both mourn and bear a double evil.

1st Antistrophe

OEDIPUS. Ah, friend,
　You are my steadfast servant still,
　You still remain to care for me, blind.
　Alas! Alas!
　You are not hid from me; I know you clearly,
　And though in darkness, still I hear your voice.

CHORUS. O dreadful doer, how did you so endure
　To quench your eyes? What daimon drove you on?

2ND STROPHE

OEDIPUS. Apollo it was, Apollo, friends
  Who brought to pass these evil, evil woes of mine.
  The hand of no one struck my eyes but wretched me.
  For why should I see,
  When nothing sweet there is to see with sight?
CHORUS. This is just as you say.
OEDIPUS. What more is there for me to see,
  My friends, what to love,
  What joy to hear a greeting?
  Lead me at once away from here,
  Lead me away, friends, wretched as I am,
  Accursed, and hated most
  Of mortals to the gods.
CHORUS. Wretched alike in mind and in your fortune,
  How I wish that I had never known you.

2ND ANTISTROPHE

OEDIPUS. May he perish, whoever freed me
  From fierce bonds on my feet,
  Snatched me from death and saved me, doing me no joy.
  For if then I had died, I should not be
  So great a grief to friends and to myself.
CHORUS. This also is my wish.
OEDIPUS. I would not have come to murder my father,
  Nor have been called among men
  The bridegroom of her from whom I was born.
  But as it is I am godless, child of unholiness,
  Wretched sire in common with my father.
  And if there is any evil older than evil left,
  It is the lot of Oedipus.
CHORUS. I know not how I could give you good advice,
  For you would be better dead than living blind.

OEDIPUS. That how things are was not done for the best—
  Teach me not this, or give me more advice.

If I had sight, I know not with what eyes
I could ever face my father among the dead,
Or my wretched mother. What I have done to them
Is too great for a noose to expiate.
Do you think the sight of my children would be a joy
For me to see, born as they were to me?
No, never for these eyes of mine to see.
Nor the city, nor the tower, nor the sacred
Statues of gods; of these I deprive myself,
Noblest among the Thebans, born and bred,
Now suffering everything. I tell you all
To exile me as impious, shown by the gods
Untouchable and of the race of Laius.
When I uncovered such a stain on me,
Could I look with steady eyes upon the people?
No, No! And if there were a way to block
The spring of hearing, I would not forbear
To lock up wholly this my wretched body.
I should be blind and deaf.—For it is sweet
When thought can dwell outside our evils.
Alas, Cithaeron, why did you shelter me?
Why did you not take and kill me at once, so I
Might never reveal to men whence I was born?
O Polybus, O Corinth, O my father's halls,
Ancient in fable, what an outer fairness,
A festering of evils, you raised in me.
For now I am evil found, and born of evil.
O the three paths! Alas the hidden glen,
The grove of oak, the narrow triple roads
That drank from my own hands my father's blood.
Do you remember any of the deeds
I did before you then on my way here
And what I after did? O wedlock, wedlock!
You gave me birth, and then spawned in return
Issue from the selfsame seed; you revealed
Father, brother, children, in blood relation,
The bride both wife and mother, and whatever

Actions are done most shameful among men.
But it is wrong to speak what is not good to do.
By the gods, hide me at once outside our land,
Or murder me, or hurl me in the sea
Where you shall never look on me again.
Come, venture to lay your hands on this wretched man.
Do it. Be not afraid. No mortal man
There is, except myself, to bear my evils.

CHORUS. Here is Creon, just in time for what you ask
To work and to advise, for he alone
Is left in place of you to guard the land.

OEDIPUS. Alas, what word, then, shall I tell this man?
What righteous ground of trust is clear in me,
As in the past in all I have done him evil?

CREON. Oedipus, I have not come to laugh at you,
Nor to reproach you for your former wrongs.
[*to the attendants*] If you defer no longer to mortal offspring,
Respect at least the all-nourishing flame
Of Apollo, lord of the sun. Fear to display
So great a pestilence, which neither earth
Nor holy rain nor light will well receive.
But you, conduct him to the house at once.
It is most pious for the kin alone
To hear and to behold the family sins.

OEDIPUS. By the gods, since you have plucked me from my fear,
Most noble, facing this most vile man,
Hear me one word—I will speak for you, not me.

CREON. What desire do you so persist to get?

OEDIPUS. As soon as you can, hurl me from this land
To where no mortal man will ever greet me.

CREON. I would do all this, be sure. But I want first
To find out from the god what must be done.

OEDIPUS. His oracle, at least, is wholly clear;
Leave me to ruin, an impious parricide.

CREON. Thus spake the oracle. Still, as we stand
It is better to find out sure what we should do.

OEDIPUS. Will you inquire about so wretched a man?

CREON. Yes. You will surely put trust in the god.

OEDIPUS. I order you and beg you, give the woman
Now in the house such burial as you yourself
Would want. Do last rites justly for your kin.
But may this city never be condemned—
My father's realm—because I live within.
Let me live in the mountains where Cithaeron
Yonder has fame of me, which father and mother
When they were alive established as my tomb.
There I may die by those who sought to kill me.
And yet this much I know, neither a sickness
Nor anything else can kill me. I would not
Be saved from death, except for some dread evil.
Well, let my fate go wherever it may.
As for my sons, Creon, assume no trouble;
They are men and will have no difficulty
Of living wherever they may be.
O my poor grievous daughters, who never knew
Their dinner table set apart from me,
But always shared in everything I touched—
Take care of them for me, and first of all
Allow me to touch them and bemoan our ills.
Grant it, lord,
Grant it, noble. If with my hand I touch them
I would think I had them just as when I could see.

[*Creon's attendants bring in* ANTIGONE *and* ISMENE.]

What's that?
By the gods, can it be I hear my dear ones weeping?
And have you taken pity on me, Creon?
Have you had my darling children sent to me?
Do I speak right?

CREON. You do. For it was I who brought them here,
Knowing this present joy your joy of old.

OEDIPUS. May you fare well. For their coming may the spirit
That watches over you be better than mine.
My children, where are you? Come to me, come

Into your brother's hands, that brought about
Your father's eyes, once bright, to see like this.
Your father, children, who, seeing and knowing nothing,
Became a father whence he was got himself.
I weep also for you—I cannot see you—
To think of the bitter life in days to come
Which you will have to lead among mankind.
What citizens' gatherings will you approach?
What festivals attend, where you will not cry
When you go home, instead of gay rejoicing?
And when you arrive at marriageable age,
What man, my daughters, will there be to chance you,
Incurring such reproaches on his head,
Disgraceful to my children and to yours?
What evil will be absent, when your father
Killed his own father, sowed seed in her who bore him,
From whom he was born himself, and equally
Has fathered you whence he himself was born.
Such will be the reproaches. Who then will wed you?
My children, there is no one for you. Clearly
You must decay in barrenness, unwed.
Son of Menoeceus—since you are alone
Left as a father to them, for we who produced them
Are both in ruin—see that you never let
These girls wander as beggars without husbands,
Let them not fall into such woes as mine,
But pity them, seeing how young they are
To be bereft of all except your aid.
Grant this, my noble friend, with a touch of your hand.
My children, if your minds were now mature,
I would give you much advice. But, pray this for me,
To live as the time allows, to find a life
Better than that your siring father had.

CREON. You have wept enough here, come, and go inside the house.

OEDIPUS. I must obey, though nothing sweet.

CREON.   All things are good in their time.

OEDIPUS. Do you know in what way I go?

CREON.   Tell me, I'll know when I hear.
OEDIPUS. Send me outside the land.
CREON.   You ask what the god will do.
OEDIPUS. But to the gods I am hated.
CREON.   Still, it will soon be done.
OEDIPUS. Then you agree?
CREON.   What I think not I would not say in vain.
OEDIPUS. Now lead me away.
CREON.   Come then, but let the children go.
OEDIPUS. Do not take them from me.
CREON. Wish not to govern all,
    For what you ruled will not follow you through life.
CHORUS. Dwellers in native Thebes, behold this Oedipus,
    Who solved the famous riddle, was your mightiest man.
    What citizen on his lot did not with envy gaze?
    See to how great a surge of dread fate he has come!
    So I would say a mortal man, while he is watching
    To see the final day, can have no happiness
    Till he pass the bound of life, nor be relieved of pain.

SOPHOCLES

Oedipus at Colonus

TRANSLATED BY
WILLIAM MOEBIUS

INTRODUCTORY NOTE

Oedipus at Colonus is probably the last play Sophocles wrote. It was produced by his grandson in 401, a few years after his death, when defeat and peace had come to Athens. The play was composed, however, when the city was fighting and under siege. A battle with enemy forces near Colonus, just beyond the city's walls, may have suggested the subject to the 90-year-old poet.

Before our eyes, the old, blind outcast is transformed into a protective spirit, a quasi-divine power to be revered and cherished. The Greeks called such spirits "heroes," meaning men whose tombs were honored and who were believed to exercise an influence extending for some distance around their graves. No extensive literary treatment of the Athenian legend and cult of Oedipus is known other than this one by Sophocles.

The theme of the family curse is treated here with the same unsparing directness as in *Oedipus the King*. Aware that his end is near, Oedipus reacts to appeals for his help as a stern judge who has earned the right to condemn because of the injustices he has endured. A strong sense of time both as destroyer and preserver permeates the play and appears notably in the choral description of the unique sacred olive, symbol of Athens, that is forever watched and protected by Zeus and Athena.

·CHARACTERS

OEDIPUS
ANTIGONE, daughter of OEDIPUS
STRANGER, a man of Colonus
CHORUS of Elders of Colonus
ISMENE, daughter of OEDIPUS
THESEUS, king of Athens
CREON of Thebes
POLYNEIKES, elder son of OEDIPUS
MESSENGER

Oedipus at Colonus

THE SCENE. *The stage represents a grove of trees. Several large rocks provide places to sit. Enter* OEDIPUS *and* ANTIGONE.

OEDIPUS. My child, Antigone, I am old and blind;
    what surroundings are these? or whose community
    have we turned up in? Who will furnish Oedipus
    with his shelter for the day? Passing through,
    hardly anything supplied to me, I get less
    than the little I put out for, but it does:
    sufferings, the continuous effects of time,
    they steady my response, as does my nobility.
    But now, look out for a seat for me, my child,
    in a public concourse or a holy grove,
    point me into it, station me inside,
    so we can clear up where we are—
    when dealing with the citizens, outsiders like us
    take note and get our obligations straight.
ANTIGONE. Father, travel-conditioned Oedipus, out there
    it looks like towers, a city crowned with them,
    if I'm not mistaken; this, a sacred setting,
    with olive, grapevine, and laurel in full bloom.
    Nightingales call on expectantly in there.
    Swing yourself down here
    on this unworked stone; you've covered
    a tremendous distance for a man your age.
OEDIPUS. Set me down, and keep me safe: I'm blind.
ANTIGONE. I'm used to it, without being reminded.
OEDIPUS. Can you make out, then, where we stand?
ANTIGONE. Near Athens; but the immediate surroundings
    I don't recognize.

[1–24]

OEDIPUS. That's what we get from every traveler.
ANTIGONE. Should I explore outside this area?
OEDIPUS. Yes, in case this site is occupied.
ANTIGONE. It is; no need to go exploring it;
  over there, I think, is the man we'll use.
OEDIPUS. Is he heading over, is he covering it fast?
ANTIGONE. Right over here. Father, stick closely
  to the present situation: he's our man.
OEDIPUS. Hello.

[*The* STRANGER *now appears.*]

      This girl who sees our way for us
  says you might be here as a special guide
  to make our darkened vision clearer . . .
STRANGER. Before you tell your tale, get off that seat.
  Putting footprints on this ground is an impiety.
OEDIPUS. What ground is this? Which god is it devoted to?
STRANGER. No intruders—not for settling on. Reaction
  to its goddesses is fear; they are daughters
  of the Earth and Darkness.
OEDIPUS. What is their official name in worship?
STRANGER. Decencies, perfect consciences,
  our folks believe. In other places
  different labels will apply.
OEDIPUS. May their reception to the suppliant be warm;
  I'm still not getting off this seat.
STRANGER. What's that?
OEDIPUS. The cornerstone of my success.
STRANGER. We won't get rid of interference
  to our society, until I have you charged
  with your offense.
OEDIPUS. No uncivil treatment for the refugee,
  stranger, but dissipate confusion here . . .
STRANGER. Be specific; then there's no uncivil treatment.
OEDIPUS. What place did we pass into?
STRANGER. What I'll say is all I know, so hear me.

It's a sacred place, in the keeping
of Poseidon, the formidable,
and Prometheus, the Titan firebearer.
You've planted your feet just where
what's called the Bronze Stoop
is located, an Athenian landmark.
In this country, we recognize
Colonus as our founder: the horseman.
We incorporate under his name.
It's a fact we give importance to
not so much in documents, as
in the way we stick together.

OEDIPUS. Then who ever lives around here?

STRANGER. Well, the people using the hero's name.

OEDIPUS. Is there one man rule, or popular consent?

STRANGER. Our chieftain is the city's royal majesty.

OEDIPUS. Who is this king and vicar all in one?

STRANGER. His name is Theseus: he inherits
his position from his father, Aegeus.

OEDIPUS. Would someone represent my case to him?

STRANGER. So that . . . he'd know of your presence
or get set to pay a visit here?

OEDIPUS. He'll find a little help quite meaningful.

STRANGER. Is there a premium on men who've lost their sight?

OEDIPUS. It's a certain consciousness I have,
and I'll explain that when I'm ready to.

STRANGER. Look, stranger, so you don't get bogged down;
you strike me as exceptional, run down
by a mystery; stay out of sight, while
I report to my fellow councillors;
Whether you remain or push on is up to them.

[*Exit* STRANGER.]

OEDIPUS. Our stranger has pushed on, has he not?

ANTIGONE. Yes, father. Now is the perfect moment
for you to open up and speak; I'm
the only person near.

OEDIPUS. Oh majesties, who look at me forbiddingly,
  who first owned the seat I'm using now,
  don't be hardened to Apollo or myself;
  after he had aired that quantity of ugliness
  about me, he announced some resting place,
  some final marker I'd reach in the long run;
  when I'd take a seat with the awesome gods
  unconditionally; stop this complicated life;
  contribute something gratifying to those
  who welcomed me, but a fatal breakdown
  to those whose welcome was to push me out.
  And I was, he promised, to receive some notice
  in the form of earthquake, thunder, or lightning-stroke.
  But even the road was unmistakeably a portent,
  when it led directly to this grove. Wouldn't you
  be first for me to make contact with as I move on,
  you use no intoxicating spirits, I am an abstainer;
  shouldn't this awesome platform no axe has bit into
  be the one that I take over? With the strictness
  of Apollo on my side, you spirits, give me ground;
  turn me loose, if I'm not something too menial.
  Go on, you gentle daughters of beginning Darkness,
  go on, Athens, named after Pallas, the great one,
  most honored city of them all—have mercy
  on these spectral remains of what was Oedipus;
  I'm not the same as I was in the beginning.
ANTIGONE. Be still. [*Music for* CHORUS *heard offstage.*]
            Some members of the old guard . . .
  they're the local groundskeepers.
OEDIPUS. I will. Turn me away and out of sight,
  so I can hear the things they're saying . . .
  the more we know, the more the situation
  may be under our control.

  [CHORUS *enters.*]

1ST STROPHE

CHORUS. Look! Who was it? Where now?
  Where is the drifter, the displaced man?
  Scan, probe, investigate this thoroughly.
  Someone restless in his old age, no one from the local scene.
  Wouldn't have moved into a marked-off area,
  where the scatheless virgins live,
  it makes me nervous just to mention them;
  when we come in contact, no conversations
  or disclosures or peepings in, just pay
  the right attention; now it can be inferred
  that there is a ritual defilement in this place:
  I've run my eye over the whole sanctuary
  without fixing its location.

OEDIPUS. Here I am. I look at voices, as the saying is.
CHORUS. Here is a sensation for our eyes and ears.
OEDIPUS. Don't, I beg you, treat me as subversive.
CHORUS. Zeus, our wall of defense, who is this old man?
OEDIPUS. Not rejoicing in his prime, commissioners . . .
  I'll be explicit: I use someone else's eyes
  to move with; so big, but I take refuge in the small.

1ST ANTISTROPHE

CHORUS. Tsk, tsk, his eyes are blind.
  A congenital defect?
  It looks rather old.
  But don't let the curses get on me.
  Move along now, give your ground.
  In the hush of that grassy duct
  what if you should slip and fall?
  So go away, get away from us; put a fair distance between.
  Understand this, man so knocked about?
  If you're making a confession to our conference,

vacate these premises at once—
the statute is explicit—and keep off.

OEDIPUS. Daughter, what should our reaction be?
ANTIGONE. Father, better be flexible and recognize
the things that count for citizens.
OEDIPUS. Well, then, help me up.
ANTIGONE. There, I've got you.
OEDIPUS. Strangers, treat me fairly;
I'm an alien, I depend on you.

2ND STROPHE

CHORUS. No one, old man, can remove your person
without your consent.

OEDIPUS. On?
CHORUS. Go on.
OEDIPUS. More?
CHORUS. Be his escort, miss. You understand.
ANTIGONE. Come, come in this direction, father.
CHORUS. A stranger on strange soil should adapt himself,
poor man, to despise
just what the city does,
and to like what it likes, too.

OEDIPUS. Well, take me, daughter, where
this reverence will be reserved
for us in this exchange of views,
so we won't be tangling with requirements.

2ND ANTISTROPHE

CHORUS. Stop! Don't step further on that outcropping.
OEDIPUS. Here, then?
CHORUS. Exactly . . . that's being alert.
OEDIPUS. Should I get down?
CHORUS. No, sit astride the crest.

ANTIGONE. Here I am, father; the next step you take
  will not be uncertain . . .
OEDIPUS. [*cries of discomfort*]
ANTIGONE. Brace yourself against my arm;
  it's close to that old body.
OEDIPUS. This cruel instability!
CHORUS. Now, poor individual, when you're settled,
  let us in on your identity—
who are you, in such sad shape?
Perhaps your birthplace is familiar?

ASTROPHA

OEDIPUS. Strangers, I have no citizenship. Don't . . .
CHORUS. What's this you're implying, old man?
OEDIPUS. Don't, please don't delve into who I am;
  don't look too hard for relationships.
CHORUS. What's this about?
OEDIPUS. I'm a messy business.
CHORUS. Let us hear.
OEDIPUS. Child, what groans shall I make?
CHORUS. Give your father, stranger,
  and your land of origin.
OEDIPUS. [*cries*] What I suffer from, my child . . .
ANTIGONE. Speak out, if it's as far as you can go.
OEDIPUS. I'll speak, I will not play with secrets.
CHORUS. Do we have to wait so long? Now hurry up.
OEDIPUS. Do you know relatives of Laius?
CHORUS. Why, yes.
OEDIPUS. Of Labdacid's line?
CHORUS. Oh, please.
OEDIPUS. Disfigured Oedipus?
CHORUS. You are that man.
OEDIPUS. Don't let my talk unnerve you.
CHORUS. [*buzzes to itself*]
OEDIPUS. I was unfortunate.
  Daughter, what is happening to them?
CHORUS. Leave. Right now.

OEDIPUS. Is this fulfillment of your promises?
CHORUS. Down payments don't determine
   what we owe. When deceptions are your business
   you won't earn your clearance,
   but pile on more indebtedness,
   you have no position here
   so pick up and get out.
   You could add to my city's liability.
ANTIGONE. Strangers, you who have your dignity,
   since you're not up to listening
   to an old man plead he meant no harm,
   then, I beg you, pity me, this little remnant,
   strangers, as I plead before you,
   strictly for my father's sake—
   I look straight into your faces with eyes that see,
   as perhaps a relative of yours may do someday,—
   I plead that you dignify this extremity,
   submitted to you as if to Zeus.
   Go on, approve a clearance
   that has no precedent,
   I plead by whatever you hold dear,
   it may be children, act of marriage,
   liability in business, or gods.
   But look around: when the gods get hold of someone,
   you never see him get away.

CHORUS. Listen here, child of Oedipus, and you, sir—
   we do feel sympathy for you in your predicament.
   But we dread the gods so much that we're
   in no capacity to answer your request.
OEDIPUS. What good is reputation or high standing,
   if it turns out superficial? Athens—
   most ceremonious to gods—they say
   affords outsiders in trouble
   their one security, their one relief.
   But the fact is, you turn me down,
   you push me back, because the name alone

inhibits you, not physical impressions
or acts . . . which I did not perform,
but I was victim of . . . I'm forced
to make a point of that mother
and father fact of mine, it's that
which causes your alarm. But how was I
at fault? I tried to stop from doing that—
not to get in trouble was my conscious aim.
There was this unfamiliar scene; then
the people I didn't know; the fatal thing
was their knowing about me. Strangers, please,
don't show me disrespect, but keep me safe.
Stand by your agreements, don't break contracts
with the gods. Keep this in mind, their eye
is out for who is reverent or the opposite:
anyone suspect in his worship has no out.
When there's prosperity in Athens, don't
let your misconduct wipe it out. Treat me
as a suppliant with full standing.
Watch over me, give me your protection.
My looks are not appealing, but don't
treat me superficially. I am sacred;
I am reverent; I come to help your city.
The general, whoever's master here,
will have the full story when he comes.
Meanwhile, don't get yourselves in trouble.
CHORUS. Very impressive old man, your argument
　　to us, not lame at all. We'll defer
　　to the decision of our superior.
OEDIPUS. Strangers, where is this maker of your policy?
CHORUS. In town, the family home. But that look-out
　　who alerted us, went back for him.
OEDIPUS. Do you think he'd feel the impact of a blindman?
　　that he would be disposed to come?
CHORUS. Of course, when he picks up your name.
OEDIPUS. How will that word get out to him?
CHORUS. It's a long way, but stories have that tendency

of wandering among travelers—when he finds out,
there's no question but he'll come; your name,
old man, haunts everyone; even if he's sound asleep,
he'll make it here express when he finds out.

OEDIPUS. May he and his city make me welcome;
    what generous man is not his own ally?

ANTIGONE. [*cries*] What shall I say? Father!
    Has my mind been wandering?

OEDIPUS. Antigone, what is it, child?

ANTIGONE. Some woman coming, yes, I see,
    riding a pony from Sicily;
    she has on one of those broad-rimmed hats
    that come from Thessaly.
    What shall I say?
    She's—no, she's not—it's me, maybe,
    that's in a daze; I warrant,
    then I disavow, and then what?
    It is she! There's the unhappy proof:
    her eyes glittering more as she gets close:
    it's definitely Ismene.

OEDIPUS. What do you say, my dear?

ANTIGONE. This is my sister; I'm seeing a friend.
    Her voice will tell you who she is.

ISMENE. To hear a father and a sister speak out loud!
    What extra happiness! It isn't easy
    to be seeing you through distraught eyes,
    nor was it an easy matter finding you.

OEDIPUS. Hello, my child; you've come—

ISMENE. Hello, father—looking . . . on disaster.

OEDIPUS. So, it's you who show your face.

ISMENE. It took some sacrifice.

OEDIPUS. Give me a hug, little one.

ISMENE. I'll give you both one.

OEDIPUS. Sisters for their father.

ISMENE. Cruel adaptation.

OEDIPUS. For her and for me.

ISMENE. For myself, I too in disaster.

OEDIPUS. But child, why come to us?
ISMENE. To break news to you, father.
OEDIPUS. Something to do with lonesomeness?
ISMENE. Strictly on my own I bring word to you;
    here's the encouragement I get from home.
OEDIPUS. Well, what are your little brothers involved in?
ISMENE. Oh, this and that. It's a complex situation now.
OEDIPUS. The things they get involved in, the kind of men
    they are, it's all a copy of the way Egyptians act.
    The man sticks to weaving on the loom at home,
    while the wife makes a go of it out in the world.
    My daughters, this was their responsibility;
    but they're so attached to home, so feminine,
    that it's you who must be burdened by this mass
    of ugliness. She left home, grew into adulthood
    just for this experience as fellow wanderer.
    She takes the old around, but the wilderness
    is not much for nourishment; her feet go bare;
    the rain is a discomfort, as is sweltering heat.
    What endurance she has! It's remarkable.
    And then, she sees us through our daily needs:
    she makes a nurse, if fathers still can keep them.
    And Ismene, you, my child, smuggled out of Thebes
    those bulletins relating to the deposition
    of my corpse, and when I was banished,
    you faithfully watched out for me.
    What's the latest story? What sort of venture
    could make you so much break with home?
    There's something wrong, something disquieting.
ISMENE. Father, all the bruising experience I've had
    trying to discover where you'd be settled down,
    I won't go into. I don't want any further despair,
    going over it again. I'm mainly here to tell you
    what has come between your sons, poor men.
    They both were on sweet terms with Creon once,
    so no one bothered with the throne, the city
    went undisturbed. They had in mind

that recent turbulence the family underwent,
when everything came crashing down at home.
Now they have a mental block, or some god interferes,
because things have settled into violence,
hankering for the throne. Your youngest
has displaced his older brother, Polyneikes;
he's off the throne, thrown out completely.
Most sources say he's found asylum down in Argos,
where he's collecting arms and friendly troops,
so he'll either rout the Thebans, his honor
is at stake, or else—
But there is a connection, father, I can't make;
it isn't straight
or comprehensible when the gods will pity you
for all the trouble and expense you've had.

OEDIPUS. Can you still afford to hope the gods were right,
  that some day I'd get this thing solved?

ISMENE. Yes, father, because it's in the latest oracle.

OEDIPUS. Which? What is this revelation, child?

ISMENE. That you're in demand, in life or death—
  the well-being of certain people is at stake.

OEDIPUS. Who could convert a man like this into success?

ISMENE. They say that for their power they need you.

OEDIPUS. So that I'll be vital when I breathe no more?

ISMENE. With the gods' support; they used to frustrate you.

OEDIPUS. It's a wobbly old man they now support,
  who in his younger days was caught off guard.

ISMENE. At any rate, Creon will be your visitor,
  you realize.

OEDIPUS. What has he to do with it? Get to the point.

ISMENE. Stick you near to Thebes,
  partition you off so that you can't get in.

OEDIPUS. What good is that, my lying by the gate?

ISMENE. They'll suffer if your tomb's not right.

OEDIPUS. That was obvious without the help of oracles.

ISMENE. They want you planted at the edge
  so you won't have some effect on them.

OEDIPUS. Then covering me with soil from Thebes?
ISMENE. Bloodguilt forbids them that.
OEDIPUS. Then never shall they have me.
ISMENE. Then someday this will hurt the Thebans.
OEDIPUS. Why? What will happen?
ISMENE. Your anger, when they stand by your grave.
OEDIPUS. Who gave you your information, child?
ISMENE. Some on-lookers at the Delphoic shrine.
OEDIPUS. Was the one in question with Apollo really me?
ISMENE. Those who just got to Thebes said so.
OEDIPUS. Which son of mine, which one found out?
ISMENE. Both; they made rather parallel discoveries.
OEDIPUS. Oh, such inhumanity! Knowing how I felt,
   they still let the dignity of offices come first.
ISMENE. This does turn my stomach, but I had to tell.
OEDIPUS. May the gods not let this violence burn out
   which they got going between these two;
   may I be the one to put an end to their dispute,
   the one they're readying their spears for now.
   May the self-appointed king not last,
   may the one he busted not come in again;
   when, in the land I felt at home in,
   I was given such a brutal push,
   and neither held back nor stuck up for
   by those sons I raised, but treated
   as expendable, and so gotten rid of,
   and publicly declared the exile.
   Wait, you say, the city granted you
   this dispensation when it knew you wanted it.
   Nonsense! The day I flared up with rage,
   dying in a stone bombardment would have satisfied,
   that was a passion seemingly for my benefit.
   But gradually my frustration got toned down,
   and I saw that I had been more furious
   than the prosecutor, over my mistakes;
   that moment the city timed to use its force
   in driving me out of the country; for assistance—

well, I was their father,
but they weren't ready to act; I came out an exile,
thrown off, always moving on, so little
was their protest. With what nature gives them,
here are my girls; but I get sustenance from them,
and refreshment, and their companionship.
For the other two, being king, official-style,
means more than the man who raised them up.
There's nothing in what I'm fighting for for them;
no help in ruling Thebes.
That makes sense, I think; this oracle ties in
with the soothsaying Apollo did for me before.
Now as for Creon—he's sent out as a detective—
and as for any others the city can produce
with such capabilities: if you want to form
a core of resistance, strangers, alongside
these reverend goddesses, deep-seated in this land,
give your city a savior, and my enemies no rest.

CHORUS. Oedipus, you're entitled to our sympathy,
 you and the children now beside you.
 You introduce yourself as savior . . .
 may I give you some constructive hints?

OEDIPUS. My friends, the guest keeps his commitments.

CHORUS. Then wash off that first contact with the spirits,
 when you were stepping on their grounds.

OEDIPUS. How does the ceremony go? Give some direction.

CHORUS. Go to that continuously flowing fountain,
 and get sacred water, so your hands are clean.

OEDIPUS. And what's this fresh material for?

CHORUS. It goes in pitchers of good workmanship;
 stop up the top and the spouts along the rim.

OEDIPUS. With what? Wooltufts or twigs? How does it go?

CHORUS. Virgin lambs' wool is your best bet.

OEDIPUS. Good. When should I perform this rite?

CHORUS. At daybreak, that's when absolution's done.

OEDIPUS. Is there a special twist involved in it?

CHORUS. Pour three times; empty with the last.

OEDIPUS. What should I put in that? Give me the prescription.
CHORUS. Strictly water and honey; no intoxicating spirits.
OEDIPUS. After the ground, gutted by the leaves, is soaked?
CHORUS. Then put down olive sprigs, nine rows in sets of three,
    and give the following prayer.
OEDIPUS. I'm listening anxiously. This is the crucial thing.
CHORUS. Since they're the Decencies to us, appeal
  to the decent spirit in their breasts,
  that they keep you, the suppliant;
  this is to be done by you or someone else.
  Whisper, don't carry on, and tiptoe out,
  no turning back. If you carry this out,
  I'll be on your side. Otherwise, I'll have qualms.
OEDIPUS. Children, were you listening to these bystanders?
ANTIGONE. We were; just designate our jobs to us.
OEDIPUS. The way is blocked to me. I am shut in
  with this inertia, and no sight—
  that makes a couple of deficiencies.
  One of you take care of these commitments.
  It only takes one person to discharge a debt—
  if he's honest—and no collective effort.
  But quickly, get it done. Don't leave me alone.
  In this unfrequented place, I couldn't get around,
  in my condition, without someone beside me.
ISMENE. I'll get it done—but I've got to find out something:
  in what space should I put this ceremony on?
CHORUS. Stranger, over there in that grove; if anything
  is lacking, there's a man in there to call on.
ISMENE. I'm taking care of this. Antigone,
  watch out for him. This man is a father.
  We don't need to keep a record
  of the work we do for parents. [*Exit* ISMENE.]

IST STROPHE

CHORUS. Bringing old evils back to life,
  that's a dreadful thing to do . . .
  still I'm anxious to find out.

OEDIPUS. About what?

CHORUS. About that strenuous crisis you once faced,
   when there was no way of getting out of it.

OEDIPUS. If you have manners, don't advertise
   the degrading things I got myself involved in.

CHORUS. Be inclusive, don't pass over anything;
   stranger, hearings are meant for hearing things.

OEDIPUS. [*groans*]

CHORUS. Come on, comply with us.

OEDIPUS. [*more groans*]

CHORUS. Steady now; you'll get whatever you want from us.

1st Antistrophe

OEDIPUS. What happened to me was the worst thing,
   the worst thing . . . I had no intention . . .
   so help me, no plan was involved.

CHORUS. It just happened, though.

OEDIPUS. It was the city that got me stuck
   in this debasing connection;
   I had no idea, the doom in that marriage.

CHORUS. I've heard, but wording this is hard,
   you spawned a litter in your mother's bed.

OEDIPUS. Strangers, even hearing that means death.
   Here, these two are

CHORUS. You're saying

OEDIPUS. My children, I have two dooms . . .

CHORUS. Please . . .

OEDIPUS. births labored by my mother . . .

2nd Strophe

CHORUS. These are the children and . . .

OEDIPUS. and the sisters of their father.

CHORUS. [*groans*]

OEDIPUS. When endless evil is undammed,

CHORUS. The victim's you . . .

OEDIPUS. The victim and the soreness.

CHORUS. It wasn't you who did it?

OEDIPUS. It wasn't me.

CHORUS. What then?

OEDIPUS. A gift—I shouldn't have taken it,
  but for sympathy, I tried to help the city out.

2ND ANTISTROPHE

CHORUS. But, shaky man! There's this! You caused a death . . .

OEDIPUS. There's this what? What are you getting at?

CHORUS. The death of your father.

OEDIPUS. You squeeze one nerve, and then another.

CHORUS. You did take a life . . .

OEDIPUS. So I did; but on that charge . . .

CHORUS. There's what?

OEDIPUS. Appeal . . .

CHORUS. Such as?

OEDIPUS. I use this defense: that I caused death,
  destroyed a personality . . . by accident.
  By being unknowingly involved, I deserve,
  by law, to get this charge dismissed.

CHORUS. Well, here's our monarch, Theseus, son of Aegeus;
  your explosive name set off his arrival here.

[THESEUS *enters, followed by guards.*]

THESEUS. In many ways up until this time I'd heard
  how your sight was brutally pricked out,
  so I knew you, son of Laius; presently,
  this way, I gain my knowledge at first hand.
  Who you are—it's clear to me,
  with that dress, those stark features—
  it's pitiful—but tell us, we are interested,
  downtrodden Oedipus, why you turn to us,
  the city and myself, you and your companion,
  unfortunate as well. Tell us this.
  I know, I had the stranger's education

as you did—abroad I faced several risks—
plenty for one man—
so whatever the stranger is, it doesn't matter;
I won't discriminate, or try for his exclusion.
Being human, I know our shares in tomorrow are the same.

OEDIPUS. Theseus, your nobility is there, though your remarks
were brief. My reply must be as modest.
As to who I am, where born, and where
I used to live, all that was accurate;
when I've specified what it is I'm after,
that will be all I have to say.

THESEUS. Explain yourself. I'll have something to work on, then.

OEDIPUS. I'm contributing my presence here—
broken-down, played-out as it is; not for study;
more important than an art object.

THESEUS. How do you rate the value of your gift?

OEDIPUS. It's something someday you will realize.

THESEUS. Well, how will its dimensions become evident?

OEDIPUS. When I die, and you have me put under.

THESEUS. It's the last rites you're asking for;
the middle you repress or abdicate.

OEDIPUS. That's the way I'm put back together.

THESEUS. The favor is small.

OEDIPUS. Look: no small amount of tension is involved.

THESEUS. Between your children and myself, you mean?

OEDIPUS. They'll make me go along with them.

THESEUS. If you want to, what good is this escape?

OEDIPUS. They wouldn't abide it when I wanted to.

THESEUS. Silly! Hard feelings won't get you anywhere.

OEDIPUS. Wait! Don't point your finger
until I've finished telling you . . .

THESEUS. Continue; I still don't get the point.

OEDIPUS. Theseus, part of the evil I suffered was unreal . . .

THESEUS. You mean the family setback, years ago?

OEDIPUS. Not that; every Greek's unhappy over that.

THESEUS. How can you be more than humanly disturbed?

OEDIPUS. How? Because my sons caused my banishment.

Being a parricide, I can't go home.

THESEUS. But now you're out—why go after you?

OEDIPUS. The words of a sacred oracle compel them to.

THESEUS. What happens, that they're so frightened of the oracle?

OEDIPUS. They'll be wiped out here unless they do something.

THESEUS. But how could our relations reach that breaking point?

OEDIPUS. Dear son of Aegeus, the gods alone
   are immune to dying and old age;
   almighty time takes the rest and lumps it
   all together; earth's vitality fades,
   man's vitality fades;
   commitment takes a final rest,
   and fraudulence goes back to work.
   Friends and towns breathe different air.
   Happiness, as each epoch ends,
   goes through a stage of bitterness
   before being restored again.
   If Thebes rates high today,
   time goes on spawning for another world
   some days and nights of another breed:
   the treaty you initialed some deft spear
   will slit without prior negotiations.
   Then down there asleep, my cold corpse
   will drink up their warm blood,
   if Zeus keeps his identity,
   and Apollo his clear sense.
   But mystery is not the subject
   I would talk about: I meant,
   in beginning this, honor to your commitment.
   Then you won't be saying what a no-good newcomer
   you let have the run of things, unless
   the gods are fooling me.

CHORUS. Monarch, not so long ago this man
   supplied a story much the same.

THESEUS. Who could block out this man's decency?
   His hearthright here as a suppliant
   is the equal of any foreign friend's;

and then he's a suppliant to these spirits,
and pays me in no minor currency.
I'm a religious man; I won't deny him clearance,
but make him my fellow citizen here on the spot.
If staying put appeals to the visitor,
I charge you with looking after him . . .
unless he'd rather go with me. Oedipus,
whichever way appeals to you, the decision
you come up with I'll abide by.

OEDIPUS. Zeus, give these people nothing but the best.

THESEUS. What did you pick? Visiting my home?

OEDIPUS. If that was the case. But here is room . . .

THESEUS. For what? Anyway I don't interfere.

OEDIPUS. for putting down the men who banished me.

THESEUS. How much it means to stick together—you can say.

OEDIPUS. If what you say is yours works out for me.

THESEUS. You can count on me; I won't let you down.

OEDIPUS. I won't swear you in like someone unreliable.

THESEUS. You'd just have my word to go on, anyway.

OEDIPUS. Then what will you be doing?

THESEUS. Doubtful of my word?

OEDIPUS. Some men are on the way . . .

THESEUS. These will handle them.

OEDIPUS. Look, leaving me here . . .

THESEUS. Don't say what I'm bound to do . . .

OEDIPUS. I'm uneasy then.

THESEUS. My pulse is not.

OEDIPUS. Didn't you get the threats?

THESEUS. No one, I am sure, is capable of taking you,
   where I am strong. Saying a lot of threats
   means saying a lot of nothing, with hard feelings.
   But if you let good sense stay in control,
   that takes care of the threats.
   If they had the nerve to talk reprisal
   when you'd turn up here, they'll soon
   find themselves out over their heads
   in a very large sea. I say to be encouraged,

even though I'm not an expert here,
but if Apollo was your dispatcher.
And though I can't be here personally,
my name looks after you; you'll have no trouble.

[*Exit* THESEUS.]

1ST STROPHE

CHORUS. This setting keeps the horse in fine condition,
    visitor—you've struck the most dynamic of our structures:
    irradiant Colonus . . .
    the nightingale perpetuates her reverberating chant
    under the slanted greenery,
    the ivy gives a cool red glow,
    the orchards encounter no resistance,
    no sun-bleaching or rainy gales;
    they put up huge stores for the god . . .
    Dionysus whirls his procession through,
    a holy entourage of women wet-nursing.

1ST ANTISTROPHE

Narcissus susceptible to dew
bursts out in bouquets, the coronet
two most mighty goddesses used to use,
and the crocus streaked with gold.
And the effervescent spring
that fans out to the Cephisus
is never thin, but keeps bubbling,
a new birth every day, perpetual rain,
here at earth's breast.
This does not put off the Muses here,
nor one controlled by Aphrodite's golden bit.

2ND STROPHE

Elsewhere I have never seen such trees survive:
they don't in Asia or down in Pelops' land;
but here, unplanted, untended, they disarm

has a cluttered style, full of devious inflections:
you'd put on first, and then you'd act!
Wouldn't it hurt to be your prisoner . . .
When I was a victim of poor health back home,
extradition would have been a lift for me;
you wouldn't extend the clearance I demanded.
When I finally got control of my emotions,
and life at home was preferable,
you discarded me, you ran me out,
no matter our being near relatives.
And now you try again; seeing how well
we get along, this city and my family,
you move in to break things up,
making mild with vicious overtones.
Should I enjoy being sociable with those
who shrug me off? Say there was a project
you were working on; one person was indifferent
and wouldn't cooperate, it made you desperate,
until his offer came, a generous dud:
wouldn't a surprise like that fall flat?
But you'll behave that way towards me:
pretty speeches, but obnoxious acts.
I'll substantiate my charge, show them
how really low you are. You come around
to sneak me back, not home, but somewhere
on some neutral ground outside your town
where my blood won't be dangerous to you.
But you're in for something else:
I'm here to stay, and retard growth
in your area. My sons inherit land,
it's theirs to die upon. My knowledge
of the Theban situation's more substantial,
is it not, because my contacts
are more accurate, Apollo, even Zeus,
his father. Here you are, stuffy speech
and polished rhetoric, but more trouble

than success is involved in terms like that.
I sense I haven't swayed you: go away.
Let us go on here. Our situation here
wouldn't be too unliveable, if it were relaxed.

CREON. You're so sure my situation will deteriorate,
when it's yours, isn't it, you're referring to?

OEDIPUS. The biggest lift for me is when you lose your case,
while all these people stand around.

CREON. Too bad, time didn't get you intelligence,
but it sure opened up your eyesore.

OEDIPUS. Your sense of humor's strange: anyone sincere,
I know, would never lay it on so thick.

CREON. Unless he was being blunt on several points.

OEDIPUS. That was nice and neat.

CREON. Your mind is not as quick.

OEDIPUS. Get out! I'll declare it publicly:
I must live here; he's not enforcing that.

CREON. I'll use your public as my witness—
if I get my hands on you . . .

OEDIPUS. Who's going to break my ties with friends?

CREON. You'll be hurting, minus one of them.

OEDIPUS. What's behind this threat?

CREON. I have one daughter of yours in custody;
I'll take the other next.

OEDIPUS. [gasps]

CREON. Next time you'll have more to gasp about.

OEDIPUS. You'd pull my child from me?

CREON. Pretty soon, the other, too.

OEDIPUS. Strangers, how will you react?
Passively? Not crack down on this kidnapper?

CHORUS. Move off, stranger, move on fast.
The way you act is not acceptable,
nor is what you did before.

CREON. She'll be taken in the nick of time,
though she may not cooperate.

ANTIGONE. [cries] How shall I escape?

What assistance is available,
from gods or men?
CHORUS. What are you doing, stranger?
CREON. It's mine. I'm not taking his.
OEDIPUS. Men in public office!
CHORUS. Stranger, your game isn't fair.
CREON. Fair it is.
CHORUS. How is it fair?
CREON. What belongs to me I take.

STROPHE

OEDIPUS. Oh you government!
CHORUS. What are you doing, stranger?
Not letting go? You'll be beaten down.
CREON. Strike the first blow, you.
CHORUS. Don't you! Such insane brutality.
CREON. You'll have my city to contend with,
if you do me harm.
OEDIPUS. Isn't this what I claimed he'd do?
CHORUS. Loosen your grip, now.
CREON. Don't run what you can't control.
CHORUS. Let go, I say.
CREON. Go get your exercise.
CHORUS. This way, this way, security guard;
the city, my city, her defense goes down;
this way; here!

[CREON's *men come forward, pull* ANTIGONE *back from the stone.*]

ANTIGONE. [*cries*] I'm being dislocated.
Strangers, oh you strangers.
OEDIPUS. Where are you leaving for, my child?
ANTIGONE. Dislocated, removed.
OEDIPUS. Hold hands with me, my child.
ANTIGONE. Impossible.
CREON. [*to his guards*] Hustle off with her.

[*Exit guards with* ANTIGONE.]

OEDIPUS. [*cries*]

CREON. Without this double agency, your movement
   is restricted. Since you make your objective
   victory, here, have one, over your friends
   and native land. You'll realize, I think,
   as time runs on, how desultory your record is,
   how at friendly pressure you hit back with spite:
   you'll always be an eyesore.

CHORUS. Stranger,

CREON. And I say, keep your hands off me.

CHORUS. I won't let you go, without them back.

CREON. I'll augment the ransom in a moment,
   because they won't be my only take.

CHORUS. How far will you go?

CREON. Pick him up, take him along.

CHORUS. That sounds incredible.

CREON. The work is almost done.

CHORUS. Unless the authorities fight back.

OEDIPUS. Shameless as the name you use,
   would you put a hand on me?

CREON. Now I say: restrict your speech.

OEDIPUS. May the holy spirits not cut off my speech
   until I curse you for your brutality—
   breaking off my contact with the world,
   never spliced from my sight before.
   May vision-perfect Helios grant you and yours
   an old decrepit life like mine.

CREON. You see, local residents?

OEDIPUS. They see both of us, how you afflict me,
   how I fend you off with arguments.

CREON. Now I'll let my will run wild . . . so I'm alone
   and rushed . . . but you're my prisoner.

ANTISTROPHE

OEDIPUS. I am miserable.

CHORUS. What nerve you have, believing
   you can bring this off.

CREON. So I believe . . .

CHORUS. No more am I a factor in the city, then.

CREON. In judicial matters, the little man
  can beat the great establishment.

OEDIPUS. Are you aware of what he's saying?

CHORUS. He won't succeed.

OEDIPUS. Zeus is conscious . . .

CREON. Yes, is conscious; you are not.

CHORUS. Isn't this contempt?

CREON. Yes, contempt you must put up with.

CHORUS. Where's our civic leadership? Where is everyone?
  This is an emergency! They're getting out of reach.

[THESEUS *enters, wearing the robes of sacrifice. Others, equally
dignified, walk beside him.*]

THESEUS. What's all this noise about? What's going on?
  What stuns you so you interrupt my sacrifice
  to the patron of Colonus, the bull the sea god gets?
  Tell me, so I'm in on this affair, just why
  I had to make this inconvenient jaunt.

OEDIPUS. My dear friend, I recognize your voice.
  The trouble that man gives me is exceptional.

THESEUS. How? Whose fault is it? Explain.

OEDIPUS. The man is Creon. Take a look at him,
  he knocks my support out from under me.

THESEUS. What do you mean?

OEDIPUS. Can't you tell what I've been through?

THESEUS. One of my lieutenants to the altars, fast!
  Break into the huddle at the sacrifice,
  and make them scramble to the rescue,
  whether cavalier or footman can participate.
  Although the roads start off on different feet,
  they cross; beyond that crossing may those girls
  not go, or I will be this stranger's laughingstock,
  stuck in such a squeeze. This is an emergency.
  Run speedily. He'll get the serious reaction

he's entitled to, he'll certainly get treatment.
We'll apply his laws to him. Not without
planting those girls unharmed here
will he get free. Your activity
does not do justice to your land
or to your family: why, to start in
on a town that figures nothing without law,
and disregard native, traditional things . . .
rush in, victimize, exploit your need . . .
you thought my city had run out of men?
was kept by slaves, or didn't exist, perhaps?
Your childhood didn't get charged up with this nonsense
around Thebes, at any rate; she does not train
guerrillas, nor would she favor you, if she found out
how brutally you treat us and our sanctities—
denying the right to safety to people in distress.
If I visited your land, even with a valid case,
I wouldn't presume a right to anything
without the stated "yes" of the authorities,
or whoever; I would recognize the practice
strangers use of filing their petition
with the citizen. You put to shame the city
you're a man of—that it doesn't deserve.
In history, that makes a pattern of our time,
you're just old and scatterbrained.
I'll go over what I've said: get someone
to bring those children back, or
be taken into custody; I speak
from my mind . . . I'm not mouthing things.
CHORUS. See, stranger, where you get? Your credentials
read, "a gentle man." Your behavior is obvious.
CREON. Son of Aegeus, the town you head is not,
as you point out, unmanaged or cleaned out;
I acted along this line of reasoning:
that one who loved my relatives
would not violate certain principles

in their upbringing. And I assumed
you did not tolerate pollution
coming from a parricide, someone
whose marriage was blighted in its offspring.
I also thought the court of Ares on the hill
was so well run, so incumbent to this soil,
it wouldn't allow his likes to settle here.
With this in mind, I sprung my trap:
I wouldn't have, had he not sworn curses
on my family and myself. I couldn't let that go . . .
I thought resistance would pay off.
Do as you please; I'm alone,
but I'll fight back.

OEDIPUS. What cold nerve! Who usurps his place,
old me, or you? The one retracing
some manslaughter for us, some marriage,
some disequilibrium, or the one
it happened to, and not by choice?
The gods were back of it, a grudge
against my ancestors, perhaps.
Don't accuse me of being degenerate
in that situation I mishandled
of my family and myself. The oracle,
remember how it ran: some children
to prove fatal to their father.
That's the charge you make, although
my parents didn't bring me up,
I was an adopted child. If I was doomed
the day I came, as it seemed afterwards,
a challenge to my father, whom I killed,
not knowing what I did or who he was,
how can you blame me for a choice
I didn't have? As for my marriage
to your sister—since you're not ashamed
to mention it—you'll be sorry
you suggested what I'll make explicit.

When you talk maliciously, I won't hold
my tongue. Her son is who I was,
how hard, god, how hard it hit;
she didn't suspect it, nor did I,
Being born to her, to marry her,
have children—she was disinherited.
But I think you're blaming us.
I married her, but not more willingly
than I report it here. I did not mean
that marriage, or my father's death
you keep alluding to, persecuting me
for that. Answer one question, then:
If someone charged at you, to take your life,
and you had no idea why, would you inquire
if he was your father, or down him first?
I think you would defend yourself, down
that apache, if your life meant anything;
you wouldn't investigate his motive.
The gods were sponsoring in my case,
so I fell. I don't believe my father's ghost
would explain it otherwise.
You make unfair allegations then, except
you think they have a certain quality,
a meaning both explicit and implied.
You flatter Theseus for his quality,
Athenians for their quality, but overlook
one thing in being generous with your praise:
that if any land knows anything about honoring
the gods, and how to worship them,
this one ranks first; yet you would detach from it
an old suppliant and sneak away
with those young virgins in your custody.
I call upon these goddesses in prayer,
I shower them with litanies:
may they come as reinforcements.
You'll learn by whom this city is policed.

CHORUS. This man, moderator, is significant;
  with his experience of calamity, he deserves our aid.
THESEUS. Let's wind up this discussion.
  While they work out their plan,
  we simply stand for it.
CREON. And what do you impose on a disabled man?
THESEUS. Get a head-start, go on in front of us—
  If you're holding the girls in this vicinity,
  you'll go and reveal their whereabouts.
  If the big fish make a run for it, that's
  no complication: they won't get free.
  Take off. You know how we caught you—
  red-handed poacher trapped just by chance—
  what you gain by fraud, and not fair deal,
  you must give up—nor do you gain more.
  You performed this sacrilege in secret,
  with what nerve! Using an accomplice,
  I am sure; that took some figuring out
  on my part, because no one all alone
  would undertake this country's overthrow.
  Does this make sense to you, or do you think
  my reactions and my speech irrelevant?
CREON. You're not to blame for what you say.
  I'll go home and do what is required of me.
  [*Exit* CREON.]
THESEUS. You, Oedipus,
  stay here, be calm. Believe me,
  unless I'm killed, I won't give up
  until I've got your girls back in your custody.
OEDIPUS. Theseus, bless your noble generosity
  and your initiative on my behalf. [*Exit* THESEUS.]

1ST STROPHE

CHORUS. With the advancing combat troops,
  where bronze means war, I'd participate,
  where they take torches to
  those about to receive the holy mysteries,

milk the goddesses of fertility give:
the golden rule of silence they observe
when they're initiated in this happiness.
Where Theseus erupts in war,
and where those undaunted virgins are,
there'll be a noise, a sound barrier
to break in all this area . . .

1st Antistrophe

or maybe he heads west,
up snowbanks in the Oian fields,
breaking through on stallions,
running a chariot race. He'll be stopped.
War as it gets on is staggering,
spear-headed by Theseus, it's staggering:
bridles glint, they're everywhere,
horses helmeted are mounted everywhere
by those who pledge allegiance
to that fine animal that Athens breeds,
and to earth-shaker, beloved son of Rhea,
turbulent Poseidon.

2nd Strophe

Are they off yet, or still standing by?
I anticipate his cause as lost, although
the stress they're under has been staggering,
suffering from a relative, that's staggering.
But Zeus plays his role, yes, every day.
I predict the game goes well.
If I had the aerial swiftness
of the dove of prophecy, I'd zoom above,
and focus sharply on that game.

2nd Antistrophe

Oh total ruler of the gods,
totally conscious, Zeus:

come to our defense,
play winner, make an end
to a well-executed hunt,
with forceful Athena, your authentic child.
With Apollo the sleuth, and his sister
who makes after the light-footed, dappled deer:
that couple might lend their assistance
to this land and its citizens with my approval.

Stranger, don't infer that this watchman
lacks prophetic truth; those maidens of yours,
here they come, I see them coming back escorted.

> [THESEUS, *with a daughter of* OEDIPUS *on each arm, moves toward the rock.*]

OEDIPUS. Where? Where? What a proposition! You mean it?
ANTIGONE. Father. Father, some god should let you visualize
  this gentleman: he's conveyed us back to you.
OEDIPUS. My daughters . . . here? Both of you?
ANTIGONE. The hands of Theseus and his followers
  kept us in one piece.
OEDIPUS. Child, come over here: let your father
  recreate the entity he'd given up for lost.
ANTIGONE. You speak out for what you put being into:
  a consolation for your lonesomeness.
OEDIPUS. Where are you, then?
ANTIGONE. Coming close.
OEDIPUS. Dearest children.
ANTIGONE. A father loves his own.
OEDIPUS. The ones a man can move with.
ANTIGONE. Their lives being equally disrupted.
OEDIPUS. We're intimate friends; if they stand by,
  I won't fall into oblivion at my death.
  Hold me close, you both, on both sides,
  steady the man who raised you; get this
  over with, this exhausting travel
  that disconnected us; and tell me what went on:

but briefly—young people should not talk too much.
ANTIGONE. He set us free, so give him your attention.
Father, it means we have less work to do.
OEDIPUS. Stranger, do not be surprised if I go on,
if of this unexpected appearance of my daughters,
I make something big—the specific joy
I feel with them could not have come about
through someone else—you set them free,
not someone else. May the gods accomplish
what I want for you, you and your land.
Only with your people have I found good faith,
politeness, and no double-crossing words—
as I use words to emphasize what I mean—
what's mine is mine through you, and no one else.
Sir, give me your right hand to shake,
and the privilege, if I have such, of a kiss . . .
How could I say that? With a life as negative
as mine, could I want to wipe it off
on someone that mess does not involve?
I won't stand for touching him. Progress
in abjection is only made by men conditioned
as I've been. We'll say good-bye,
and you keep these remains intact
until this day's gone by.
THESEUS. Even if you amplified this utterance still more,
about how pleased you are to have your children back,
I would not be surprised, even if you let them
have their say before my own. I'm not put out.
We aim to build our life with acts, not words.
So, for example, we were not bluffing
when we swore our oath, old man.
We recovered them unhurt by their assailants.
Well, why inflate a real accomplishment?
Turn to those two for the actual happening.
A bit of news I obtained as I came over here
I also bring: its implications are enormous,
you might study them. In government

everything is scrutinized.

OEDIPUS. What is it, Theseus? Come out with it,
so I'm not in a state of bafflement.

THESEUS. It's about a man: they say the city
you belong to is different, but that
you're relatives; back at Poseidon's altar,
where I was interrupted at my sacrifice,
he was on his knees.

OEDIPUS. Where was he from? And wanting at that monument?

THESEUS. I do know what he wants: a short interview
with you, they say . . . the punch line, as it were.

OEDIPUS. What's his motive?

THESEUS. His motive in approaching you, I'm told,
is to dislocate you, on a permanent basis.

OEDIPUS. Who would this be, taking this seat over?

THESEUS. Think of someone from Argos you're related to,
who might want a meeting to that point . . .

OEDIPUS. Let's drop the subject there, my friend.

THESEUS. Somehow it affects you?

OEDIPUS. Don't press.

THESEUS. Press what? Say.

OEDIPUS. When I hear that, I know this agent's identity.

THESEUS. Who, then? What should I condemn him as?

OEDIPUS. My son. Unacceptable. I could hardly put up
with such a distressing voice.

THESEUS. But why? Can't you be an audience,
still have your own reaction?
How does it hurt to hear him out?

OEDIPUS. Sir, I'm his father and I hate his tone.
Don't push me to the breaking point.

THESEUS. But suppose that seat makes it compulsory?
Better not prejudge the case a god upholds.

ANTIGONE. Father, I'm young to be advising you,
but be sensible. Let this man's intention
be fulfilled, and his expectations from the god;
give in to us, and let our brother come.

What's wrong with hearing someone's case?
Speech serves as some evidence for things
he might do to you—you gave him life:
so that no matter what he does,
the worst that son can do, yet still it's wrong
for you to act that way to him. Give in.
The problem child, and acute dissension run
in other families as well; but when
the charms of dear ones hold us back,
we respond somewhat differently inside.
If you reflect, not on just this moment,
but on the past history of your punishment
related to your mother and your father,
if you study that, I think you'll realize
what bad results bad tempers get.
Your reply to this can't be very strong
if your own eyes serve to illustrate.
Give in to us: there's no use sulking
when the claim is fair; your holding out
when your case has met success
is not the right kind of gratitude.
OEDIPUS. Daughter, I'm in no frame of mind for it,
    but I'll agree, since he's a friend of yours.
    Don't let him curtail my activity.
THESEUS. I'll deal with this, I need no reminding;
    this isn't propaganda, but you know
    how we've responded in your case,
    and if the gods do help us out. [*Exit* THESEUS.]

STROPHE

CHORUS. The man who wants to live
    over normal life expectancy
    is only playing a hunch,
    and I see right through him—
    since the days are long and many
    that pack the pains in close together;

and where a man is short of time,
comfort is not what you see him with.
There's the undertaker, the impeccable,
there's Hades, when out shines our fate
without the ado of wedding song,
instrument or dance,
there at last is Death.

ANTISTROPHE

Better not be born
than have to argue it.
If you're in the picture though,
best go out the way you came and fast.
In view of this case of silly oversight,
who can dodge frustration or anxiety,
cold wars, civil wars, and violence,
slayings and mass murders?
Your pension then awaits you:
impatient, unwelcome, not appreciated, weak—
old age is your indemnity—
the ravages of all this ugliness.

EPODE

And here's the victim, I'm not the sole example:
like a bluff up north subject to the pulverizing influence
of rough water in the wintertime,
in his full height, he's subject to the continuous assault
of all the waves of insecurity combined,
sweeping from the sinking sun,
and from the rising, and the noonday,
and from the tides at night.

[*Enter* POLYNEIKES.]

ANTIGONE. Here is the visitor; father, it's unusual
   for a man to have tears streaming down
   as he approaches you.
OEDIPUS. Who is he?

ANTIGONE. The one I made you change your mind about,
   awhile ago; he's here: it's Polyneikes.
POLYNEIKES. What shall I do. Let the tears fall
   over my own extreme condition,
   or at the sight of this old man, my father?
   Someone I've caught up with. They're with him.
   On someone else's land. With the shrunken clothing
   they were tossed out in—Old Man Squalor
   is a tough one to get used to for an old man,
   his hair, all tangled, getting blown about,
   his head where the eyes are all punched out.
   And food—I'd guess that what he's carrying there
   for his stomach is just like all the rest.
   This knowledge is too late, when I myself
   am down to nothing: I admit
   I am the most execrable person in the world—
   for what I've done and failed to do.
   You'll hear it from me. I know it.
   But Dignity in everything sits by Zeus' throne . . .
   Father, may she be by your side.
   You went wrong until a certain point,
   but you've had no compensation since . . .
   You're being so quiet. Why?
   Father, say something!
   Don't turn me back! Have you no response?
   Then you disown me, send me off unheard,
   and won't say what you stand against?
   Daughters of this man, common blood with me,
   activate his tongue, it's stuck or blocked . . .
   so as the minister of the god,
   I won't be given disrespect,
   dismissed without a sound.
ANTIGONE. Then tell us what you're here for.
   Travel has conditioned you; keep
   your answer to the unresponsive going
   on any theme, amusing, bothersome, or simply pitiful.
POLYNEIKES. Then I'll go on. Thanks for cueing me.

The god was my first agency of relief,
but I got leave to go in here
from the high official of this land:
he granted freedom of speech and audience
when I left. I'd appreciate the same
from you, oh strangers, as to my sisters
and myself; the same, too, from my father.
Father, I want to tell you what I came about.
I was exiled from my home at the time
I should have occupied the throne
of your imperial command, having grown up
the elder in the family. Eteocles,
younger than I am, has expelled me
from the land instead: he didn't argue it,
he didn't put up muscle or experience
to prove his case but got the city on his side.
I'm telling you that I'm the one
to do your vengeance. The oracles agree,
I understand. While with the Dorians
in Argos, I've attached Adrastos to me
as an in-law, and I've won adherents
to my cause, men
who earned a name for spear-handling;
so when I make a seven-point attack
on Thebes, I'll either die on top,
or run those outlaws off the land.
Why make this special trip, then?
Father, to you my prayer's addressed,
for myself and for my fighting men;
we now encircle Thebes with seven shields
and seven spears. There's the marksman
Amphiraus, who's most efficient with the spear,
and at taking omens. Second, there's Tydeus,
the son of Oineus, from Aetolia. Third,
the Argive Eteoklos. Fourth, Hippomedon,
pressed into service by his father Talaos.
Fifth, Capaneus, who would send the town of Thebes

up in a holocaust. Arkas, the sixth partisan,
is a priestess' son, named after his mother,
who bore him out of wedlock, he's Atalanta's
true loyal son. Then here am I, your son . . .
if not yours, then some ugly doom's,
and they still call me yours: I head up
the fearless Argives bound for Thebes.
Father, for your own good, for your children's sake,
we make our prayer, we plead especially
with you—bend your tremendous wrath
away from me, the outsider, and towards
my brother as a penalty for ousting me,
for excluding me from home.
If oracles have a basis we can trust,
anyone you align with boosts his strength.
But my answer to you is "change your mind,"
by the family gods, by old family ties,
take sides with me, we're beggars,
both of us, outsiders: you're an outsider.
We play up to others for our living,
you and I; our life is not that stable.
And how the man who runs our house
can chuckle and display his wealth.
If you join up with me, then shortly
I'll have him swept out, and you
installed back in your old residence,
myself as well, and force him into exile.
If you go along, what claims then I can make!
If not, I won't be able to pull through.

CHORUS. Since Theseus was his sponsor, Oedipus,
   tell him how things stand; then
   authorize his departure.

OEDIPUS. People, if Theseus hadn't fallen in with him
   over on that ground of public sanctity,
   hadn't promoted him, thinking that his speech
   should get attention, he'd have gone without
   my high-sounding name. Now it's his right

to act as audience to things that won't
add jolliness to his career. Criminal!
Holding on to kingship and high function,
which now your brother has in Thebes,
and letting your own father down,
cancelling his citizenship; you weep now
at what then you clothed him in, now
that your existence is as low as mine:
not for weeping at, but for shouldering
while I'm alive, a memento of your bloodiness.
You give me one frustration day by day
to nibble on—you're the one who shut me out.
Because of you I tramp around each day
asking someone else for life. Had I not raised
these nurses, my two daughters, would it exist,
now would it, here, what's left of me?
They land me out of trouble, these nurses do,
they're men, not women, when it comes
to joint endeavors. Someone else had charge
of raising you: it wasn't me. And so
there's no extension of your happiness
to look forward to, if these spears
go into action against Thebes.
You won't break that city down, until
you've gone down smeared in blood,
same as your brother. Those revenges
that I once was subject to I now invoke
to join me as my allies; so you will judge
it's good to hold your father in awe, and not
despise him, if he's blind and you so fine,
his sons. These girls were not like you.
Revenges rule your suppliant's bench, your throne,
if that square deal they used to talk about
so long ago is still around, attending
to the ancient laws of Zeus. You'll wander,
you'll be spat upon, I won't be your father,
you miserable extremist, you'll take along

those revenges I invoke on you; by using spears
you will not gain control of land you grew up on,
you will never regain Argos in the valley,
but you'll die under a brother's hand,
and kill the one who shoved you out.
This is the curse I put on you, and I invoke
the hateful gloom of the fatherhood of Tartarus,
that he make you remote; I invoke these goddesses,
and Aggression, that by its awful hatreds
you'll be crushed. You've heard it, so be gone;
relay this happening to all the Kadmeians,
and to your loyal partisans; hereby Oedipus
awards these prizes to his children.
CHORUS. Polyneikes, your about-faces
    I don't like: hurry up and leave.
POLYNEIKES. What failure looms for me,
    and for my partisans! Operations
    based in Argos reach this impasse . . .
    So let down, but I can't break the news—
    recall my partisans—there's no room
    for argument against odds like these.
    Sisters, you who share my blood,
    you hear the damning evidence
    my father has come out with,
    but, for the gods, if his curses stick,
    and you make it home, don't rule me out,
    but give me a decent burial.
    There's no less credit for helping me
    than for the energies you've spent on his behalf.
ANTIGONE. Polyneikes, please come to terms.
POLYNEIKES. Which, my dear Antigone? Speak.
ANTIGONE. Pull back your troops—to Argos:
    your city will be saved and so will you.
POLYNEIKES. That's impossible. The army won't fall back . . .
    I'll be accused of spinelessness.
ANTIGONE. Young man! What makes you so distracted?
    What does wiping out your own city gain?

POLYNEIKES. It saves the embarrassment of being a laughingstock,
  were I to run away; I'm older than my brother.
ANTIGONE. See how you make the oracle concrete,
  though you grieve for both impending deaths?
POLYNEIKES. His will be done. We can't shift our position.
ANTIGONE. I am appalled. Who can stand listening
  to this man's talk, the things he spouts?
POLYNEIKES. My language isn't trivial; a true commander
  talks supremacy and not defeatism.
ANTIGONE. Young man, this, then is your decision.
POLYNEIKES. Don't tie me up; having run across my father
  and his Furies, I have a heavy doom ahead,
  an ugly one. May Zeus grant you his blessing,
  if you do for me what I've asked,
  dead, not alive, when you have me back.
  Let me go now; say good-bye.
  You won't see my eyes blink again.
ANTIGONE. I'm appalled.
POLYNEIKES. No, don't weep.
ANTIGONE. As you head down to Hades of the sinking gaze,
  who wouldn't breathe heavily for you?
POLYNEIKES. If I have to die, I do.
ANTIGONE. Unless you accept my terms.
POLYNEIKES. Don't nag me with what I'm not allowed to do.
ANTIGONE. Then I can only be unhappy, being cut off from you.
POLYNEIKES. My luck runs out, the way the situation stands;
  I pray the gods you not get hurt—so you deserve.

[*Exit* POLYNEIKES.]

1ST STROPHE

CHORUS. Dismal feelings of depression turn up fresh and new
  with the visitor who lacks his sight:
  a foregone conclusion, perhaps.
  Silly for me to answer for the status
  of the earth-demons.
  Time's scope, time's scope

includes the whole continuity;
gives this emphasis, and that another day.

[*Thunder begins.*]

The air is rumbling! Zeus!

OEDIPUS. My children, you, the rest of you,
  go fetch Theseus, a man of noblest quality.
ANTIGONE. Father, what would you impose on him?
OEDIPUS. The thunder of this Zeus
  who makes us relevant
  points me to Hades. Bring him at once.

1st Antistrophe

CHORUS. Listen, the increase in volume of this rumbling!
  There's no expressing it, Zeus turns it on.
  My heart palpitates.
  Again the streak of burning lightning
  in the sky. What is it coming to?
  Numinous. Explosion not for nothing,
  not short of its effect.
  Oh universal air, oh Zeus!

OEDIPUS. Children, it's today; the gods were right.
  There is no turning back.
ANTIGONE. How do you know or figure that?
OEDIPUS. I know what it means.
  Go to his majesty, the prince,
  and bring him here at once.

2nd Strophe

CHORUS. Stand by, stand by, hear it again!
  It extends all over, this clapping boom!
  You're kind, oh spirit, you're kind
  if you deliver this blighted object
  to his mother earth.
  May I participate in your steady beat

and not be passed a bogus grace
for having seen this human image
I cannot repress.
Oh Zeus high above, we call on you.

OEDIPUS. Well, is he here? Daughters,
    as long as I'm still breathing
    I'll make sense to him, when he arrives.
ANTIGONE. What pact is this you want with him?
OEDIPUS. It's not a matter of my suffering now,
    but of a specially significant clearance
    that has just now been granted me.

2ND ANTISTROPHE

CHORUS. But then, but then, child, hurry up!
    You might still catch him
    at his seaside rock-hollow,
    where he dedicates the shrine
    for bulls, the god Poseidon's sacrifice.

[THESEUS enters.]

He comes.
The visitor considers you, the city
and its favorites, worthy recipients
of a tidy benefice;
give him your immediate and close attention, prince.

THESEUS. What touched off these blasts in your vicinity,
    zeroing in on citizens, but on Oedipus especially:
    Zeus thundering, or pounding us with hailstones?
    That's the usual case, when there's a stormy sky . . .
OEDIPUS. Prince, I welcome you; the god set up
    an opportunity along this road.
THESEUS. What's been happening, son of Laius?
OEDIPUS. My time's run out, and I don't want
    my death to break the promises
    I made to your city and to you.

THESEUS. But what says that is next?
OEDIPUS. The gods confirming what they mean—
in their communication, they don't lie.
THESEUS. Old man, what manifests are you speaking of?
OEDIPUS. The heavy concentration of the thunder,
and that barrage of lightning bolts
streaming from an invincible hand.
THESEUS. You're right. I see you have the god-given sense
of relevance and honor your commitments.
What now? Tell us what we have to do.
OEDIPUS. Child of Aegeus, I will let you see
what the city will inherit—it won't be
diminished by your old age. The setting
I'm to die in I'll prescribe myself,
with no escort in the way; reveal
this place to no one,
nor in what area it lies. It will confer on you
the everlasting strength of numerous shields,
and the spears of foreign countries.
When you've found out, don't stir up
conversation on such secret things,
as you go out alone: because I can't tell
just any of these citizens,
or even my children, though we're on good terms.
Always keep the secret; when you reach the end,
then pass it on to the next-in-line alone,
and let him leave word with his successor.
That way you'll immunize your city to assault
from Theban men. Most governments,
even though established in a state of happiness,
easily grow self-centered. The gods
focus on abundance once, and then again
they focus their attention; when someone
has neglected sacred things, he's going mad.
May you, son of Aegeus, avoid that experience.
Now that you've heard, I'll quit lecturing;
let us go in, and not turn back. Children,
you walk in back of me.

[OEDIPUS *rises, without assistance, and begins his slow departure from the stage. His daughters look on in amazement.*]

They're calling me
new leader, just what they were to their father.
Go away now, don't hang on to me,
let me find the sacred tomb myself,
so my conclusion's hidden under ground.
This way, take this way now. This way Hermes
leads me, and the goddess of the underworld.
Secret illumination, once upon a time my own:
now my vitality is taken far from you.
So I go my way, my life over and fulfilled,
to Hades, to hide myself. Most precious stranger,
may this land, yourself, and your subordinates
have a large share of happiness; and in success
remember by my dying your constant open-mindedness.

[*Exit* OEDIPUS, *flanked by his daughters, followed by* THESEUS, *through an arbor directly behind the rock, from which* THESEUS *will finally emerge, after the* MESSENGER's *speech.*]

STROPHE

CHORUS. If it is my right to worship, if prayers will do
    for the goddess without epiphanies and you,
    lord of benighted things, Hades, Hades,
    do not weigh me down . . .
    don't hit the stranger with some woeful fate
    down on the plain of shades below,
    the house of Styx.
    The punishments you have arrived at
    are many and even absurd:
    the just spirit raises some men back up again.

ANTISTROPHE

Oh, goddesses of earth, and wild undefeated creature
who sleeps down by the gates that many strangers pass;

who whines out of caves, on untamed watch by Hades' side,
so the abiding story goes . . .
Oh, son of Earth and Tartarus, you I beseech
not to interrupt the passage of the stranger
scheduled for the underworld.
On you I call, who always sleep.

[*The* MESSENGER *arrives, from the side.*]

MESSENGER. Citizens! I should make it brief, and say
   that Oedipus is dead. But the meaning
   of what happened, the actual event,
   I couldn't talk about in brief.
CHORUS. The poor man died?
MESSENGER. You should be informed how he
   went out of this existence.
CHORUS. How? Did the patient have it easy,
   was it in godliness?
MESSENGER. It is something you can marvel at.
   You were close by and saw him off:
   he took steps over there without
   using any friend of his as escort,
   but took the lead of all himself.
   When he reached the way that drops down in,
   bronze fixtures there are planted in the earth,
   he stood on one path of the many issuing therefrom,
   beside the hollow urn, that cornerstone
   of friendship between Peirithoos and Theseus.
   Setting himself between the leaper's ledge
   and a prickly thorn, off from a marble tomb,
   he sat, removed his dirty clothes . . .
   and then called and made his daughters
   bring him fresh spring water in pitchers
   from somewhere. Out on the eminence,
   the overlook of greens-keeping Demeter, they went,
   and carried out his orders then and there;
   they showered him, clothed him as is usual.
   When he was satisfied that all was done,

that no obligations had been missed,
Zeus rumbled from inside the earth,
the girls shivering when they heard.
They fell down at their father's knees,
and cried, and beat their breasts,
and at the top of their lungs were clamoring,
and wouldn't stop. Listening to their screams,
he held them in his arms, and said, "Children,
today your father is not with you any more.
Everything about him dies: this rigorous attention
to his needs now may be dropped. Children, I know,
it leaves you numb. But one thing can be said
to alleviate all the soreness: the love
I felt for you, more than anyone would give, which
the life you face from now on is deprived of."
Arms locked together, they wept and sobbed.
When their effusion was over with, and no noise
any more rang out, a silence came; then someone's
voice suddenly screamed out at him, so that
it made all our hair stand up suddenly
fear-stricken: it was the god calling him
from everywhere: "You there, you there, Oedipus!
What are we waiting for? for so long is your progress slow."
When he realized that a god was indeed addressing him,
he called for Theseus, the monarch, to approach,
who did then come, and Oedipus said, "Dear man,
with your handshake make the ancient pledge
to them; my daughters, make the same to him.
Promise never to betray them selfishly,
and always do what you know is best for them."
Since he has integrity, he made his pledge
to do these things, and did not object.
When that was done, Oedipus turned then
to his daughters, in his blind hands held theirs,
and said: "Children, you who have lived up
to your integrity, you must exit from this place;
you are not authorized to see these things work out,

nor to hear our responses. Step back at once.
Only high-ranking Theseus may learn the way it's done."
These things he talked about we listened to
together. Then we walked those maidens out,
ourselves in grief. After leaving, we turned back
a moment later, looked all over but he wasn't there;
our prince was, holding up his hands to shade his eyes
against something phenomenally frightening
shining out, intolerable to sight.
We saw him do obeisance to Earth
and the Olympian gods all in one breath.
So, how he died no one in the world can talk about
except one person, Theseus. What actually
set it off was not the thunder of the fire-bearer,
or a hurricane timed precisely for that moment,
but some agent of the divine world, or else
those encased in comfort under earth
were kind enough to open earth a crack . . .
The man you made your farewell gestures to
was not moaned over or suffering from illness,
but in terms of human life, one to be marvelled at.
Those who impugn my sanity, think
I'm being irrational, we part company.

CHORUS. And his children, and those friends of his
who went up in his party, where are they?

MESSENGER. Not far from here; with their expressive cries,
they identify themselves in their approach.

[ANTIGONE *and* ISMENE *make a final entrance from the side.*]

1ST STROPHE

ANTIGONE. Oh dear. Oh my. So. So is there
of what existed of our father,
survived its terrible growth,
not one whit for us poor things to mourn over?
One on whom we expended so much toil and energy,

it turns out what we get from our impressions and experiences
is imponderable . . .
CHORUS. What is this about?
ANTIGONE. You interpret it, my friends.
CHORUS. He passed away . . .
ANTIGONE. So you'd take it to heart especially.
  Why then, it was not at war or on the sea
  that he was taken away;
  but an anonymous landscape swallowed him,
  how, no one knows. My misfortune is
  to have passed on to us
  a disintegrating night over our eyes.
  How can we feed ourselves the minimum
  away at these loose ends, or tossing on the sea?
ISMENE. I don't know. The mass murderer himself,
  Hades, should run off with me; then old father
  and poor me, we'd be dead together.
  The life ahead for me is not liveable.
CHORUS. Now such a fine pair of children
  should not let the intervention
  of a god (which should be accepted)
  heat them up too much.

1ST ANTISTROPHE

ANTIGONE. Even mean things got a good response:
  this entirely unappreciated man I did appreciate,
  when I could lend my arms' support.
  My father, my friend,
  dressed for always in the darkness of the earth:
  in me you have an admirer, though you're gone.
CHORUS. He has completed his role.
ANTIGONE. The role he wanted to play.
CHORUS. Which one?
ANTIGONE. Dying on the strange soil he wanted to.
  A pleasant shade perpetually over his bed below,
  a grief whose cries are not suppressed:

father, these tear-filled eyes weep over you;
to wipe them clear of sadness is impossible.
Oh, dying on the strange soil you wanted to,
but you died leaving me behind.
ISMENE. It's difficult; with our father gone,
what's in store for us?
CHORUS. But his life wound up solidly—
dear children, don't drag out this complaint.
Evil exempts no one.

2ND STROPHE

ANTIGONE. Let's move on again.
ISMENE. What will we do?
ANTIGONE. My instinct is . . .
ISMENE. Is what?
ANTIGONE. To visit the region of the offering-place . . .
ISMENE. To whom?
ANTIGONE. Where our father is. [*She cries.*]
ISMENE. But are we authorized? You don't see?
ANTIGONE. Why do you pester me with that?
ISMENE. It's that way because . . .
ANTIGONE. Why that excuse?
ISMENE. He had no burial; it's a special case.
ANTIGONE. Lead on; then finish me.
ISMENE. How would a shattered life be liveable
if there were no escape, no one but myself?

2ND ANTISTROPHE

CHORUS. Dear girls, don't get upset.
ANTIGONE. Where can I run?
CHORUS. You two ran away before.
ANTIGONE. So . . .
CHORUS. So you wouldn't fare ill.
ANTIGONE. I know.
CHORUS. What are you considering, then?
ANTIGONE. I don't see how we're getting home.

CHORUS. Don't take the trouble to.
ANTIGONE. It's difficult for us.
CHORUS. It was before, especially.
ANTIGONE. Then it was unfeasible; now it's out of the question.
CHORUS. An ocean of trouble.
ANTIGONE. Oh dear. Where will we go, oh Zeus?
Now what promised land does the spirit guide me to?

[*Enter* THESEUS.]

THESEUS. End your grieving, children. Those on whom
the night of the ground, a blessing, falls,
need no show of grief: it is looked down upon.
ANTIGONE. Oh, son of Aegeus, we prostrate ourselves before you.
THESEUS. Children, what is it that you require?
ANTIGONE. We want to see our father's tomb ourselves.
THESEUS. You're not authorized to go in there.
ANTIGONE. What do you mean, prince, high authority of Athens?
THESEUS. Children, he discouraged me
from letting people in those grounds,
and from talking over with anyone
that sacred grave he has.
He said I would fare well that way,
and preserve the land from noxious influence.
Our native spirit was the audience,
Sworn Commitment alert to everything.
ANTIGONE. If that was his intention, let it stick.
Return us to the other world of Thebes;
we might still prevail against that fratricide.
THESEUS. I will accomplish this, and anything
that is in your interest, I'm set to do,
or in his below, who's on new avenues,
for his sake. I won't slough it off.
CHORUS. Now end the grieving, start it up no more.
This process is on high.

SOPHOCLES

Philoctetes

TRANSLATED BY
EDWIN DOLIN AND ALFRED SUGG

INTRODUCTORY NOTE

The *Philoctetes* is perhaps the most complicated Greek tragedy that
has survived. Philoctetes has been abandoned on a deserted island,
because of an offensive wound, until an oracle is made known
which says that he must be brought to Troy, if the Greeks are to
win. This task is undertaken by Odysseus, well aware that Philoctetes hates his former comrades and none more than the wily Itha-
can. To accomplish his aim, Odysseus uses a young noble, Achilles'
son, Neoptolemos, whom he orders to gain Philoctetes' confidence
by lies and then, at the opportune moment, to seize the famous
bow, which is Philoctetes' one means of defense. The strain of this
intrigue on each of the characters is immense. Neoptolemos wavers
between sympathy for the suffering outcast and disgust at his own
lies on the one hand, and desire to win the war and satisfy the
Greek army on the other. Philoctetes is torn in all directions: affection for his young visitor, bitterness at having been deceived, hatred
for the Greek leaders, fear of his own destiny, and the longing, re-
pressed but not extinct, for accomplishment and act. Odysseus can
be condemned as merely a villain, but the case is hardly so simple.
Behind his cynicism is the disillusion of the man who has lived
long and known too well the fluidity of values and the weakness
of humans. To fight is not his choice. The point is made by Philoctetes himself that Odysseus had to be compelled to enter the war.
Once involved, he can see no alternative to success and accepts any
risk and stratagem to gain that end.

Philoctetes was produced in 409 and won first prize with the
other plays of its tetralogy. Their names are not known.

CHARACTERS

ODYSSEUS, king of Ithaca
NEOPTOLEMOS, son of Achilles
CHORUS of sailors, subjects of NEOPTOLEMOS
PHILOCTETES, son of Poias
MERCHANT
HERAKLES
(silent) MAN with MERCHANT

Philoctetes

THE SCENE. *The stage is empty; an apparently deserted coast relieved only by a cave opening and, in the background, a volcanic peak.*[1] *The* CHORUS *enter, alert for danger. When they see that all is clear, one gives a signal back toward the beach, while the others take up perimeter positions.* NEOPTOLEMOS *enters, followed by* ODYSSEUS.

ODYSSEUS. This is it, the beach of Lemnos. A lonely place in the
middle of the sea where no one ever sets foot. Not even a house!
You know, boy, standing there, you remind me of your father.
You have a lot to live up to as the son of Achilles. He was a great
man, Neoptolemos, far the best of us all. It was right here, a long
time ago, they ordered me to put Philoctetes out. I did it, because
they told me to. He was sick; his foot was eaten away, draining
from infection. With his screaming we had no chance to touch
a libation or a sacrifice to the gods. His screams were inhuman!
There wasn't a place in the whole camp you could get away from
them day or night. Because of him, anything religious we did
would have been a sacrilege. But do I have to talk about that?
It's a long story and there's not much time. If he finds out I'm
back, my whole plan would be finished, the whole thing! Yes, I
have a plan that I think will take him—and soon. Now, the rest
is up to you. Just follow orders. Take a look. There's a cave
somewhere. It had two openings; that way in winter he has two
places to sit in the sun, and in summer he can sleep with a breeze

---

1. The nature of the "Lemnian fire" mentioned in the *Philoctetes* is
obscure. It was probably not volcanic. However, this is the explanation in
standard commentaries. It is kept in this version because it is traditional
and could be useful in a production.

that goes right through. Down to the left you might see a spring
of clear water. It could still be running. Go ahead, but no noise!
When you find it, let me know if he still lives in the same place
or has moved away. Then I'll explain the rest, so you'll know
my plan. We're going to do this together.

NEOPTOLEMOS. Odysseus, sir, this is easy. I think I see the cave—

ODYSSEUS. Up high or lower. I can't tell where you mean.

NEOPTOLEMOS. Up here. And I don't hear anyone moving around.

ODYSSEUS. Careful. He could be asleep, inside.

NEOPTOLEMOS. The place is empty. Nobody's here.

ODYSSEUS. Isn't there anything? Food or furniture, the things a man
needs to live?

NEOPTOLEMOS. Some leaves tramped down, like a bed.

ODYSSEUS. Nothing else? Nothing?

NEOPTOLEMOS. Wait! It's solid wood. A cup! Whoever worked on
it didn't know what he was doing. And here's the makings for
a fire.

ODYSSEUS. That's his treasure you've found there. Now—

NEOPTOLEMOS. There's more—! Rags, warm and full of pus—

ODYSSEUS. All right, we know the man lives here; and he's close by.
How far could he walk with his leg eating at him like slow
death? Either he's looking for something to eat, or maybe he
knows some herb to stop the pain. Would you send this man
here as lookout? I don't need any surprises. He'd rather get me
than all the rest of the Greeks put together.

[NEOPTOLEMOS *complies.*]

NEOPTOLEMOS. He'll watch for anyone coming. Is there something
else? You were going to explain—

ODYSSEUS. You're Achilles' son. You mustn't forget what your family stands for. You have to be true to it here just as much as
anywhere else. And not just by fighting. That's important, of
course; but if I tell you something new, something you haven't
even heard about till now—remember, you came as a soldier to
carry out a mission.

NEOPTOLEMOS. What do I do?

ODYSSEUS. You're here to get Philoctetes—by talking to him, by tell-

ing him just what he wants to hear, by fooling him with a story
until you have him, mind, heart and soul. When he asks who
you are and what way you came, say you're Achilles' son. About
that don't lie. But about your trip—say you're sailing home.
You're out of the army, for good. Why? You hate it. There's
nothing between you and them, only hate. After they sent for
you and begged you to leave home to be with them as their
only hope for defeating Troy, when you got there and asked for
Achilles' armor, they said "No." You didn't deserve your father's
armor? Who else has a right! But they handed it over to someone else. Yes, to Odysseus. Say that; and add anything against
me you want—insults, contempt, anything. Because none of that
will hurt me. But if you don't do what I'm telling you to do, you
will hurt every man fighting right now at Troy. Because unless
this man's bow is taken from him first, you haven't got a chance
of defeating Troy. But why *you* instead of me? Because he'd
trust you. You'd be safe. You could say that you'd quit the army.
Me? I swore the same oath they all did about staying in this war
till the end. I had no way out then, and I've no way out now.
I've been part of everything they've done from the beginning.
So if he gets *one* look at me while he has that bow, I'm finished.
And I'll take you down with me, too, just because I am who I
am and we're here together. So, as I said, there *has* to be a plan:
that bow cannot be beaten in a fight. It has to be stolen, and you
have to do it. I know: you aren't the type to tell this kind of story,
to think it out rationally and then lie to get what you want. I
know that. But do you want to win, to be first? Then do what
you have to do. As for what's right—we *will* look right, later.
But now, just for one little hour, forget about what the world
will say, forget about yourself, let me decide. And then, for the
rest of your life, show the world that no one has more respect
than you do for everything good and sincere.

NEOPTOLEMOS. Odysseus, there are some things I don't even want
to talk about. How am I going to do them? No, I'm not the type
to lie to get what I want. And my father wasn't either—so I've
been told. But I have nothing against taking this man by force,
without tricks and lies. Let him fight. Nobody with one leg will

stop as many as we are. Still, it's true, they sent me here to help, and no one is going to say I've been disloyal. But, sir, I would rather fail and be right than win and know I've been wrong.

ODYSSEUS. Yes, you are your father's son, Neoptolemos. Oh, I was young once. I was like you. To get things done I went for my sword. I never bothered with what a few well-planned words could do. Now—I know from experience what brings results: to get people to do what you want, it's what you say that counts.

NEOPTOLEMOS. Then tell me what to say. If it's not a lie, I'll—

ODYSSEUS. I've been telling you. My plan is to take Philoctetes by a lie.

NEOPTOLEMOS. Why? What's wrong with trying to argue and reason with him?

ODYSSEUS. Reason with *him?* Hopeless! And you couldn't take him by force either.

NEOPTOLEMOS. Why? What's he got? It must be good.

ODYSSEUS. If he gets one shot with that bow—you're dead.

NEOPTOLEMOS. That good . . . There's no way to get in up close?

ODYSSEUS. No, unless you try deception. That's my approach.

NEOPTOLEMOS. So you don't think it's wrong to tell lies?

ODYSSEUS. Not when it's either that or death.

NEOPTOLEMOS. But is it possible to have the nerve to tell him what you said—and act sincere?

ODYSSEUS. It should be when it's for yourself.

NEOPTOLEMOS. Why should *I* care? Suppose he doesn't come to Troy—

ODYSSEUS. Troy can only be captured with his bow. It's as simple as that.

NEOPTOLEMOS. I thought you all said I was the one who was supposed to capture Troy.

ODYSSEUS. Without *you* the bow couldn't do it; but neither can you without the bow.

NEOPTOLEMOS. Maybe you're right. Like hunting. Sometimes there's no other way, except with a trap.

ODYSSEUS. And remember, this way you'll win two trophies, where you thought there would be only one.

NEOPTOLEMOS. If I knew what you meant, I think I'd be ready.

ODYSSEUS. They're going to say you have both: courage, of course, but intelligence, too, one as much as the other.

NEOPTOLEMOS. All right, I'm not going to worry from now on. I'll do it.

ODYSSEUS. Do you remember what I told you?

NEOPTOLEMOS. I do, and now I understand it. Don't worry. I'm with you—all the way.

ODYSSEUS. Then stay here till he comes. I'm leaving, so he won't see I'm here too. The lookout there—I'll take him back to the ship with me; then—I mean, just in case you and your men seem to be taking longer than you should, I'll send him right back here. This is the man I'll send, but it will be part of our deception: he'll be dressed like the captain of a merchant ship, in case there's any confusion. Now son, he'll be talking a kind of code, so listen, and pick up your cue any time it helps. I'm heading for the ship. Now it's up to you. May we two be led by that god who guides in the darkness of deception, Hermes; and may we be led by Athena, too, the goddess of success for our army and for our country—she who always keeps me from death. [*Exit* ODYSSEUS *and lookout.*]

1ST STROPHE

CHORUS. —Sir—sir, we're strangers here; anyone we meet is bound to be suspicious.

—Tell us what to say.

—And what we should cover up.

—Tell us. You're the one who gives *us* orders.

LEADER. Sir, what the men mean is, what do *you* think? Because if the problem is about having a plan, and deciding what to do, we know who's going to decide better: the one who has authority from the gods, the one who has power from Zeus—

CHORUS. —Because Zeus gave it to him

—and to his father and to all his fathers before him.

LEADER. Son, *you* have that power. It's come to you through the ages. No one knows how old it is.

CHORUS. —*You* give the orders.
  —What should we do?

NEOPTOLEMOS. For the moment—if that's what you mean—you may want to take a good look at the lay of the land on this cliff. There's nothing to worry about, not *now*. Go on, take a look. But he's dangerous! Make no mistake about that. And when he gets here—Oh, yes, he's on the way. And when he comes, watch my hand. When you see the signal, try to give me whatever help I need.

1st ANTISTROPHE

CHORUS. —We have been watching you, sir.
LEADER. For quite a while now we've been watching, and worrying.
CHORUS. —We're ready to do what's good for you—
  —and not what's good for somebody else.
LEADER. Right now, could you say where *he* is?
CHORUS. —He might be lying out there, right now.
  —But where?
  —We don't want to be caught by surprise.
  —It would help us if we knew—
  —Is he holed up someplace?
  —Or out in the open?

NEOPTOLEMOS. As for where he lives, see! There! Two doors, front and back, with stone for a bed . . .
LEADER. Poor man. But where *is* he now?
NEOPTOLEMOS. Isn't it obvious? He has to eat, so he's gone out after food. He's someplace near, laboring along, step by step. That's how they say he stays alive: hunting wild animals with his bow. It's hard for him; you don't know how hard. And people say there's no way he can do anything about what's wrong with him.

2nd STROPHE

CHORUS. —You can't help but feel sorry for him. *I* do.
LEADER. You think what it is to be lonely even for a while, and then you think what *his* life is. He's not alone for some reason that

will change; he's alone for good, and nobody cares if he lives
or dies.

CHORUS. —It's hard to think of being sick with *anything* when
there's nobody to take care of you, but what's it like to be sick
with a pain that would make a savage out of you, day in and
day out?

—I can almost feel the panic he must feel when there's something he *has* to have—like food or water, and he can't find it.

—How can he keep it up?

—The gods are hard.

—But that's how it is with ambition. Great men; great families!

—The higher they reach, the farther they fall.

—A plain man's life is best.

2ND ANTISTROPHE

LEADER. Take him. *He's* from a great family; maybe there's no one
greater than he was.

CHORUS. —He had everything. Now, what's left?

—Nothing.

—He lives on here, all by himself—

—No, there's animals near. *His* neighbors have stripes and fur!

—And hasn't he got pain to keep him company? And hunger,
too?

—And even a voice, that always answers his screams; his echo,
that comes back from out there, and goes on and on—

NEOPTOLEMOS. What about it? All of a sudden you'd think we were
face to face with some mystery that we can't explain. There's no
mystery! Not for *me*! If you'll let me say what *I* think, it can all
be explained in one word: the gods! From beginning to end,
what's happened to Philoctetes is the will of the gods. Back then
it was a goddess, the Golden One, Chrysē: she let the snake get
him. She didn't have pity on him, did she? And the same thing
is true right now. The gods are behind his suffering, and his
loneliness, too. The gods: thinking, planning—deliberately!—so
that he can't move against Troy with his fatal arrows—the gods
gave them to him, didn't they?—until the time comes. Now;

this is the time; the time when it's said Troy will fall because of his bow.

3RD STROPHE

LEADER. Don't talk, boy.

NEOPTOLEMOS. Why?

LEADER. A sound! Out there. Like someone tired or hurt.

CHORUS. —Listen. This way?

—Or this?

—I hear it! Like a man forcing himself on, step by step.

—A voice! Listen!

—He sounds exhausted, finished—

LEADER. It's still far off, but clear. No doubt about it.

3RD ANTISTROPHE

LEADER. Son, please—

NEOPTOLEMOS. What?

LEADER. Think hard. Because he's not someplace else now. He's here.

CHORUS. —And that's not the music of any shepherd coming home from the fields playing on his pipes.

[*A scream is heard from offstage.*]

—God, how the sound carries.

—Maybe he stumbled.

—Or else he sees this coast, with no harbor, where no ships ever come in.

—That sound!

[PHILOCTETES *appears at the cave entrance holding a bow.*]

PHILOCTETES. Strangers! You stopped? Here? There's no harbor for your ship, no people. But who—? Would I be right if I said you—your clothes, *they're* Greek. For me that's welcome enough; but could I hear your voice? Though maybe you're so surprised, you can't talk. Or even think. I know, I don't look human any more. Are you thinking that you maybe ought to stay away from me? You're scared. Please, I'm alone. That's what's made me like this, being left here by myself. If you know what pity is, talk to me. Are you friends? Answer me. We could at least expect that much from each other. *I*'ve spoken. How could you fail—?

NEOPTOLEMOS. All right. First, we're Greeks. That was your question, wasn't it?

PHILOCTETES. Even the sound of your voice! I've waited so long just to be spoken to by someone like you! But son, why? What got you to land here? Maybe you had to, or was it an impulse? What wind brought you? Any wind—it doesn't matter; to me it's the best. Tell me. Everything! Who are you?

NEOPTOLEMOS. I was born in the middle of the sea, on Skyros. I'm bound for home now. My name is Neoptolemos. I'm the son of Achilles. I—

PHILOCTETES. "Achilles?"

NEOPTOLEMOS. Yes, I've told you everything.

PHILOCTETES. What joy to hear your father's name! And Skyros, too! I remember your grandfather, Lycomēdes, though he was an old man when I last saw him. What brought you to sail past here? Where did you sail *from?*

NEOPTOLEMOS. From Troy! Yes—*now* I'm sailing from Troy.

PHILOCTETES. But you weren't in the fleet with us when we started against Troy—

NEOPTOLEMOS. What do you mean "we?" Don't tell me you had anything to do with that—

PHILOCTETES. Son, you mean you have no idea who you're looking at?

NEOPTOLEMOS. How can I recognize someone I've never met before?

PHILOCTETES. Surely *someone* has mentioned my name! Or said something about what I've been going through all this time! Nothing?

NEOPTOLEMOS. Nothing. I don't know what you're talking about.

PHILOCTETES. It seems I'm more an outcast than I've thought through the years. How the gods must hate me! Not a word? No news of my trouble has reached home, not any place in Greece? Not— no, I see it all. They've kept quiet. They would! They're the ones who threw me out. Of course, they've kept it to themselves. They're not human. I expect it's given them a laugh, though,

through the years, all the time that my sickness has been growing worse. Not just growing, flourishing! I'll *tell* you who I am,
boy. I'm a man the son of Achilles might have heard of, because
I'm the man Herakles chose to leave his bow to. He gave it to
me on Mount Oita, when he died. I'm the son of Poias, I'm Philoctetes. The man the two great generals and the lord of Ithaca
dishonorably deserted on a desert island. Yes, deserted! . . . When
he was all but dead from the savage, bloody bite of a killer snake!
Alone, child, and crippled. With a sickness that wasn't human,
they put me out here when they saw it from the open sea, sailing
from the Isle of Gold. They *left* me here! The seas had been
rough, I remember; I guess I was tired and fell asleep. That must
have tickled them! How easy to sail away and leave me here
asleep in a cave on the beach! Oh, they tossed me a little food,
whatever they happened to have, and a wad of rags you might
give to a beggar. Think about it, boy—what it must have been
like, that first moment when I woke up; when I stood up after
that sleep and began to realize my ships and all the ships I had
sailed with were gone! There was no one to share my misery,
let alone help me. I had to do *something*. So I looked, carefully,
everywhere, but there wasn't anything but pain! And that was
everywhere, son. That didn't desert me for a minute. Oh, time
didn't stop. I wasn't that lucky. I had things to do. I had to worry
about everything myself; this little house, food. It's true that
shooting game wasn't any problem. With this bow I could kill
wild doves on the wing, but imagine what it was like for me
to pick up what I'd hit. Hobbling, stumbling, dragging this foot,
gritting my teeth at every step. It was the same when I had to
have drinking water or break up firewood, if the frost came in
winter. I managed to drag out after it. But then when I had the
wood, there was no fire here to light it with. So I scraped stones
together. Stones! But I knew the spark was buried there inside—
and I did it, I made it shine out, bright! And that light is what
keeps me from death, still. When you get right down to it, that's
all a man really has to have: fire, and a place to live. No, that's
wrong. He needs one other thing: not to be sick as *I* am.—Wait,
boy, you haven't heard about my island. Listen! Oh, it's not a

place a traveller would even get close to of his own free will. You can see, there's no harbor. There's no profit to be turned here, no people to sell anything to or be friends with. No sensible man would come here. Of course, some *have* come. Sure! Without wanting to. That kind of thing might happen a lot in a man's whole lifetime. But not one of those who came, boy—Oh, they found words to say they felt sorry for me. Maybe I'm being unfair; maybe they even felt sorry, really, inside, and gave me a little food, or maybe a coat. But when it came down to *doing* something about the way they felt—I mean, even when I asked them to bring me home, safe, they. . . . It's been ten years now. Dying from hunger and misery, all the while feeding this sickness that eats me up and never has enough! Do you see—that's what Agamemnon and Menelaos and the great Odysseus did to me, son. May the Olympian gods grant that some day they pay for it![2]

CHORUS LEADER. What you said, Philoctetes, about the strangers who landed here—I think *I* feel sorry for you just as much as they did.

NEOPTOLEMOS. And I—even more, because, in a way you don't know, I'm a witness to the truth of what was done to you. You see, I've had some experience myself with the sons of Atreus and the great Odysseus. And their ways!

PHILOCTETES. How did they get to *you?* The bastards. What could they have done to make you feel some of my bitterness?

NEOPTOLEMOS. If there were only some way I could *do* something about what I feel inside, then Mycenae and Sparta would find out that little Skyros, too, is the mother of men! Men who aren't afraid to stand up for what they know is right.

PHILOCTETES. You *are* my son when you speak like that. Go on, tell me why you hate them so much.

NEOPTOLEMOS. It will be hard, but I'll tell *you* what they've done to humiliate me. You see, I didn't get to Troy until fate had come to take my father.

PHILOCTETES. Wait. Before you go on—Achilles? Dead?

NEOPTOLEMOS. Yes, he's dead. Killed.

2. Here Neoptolemos may give the prearranged signal to the chorus.

PHILOCTETES. Who . . .

NEOPTOLEMOS. It wasn't a man. No man could have killed him. It was a god. They say it was Apollo, with an arrow that only he would have known how to guide to its mark.

PHILOCTETES. What is death? A little thing, when he that killed and he that fell were both possessed of such nobility. I . . . you started to tell your story. It is hard for me not to hear you out, and hard, too, not to give in to the grief I feel for your father.

NEOPTOLEMOS. You have enough troubles yourself. Why grieve for those of the people near you?

PHILOCTETES. You put that very well. But please go on. No, go back and start again the story of how they insulted you.

NEOPTOLEMOS. They came to get me, in a ship all rigged out to *look* good. Two of them came, this "godlike" Odysseus and Phoinix, my father's old teacher. And what a story *they* had. I took it for truth, whether it was true or not. They said that, since my father was dead, it would be impossible for anyone but me to capture Troy. With that kind of argument, my friend, it didn't take them long. I could hardly wait to set sail. First, because I longed to see my father before they buried him. I never *had* seen him, you know. But there was also the chance that what they'd said about Troy—I mean, I can't deny I thought I might do what everybody else . . . capture Troy! Two days later I was there. The sea, the wind, everything seemed to push me on. A perfect crossing to Sigeion—how I hate the place! I had barely got off the ship when it seemed the whole army was around me, taking my hand, shouting greetings. I heard it over and over from all sides that I looked so much like my father that they thought it was him, alive again. He was there, all right, stretched out on the beach, dead. And—I just felt deserted. I stood by his funeral pyre, crying. Then, after a while, I searched for Agamemnon and Menelaos. Where else should I have turned? I *thought* they were my friends. I asked them for my father's armor and the rest. You know what they had the nerve to say to me, his own son? "You're welcome to take what belonged to your father," they said, "But the armor . . . another man already has it, the son of Laertes, Odysseus." I jumped up, my eyes full of tears.

I really felt the most terrible pain! "How did you dare," I said, "how did you have the nerve to give my armor to somebody else without waiting to find out what I had to say about it?" Then *he* spoke up, Odysseus. He was nearby somewhere. Men like him are never very far away. He said, "Yes, boy, they've given the armor to me. And it was only fair, since I was the one who brought it off the field. Safe. And your father's body, too. They gave the armor to me because I was there when it counted." I was so mad I began to lash at him with every insult I could think of. I didn't leave anything out. I was going to have them *hear,* at least, what kind of a man was going to have my armor for himself. And he took it, for a while, standing nearby. You know how cool he is. But the things he had to hear stung so deep that he answered me: "Away some place, weren't you," he said, "where you shouldn't have been, weren't you, while *I* was there? And now that you've had your say, I'll tell *you* something: there's not a chance you'll take the armor with you when you sail back to that Skyros of yours!" That's what I had to take, so now I'm going home, leaving what was mine by rights in the hands of that liar and son of a liar. But why blame him? The guilty ones are the ones in *command.* An army's just like a city or a country. It depends on its leaders. If the men in it do wrong, it's because that's what they're told and taught to do. That's all. I've told it. And may any man who's sick of the Atreidae be as much a friend to the gods as he is to me.[3]

STROPHE

CHORUS. Earth—
  You with your mountains
  You who feed us all
  Mother of Zeus himself
  Goddess whose power is over the great stream of Paktōlos and
    its gold
  We called to you then too
  When against this boy pressed all the arrogance of the Atreidae

---

3. Here Neoptolemos may give the prearranged signal to the chorus.

When they were handing over his inheritance from his father—
O hear us in your glory you who ride lions that kill wild bulls—
When his inheritance with all the respect that it should have
Was being handed over to the son of Laertes, Odysseus.

PHILOCTETES. You *are* friends! The signs of pain you show me seem
to match mine point for point. We sing the same bitter music,
so that I can see—all of this is the work of the Atreidae. And of
him, Odysseus. You don't have to tell me, because I know. He'd
do or say anything underhanded, if he thought it would help
him win out over some poor man in the end. That's no surprise, not to *me!* Except I am surprised that the others—men like
Ajax—would have stood for it. Where was Ajax? He must have
been there.

NEOPTOLEMOS. No, he wasn't. If he had been, they would never
have robbed me.

PHILOCTETES. What? Him too? Ajax? Dead?

NEOPTOLEMOS. You might as well accept it. For him the light has
gone.

PHILOCTETES. But men who shouldn't be alive at all—there's no way
for *them* to die. Not Diomedes or Odysseus, that bastard son of
Sisyphus, the old fox who outsmarted death itself.[4]

NEOPTOLEMOS. You can be sure of that. In fact, as things are now,
those two are the big men in the Greek camp. They're positively
flourishing!

PHILOCTETES. There's one more friend I'd like to hear about. One
more good man. He . . . back then, he *tried* at least to block that
crew. He understood what was right. Nestor of Pylos, what
of him?

NEOPTOLEMOS. He's alive. But things aren't going well for him, not
now. His son is gone, Antilochus, a son who stood by his father
to the last.

---

4. "The old fox who outsmarted death itself" has been added by the
translators. Sisyphus was well known to Athenian audiences as the arche-
type of the tricky deceiver. The most famous story about him told how he
cheated death itself. Many legends claimed that Sisyphus, not Laertes, was
the father of Odysseus.

PHILOCTETES. Ajax, Antilochus . . . I didn't think there was anything you could tell me that would hurt as much as . . . I'm not interested in hearing more, when those two are dead, while Odysseus is there—alive—

[PHILOCTETES *points toward Troy, which is also the direction in which* ODYSSEUS *is hiding.*]

where *he's* the one who should be a corpse, and not them.[5]

NEOPTOLEMOS. He knows all the tricks. Still it is true, isn't it, Philoctetes, that even a man as sharp as he is can trip himself up?

PHILOCTETES. Wait a minute! By all the gods where was Patroklos? There was no friend as close to your father—

NEOPTOLEMOS. Dead too. I can put it in a few words: war never takes away a worthless man, if it can help it. No, it's very careful to go after the good.

PHILOCTETES. I'm a witness to that, too. And it makes me think of a worthless character I'd like to find out about. *How* he could talk!

NEOPTOLEMOS. I told you Odysseus was alive, didn't I?

PHILOCTETES. Not him; someone else—Thersites. There was a man who could have said what he had to say and got it over with. No one was stopping him. But he wouldn't, he—

NEOPTOLEMOS. I didn't see him, but I heard he was still alive.

PHILOCTETES. Of course! Since nothing corrupt has ever yet been wrecked. The gods take good care of them. It looks as though they're *happy* when they can send any hard, two-faced fraud back from darkness and death: but the good, open men—they help them down. How can you make sense of it? Oh, it's easy to say that what the gods do is right, but, from what I see, they're wrong.

NEOPTOLEMOS. While you were talking I was thinking of home, out there in the sea, Philoctetes, across from Mount Oita, your

5. The translation is designed to render an ambiguity in the Greek, which can mean both a) Odysseus is alive when *he* should be dead, not the others, and b) Odysseus is actually here again when *he* should be called a corpse, not them.

father's mountain. From now on I . . . well, I'm going to be careful, that's all. Careful, anyway, to keep a long way between me
and the Atreidae and Troy. That's the place where the little men
are bigger than the brave, where the weak have power and what's
good dies. I've decided. Why should I try to get along with men
like that? Skyros and its rocks will be good enough for me. It
will be good to be home. I'm going now, back to the ship. And
you, Philoctetes, good-bye! Good-bye and good luck. I pray to
the gods to set you free from this disease. That's what you want.

[*to his men*] Let's go. We want to be set to push off the minute
the gods give us the right wind.

PHILOCTETES. You're not going, son!

NEOPTOLEMOS. Yes. If I'm out of sight, I'll miss the right time to
push off. I have to be right there.

PHILOCTETES. Please, my son, I beg you, in the name of your father,
your mother, of everything you love at home, of all that's sacred
to you, don't leave me *alone* like this! You've seen what I have
to live with here yourself; besides what I've told you. I know you
have other things to do, but spare me a passing thought anyway!
I know what you'll have to put up with if you take a cargo like
me. But, please, do it anyhow. Remember what we were saying
just now—that for men who are noble and true to themselves,
the enemy is dishonor. The real glory comes from doing what's
honorable and right. If you fail in this, you will take away from
here the kind of reputation a man like you wouldn't want. Take
me and the greatest glory will be yours—the memory of it will
never die, if I get home alive to the hills of Oita. Come, please—
it's just for one day. No, not even for a whole day. Just steel your
nerves and do it! Put me aboard any place you want, but take
me away! In the hold, the bow, back in the stern with you, where
there's least chance the others will mind. Say "Yes." In the name
of Zeus, Zeus who protects suppliants, say "Yes," son. Let me
persuade you. Look, here I am on my knees, though I'm lame
and can hardly do it. Don't leave me alone, where no human ever
sets foot. If you won't take me home with you, then get me safe to
Euboea, the island of Khalkōdon. From *there*, it's no great trip

for me to the sheep country of Mount Oita and the ridge of Trachis and the good river Spercheios. There you could show me to my father, though for a long time what I've been afraid of is that he's passed away and left me. You see, I sent for him, by everyone who's landed here, begging and pleading with him to save me and send me home by himself. So he must be dead, or else—yes, that must have been the reason: those others who were here, whom I asked to go to him for me, they didn't think what I asked for was important, so they hurried on home for themselves. But this time it's different. Because you won't have to take a message. You can take me yourself. Yes, *you*. Save me. Because you can feel sorry for me; because you can see—right here!—how nothing in life is certain or trustworthy. It can all change in a minute. The right thing is to be careful while you can. When life is good, that's exactly when you have to watch yourself the most, or you can be dragged down before you know what's happened.

ANTISTROPHE

CHORUS. —Sir—

—Have pity on him.

—Think about what struggles he's had, what hardships. I couldn't help thinking, sir when he was telling about himself, suppose the same thing happened to someone close to me—but the gods forbid.

CHORUS LEADER. Sir, if you hate the Atreidae as much as you say because of what you lost in their crooked business, I'd try to turn it to a profit. I'd go right where he longs to go. On a good swift ship.

CHORUS. —Take him home.

—That way we'd stay clear of the wrath of the gods that's bound to come.

NEOPTOLEMOS. Think what you've said. It's easy enough to stand here now and say you're ready. But when you've had your fill of being next to disease like this, you may have second thoughts.

CHORUS. —Not me!

—I'm not two-faced, whatever else.

—Never!

—No matter what happens, you won't be able to blame me for that.

NEOPTOLEMOS. Well, I wouldn't want our friend to think that *you* had what it takes to make a hard decision, while I didn't. So if the decision is made, let's put to sea. Have him come along quickly: my ship will take him. May the gods help us get out of here first, and then make it the rest of the way to where we want to go.

PHILOCTETES. This day is the sweetest of my life because of what you've done for me, *all* of you. If only there were something I could do to show you how grateful I am! Let's go, son, as soon as the two of us have prayed and humbly asked the blessing of this home here, if it can be called a home. Besides, you should see what I made do with, how I found the strength for it. I'm the only man, maybe, that could have. Just the look would have been enough to break another man's nerve. But for *me* there was no choice, so I learned, bit by bit, to get along, no matter how bad it was.

CHORUS. —Wait.

LEADER. Let's find out about this, sir.

CHORUS. —Two men.

—One of them from your ship.

—The other looks like a foreigner of some kind, sir.

—Headed right this way.

—Maybe you ought to find out what they have to say before you go in.

[*Enter* MERCHANT *with another* MAN.[6]]

MERCHANT. You must be the son of Achilles!—I thought so! I got this fellow to come along with me to show me where you were. He and two others were back at your ship, guarding it, the way

6. The Merchant is probably Odysseus. This would be obvious to Neoptolemos if the sailor with the Merchant were the Sentry who exited with Odysseus in the Prologue. It was this Sentry who was supposed to return disguised as a Merchant. If he reappears undisguised, the one in the disguise must be the master of deception, Odysseus.

I figure. Who would have thought it was *your* ship anchored there? Not me, I'll tell you. You don't know me. I'm just a business man, a trader—but I have my own ship. Not too big, but, well, you'll never guess. I was sailing from Troy for home— Peparēthos, just a little island, but it turns out the best wine in the world, I'll tell you, and it's not too far from where you come from.[7] Anyway, when I heard that all the sailors were with *you,* I just couldn't go on without coming right out and telling you something which I hoped you'd thank me for. My guess is you don't know anything about what's going on, even though you're the thing it's all about. Right? Well, I'm here to tell you. The Greeks have decided on new plans as far as you're concerned, not just plans either—deeds, being done right now! With no more delays—

NEOPTOLEMOS. Stranger, or should I say friend? I see the care and concern you have for me. And I *am* grateful; so unless I'm not who I think I am, I will remember what you've done. Go ahead, tell me exactly what you meant. The Greeks have a new plan and you know what it is?

MERCHANT. They're already following you with ships—I mean, the old man, Phoinix, and the Athenian leaders, the sons of Theseus.

NEOPTOLEMOS. Is their idea to take me back by force or to persuade me into it?

MERCHANT. I don't know. I can only say what I heard.

NEOPTOLEMOS. Can Phoinix and the men with him be working so hard to do a thing like that for the Atreidae?

MERCHANT. I'm here to tell you that's what's being done. You can count on it. *They*'re not stalling.

NEOPTOLEMOS. But I'd have thought that in something like this Odysseus would have seized the moment and sailed to speak for himself. Could it be that he hung back because he was afraid?

MERCHANT. Odysseus? How could Odysseus have come? When I put to sea, he and Diomedes were getting set to go after some other man.

7. "Just a little island" as well as "and it's not too far from where you come from" are added by the translators. The Athenian audience knew Peparēthos was a small island near Skyros.

NEOPTOLEMOS. Who? You mean there's someone Odysseus went
after by himself?

MERCHANT. Once there was a man. . . . First, tell me, who is this
man with you? Keep your voice down.

NEOPTOLEMOS. This, my friend, is someone you must have heard
about, Philoctetes!

MERCHANT. Look, don't ask me about the rest of it. For your own
good, get out of here as fast as you can. Put to sea—

PHILOCTETES. What's he talking about, son? Maybe this trader wants
to sell me out for a profit. What's this story he's telling as though
he had you in a dark corner?

NEOPTOLEMOS. I don't know yet *what* he means. But you're right—
whatever it is, he ought to bring it out into the light in front of
you and me and these men here, too.

MERCHANT. Oh, sir, you're Achilles' son. I'm just a poor man. You
won't get me in trouble with the army? I mean, if you told them
that I talked about things I shouldn't have, it would—well, I
mean the Atreidae have paid me back for anything I've done,
paid me well, too, considering I'm a poor man.

NEOPTOLEMOS. I consider the Atreidae my enemies. This man here
is my best friend, because he despises the Atreidae. If you're really
here to help *me,* then don't hide anything you've heard; speak
out in front of us all.

MERCHANT. Young man, you ought to think about what you're taking on.

NEOPTOLEMOS. I *have* been thinking about it.

MERCHANT. Oh? Then what happens will be your responsibility,
not mine.

NEOPTOLEMOS. Yes, it will. Now talk.

MERCHANT. I will. The two men I mentioned—Diomedes and the
great Odysseus—they sailed in pursuit of Philoctetes. They swore,
both of them, as I understand it, to bring him to Troy, either by
talking to him and persuading him or by sheer physical force.
All the Greeks standing around heard this plainly, from Odysseus. He was the one that did the talking. *He* had more nerve
than his partner for what they were going to do.

NEOPTOLEMOS. But why *this* man? It's been a long time. Why now
all of a sudden did the Atreidae start worrying about him?

They'd thrown him out, hadn't they? And gone along with it
for years and years? Don't tell me they suddenly just missed
him and wanted him back! Or was it they were forced by the
gods to make retribution for what they had done? Was it the
gods? Who makes men pay for the crimes they commit?

MERCHANT. Oh, maybe you didn't hear that part of it before. *I* can
explain it all. You see, there was a prophet—a man of noble birth,
one of Priam's sons, in fact, whose name was Helenos. One night
Odysseus—yes, Odysseus who's been called every dishonorable
and humiliating name—went out, all alone, and captured him
by a trick. He brought him back all tied up and showed him to
the army. That's quite a trophy to win by deceit. As I said, it
turned out this Helenos was a prophet and he talked. He told
them all he knew about the future and especially that they would
never capture Troy unless they talked to Philoctetes here and
persuaded him to come back from this island where he lives
now. When Odysseus heard the prophet say that, without a moment's hesitation he promised he would bring the man back and
show him to the army. He said he thought he would get Philoctetes to come definitely of his own free will; but, if he refused,
then against his will. And he said if he failed in *this,* he wanted
anybody who would to cut his head off. That's the whole story,
son. And if I can offer you some advice, you should take what
I say seriously. And work fast! For your own sake and anybody's
you care about.

PHILOCTETES. What else am I going to have to suffer? He swore, did
he? That befouling blight swore he'd *persuade* me to be shipped
back to Troy? There's about as much chance of that as of my
being "persuaded" to come back up into the light after I'm dead
in Hades, the way *his* father did.

MERCHANT. That may be. I don't know. But I do have to get back
to the ship. As for you two, may the gods be with you, and help
you do what is best.

[*Exit* MERCHANT *and other* MAN.]

PHILOCTETES. Did you hear that, son? What kind of a mind must
Odysseus have to make him think he could find words soothing
enough to bring *me* back in a ship and show me off in front of

the Greeks? No! I'd sooner listen to the enemy that *I* hate most, the snake that made me a cripple. But there isn't anything he wouldn't say, anything he wouldn't have the nerve for. And now I know why he's going to come. Let's move, son, while there's plenty of open sea between Odysseus' ship and us. Let's go. There's a right time to do things, remember, that you can miss if you don't move fast. Action now; afterwards, some sleep and rest.

NEOPTOLEMOS. But what about the wind? Now it's steady against our course. When it lets up, we'll—

PHILOCTETES. It's always good sailing when you're getting away from what's bad for you.

NEOPTOLEMOS. But—of course, the wind's against *them,* too.

PHILOCTETES. The wind's never against pirates when they're out to steal and grab something by force.

NEOPTOLEMOS. Well, if that's the decision, let's move—inside; isn't there anything inside you need and would especially like to keep?

PHILOCTETES. There *are* things I need, though it's not much to choose from.

NEOPTOLEMOS. What could there be that isn't on my ship?

PHILOCTETES. An herb I use for keeping this wound quiet; it puts it to sleep completely.

NEOPTOLEMOS. Bring it out. There's nothing else you really want?

PHILOCTETES. Maybe an arrow for this bow fell without my noticing. I wouldn't like to leave it for anyone else to take.

NEOPTOLEMOS. Is that the famous bow you're holding?

PHILOCTETES. Yes, this; in my hands.

NEOPTOLEMOS. Do you think I could look at it, from up close? Could I hold it in my hands? I would treat it . . . like a god.

PHILOCTETES. My son, *you* can. The bow will be yours and so will anything else of mine you need.

NEOPTOLEMOS. It will? Because I want . . . I mean, I want to, and I'd do it, if I were sure it's the right thing. If it's not—

PHILOCTETES. The gods love words like that, son. Yes, it *is* right, since who but you gave me the chance to see this day's brightness? Isn't it you who raised me up when I was buried by my enemies and put me beyond their reach? Don't worry—the bow will be yours to handle—

[NEOPTOLEMOS *touches the bow.*]

Between us to give and receive.

[PHILOCTETES *does not give up the bow, but takes it back.*]

You will be able to say you're the only human who's touched it; in return for doing something that took courage and will be long remembered. That's how *I* got it, too, you know. Because of what I did for someone else, when it was hard.

NEOPTOLEMOS. I'm glad I've seen you and have you as a friend. For to have as a friend someone who repays those who help him is better than having anything else in the world. Weren't you going inside?

PHILOCTETES. Yes. And I want you to come, too. This sickness needs to have you by me; for help.

[*Exit* PHILOCTETES *and* NEOPTOLEMOS *into the cave.*]

1st Strophe

CHORUS LEADER. I can't say I *saw* it, but I heard what happened long ago to someone who came close to the bed of a goddess, the wife of Zeus. The god of all power tied the man onto a whirling wheel and left him there.

CHORUS. —Yes, I remember.
—Except for him, there's no one I've ever heard of—much less seen—whose life turned out worse than this man's here.
—But Ixion, that other man, was a killer, and, as you said, came close to a goddess. This man never hurt anyone or took anything that wasn't his: a good, plain man who never looked for trouble.
—Just the same, he's lost and dying here. What did he do to deserve it?
—I keep thinking; how did he—?
—What?
—Alone, with no way to get away from the sound of the surf, pounding like that, everywhere. How did he—?
—He should have broken.
—How did he—keep on living?

1ST ANTISTROPHE

LEADER. In a place where there was no neighbor—no one to listen when he screamed even. Only an echo, an aching echo, with blood in it.

CHORUS. —No one but himself to go to when the hot gore in his wound started to run, and his foot felt like there was a savage animal trapped inside.

—No one to put it to sleep with some soothing herb, from the earth that gives us food to live.

—Stumbling when he walked, like a baby when its mother's not there—

—Going the only way he knew how to, to get what he had to have.

—Whenever that curse would let him go, whatever it is that eats away at his heart.

2ND STROPHE

LEADER. And his food? Not bread, like we have, that we owe to the earth, may she bless us. There wasn't any bread around for him to pick up, or anything else, either, that ordinary people sow and reap and eat.

CHORUS. —What he put in his stomach was only what he hit with that bow and those arrows, fast as birds.

—Is that living?

—To go ten years without the warm taste of wine?

—To find water, if he could, in any stagnant pool?

—That's what he had to drink.

2ND ANTISTROPHE

LEADER. But now that he's joined up with a boy from a great and famous family, his luck has changed. He'll be happy in the end. He'll have power and respect, instead of—

CHORUS. —This boy is taking him across the sea in a ship, after months and months, to his father's home and his grandfather's—

—To where the nymphs of Malis live.

—To the banks of the river Spercheios, where the man with the
  bronze shield, Herakles, came close up to the gods—
—Closer and closer, in the fire that the gods sent so that all could
  see—
—In that fire on the top of Mount Oita.

[PHILOCTETES *and* NEOPTOLEMOS *have emerged from the cave be-*
fore the end of the CHORUS' *stasimon.*]

NEOPTOLEMOS. Why have you stopped? You don't talk. You stand
  there, paralyzed.
PHILOCTETES. Ahh!
NEOPTOLEMOS. What is it?
PHILOCTETES. Nothing serious. Keep going, son.
NEOPTOLEMOS. Is it the sickness, again? You're not in pain?
PHILOCTETES. Me? No, not that. In fact, I just felt better. O gods!
NEOPTOLEMOS. You're moaning. Why call to the gods, if—?
PHILOCTETES. Only so they will come and be kind. They can save
  us. Ahh!
NEOPTOLEMOS. Something's happened to you. Why don't you say
  anything? Tell me! You look as though you're in serious trouble.
PHILOCTETES. I'm finished, son. I won't be able to hide it, not from
  any of you. Ahhh! There it is, right through me; right through!
  I can't stop it. I'm finished, son. It bites, it tears. Oh!—oh, oh, oh![8]
  In the name of the gods, son, if you have a sword ready, hit the
  end of my foot. Cut it away. Quick. Don't worry about killing
  me. Do it, boy!
NEOPTOLEMOS. What's happened all of a sudden? What could make
  your voice sound like that, so hopeless?
PHILOCTETES. Son, you know.
NEOPTOLEMOS. Tell me.
PHILOCTETES. You know, son.
NEOPTOLEMOS. What is it? I *don't* know.
PHILOCTETES. You do, you do! Oh, oh, oh!

8. From here to the end of Philoctetes' speech may be an interpolation,
since Philoctetes' reference to his foot would seem to make it impossible for
Neoptolemos to imply that he doesn't know why Philoctetes is in pain.

NEOPTOLEMOS. You're sick. It's awful how it crushes you.

PHILOCTETES. It does, yes. I can't even tell you how! Only, if you can pity me—

NEOPTOLEMOS. What should I do?

PHILOCTETES. Don't betray me out of fear. You see, this sickness only comes once in a while. It's been gone a long time. I guess it's had enough wandering. [PHILOCTETES *slumps*.]

NEOPTOLEMOS. Here! You *are* suffering! I see it. You've been through everything! Do you want me to take hold of you? Do you want me to touch you?

PHILOCTETES. Not that, no. But the bow—a minute ago you asked for it. Take it, but keep it safe, until this attack is over. It's close now; when the pain is worst, I'll fall asleep. Till then there's no stopping it; so while I'm sleeping—! By the gods, I beg you, don't turn the bow over to them, no matter what they do. They might have some smart plan—but don't let the bow go. Because you could kill us both. I'm helpless now, and depend on you.

NEOPTOLEMOS. Don't worry. I know what I'm doing. No one will have the bow except you and me. Hand it here. And good luck go with it.

PHILOCTETES. Here—take it, son. But humbly ask for the gods' blessing. The gods can be hard on us when we come so close to greatness. Pray the bow doesn't bring you misery; pray it doesn't do for you what it did for me and him who had it before me.

NEOPTOLEMOS [*praying*]. O gods, answer this prayer for both of us. May we sail with a fair wind and no problems to whatever place the gods think best and for which our plans are made.

PHILOCTETES. My boy, I'm afraid that in spite of your prayer, you won't get what you want. See? The blood is running again from deep inside. Something's going to happen. Oh, no! Ohh! I know what you're going to do to me, foot! Coming closer—close, close! Ohh, oh.

[*to the* CHORUS *as well as to* NEOPTOLEMOS]

Do you see what it's like? But don't leave me! Ai-eee! Odysseus, my friend, if only this pain were stabbing you—right through the chest! Ahhh! Ahhh! *Again!* Ahhh! And that pair of two-faced generals, Menelaos, Agamemnon. If only the two of you were feeling this sickness, instead of me, and for just as long a time. Ohh! Death, death! Here I ask for you day after day, but you can never come. O child, you *are* your father's son, you're brave and generous; take me, use the fire of Lemnos—

[PHILOCTETES *points to the volcano.*]

set me on fire. I'm begging you to do it. Remember what your family stands for. Didn't I do the same thing once myself?— when I decided to set fire to Herakles, in return for this bow, the bow *you're* keeping safe now. Will you, boy?—Will you? Won't you say something? What is it, son?

NEOPTOLEMOS. For a long time there's been nothing but pain for me, thinking about this trouble—and you.

PHILOCTETES. But, son, there's reason for hope, too. The sickness comes quickly and it goes away again, just as fast. Only please, don't leave me here alone.

NEOPTOLEMOS. Don't worry. We'll wait.

PHILOCTETES. You'll wait?

NEOPTOLEMOS. I mean what I say.

PHILOCTETES. Son, I won't ask you to take an *oath*.

NEOPTOLEMOS. There's no need. It's simply not possible for me to go without you.

PHILOCTETES. Give me your hand on it.

NEOPTOLEMOS. Here. I'll stay.

PHILOCTETES. Now! Take me there! There!

NEOPTOLEMOS. Where?

PHILOCTETES. Up!

NEOPTOLEMOS. Are you out of your mind again? Why are you staring at the sky?

PHILOCTETES. Let me, let me go!

NEOPTOLEMOS. Go where?

PHILOCTETES. Just let me go!

NEOPTOLEMOS. No, I won't.

PHILOCTETES. Take hold and you'll kill me.

NEOPTOLEMOS. There, I let you go. You know what you're saying, don't you?

PHILOCTETES. Earth, I'm dying. Take me and hold me. I can't stand
up, not any more. This evil thing won't let me.

NEOPTOLEMOS. I think he'll be sound asleep in a little while. There,
his head is drooping. And look, he's covered with sweat. There—
the vein has burst; the blood's pouring from his foot. Let's leave
him in peace, men, so he can go to sleep.

STROPHE

CHORUS LEADER. O god of sleep, you don't know bitter pain and
never will know it.

CHORUS. —Hear us, god of sleep, please; we pray to you.

LEADER. Lord, *your* life is happy and blessed.

CHORUS. —Please come, for us; be kind—

LEADER. His eyes are held in warmth and light. Keep him bound
in that peace, Lord.

CHORUS. —Healing god, we pray to you; please come.

LEADER [to NEOPTOLEMOS]. Son, please: think what to do now.
What worries me is what might happen. Do you see?

CHORUS. —Are we going to wait for—?
—Why?

LEADER. It's important to act, you know, when you have a chance.
In just a minute—if it's the right one—a man who grasps all the
consequences can gain great power.

NEOPTOLEMOS. Even if *he* can't hear anything, *I* can still see. And I
see this: We caught the bow in our trap. But it won't do any
good if we sail away without *him*. His is the glory of success;
he's the one the gods said to bring. I might find myself boasting
of what I'd done, when nothing had happened. Only my lies
would be left for the world to remember.

ANTISTROPHE

LEADER. The gods will look after that, son. But for now, you answer
me. And answer with just a word. That's enough; because sleep
isn't really sleep for the sick. It has eyes to see.

CHORUS. —Please. Take a long look as far as you can—

LEADER. Do you see how you can do "you-know-what" without his even knowing it's being done? But if you meant what you said about this man, it's just common sense that there's going to be trouble and no way out of it, either.

EPODE

CHORUS. —The wind is good, my son! The wind is with us!
—And the man has no eyes to see.
—What does *he* have on his side?
—For him stretched out there, it's dark night.
—Sleep is sound in this warm air.
—He has no control, not over anything, not his feet or his hands.
—In fact, it's as though he was dead, stretched out there.
LEADER. Do you see? Well? Are you missing your chance? Missing your only chance? I've been thinking, and I say the best way is the safest way.

NEOPTOLEMOS. Shhh! Watch. His eyes moved. He's lifting his head.
PHILOCTETES. I was asleep. What a wonderful light! Strangers, you did keep watch by me! I didn't think you would, my boy! I didn't think your pity would make you wait here to help. Those fine generals, the sons of Atreus, couldn't stand to do what you did. But you could, son, because you've grown up like your noble father. You decided it wasn't so hard, in spite of the sound and the smell. Well, it looks as though we can forget my troubles for a while, son, because they're over now. Will you lift me up yourself? *You* get me on my feet, son. We can start for the ship as soon as I feel a little better. Nothing should stop us from sailing.
NEOPTOLEMOS. Well, it *is* good to see you out of pain and still alive. I wasn't sure. The way things were going, it looked as though you were dead. Try to get up now. Or, if you'd like it better, the men will carry you. They won't mind, not when it's what you and I have decided together.
PHILOCTETES. Thank you, my son. Get me up any way you want. But there's no need for them to suffer from the smell before they have to. There'll be enough for them to put up with when we're together on the ship.

NEOPTOLEMOS. Yes, that's right. Here—try to stand. You get a grip, too.

[NEOPTOLEMOS *helps* PHILOCTETES *up.*]

PHILOCTETES. Don't worry. I'm used to it, you know, and that will get me up.

NEOPTOLEMOS. Oh God! And me? What's next for me?

PHILOCTETES. I don't follow, son. Where are you?

NEOPTOLEMOS. Where there's nothing more to say and no way out.

PHILOCTETES. For you? No way out of what? Don't say that, child.

NEOPTOLEMOS. But that's what's happened. That's where I am.

PHILOCTETES. It isn't my disease, is it? Is it so bad that you've changed your mind and won't take me aboard any more?

NEOPTOLEMOS. So bad? Everything's bad when you try to do what's against the way you were born to live.

PHILOCTETES. You? Against what you were born for? But you *are* your father's son, if what you do and say is helping a good man.

NEOPTOLEMOS. I know what they'll say about me; and that's what hurts.

PHILOCTETES. There's nothing wrong in what you're doing, but as for what you say—

NEOPTOLEMOS. O Zeus, what am I going to do? Go wrong a second time by hiding what I shouldn't, when I've already told a story I despise?

PHILOCTETES. Maybe *I'm* wrong, too—because I can't understand things, but doesn't this man act as if he's going to betray me and sail away leaving me here?

NEOPTOLEMOS. Leave you? I won't do that. But to make you go when you don't want to—that's what hurts me, and has for a long time.

PHILOCTETES. What can you mean, my son? I don't understand.

NEOPTOLEMOS. I won't hide anything from you. You have to sail to Troy where the others are, the whole army and the Atreidae.

PHILOCTETES. What did you say?

NEOPTOLEMOS. Don't be upset before you *do* understand.

PHILOCTETES. Understand? What are you going to do to me?

NEOPTOLEMOS. First, save you from this misery; and then go with you to defeat Troy.

PHILOCTETES. That's what you're going to do, in all sincerity?

NEOPTOLEMOS. It has to be. Listen, and don't you get mad, too.

PHILOCTETES. I'm betrayed, finished. What have you done to me, stranger. Give the bow back. Quick.

NEOPTOLEMOS. I can't. It's right for me to listen to those in command, and it's for my good, too.

PHILOCTETES. Fire! You're the fire, inhuman. You deceived me—a deliberate vicious lie. Look at me. Have you any sense of human decency? I asked for help, I begged. And you? The bow kept me alive. Now you've got it. Son, give it back, please. I beg you. I ask you in the name of the gods that your father honored, don't take my life away from me. No? He won't talk any more. That's his answer—to turn his head away as though he'll never let go of it.—There—coves and cliffs by the sea, animals I live with on the mountains, rocks worn down and broken: you're my old friends. You and I have been here together. I'll talk to you— there's no one else to listen. I'm going to cry out to you exactly what the boy's done, this son of Achilles. He's taking me to Troy, though he swore he'd take me home. He solemnly gave me his hand and took the bow, and now he's keeping it, the sacred bow, the bow of Herakles, son of Zeus. He wants to hold it out in front of the army as his own. And he's taking me there as if I'd fought against him with all my strength and he'd won. He doesn't see that he's caught a corpse, no more real than the shadow of smoke. If I had my strength—then he wouldn't have taken me, because even as it is, he had to do it by a trick! But I was a fool, and it worked. What can I do now? Give it back! Now! Be yourself again! Yes? You won't talk. It's over. My cave, you with two doors, I'm coming back to you without my weapons, without any way to get food to live. Inside, I'll dry up alone. Not birds, nor wild animals from the mountains will be killed by my bow. But me! And they'll feed on me as I once fed on them. I used to be the hunter; now they'll hunt me. With my own blood, I'll pay back blood—all because of someone who seemed so good!

I won't curse you yet; not till I find out if you're going to change. If you're not—curse you! Die!

CHORUS. What should we do? It's your decision now, sir, both as to us sailing and agreeing with what he said.

NEOPTOLEMOS. I'm sorry for him . . . sorry. And this isn't the first time. All along, I've felt—

PHILOCTETES. Act on what you feel, boy, in the name of the gods! If you take me by lies and deceit, can you blame people if they despise you?

NEOPTOLEMOS. Ohh. What should I do? If only I had never left Skyros! If only things were different—!

PHILOCTETES. You aren't evil. You must have learned this kind of thing from men who are. That must be why you came. But now, give others what by rights is theirs, and sail away. Let me have my bow.

NEOPTOLEMOS. Men, what should we do?

[ODYSSEUS *appears from his hiding place.*][9]

ODYSSEUS. Stop! That's the worst thing you could do. Let *me* have that bow. Step back.

PHILOCTETES. Who's this? The voice . . . Odysseus?

ODYSSEUS. Odysseus, without a doubt. You're looking right at him.

PHILOCTETES. Then I . . . I've been sold out! He's been behind this all the time; it was his hand that took away my bow.

ODYSSEUS. Without a doubt. We're agreed.

PHILOCTETES. Boy, give the bow back. Let me have it.

ODYSSEUS. Give it back? No, he'll never do that, not even if he wants to. And the fact is you'll come, too, right along with it. Or they'll force you.

PHILOCTETES. Me? You scum! You have the nerve to say they'll force me to go?

ODYSSEUS. Unless you do it of your own free will.

PHILOCTETES. You, earth of Lemnos. And you, fire of Hephaistos,

9. He is still wearing the merchant disguise. That, at least, is the implication of the words "Who's this? The voice . . . Odysseus?" which indicate that Odysseus is only recognizable by the sound of his voice.

with power over all, are you going to stand for him taking me away from you by force?

ODYSSEUS. You want to know who has the power here? It's Zeus! *He's* the one who made the decision. I just carry out his orders.

PHILOCTETES. No wonder people despise you! Excusing yourself with lies that make liars out of the gods.

ODYSSEUS. No. I'm making what they said come true. You must make this journey.

PHILOCTETES. No.

ODYSSEUS. Yes. You must obey.

PHILOCTETES [*groans*]. If that's so, then my father begot me to live in slavery, not freedom.

ODYSSEUS. No, he begot you to live like the best men there are—I mean the men with whom you must raze Troy to the ground.

PHILOCTETES. Never! No matter what happens to me! Not while I have this high mound of earth beneath me—

ODYSSEUS. What are you up to?

PHILOCTETES. In a moment this head will split on the rocks down there.

ODYSSEUS. *Grab* him. Don't give him the chance.

[PHILOCTETES *is seized and held by the arms.*]

PHILOCTETES. My hands! Do you see what happens to you when you've lost the bow-string that you love; when you're ambushed —by him!

[*to* ODYSSEUS] You! Is this all you ever do: *use* other people? and break them? Like now, playing on my hopes until you trapped me, all the while hiding behind this boy, whom I didn't know. He was too good for you, but just right for me. What did he know except to do what he was ordered to do? Now, see how he's suffering because of his mistake and what it's done to me. But you—with your scheme that only you could see through—step by step, you taught him, against his nature, how to be an expert in evil. And now me! You have the gall to tie me up and take me away from the very rock where you had me thrown in the first place, without friends or home, ban-

ished from the world, a corpse in the midst of life! Curse you!
How many times I've said that prayer, but it's no use. The gods
won't give me even one thing I want: here you are, alive and
glad of it, while *I* suffer, just because I *am* alive with all these
troubles, while you, gloating—you and those two-faced generals,
the Atreidae. And to think you're doing all this on their orders,
when *you* were the one who only sailed with them in the first
place because you were tricked and forced into it, but *I* went of
my own free will. With seven ships. And what did it get me?
They threw me out. That's your story; they say *you* did it.

[*to everyone*] And now you want to take me away? But why?
What good will it do you? *I*'m nothing. As far as all of you are
concerned, I could have been dead long ago.

[*to* ODYSSEUS] So why? The gods curse you! Am I not still a
cripple? Don't I still smell? If I come with you, can you set fire
to any sacrifices to the gods? Can you pour libations without
sacrilege? Those *were* the excuses you gave for getting rid of me.

[*to everyone*] Curse you all! Die. And you will die because of the
wrong you've done, if the gods care about justice. And I know
they care, because you would never have come for a man as
ruined as I am, unless there were some force from the gods
driving you.

[*He prays.*] But earth, you listen! You earth, where my fathers
lived. And you, gods on high who see what men do, punish them
all some day, no matter how long it takes, if you pity me. Let my
life go on as pitiful as it is; but still, if I could only see them destroyed, I'd think I was rid of my disease.

CHORUS LEADER. Odysseus, he's a hard man, and what he said—that
he won't give in, no matter what—that was hard, too.

ODYSSEUS. There's a lot I could say to answer him, if circumstances
would let me. But, for now, I can tell you just this one thing:
whatever I have to be, that is what I am. If what's called for is
honesty and nobility, you couldn't find anybody with more than
I have. But there's one thing I want absolutely above everything
else—to win. Except against you. For you, though it's not like
me, I'm going to stand aside.

[*to the men holding* PHILOCTETES] Go ahead; turn him loose, and don't touch him again. Let him stay here.

[*to* PHILOCTETES] We don't need *you,* not if we have the *bow.* Because there's somebody else who knows how to use it—Teucer, and he's with *us.* Besides, I think I'd be no worse a master of it than you, and no worse at using it either! So who needs you? Good-bye. Have a good time walking back and forth around your Lemnos.

[*to* NEOPTOLEMOS *and the* CHORUS] Everybody else, come on.

[*to* PHILOCTETES] And maybe the bow you were given for being so noble will bring me the glory that you were supposed to have.

PHILOCTETES. What? You mean *you* are going to use my bow at Troy?

ODYSSEUS. Don't waste your breath. I'm already on my way.

PHILOCTETES. And the son of Achilles? Are you leaving? Without another word?

ODYSSEUS [*to* NEOPTOLEMOS]. Keep moving. Don't even look, though you *are* so noble and generous. You might just spoil our good luck.

PHILOCTETES [*to* CHORUS]. And you, my friends? You too, are you going to leave me alone, without pity?

CHORUS LEADER. Our captain is this boy. We back up anything he tells you.

NEOPTOLEMOS. Well, I'll be called soft-hearted, but—stay here anyway, if that's what he wants; at least until the men on board get the ship ready and we've prayed to the gods. And maybe, before we go, he'll start thinking our way.

[*to* ODYSSEUS] Shall we go?

[*to* CHORUS] Men, when we call for you, come along quickly. Don't wait.

[*Exit* NEOPTOLEMOS *and* ODYSSEUS.]

1ST STROPHE

PHILOCTETES. So, my cave in the rocks—melting hot and cold as ice—so *this* was what was coming: I won't ever leave. I'm going to die here with you—so full with the pain I brought. What will happen to me as the days drag by, one after the other? What hope do I have for food to live?—Up there in the sky, where the winds shriek, the seabirds won't be afraid, not any more. They'll fly on. I can't stop them.

LEADER. But this is what you chose, isn't it?

CHORUS. —It's a hard, terrible thing, but you asked for it.

LEADER. What you have to face now is your own decision.

CHORUS. —Nobody's *forcing* you to stay here.

LEADER. Just now, you had your chance for a better life, and you chose a worse—

1ST ANTISTROPHE

PHILOCTETES. So—there's no hope. I've had to take so much I'm not even a human being any more. From now on I'll be alone; alone till the end. Aeee! Aeee! Never again to get food with my arrows—swift as birds themselves, my arrows! Never again to feel my hands on the bow—hands steady and sure! Words did this to me. How could I have known how treacherous they were or what a lying heart they came from?

LEADER. But the gods are the ones who did it, the gods! It's *their* work.

CHORUS. —Not mine.

—No.

LEADER. *I* didn't lie to you.

CHORUS. —So take that terrible, bitter curse and turn it against other people.

LEADER. Because the fact is I'm offering you friendship. Don't reject it; please—

2ND STROPHE

PHILOCTETES. *He* must be sitting there right now on the edge of the grey sea, laughing at me, waving the bow! The bow that kept me alive, the bow that no one ever held. Listen to me, my bow! They forced you out of my hands. How desperate you must be, if you have a heart and can feel, to know that I, the friend of Herakles, will never use you again; to belong to someone deceitful and two-faced! And what are you looking at now? Acts of despicable treachery? The face of a man I hate? A thousand schemes arising against me?

LEADER. Surely you will admit that it's right to talk about the good a man does, and to turn away if someone who won't admit it runs him down out of spite!

CHORUS. —After all, he only did what he was told.

—He followed orders, just like any other soldier.

LEADER. And it wasn't just for himself. He did it for the army, for everybody—

2ND ANTISTROPHE

PHILOCTETES. You birds that I hunted, you animals with your wild eyes, who find your food on the mountains, you'll never run away from me again. My hands have no weapon to make you afraid. I'm weak, helpless. There's no defense here, nothing to frighten you! Come on! Now's a good time to take blood for blood, to glut your mouths on my rotting flesh. My life will be over soon. What can I live on? Can anybody live just by breathing air, if he has no way to get any of the things that the earth gives us to live on?

LEADER. Please, in the name of the gods, if you have some respect for other human beings who are trying to be close to you and to help you—won't you see, won't you understand? It's up to *you!*

CHORUS. —You don't need to keep on struggling with death here.

—It's too pitiful! It's too hard!

—It's unendurable to try to live with death—

ASTROPHA

PHILOCTETES. Again! There, again! You won't let me forget the pain I've had so long. Nobody else who's come has been as good as you. Why did you destroy me? Why have you done this?

LEADER. What do you mean?

PHILOCTETES. If you—even *you* thought you'd take me to Troy, when I despise and loathe it—!

LEADER. But it's for the best.

PHILOCTETES. Leave me alone! Go on!

LEADER. That's just what I wanted to hear!

CHORUS. —That's the order we've been waiting for.
    —Come on! Let's go!

LEADER. To the ship, men. Every one to his place!

PHILOCTETES. No! Please! I beg you in the name of Zeus, who fulfills a man's curse!

LEADER. Easy now—

PHILOCTETES. Friends, stay! In the name of the gods!

LEADER. Well?

PHILOCTETES. Aeee! Aeee! This life, this life . . . What can I do?
    Foot! You—what will I do with you from now on?—Friends!
    Come back again!

LEADER. What for? You made your decision. Inhuman as it was, it
    was plain enough—

PHILOCTETES. Surely you won't hold against me what I say when
    I'm crazy. I can't think straight. The pain is pounding, pressing
    me—I panicked—

LEADER. Come on, then! Don't suffer. Do what we've been telling
    you to.

PHILOCTETES. Never. Never! That's final. Not even if the god of fire
    and lightning comes with thunder and burns me in flames! I'm
    finished with Troy and the men there, all of them who had the
    heart to throw out this crippled body, this foot!
    [*to* CHORUS] Friends, listen. Would you do me just one favor?

LEADER. What do you mean?

PHILOCTETES. If you have a sword some place, or an axe, or any
    weapon, would you give it to me?

LEADER. What's your plan?

PHILOCTETES. To hack it off—my head, my feet, everything! I can't
    think of anything else—to kill—!

LEADER. What?

PHILOCTETES. —and find my father.

LEADER. Where?

PHILOCTETES. Down. Among the dead. At least he's not in the *light*
    any more. Ah, my country, my father's country, if I could only
    see you! I must have been out of my mind, when I left your
    sacred stream and went to help the Greeks, my enemies! And
    what am I? I'm nothing!

LEADER [*to* PHILOCTETES]. *I'*d already be in my ship by now, except we could see that Odysseus was near, coming this way, to us; and the son of Achilles with him.

[PHILOCTETES *exits into the cave, as* NEOPTOLEMOS *and* ODYSSEUS *enter.*]

ODYSSEUS. What's your hurry? Would you be kind enough to tell me? It must be important.

NEOPTOLEMOS. I'm going to make up for the mistake I made before.

ODYSSEUS. That sounds serious. What mistake?

NEOPTOLEMOS. When I obeyed you and the whole army—

ODYSSEUS. What did you do that was so wrong for you?

NEOPTOLEMOS. I destroyed a man by a cheap, cynical trick. I lied.

ODYSSEUS. To whom? Wait! You're not going to ruin things, are you?

NEOPTOLEMOS. Ruin things? No. I'm going to Philoctetes and—

ODYSSEUS. And do what? I'm beginning to worry.

NEOPTOLEMOS. Go back to the man I took this bow from—

ODYSSEUS. O Zeus! You can't mean you want to give it back!

NEOPTOLEMOS. Yes. I got it by lies and I would be keeping it by lies.

ODYSSEUS. In the name of the gods, tell me, are you playing games with me?

NEOPTOLEMOS. If telling the truth is playing games—

ODYSSEUS. You're the son of Achilles. What kind of talk is this?

NEOPTOLEMOS. Do I have to repeat everything two or three times?

ODYSSEUS. I wish you hadn't said it even once.

NEOPTOLEMOS. Well, now you know. I've said all I'm going to.

ODYSSEUS. Someone will stop you from doing it—

NEOPTOLEMOS. Who?

ODYSSEUS. The whole army. And I'll be one of them.

NEOPTOLEMOS. You may be smart, but what you're saying isn't.

ODYSSEUS. And you? Neither what you say nor what you're trying to do makes any sense.

NEOPTOLEMOS. If I'm right, though—that's better than being smart.

ODYSSEUS. Right? How is it right to give back everything my plan has gained us?

NEOPTOLEMOS. It was contemptible. I'll try to make up for it.

ODYSSEUS. Aren't you afraid of what the army will do?

NEOPTOLEMOS. If I'm on the side of right and truth, you can't frighten me.

[ODYSSEUS *reaches for his sword.*]

And you can't *force* me to obey you, either.

ODYSSEUS. Is that so? You know we could fight *you* instead of the Trojans.

NEOPTOLEMOS. What is going to happen *will* happen.

ODYSSEUS. You can see my hand on my sword, can't you?

NEOPTOLEMOS. And you'll see mine there, too—just as fast.

ODYSSEUS. No—I'll let you alone. But I'll tell the whole army and they'll make you pay for it.

NEOPTOLEMOS. That makes more sense. Keep on like that and maybe you won't find yourself tripped up again.

[ODYSSEUS *exits.* NEOPTOLEMOS *calls into the cave.*]

Hallo! Philoctetes, do you hear? Come on out of your cave—

PHILOCTETES [*offstage*]. What's the yelling outside? What do you want me for? Do you need something, my friends? What is it?

[*He enters and sees* NEOPTOLEMOS.]

Ahhh! It's trouble.

[*to* CHORUS] Have you brought more misery to add to what I already have?

NEOPTOLEMOS. Don't worry. Listen to what I've come to say.

PHILOCTETES. I listened to you before and believed you. See what happened!

NEOPTOLEMOS. Isn't it possible to change—even to be sorry?

PHILOCTETES. That's just the way you talked when you were stealing my bow: so honest and sincere, and treacherous as death underneath!

NEOPTOLEMOS. But not *now!* I want you to tell me whether you're determined to stay here, or to sail with us.

PHILOCTETES. Stop. No more words. You're wasting your breath.

NEOPTOLEMOS. That's your decision?

PHILOCTETES. Yes, more than words can express.

NEOPTOLEMOS. Well, I hoped you might listen to what I had to say. And agree. But, if I haven't found the right way to talk to you, I'm through.

PHILOCTETES. I mean it. You'll waste your time. You'll never have me on your side, not after lying to me to get my bow. And after *that* you come and tell me where *I*'m wrong! Your father was the finest of men; you're the worst. Curse you all: first, the Atreidae; then Odysseus, and you.

NEOPTOLEMOS. No more curses. Here, in my hand—take the bow.

PHILOCTETES. What! Another trick?

NEOPTOLEMOS. No. I swear it. By all that is most sacred, by the power of Zeus that is over all.

PHILOCTETES. I . . . Those words are good, if they're true—

NEOPTOLEMOS. I'll prove it. Here, hold out your hand, take your bow again.

ODYSSEUS. And I say "No!" With gods as my witness: I forbid it in the name of the Atreidae and the whole of the army!

PHILOCTETES. Whose voice is that, son? Did I hear Odysseus?

ODYSSEUS. You did. I'm close by. Because I'm going to force you to go to Troy whether the son of Achilles agrees or not.

PHILOCTETES. You'll be sorry, if this bow works.

[PHILOCTETES *draws the bow, but* NEOPTOLEMOS *grabs his arm.*]

NEOPTOLEMOS. No! Don't. Don't shoot!

PHILOCTETES. Let me go. Please, son, let me—

NEOPTOLEMOS. How could I—

[ODYSSEUS *exits.* PHILOCTETES *groans.*]

PHILOCTETES. That's the enemy. Why didn't you let me shoot him?

NEOPTOLEMOS. That's not a good thing, either for you or for me.

PHILOCTETES. This proves one thing, anyhow; the leaders of the army, the liars they send out to talk for them—they're gutless when it comes to a fight; but when it's only a question of words, they're ready for anything.

NEOPTOLEMOS. Never mind. You *have* the bow. So now there's no reason to be angry or blame me.

PHILOCTETES. No, there isn't. You showed who you are, son. You proved your father wasn't Sisyphus, the liar, but Achilles the greatest man of us all when he was alive, and the greatest now, too, among the dead.

NEOPTOLEMOS. I'm glad to hear you praise my father. And me, too. But there's something I'd like to ask of you. Listen. Please! There are terrible things that we have to suffer because it's the gods' will. But if the troubles are our own choice, as *yours* are, then it's not right for other people to feel sorry for them. You've turned savage; you won't listen to anybody! Even when someone on your side tries to show you where you're wrong, you have nothing to do with him. You think he's your mortal enemy. But just the same, I'll try. I call on Zeus to be my witness. Try to understand what I'm saying. Write it deep so you can remember; your sickness and hurt come from the *gods*. You came close to the guard who protects Chrysē, the Golden One. Her sacred ground is uncovered and open, but the snake, who lives there with her, is covered over and secret. Listen: there will never be rest from the sickness that drags you down, so long as the sun rises there and goes back down again here, until you go, yourself, of your own free choice, to Troy; until you meet the two sons of Asklepios, who are with us there and who will heal your sickness; until with *me,* and with the bow, you conquer Troy. How do I know it? This time *I* will tell you: we have a prisoner from Troy, a famous prophet, Helenos, and he says that's how it must be. Exactly. And more than that: he says that the war will be over this summer, that Troy will fall. He's ready to stake his life that this is true. So now that you know, can't you agree, willingly? Remember what you're going to get, besides being chosen as the first man in the army: first, you'll be in the hands of those who can cure you; and second, when you conquer Troy—that source of so much sorrow, you'll have reached the highest glory of all.

PHILOCTETES. What good is living? Why am I still here? Why? Why not down with the dead in Hades? What to do . . . Can I refuse him, when he *is* on my side? Should I give way? And if I do, after all that's been done to me, can I go out into the light of day again in front of everyone? Who will I want to talk to? And my eyes, you've seen everything that's happened to me. Can you endure seeing me with those who ruined me, the Atreidae and Odysseus? It's not the pain of what's already happened that hurts; it's as though I could see ahead to what else they're going to do. Because once a man's mind brings evil into the world, it doesn't stop there; his mind tries to make the evil grow until it's perfect. And what about you? It's hard to believe you mean this. *You* should never go to Troy yourself and you ought to be trying to keep me away. Didn't they insult you and steal your father's armor?[10] Are those the men you want to fight beside? And you're pushing *me* to go there? No, son, no! Do what you swore you would; take me home. And *you* stay home, too; stay in Skyros. Let them go their own way to nothingness. Do it my way and you'll have twice as much gratitude from me and twice as much from my father: because you won't be helping evil men and you won't be like them, either.

NEOPTOLEMOS. What you're saying might be the best thing to do, I can see that. But even so, I'm asking you, please, trust in the gods; trust *me,* and sail away from here with me, because I'm your friend.

PHILOCTETES. You mean, with my foot like that, go to Troy in front of Agamemnon, my mortal enemy?

NEOPTOLEMOS. No, not enemies, men who will stop the infection, so you can walk, without pain. They'll make you well!

PHILOCTETES. Do you realize what you're telling me to do?

NEOPTOLEMOS. Only what I believe will be best for both of us.

PHILOCTETES. Can you really say that and not be afraid of what the gods think of you?

10. The manuscripts have at this point: "men who, in the judgement about your father's armor, decided poor Ajax was inferior to Odysseus." Most editors consider these lines an interpolation, because a) earlier in the play it has been established that Philoctetes knows nothing of recent events at Troy, except insofar as Neoptolemos tells him, and Neoptolemos does not tell him of this event; b) even if Philoctetes knew about the army's decision against Ajax, for him to mention it here would be hard to understand, since the implication of the event is that Ajax was as ready as Odysseus to accept Achilles' armor and thus to do an injustice to Neoptolemos, whereas Ajax earlier in the play, was defined as one of the just men at Troy, as opposed to Odysseus, Diomedes, and the Atreidae.

NEOPTOLEMOS. I can, yes; because there's nothing wrong with trying to help.

PHILOCTETES. You mean help the Atreidae—or me?

NEOPTOLEMOS. I think I'm your friend. That's what I'm saying.

PHILOCTETES. You? *My* friend? When you're ready to let my enemies get their hands on me and—

NEOPTOLEMOS. Can't you understand? Has your suffering made you so superior, so arrogant—

PHILOCTETES. If you keep on like this, you'll break me. I know it.

NEOPTOLEMOS. I'm not the one who'll break you. You *don't* understand—

PHILOCTETES. Don't I know that the Atreidae threw me out?

NEOPTOLEMOS. But now it's different. They're going to bring you back.

PHILOCTETES. Never! If you're saying I should go to Troy myself, of my own free will—

NEOPTOLEMOS. Then what? If nothing *I* can say makes any difference—nothing—Then I guess the best thing is for me to stop talking. And for you to live the way you do, with no cure.

PHILOCTETES. I'll have to take whatever's in store for me. You can't do anything about that. But what you promised when you touched my right hand—to send me home—please, son, keep your promise, and don't delay any more. Don't ever mention Troy again. I've cried and grieved enough.

NEOPTOLEMOS. If that's the decision, then let's be on our way!

PHILOCTETES. You *are* brave! You *are* true to your father.

NEOPTOLEMOS. So, steady. Try to walk with me.

PHILOCTETES. I will, as best I can.

NEOPTOLEMOS. What will I do when the army turns against me?

PHILOCTETES. Don't worry about that—

NEOPTOLEMOS. No? Suppose they destroy my home and country?

PHILOCTETES. I, beside you—

NEOPTOLEMOS. To help? How?

PHILOCTETES. With the bow of Herakles—

NEOPTOLEMOS. Yes?

PHILOCTETES. I won't let them get close to your home.

NEOPTOLEMOS. Then pray to the earth here for the last time. And start on the way.

[HERAKLES *appears on the rock where* ODYSSEUS *disappeared.*]

HERAKLES. Not yet on your way, not yet, Philoctetes.
  Not till you've listened to what *I* have to say.
  Yes, it is the voice of Herakles you hear.
  It is Herakles you see.
  For you, I've left Olympos and come here.
  I've come to tell you of what Zeus has planned.
  And to hold you back from the journey you've begun.
  Listen, do you hear? Listen to what I shall say.

First of all, you remember what happened to me, all the troubles that I had, and how I bore my suffering through to the end, when my courage was proved. As you see, the glory of it can never die. Well, you too—yes, *you* have to face your fate: accept your suffering and out of it leave a memory that will not die. Go with the man beside you. Go to Troy. There, first of all, you will be cured of the terrible sickness. And then, when you have been judged the best man of the army because of your courage, you will use my bow to take the life of Paris, who is to blame for this evil. You will conquer Troy and send the spoils, the army's prize of honor, back to your home, to your father, Poias, where he lives in your own country on the heights of Mount Oita. But any spoils that *you* receive from this army—bring them, as a tribute to my bow, up to my pyre.

[*to* NEOPTOLEMOS] Son of Achilles, I am speaking for you, too. For you cannot take Troy without him, nor he without you. The two of you are like a pair of lions that range the same plain, side by side. You must protect him, and you, Philoctetes, must guard him. I will send Asklepios to Troy to cure your sickness. For Troy must be taken a second time with my bow. But remember! Both of you! When you've conquered, when the earth is yours, respect what belongs to the gods. Everything else comes second to this in the eyes of Zeus, the father; second to that respect which does not die with men. What they do well in their lives lives on. It cannot end.

PHILOCTETES. How I've longed to hear your voice! You *have* spoken to me. You *have* come, at last. I believe what you say. I won't refuse.

NEOPTOLEMOS. And this is the way *I* want it to be.

HERAKLES. Then don't wait. Go and do it. This is the time. This is the wind, blowing astern, pushing you on.

PHILOCTETES. Then let me say good-bye, as I start on my way. Good-bye, my house. You and I kept our watch together. Good-bye, you nymphs who live in the streams and the meadows. Good-bye, you deep, strong roar of the surf. And you, rocky cliff, where so many times I felt the rain hit my face, even in the dark of my cave, when the storm winds blew. So many times the mountain of Hermes sent the echo back to me when I cried out in wild storms of pain. Good-bye now, you springs of clear water I drank. I'm leaving you. I'm leaving you now for good, though I never thought it could be. Good-bye, Lemnos, here in the middle of the sea. Grant me fair winds and a smooth course to where the great goddess, Fate, brings me—where my friends would take me, and where the god who subdues all things has ruled that I must go.

CHORUS. Let's go, yes, all together—and pray to the sea-nymphs to bring us home safe.

[*They all exit.*][11]

11. An alternative final stage direction is:
     [NEOPTOLEMOS, PHILOCTETES, *and* CHORUS *exit.*
     ODYSSEUS *takes off the mask of* HERAKLES *and smiles.*]
This view of the play, while not accepted by most scholars, meets with the approval of others and has much to commend it. The translators believe it to be correct.

EURIPIDES

Andromache

TRANSLATED BY
JENE A. LARUE

INTRODUCTORY NOTE

The *Andromache* is one of several Greek tragedies concerned with the psychology of women and marriage. In this case, the husband is absent. The two rivals for his affections confront each other and themselves in a series of desperate and character-revealing situations. Various men are no less pungently and specifically drawn. The plot brilliantly supports this interest in character portrayal, but has occasioned the charge of lacking unity. In fact, there is one climax a little past mid-point. But whether the play's effectiveness suffers from this apparent division into two parts is arguable.

Ancient sources claimed the *Andromache* was not produced in Athens. This could be true, since no accurate information is available as to date of production, success in competition for prizes, or position in a tetralogy. The play's anti-Spartan tone leads many scholars to believe it was written during the 420s and produced outside Athens, possibly in Argos.

CHARACTERS

ANDROMACHE

NURSE

CHORUS of Phthian Women

HERMIONE, wife of Neoptolemos

MENELAOS, king of Sparta, father of HERMIONE

CHILD, son of ANDROMACHE and Neoptolemos

PELEUS, father of Achilles

SERVANT of HERMIONE

ORESTES, son of Agamemnon

MESSENGER

THETIS, goddess, wife of PELEUS

Various attendants

Andromache

THE SCENE. *Achilles' district of Phthia in Thessaly.* ANDROMACHE *is a suppliant at the shrine of the goddess* THETIS, *which is near the home of Neoptolemos, Achilles' son.*

ANDROMACHE. From the city of Thebes, Splendor of Asia,
  With all the golden glitter of my dowry
  I came long ago to the royal hearth of Priam,
  Given as wife to Hector to bear him children.
  My name is Andromache,
  An object of envy in former times,
  But now, if anyone deserves the title,
  Call me the most unhappy woman on earth.
  I looked upon my husband dead at Achilles' hands
  And saw the child I bore him, Astyanax,
  Hurled down from the steep towers of the city,
  When the Greeks captured the land of Troy.
  From what was once the freest home of all
  I now have come to Greece to be treated like a slave,
  A spear-prize for Neoptolemos, the islander,
  His choice selection from the Trojan spoil.
  Now these lands which border Phthia and the city of Pharsalia
  I call my home, where Thetis, goddess of the sea,
  Lived once with Peleus apart from men,
  Shunning the crowd. Because of the goddess' marriage
  The people of Thessaly call this place "Temple of Thetis."
  Here the son of Achilles has his home,
  And allows old Peleus to rule this Pharsalian land,
  Not wanting to take the scepter while the old man lives.
  And I, lying with Achilles' son, my master,

Have born a male child into this house.
My lot was hard enough before,
But I always held the hope that my son, if he lived,
Could offer me protection and defense against destruction.
But since my master, disdaining the bed of a slave,
Has taken the Spartan Hermione in marriage,
I'm driven mercilessly by troubles at her hands.
That woman claims that by some secret drugs
I've made her childless and hateful to her husband,
She claims I want to take her place inside
By forcing her out of that very bed
Which I did not willingly accept in the first place
And now I've left forever. Great Zeus knows
I shared this bed against my will.
But all my words are useless. She intends to kill me
And her father Menelaos assists her plans.
Even now he's in the house—
Just come from Sparta for this very purpose.
In fear I have come as a suppliant to this nearby shrine
Of Thetis in hope she might prevent my death.
For Peleus and his descendants respect this shrine,
As a monument to the sea-nymph's marriage.
My only child I've sent away in secrecy
Into another house for fear he may be killed
Because his father is not here to help.
He's off at Delphoi paying the penalty
For his former rashness against the Loxian god;
When once he went to Pytho and demanded
That the god must pay for murdering his father.
He's gone to beg forgiveness of his faults
And render the god more kindly in the future.
NURSE. Mistress—for I do not fear to use that name
　　Since that is what I judge it right to call you.
　　At home, when we dwelled in the plain of Troy,
　　I loved you then and your late husband—
　　And now I come with news, although I am
　　Afraid one of our masters will notice me,
　　But yet I pity you. Terrible plots

Menelaos and his child have set against you.
You must be on your guard!
ANDROMACHE. Dearest sister slave—for that is what you are—
You address a former queen, who now is ruined.
What are they doing? What plots do they weave
In their determination to kill me, helpless as I am?
NURSE. Unhappy woman, they intend to kill
The child you sent away in secrecy.
ANDROMACHE. Oh no! She learned my son was sent away?
Where did she find out? Unhappy me, I'm ruined.
NURSE. I don't know how. I got the news from them.
Menelaos has left the house to get him.
ANDROMACHE. I'm done for! My baby, those two vultures will
Kill you, while your so-called father is off at Delphoi.
NURSE. If only he were here, it wouldn't be so bad,
But now you're lost and without friends.
ANDROMACHE. And is there no report of Peleus' arrival?
NURSE. He's too old to help, even if he were here.
ANDROMACHE. And yet I've sent for him far more than once.
NURSE. And do you think the messengers will pay you any heed?
ANDROMACHE. Why should they? Are you willing to be my
messenger?
NURSE. What shall I say, after I'm gone so long?
ANDROMACHE. You're a woman. You will find a way.
NURSE. It's dangerous. Hermione is not a stupid guard.
ANDROMACHE. You see? Renounce your friends when they're in
trouble.
NURSE. That's not true. Don't reproach me with that.
I'm going, no matter what I suffer.
My life is not worth saving, for I am but a woman and a slave.
ANDROMACHE. Go then,
While I in anguish reach the heights of heaven
With the lamentation, groans, and tears which are my lot.
Inborn in every woman is some strange pleasure
To have her sorrows on her lips without relief.
And my luck is to lament not one, but many:
The city of my father and Hector killed,
The stubborn fate to which I'm yoked,

Having fallen into slavery undeservedly.
You should not say that any man is truly happy
Before you've seen the final day of death,
And how he passed it on his way from earth.

No marriage did Paris lead to lofty Ilion, but doom,
 When he brought lovely Helen to share his marriage bed.
On her account, oh captive Troy, swift Ares
 With a thousand ships from Greece levelled you with spear
  and flame,
And my poor husband Hector about the walls of Troy
 Was dragged behind the chariot of sea-born Thetis' son,
And I was led from my bedroom down to the shore of the sea,
 With the hateful veil of slavery cast upon my head.
Many were the tears that ran down my cheek, when I left
 Behind my city and chambers and husband in the dust.
Ah poor unhappy me! Why must I still behold the light of day
 As the slave of Hermione? Worn out by her oppression
I've come as a suppliant to this statue of goddess Thetis.
 Like a gushing spring among the rocks I melt away in tears.

[*Enter* CHORUS.]

1st STROPHE

CHORUS. Oh lady, you who sit a suppliant at Thetis' chamber and
 shrine,
  and never leave this place.
Phthian though I am, I come to you, an Asian,
  if only I might
Discover some cure for these harsh troubles,
which have enclosed Hermione and you in hateful strife.
  Unhappy girl who share
  A double bed with Achilles' son.

1st ANTISTROPHE

Know your lot. Consider the unhappy state to which you have
 fallen.
  A girl from Ilion,

You do not hope to strive with those of Spartan birth?
    Leave the guest-receiving
House of Thetis, goddess of the sea.
What good does it do you to waste away in your unhappiness
    At the insistence of your masters?
Their power overtakes you. Why struggle in vain,
    When you are nothing?

2ND STROPHE

But come now. Please leave this bright and splendid temple of
    Thetis.
    Think! You're only a slave
      in a foreign land
        Without a single friend,
You miserable, helpless girl.

2ND ANTISTROPHE

Woman from Ilion, you're the sorriest sight
    To come to my master's house.
Yet I keep silent from fear,
    Although I pity you,
That the child of Zeus' daughter may notice my sympathy
    for you.

[*Enter* HERMIONE.]

HERMIONE. I come with golden splendor on my head,
    With luxury of dappled gowns to grace my skin,
    Not from Achilles nor from Peleus
    Do I hold these gifts, but from the Spartan land.
    My father Menelaos gave me these,
    Along with many other gifts.
    So I am free to speak my mind
    And answer all of you as I wish. But you,
    You're just a slave, a woman taken by the spear,
    And yet you hope to force me out, and take my place.
    Your drugs have made me hateful to my husband.
    Because of you my womb will bear no child.

You Asians are good at just such tricks,
But I'll put a stop to your dirty plans.
And this house of Thetis won't help you then
With all its shrines and altars. Soon you'll die.
If any god or mortal wants to save you,
You must forget those lofty thoughts of yours
And bow to me! Then sweep my house, and wash
My floors with Acheloos' water from my golden pails.
Learn where you are! There is no Hector here,
No Priam with his gold. This is a Greek city!
You scum! You sank so low you had the cheek
To sleep with the son of the very man who killed
Your husband, and even bear him children.
That's what it is to be a foreigner.
Father and daughter, son and mother,
Brother and sister, all sleeping together.
And murder makes it possible. No law against it.
Don't bring your filthy customs into our land.
It's not proper for a man to have two wives.
A man who wishes to avoid domestic trouble
Loves one woman and keeps his eyes on her alone.

CHORUS. A spiteful thing is a woman's mind,
And particularly hostile to a rival wife.

ANDROMACHE. Ahh!
What good is youth for humankind,
When in the young there is no love of justice?
I fear my slave's condition will hinder me
From speaking out my thoughts, although I'm right.
On the other hand, if I should win, I'd pay for my victory,
    I'm afraid.
The high and mighty have no use for better
Arguments, which come from lesser folk,
But all the same I don't intend to betray myself.
Tell me, young girl, for what good reason
Would I prevent you from your rightful marriage?
Because I think Sparta less than Troy?

Is Troy's luck better? Is it a free woman you see?
Or is it my youth and fine figure,
The greatness of my city and trusty friends,
Which prompt me to usurp your place?
Or that I might bear sons instead of you—
So they'll be slaves and weights around my neck?
Or will anyone endure my children as kings of Phthia,
If you fail to generate an heir?
Or do the Greeks love me for Hector's sake—
And was I unknown in Troy, and not a queen?
No drugs of mine have made your husband hate you;
It's simply that you're not fit to live with.
Here's a love charm too: it is not beauty, my girl,
But our good behavior which charms our bed-fellows.
If you are irritated in any way, Sparta is an important thing,
Skyros, your husband's home, means nothing to you.
You flaunt your wealth. As far as you're concerned
Menelaos is greater than Achilles. That's why your husband
   hates you.
A woman ought to love her husband, not strive
With him, even if he is a worthless sort.
If you married a king in snowy Thrace up north
Where one man shares his bed with countless women,
What would you do? Kill them all?
You'd simply show how sex-starved women are.
It's disgusting! Though our disease is worse than that
Of men, but we attempt to cover it.

Oh dearest Hector, for your sake I even
Loved your concubines, when Kypris got the best of you.
And to your bastard children I often gave
My breast in order not to cause you grief.
He approved, and loved me for this good behavior.
But you're afraid to let your man outside—
You won't permit a drop of dew to touch him!
Helen loved her man as much—didn't she?

Won't pay to follow your mother's example, my dear,
Sensible children ought to avoid a mother's bad habits.
CHORUS. My lady, so far as is in your power,
Please heed my prayer and come to an understanding.
HERMIONE. What are all these haughty words and arguments?
You think you're virtuous, but I am not?
ANDROMACHE. No, you're not, so far as your present argument is
concerned.
HERMIONE. I hope I never share your point of view.
ANDROMACHE. So young and yet you speak so shamelessly.
HERMIONE. But you don't merely talk. You do your best against me.
ANDROMACHE. Can't you bear the pangs of love in silence?
HERMIONE. Why? Isn't love the most important thing for women?
ANDROMACHE. When they love honestly; if not, it's bad.
HERMIONE. We don't follow your barbarian customs here.
ANDROMACHE. No matter. Here or there—shameful deeds bring
shame.
HERMIONE. You're pretty sharp. But you'll perish all the same.
ANDROMACHE. Don't you see this statue of Thetis looking down
on you?
HERMIONE. Yes,
She hates your land because of Achilles' death.
ANDROMACHE. That mother of yours, Helen, killed him, not I.
HERMIONE. You still attempt to aggravate my wounds?
ANDROMACHE. All right. I'm silent and I stop my mouth.
HERMIONE. Just tell me one thing for which I came.
ANDROMACHE. I'll only say your mind is not what it should be.
HERMIONE. Do you intend to leave this holy shrine of Thetis?
ANDROMACHE. If you grant an amnesty; otherwise I'll never move.
HERMIONE. It's settled, and I'm not going to wait until my
husband comes.
ANDROMACHE. And I'm not going to hand myself over to you
before he does.
HERMIONE. I'll burn you out. So much for you.
ANDROMACHE. Go ahead and burn. The gods will notice this.
HERMIONE. I'll tear apart your flesh with savage wounds.

ANDROMACHE. Kill! Bloody the altar of the goddess. She'll
    remember you!
HERMIONE. You savage, you, so bold of heart,
    You'll wait out even death? I'll drive you out
    From your seat soon enough, and you'll go willingly.
    I've got just the bait for you. But that's enough of talk,
    The deed itself will show you soon enough.
    Just sit tight, my girl, for even if hot lead
    Welded you in place, I'll pry you loose before
    Achilles' son, in whom you trust, will come.
ANDROMACHE. I trust in him—how strange that god has found
    For mortals the cure for every creeping beast.
    But as for that which is far worse than any
    Snake or fire—no one has found a cure for an evil woman.
    What a curse we are for men on earth!

1st Strophe

CHORUS. That was the first beginning of our great troubles, when to
    the vale of Ida came
    Hermes, son of Zeus and Maia,
    Leading a chariot with three
    Goddesses—heaven's fairest,
    All fitted out for struggle in a contest of beauty
            Beside a herdsman's hut.
    A young shepherd was there alone,
            A fire and a
            Lonely camp.

1st Antistrophe

When the goddesses reached the vale enclosed by lofty trees,
        In mountain streams they washed
        Their bright and gleaming bodies.
        And vying with one another in extravagant promises
They next drew near the son of Priam,
Straining to persuade. The Cyprian won with words of guile.
        Sweet they were perhaps,

But bitter ruin they brought on Troy,
      Poor Troy,
And all her lofty towers.

2ND STROPHE

Would that his mother had cast this
   Evil, Paris, over her head
         Before he
      Settled Ida's rock,
When next to the prophetic laurel
Kassandra shouted out to kill him,
The great instrument of ruin for Priam's land.
Every elder, every man, she approached and begged
      To kill the helpless child.

2ND ANTISTROPHE

If she had won her way, then on the Trojan women
      Would be no yoke of slavery,
         My lady,
      As queen you'd rule your home.
Hellas would not have loosed the woes of war
      About the dusty plain of Troy,
Or young spearsmen roamed for ten long years.
Our beds would not be empty of our husbands,
      Nor old men
      Orphaned of their children.

[*Enter* MENELAOS.]

MENELAOS. I've come with the child you've sent away into
   Another house without my daughter's knowledge.
   So you were sure this statue was going to save you
   And those who hid the boy? But it's all up now.
   You're not as smart as Menelaos is, woman.
   If you don't vacate this place immediately,
   The boy will die instead of you.
   Just think on that.

Do you want to die or let the boy perish
For the wrong you did me and my child?
ANDROMACHE. Oh reputation, reputation! You've puffed up
  A thousand puny men and made them think they're great.
  Those men who have an honest reputation
  I'll gladly praise; but the shams who have only luck,
  I hold them next to nothing—they're only made of chance.
  So you're the mighty general of all those Greeks
  Who took Troy away from Priam—you worthless scum!
  Do you take on these airs for your little baby girl
  And pick a fight with a common slave?
  You weren't worthy of the trip to Troy,
  Nor did Troy deserve a thing like you.
  (The famous men are those who seem to be so good,
  But on the inside they're just like everybody else.
  Unless they're wealthy. Wealth, you know, is power.)[1]
  Come, Menelaos, let's finish our discussion.
  Suppose I'm dead and your daughter is to blame.
  Do you think she could avoid the taint of blood?
  And in the common eye you would share her guilt.
  As an accomplice you would be forced to do so.
  But if I escape death, you'll kill my only child?
  You think his father will submit to that?
  At Troy he wasn't known as such a coward.
  He'll go where he must; you'll see his deeds
  Are worthy of old Peleus and his father Achilles.
  He'll run your daughter right out of the house.
  Then what will your story be to find her another man?
  You'll claim her virtue couldn't stand a vicious husband?
  She'll soon be known for what she is. Then who will marry her?
  Or will you keep her without a husband in your home
  Until she's grey and wrinkled? You wretched man!
  Don't you see the flood of grief you'll cause yourself?
  Wouldn't you prefer to let the girl be cheated

---

1. The lines in parentheses are possibly an interpolation.

A thousand times than suffer all this grief?
You really shouldn't add big problems to small,
Nor, if we women are a worthless lot,
Should you drag down men to match our level.
For if, in truth, I charmed your child with drugs
And blocked her womb from childbirth, as she claims,
I'm quite prepared to quit my sanctuary
And stand trial willingly before your son-in-law
In whose eyes I'm no less guilty, if I made her childless.
That's my account. But I fear one thing alone—
Your penchant for fighting over women;
For a woman too you wasted pitiful Troy.

CHORUS. That's enough. You talk too much for a woman.
Have you too completely lost your senses?

MENELAOS. Woman, these matters are petty, as you say,
Concerns unworthy of my reign and Greece.
But don't forget that whatever someone wants
Is more significant for him than any sack of Troy.
To be defrauded of a marriage bed is no small concern,
And so I stand an ally to my daughter.
Whatever other sorrows a woman might bear take second place,
But if she's lost her husband, she's lost her life.
I don't mind if my son-in-law orders about my slaves
And thus I claim the right to order his about.
Among friends—real friends—there is nothing private,
But all their goods are held in common.
While I await my men, I'd be a stupid fool,
If I didn't look out for my own best interests.
Well—
Get up and out of the goddess' shrine.
If you are willing to die, the child escapes his fate,
If you're not, then he dies by my hand.
One of you must leave the light of day.

ANDROMACHE. Ahhh!
This is a bitter choice you've given me—
No matter what I choose my fate is wretchedness.
Oh you who do great wrongs for no great cause,

Hear me. Why kill me? For what good reason?
What city have I betrayed? What children of yours have I
    killed?
Whose home have I burned down? I was forced to my master's
    bed.
Why not kill him? He's to blame, not I.
You disregard the cause and push the blame on me.
These awful sorrows, my poor unhappy fatherland,
What troubles I endure. Why did I have to bear children
To add another burden to the one I bear?
When there's trouble enough at hand?
I saw the bloody death of noble Hector,
Dragged in the dirt behind Achilles' chariot,
And I was witness to the pitiful burning of Ilion.
And as a slave I embarked upon an Argive ship—
Dragged by the hair. Then when I came
To Phthia, I married Hector's murderers.
What's left in life that's sweet? What should I consider—
My present woes or the sorrows of the past?
This one dear child was the very light of my life,
Whom now these men intend to kill.
Oh no! Not for me—not to save my petty life.
There is some hope in him, if he can live.
But for me not to die on his behalf would be disgraceful.
Now look. I leave this altar. I'm yours
For slaughter, butchering or garroting.
My child, the mother who bore you goes down to Hades
So you might live. If you escape your fate,
Remember me, your mother, and what I suffered.
Go to your father and cover him with kisses.
Weeping and embracing him, tell him what I've done.
For all men their children are the very soul of life.
The childless ones may well be scornful;
They suffer less, but their happiness is a paltry one.
CHORUS. I pity you as I listen. For all mortals
    Such burdens are cause for tears, even if they're not our own.
    Menelaos, you should reconcile your daughter

To this woman, and free her from distress.
MENELAOS. Men! Seize the woman. Throw your arms around her.
  She won't think my words are nice.
  In order to coax you from the holy altar
  I held before you the threat of your son's death
  And lured you into my hands for slaughter.
  Perhaps now you realize your situation.
  As for the child, my daughter will decide
  Whether to kill him or let him live.
  Now get inside the house. Since you're a slave,
  You must learn not to insult free folk.
ANDROMACHE. Oh no! You've tricked me. I'm betrayed.
MENELAOS. Tell it to everyone. I won't deny it.
ANDROMACHE. Is this considered wisdom back in Sparta?
MENELAOS. At Troy too. Eye for eye, and tooth for tooth!
ANDROMACHE. Do you think there are no gods to punish you?
MENELAOS. I'll think about that when the time comes. You die first.
ANDROMACHE [*indicating her son*]. And this little bird, snatched
    from under my wing?
MENELAOS. Not my concern. My daughter can kill him, if she likes.
ANDROMACHE. Ah no! Then you're as good as dead, my child.
MENELAOS. I wouldn't say his expectations are too good.
ANDROMACHE. Oh you Spartans, hateful to all men,
  With your deceitful counsels,
  You masters of lies, crafty schemers,
  You twisted, sick contortionists,
  Who think in circles all the time,
  How unjustly you win your fame in Greece!
  What are you noted for? A thousand dirty murders?
  And what about your sordid greed for money? You say
  One thing, but hide another in your minds.
  Damn you all! Death is not so hard on me
  As you may think. For I lost my life
  On that very day unhappy Troy was wasted,
  And my great husband Hector, who often sent
  You running back to the safety of your ship like the coward
    that you are.

But now against a woman you become a frightening warrior.
Well go ahead and kill me! But you and she
Will feel the sharpness of my tongue before I go.
So you're the one who rules in Sparta now?
Well I had my day at Troy. And if you think I'm badly off,
Don't feel too proud because you could get yours!

[*Exit* ANDROMACHE, MENELAOS, *and* CHILD.]

1ST STROPHE

CHORUS. Oh, I shall never praise a double set of beds for men
     nor children springing from two wives.
Strife and grief are what they bring into the home.
In marriage let a man love one bed only
     and share it
   not with other women.

1ST ANTISTROPHE

Nor in our cities is a double set of rulers
     better than a single prince.
More than one bring plague on plague and discord to the state.
     Even when two men work together on a single song
    the Muses love
   to bring on strife.

2ND STROPHE

Or when the swift winds are tossing sailors all about,
Two minds in conference above the rudder are less than one,
And a multitude of wise men are far weaker than
    A simple brain which is in complete control
All power belongs in a single hand at home,
And in the state, whenever there is need
   to find success.

2ND ANTISTROPHE

This Spartan girl, daughter of Menelaos, has showed
that well enough. She's breathing fire against this second wife

She's killing this wretched girl from Troy
and her baby too—all from hateful strife.
It's a godless, lawless, spiteful crime!
But still, my queen, the time of retribution will come
for these deeds of yours.

And now I see
This pair closely tied coming from the house
Under the sentence of death.
You, poor woman, and you, unhappy child,
Who die for the sake of your mother's marriages,
Though you're not to blame
And no cause of this trouble to the kings.

Strophe

ANDROMACHE. Look at these hands
All bloodied from the rubbing of the ropes.
I am sent below the earth.
CHILD. Mother, mother. I go down with you
Underneath your wing.
ANDROMACHE. An unhappy victim,
Rulers of this Phthian land.
CHILD.   Father,
Come help us now.
ANDROMACHE. My dear child, you'll soon lie close
To your mother's breast—
A corpse beneath the earth.
CHILD. Oh no! What's happening to me?
You and I are ruined forever.
MENELAOS. Get going beneath the earth. You two are enemies
From enemy territory. Both of you will die
By two separate fates. My vote kills you,
The mother; the child will die
By my daughter Hermione's decree.
For it's madness to let your foes go free,
When you can kill them and wipe away the fear forever.

ANTISTROPHE

ANDROMACHE. Oh my husband Hector,
  Son of Priam, if only I had you
  With spear in hand to stand by my side.
CHILD. Unlucky me! I wish I could find
  A song to turn away my fate.
ANDROMACHE. Pray, my son,
  Get down at your master's knees.
CHILD [*kneeling*]. Dear friend, please don't kill me!
ANDROMACHE. My eyes are wet with tears.
  I weep like a spring
  Flowing from a shady rock.
CHILD. Ohhh! What way out of these troubles?
MENELAOS. What's all this begging? I'm like a rock,
  Or a cold, unfeeling wave of the sea.
  All my help is for my relatives.
  I've got no cure for you, especially since
  I spent so much of my life just
  To take Troy and your mother.
  This is the good you will get from her
  To go to Hades' place underground.

CHORUS. And now I see old Peleus drawing near,
  Hurrying on his ancient feet.
PELEUS [*speaks as he is entering the playing area*].
  All of you—and yes, you, standing over this butchery—
  What is all this? How did it come about?
  Why does the entire house stink with death?
  And what are these illegal plots of yours?
  Menelaos, cease! Don't rush on without the law.

  [*to his slave*] Quicker there fellow! This is not the time for
    leisure.
  I wish I had my youthful strength again.
  First thing to do is breathe a fresh wind of
  Encouragement into this woman's sails.

Tell me, on what charge do they bind your hands
And drag you and the little boy about?
You are like a sheep with a lamb underneath you,
Led to slaughter, while I and his father are far away.

ANDROMACHE. Old sir, these men drag me away, as you can see,
To die with my little child. What can I say?
In desperation I sent for you not only once,
But at least a thousand times.
You've heard of the strife that reigns within the house;
My quarrel with his daughter is costing me my life.
And now from the very altar of the goddess Thetis,
Who bore your noble son to you, and whom
You worship as the marvel of your life,
From this sacred altar they've dragged me away by force.
Without trial or condemnation, and without
Awaiting those absent from the house.
But knowing that I was alone with the child,
Who had caused them no harm, they planned to kill us.
I beg of you, old father, falling before
Your knees—my hands are tied and cannot
Touch your dear face in supplication—
Protect me by the gods, or I shall die;
Death—painful for me, but disgraceful for you, old man.

PELEUS. I order these bonds to be loosed before someone gets hurt,
And set free the woman's hands.

MENELAOS. And I forbid it—I who am no less than you,
And in her case my authority is even greater.

PELEUS. What's this? Do you come here and rule my house?
Isn't it enough to lord it over Sparta?

MENELAOS. It was I who took her as a captive from Troy.

PELEUS. My own grandson received her as his prize of honor.

MENELAOS. What's mine is his, and his is mine. Not so?

PELEUS. To help them, yes. Not to harm or kill!

MENELAOS. You'll never take her from my hands.

PELEUS. You want your head bashed in with this scepter?

MENELAOS. Just try it and you'll see what happens. Come on!

PELEUS. Do you consider yourself a man, you base creature?

How could you be worthy of that name?
You who lost your wife to a worthless Phrygian,
When you left the house unguarded and unlocked,
As if you had a virtuous wife instead of
The foulest of them all. Not even if one wanted,
Could a Spartan girl be virtuous.
They leave their homes with the young men.
With naked thighs and skirts drawn up they wrestle
And race with boys in common contests.
It's no surprise at all that your women
Haven't learned to guard their chastity.
Why not ask Helen, who left her family gods behind
And went running off with a young man to a foreign land?
And for this woman you gathered a band
Of Greeks and led them off to Ilion,
When you should have spit at her and not moved a finger.
For once you found out what she was, you should
Have let her stay, even paid to keep her there.
But that thought didn't pass your feeble brain.
Instead you led a host of noble souls to death.
You left old women childless in their homes.
From grey-haired fathers you took their noble children.
And I am one of these old men. In my eyes
You are Achilles' murderer—you filthy scum!
But you alone came back from Troy without a wound,
With all your lovely armor still intact,
In the same fine condition as when you left.
I told my grandson not to marry your relations,
Nor take the offspring of a bitch into the house.
They carry their mother's shame. (Take care,
Oh suitors, to win the daughter of a decent mother.)
And in addition there's your offense against your brother—
Encouraging him to kill his innocent daughter like a fool.
So afraid you were that you might lose your useless wife,
And then when you took Troy—I'm at that point—
You failed to kill the woman when you had her in your hands.
No!

You took one look at those fine breasts of hers
Then threw away your sword and took a kiss,
Fawning on that treacherous bitch.
You were worsted once again by Cypris, you coward!
Then coming to my grandson's house when he's gone you sack
The place and shamelessly attempt to kill
A helpless woman and her child. But he will make
You pay for this, you and that daughter of yours in the house,
Even if he is a bastard three times over.
Quite often dry land outproduces rich,
And many bastards are better than noble-born.
Now take away your daughter. It's better
To get a poor but honest in-law
Than one who's rich but base like you—you nothing!
CHORUS. From a small beginning the tongue contrives
      Great strife for men. This is what wise men
      Guard against—a struggle among friends.
MENELAOS. Why then is one to say old men are wise,
      Even those who seemed to be the sages of the Greeks,
      When you, old Peleus, of noble birth,
      Related to me by marriage, say things shameful for yourself,
      And heap rebukes on me all for some damn foreign woman,
      Whom you should have driven beyond the Nile,
      Beyond the river Phasis, and kept encouraging me to do as much,
      Since she comes from Asia, where countless of our Grecian
      Men fell victim to the spear—and died!
      She shared in your own son's death,
      For Paris, who killed your son Achilles,
      Was Hector's brother, and she's the wife of Hector.
      And yet you enter the same house with her
      And deign to share your food with her,
      You even allow her to produce her hateful children.
      And I, with your best interests at heart as well as mine,
      Wanted to have her killed, but she is snatched from me.
      Well listen then; it won't hurt to hear some reason.
      If my child is proven sterile, and from this one
      Children are engendered, will you make them rulers

Of this Phthian land, and will barbarians
Lord it over Greeks? Then am I daft
For hating such injustice, while you are sensible?
And now consider this: if you gave your child
To some citizen and she suffered thus,
Would you sit by silent? I think not.
But for a foreign woman you hound your closest relatives?
Indeed, a husband and wife have equal strength,
When a woman is cheated by her husband,
Even so when a man has an unfaithful wife in the house,
The man has strength of hand to right his wrongs.
A woman's strength is in her friends and parents.
Well, don't I have the right to help my own?
Old man, you're senile. By bringing up my command
You'd help me more than by remaining silent.
Not willingly did Helen suffer grief.
It was the doing of the gods,
And this raised the Greeks to eminence.
We knew nothing then of arms and battle,
But soon we scaled the very heights of bravery.
Familiarity is the teacher of all mortals.
And if I cast my glance upon my wife,
And restrained myself from killing her, it was a wise decision.
I wished you had not killed your brother, Phokos.
My argument is a gentle one, not filled with anger.
If you lose your temper, you may run off at the mouth,
But I consider forethought advantageous.
CHORUS. Bring this to an end at once—that's best,
Before you both regret these useless words.
PELEUS. A shame that customs are so bad in Greece.
When armies set up trophies over enemies,
The fighters of the battle receive no glory,
But the general wins all the reputation.
The one who shakes his spear among ten thousand others
And does but one man's work takes the greater praise.
So high and mighty in the city government,
They think they're better than the people, when they're nothing!

The ordinary man is so much wiser,
If he only has a bit of guts and purpose.
So your brother and you were so important at Troy,
Who sat in splendor of the high command,
Exalted by the toil and work of others!
I'll show you not to think of me as any
Less an enemy than Paris, lord of Ida,
Unless you leave this house as soon as possible—
You and that childless girl of yours.
When my son, if he is my son, catches her
He'll drag her by the hair through all the house.
That sterile cow will not allow another
To bring forth children, since she herself is childless.
What? If she alone cannot produce,
Does she intend to keep us all from children?
Damn you slaves! Get back from her so I can see
If anyone will hinder me from freeing her.

[*to* ANDROMACHE] Lift yourself up. Even though I'm trembling,
I'll loose these ropes entangled round your wrists.
You beast, look at her bloodied hands!
Did you think you were tying up a bull or lion?
Were you afraid she'd grab a sword and defend herself?
Little one, come here. Creep beneath my arms
And help me free your mother. I'll rear you up
In Phthia to be a hateful enemy of these Spartans.
If the glory of the spear and din of battle
Are taken from them, they're next to nothing.
CHORUS. An old man is often uncontrollable
And the quickness of his temper is hard to guard against.
MENELAOS. You're much too forward with your abuse.
Here in Phthia I will commit no wrong by force,
Nor will I suffer any wrong by force.
And now—there's no time for quarreling—
I must be off. There is a certain city, a place
Not far from Sparta, which was formerly friendly
But now commits aggression. I've got to set out

On campaign and force her beneath our hand.
When I've put everything in order there,
I shall return. Then face to face with my son-in-law
I'll talk the matter over and hear his side.
If he restrains the woman and shows respect for us, hereafter,
He'll receive respect in turn. But if in anger
He tries our patience, he'll soon find out what anger means:
He'll find acts to match his acts.
As for all your words, I endure that easily.
Despite your voice, you're nothing but a shadow—
Completely helpless, nothing else but talk.

PELEUS. Come here, my child, and stand beneath my arms.
And you, poor woman, have found a calm and windless
Harbor as refuge from this savage storm.

ANDROMACHE. Old man, may the gods bless you and your family
For saving the child and me from death.
Be careful that these men don't lie in ambush
On some deserted road and take me by force.
They see you're old and feeble, and I am helpless.
The boy is just an infant. Take care that
We don't escape now only to be captured later.

PELEUS. Please! None of your womanish fears now.
Go ahead. Who will lay his hands on you?
Whoever does will soon regret it,
For I rule over Phthia with the blessing of the gods,
And have a mighty troupe of cavalry and many soldiers.
I'm still upright and not as old as you may think.
Despite my age, if I just look at him,
He'll run away like the coward that he is.
An old man is stronger than many young ones, if he's brave.
What good is size and strength, when you have no heart?

STROPHE

CHORUS. I'd rather not be born, if not of noble parents
And sharing in a house of wealth and property.
For if some awful calamity falls, there is
No scarcity of help for

The noble-born, who from their honored houses win
Glory and reputation; the famous deeds of noble men
Are not diminished by time. Their glory
    Glows, even when they're dead.

ANTISTROPHE

Better not to win a shameful victory
Than to overthrow justice with spite and force.
Although at the present this may seem sweet to men,
In the course of time it grows
Barren and becomes an object of reproach.
This way of life I've always praised and adopted for myself:
    Don't let unjust power hold sway in your home
    Or in the government.

EPODE

    Old man, son of Aiakos,
Now I believe that you wielded your famous spear
In the battle of the Lapiths and the Centaurs;
That on the ship called *Argo* you sailed the hostile sea
    And passed through the Clashing Rocks
    On that sea-journey for fame;
And that when Herakles, the son of Zeus,
In the distant past covered the city of Ilion with gore,
You shared his glory with him,
    And then returned to Greece's shores.

NURSE. Oh dearest ladies, how evil follows evil on this day.
    The mistress of the house, I mean Hermione,
    Abandoned by her father and realizing
    What a dreadful thing it was to try to kill
    Andromache and her little child wants to die herself.
    She fears her husband—afraid she will be cast away
    Disgracefully in punishment for what she did,
    Or even die for attempting to kill those who should not be killed.
    The servants on watch have just prevented her
    From tightening a noose about her neck,
    And snatched a sword from her right hand

Remorse has filled her heart and she realizes
That her former deeds were foolish ones.
My friends, I'm completely exhausted from stopping her
From suicide. Please go within the house
And persuade her not to kill herself.
Perhaps your new faces will be more persuasive
Than those of old, accustomed friends.
CHORUS. Listen—we hear the cries of the servants
Within, echoing your awful message.
Apparently she is going to show us the extent
Of her grief caused by her misfortune
Look there! She's escaped her servants' hands
And rushes out in her longing to die.

[*Enter* HERMIONE.]

1ST STROPHE

HERMIONE.   Poor me!
I'll tear out my hair
And scratch my cheeks to bits.
NURSE. My child, what are you doing?
Don't disgrace your body.

1ST ANTISTROPHE

HERMIONE. What do I care about this veil on my face?
        Away with it!
NURSE. Child, cover up your breast; pull your clothes together.

2ND STROPHE

HERMIONE. Why should I cover myself?
It's quite clear now and not concealed,
What I did against my husband.
NURSE. Do you grieve that you tried to kill his other woman?

2ND ANTISTROPHE

HERMIONE. Yes,
Now I lament
My rashness then.

I'm cursed,
Cursed before men.
NURSE. Your husband will forgive your mistake.

ASTROPHA

HERMIONE. Why did you snatch
  The sword from my hand?
  Give it back, my friend, give it back
  And I'll thrust it through my side.
  Why do you stop me from the noose?
NURSE. What? Am I to let you kill yourself, mad with frenzy?
HERMIONE. Oh my fate!
  Where is there a fire to consume me?
  Where is there a rock to climb—
  A way to the sea or to the mountain forests,
  Where I can die and join the blessed dead?
NURSE. Why all this grief? Calamity from god
  Comes to every mortal sooner or later.
HERMIONE. Father, you abandoned me on the shore—
  All alone on the shore, far from every ship.
  He will destroy me. Never again shall I inhabit
  This my bridal house.
  What altar should I supplicate?
  Or as a slave am I to fall at the knees of a slave?
  I wish I were a dark blue winged bird,
  Flying from this Phthian land,
  Or the first boat of pine
  Which reached the end of ocean.

NURSE. My dear, I did not approve of your intemperance then,
  When you wronged that Trojan woman,
  And now I do not like this intemperate fear of yours.
  Your husband will not disregard his marriage ties
  Because of some barbarian's cheap rhetoric.
  He did not get you as a captive from Troy,
  But as the child of a noble father with a handsome dowry
  From a city of more than average prosperity

Your father hasn't abandoned you, as you fear;
He won't allow you to be exiled from this house.
Don't carry on out here and bring yourself to shame
Before the eyes of everyone.
CHORUS. Look there! Some foreign stranger approaches.
See how he hastens his steps toward us.

[*Enter* ORESTES.]

ORESTES. Ladies, tell me—is this the royal home of Achilles' son?
CHORUS. Yes, it is. But will you tell us who you are?
ORESTES. I'm the son of Agamemnon and Cyltemnestra.
Orestes is my name. I'm heading for the oracle
Of Zeus at Dodona. And since I came to Phthia,
It occurred to me to inquire about my cousin—
To see if she's alive and prospering.
I mean Hermione of Sparta. Even though
She's living far from me, she's as dear as ever.
HERMIONE. Oh child of Agamemnon, you've appeared like a safe
    harbor
For the sailor who has weathered winter's storms.
At your knees I beg of you to pity
My unhappy fate. I have no suppliant's wreaths for you,
And so I'll throw my arms about your knees.
ORESTES. Wait!
What's the matter here? Am I mistaken or do I see
The queen of the house, Menelaos' daughter?
HERMIONE. Yes, the only child that Helen bore
To my father. You should know it all.
ORESTES. Healer Apollo, free us from these troubles.
What's the matter? Do you suffer at the hands of god or mortal?
HERMIONE. Partly on my own account, partly on my husband's,
And partly because of some god. I'm completely ruined.
ORESTES. What trouble could a woman have, who still
Is childless, except the troubles of a marriage bed?
HERMIONE. That's exactly what my trouble is. You've guessed
    it well.
ORESTES. Does your husband love another woman more than you?

HERMIONE. Hector's wife, the captive taken by the spear.

ORESTES. That's a sorry tale: one man with two wives.

HERMIONE. That's how it is. I only tried to protect myself.

ORESTES. You didn't plot against your rival, as women usually do?

HERMIONE. Death for her and her bastard son.

ORESTES. Did you kill her, or did something intervene?

HERMIONE. The old man Peleus who honored the wrong ones.

ORESTES. Did anyone share the murder plot with you?

HERMIONE. My father, Menelaos, who came from Sparta.

ORESTES. And was he worsted by the old man?

HERMIONE. He had respect for Peleus. He's gone and left me alone.

ORESTES. I understand. And you fear your husband for your actions.

HERMIONE. Yes.

He'll kill me—and with justice. What am I to say?
But I beg of you by Zeus who guards our family—
Send me away as far as possible from this land
Or to my father's home. The very house seems to have
A voice which shouts for my departure.
The whole land of Phthia hates me. And if my husband
Returns from Apollo's oracle and finds me here,
He'll kill me on these base charges. Or shall I be a slave
To the bastard-spawning woman whom once I ruled?
Someone may ask, "How did you fall so low?"
The visits of evil women ruined my life.
They talked to me and puffed up words like these:
"Will you allow that slave, that prisoner of war,
To share your husband's bed with you?
By the gods in heaven, not in my house she wouldn't.
She wouldn't have my bed and keep on living."
I listened to the deceitful lies of these sirens,
These base but clever babblers of vicious words.
And I was puffed up by my foolishness. Why did I
Spy out my husband's every action, when I had all I needed?
Great wealth was in my hands and I ruled the house.
I could have born legitimate children;
Her bastards would have been half-slaves to mine.
But never, never—it cannot be said enough—

Should a man with any sense who has a wife
Let other women approach his wife at home.
For they are the teachers of base and evil deeds.
For one has something to gain by destroying a marriage,
Another has slipped and wants to bring a friend along.
And many are filled with lust. And so the homes
Of men are sick and troubled. Be on your guard
Against this evil and lock your doors with bars and levers.
For female visitors from outside the house
Have never brought one healthy thing—only grief and misery.

CHORUS. You speak too harshly against your own kind.
Although that can be forgiven, none the less
We women ought to pretty up these female vices.

ORESTES. It was a bit of good advice—whoever
Told us to listen to both sides of any argument.
I learned about the confusion in this house,
About the strife between you and Hector's wife,
And then stood by on watch to see if you
Would stay, or if in terror of the attempted murder
Of the slave you would turn and run away.
Your letters did not bring me here. I came
To see if we might talk, as now we do,
And then escort you away. You were mine before,
But now you live with this man because of your father's
    cowardice.
Before attacking Troy he gave you
To me, then later promised you to your present husband
On condition that he would help to sack the Trojan citadel.
And when Achilles' son returned from Troy,
I excused your father and begged him, Achilles' son,
To give up his marriage with you. I told him of my
Unhappy fate and the evil spirit upon me,
I argued that I would not easily be able to marry
Outside the family, since I was in exile for the crime of murder.
But he merely insulted me about my mother's murder
And chided me about the bloody fiends which followed me.
I was humbled by that unhappy family fortune.

I suffered, yes, I suffered, yet still endured.
Unwillingly I left, deprived of your hand in marriage.
But now, since your luck is bad and circumstance
Has left you at a loss for what to do,
I'll lead you away and deposit you in your father's hands.
Close kinship is a wondrous thing, and in evil times
There is nothing better than a dear relation.

HERMIONE. My father will take care of my wedding plans.
It's not my decision to make.
But send me away from here as quickly as possible
So my husband won't return and take me by surprise,
Or the old man Peleus find me missing from the house
And send a team of horsemen in hot pursuit.

ORESTES. Don't worry about the old man. And as for Achilles' son
Don't fear him for his outrages against me.
He won't escape the tightly woven net
Of death I've set for him.
No more. I shall not say anymore.
But the rock of Delphoi will soon know the outcome.
And if my allies in the land of Pytho
Hold fast to their sacred oaths, I, the mother-killer,
Will teach him not to marry a woman who belongs to me.
He'll soon regret that he asked Apollo to pay
For his father's murder. Not even a change of heart
Will help him, when the god exacts his punishment.
At the god's hand (with the help of my accusations)
He'll perish basely. Then he'll know my hate!
For god overthrows the fortune of one's foes
And does not permit these high and mighty thoughts.

1st Strophe

CHORUS. Oh Phoebus, who fortified the rock of Ilion with a
      mighty wall,
    And you Poseidon, rider of the sea
        on dark grey horses,
    What fury drove you gods
    To wreck your handiwork?

And for mad Ares, master of the spear,
Why did you throw down unhappy Troy, destroy unhappy
    Troy?

1ST ANTISTROPHE

Many chariots and fine horses you set on the river banks
And many men you set to bloody struggles
    that win no prize nor garland.
They are dead and gone, dead and gone
    are the kings of Ilion.
Nor does fire yet shine on the altars of Troy.
To please the gods with fragrant smoke of incense.

2ND STROPHE

Gone the son of Atreus, victim of his wife's deceit,
And she in turn has received bloody death for death
    at her children's hands by god's will.
The god's command turned the son of Agamemnon against her,
    when he set forth from Argos
    and came to the holy temple at Delphoi.
    Mother-killer!
Great god in heaven, Phoebus,—how can I believe this?

2ND ANTISTROPHE

And in the marketplaces of the Greeks
Countless mothers lament their unhappy sons.
    Wives have left their homes
    for other men.
Not to you alone, nor to your friends, have these sad sorrows
    fallen.
    Sick, all Hellas is sick.
And through the fertile fields of Troy
Has passed the pest of war, dripping slaughter.

PELEUS. Women of Phthia, I have a question.
    Answer me clearly. I've heard a rumor
    That Menelaos' daughter has left the house.

In haste I've come to learn the truth.
For when our friends are gone,
It's up to those at home to watch over things.
CHORUS. Peleus, your information is correct. It's not right
For me to hide the evil state we're in.
The queen has left the palace and has gone into exile.
PELEUS. What did she fear? Tell me all.
CHORUS. She feared her husband would throw her out.
PELEUS. Because of the plots she laid against the boy?
CHORUS. Yes, and in fear of the captive woman.
PELEUS. Did she leave with her father or someone else?
CHORUS. Agamemnon's son led her from the land.
PELEUS. What does he intend? Does he plan to marry her?
CHORUS. Yes. And he also plans to kill your grandson.
PELEUS. In ambush or will he fight him face to face?
CHORUS. An ambush in the holy temple of Apollo with the help of
    Delphoians.
PELEUS. Oh no! That's terrible. Someone go as quickly
    As possible to the temple at Delphoi
    And inform our friends there of this plot,
    Before Achilles' son is killed by his enemies.

[*Enter* MESSENGER.]

MESSENGER. Unhappy day!
    What a gloomy fate to bear the news I bear
    To you, old man, and to my master's friends.
PELEUS. No! My heart foresees your message.
MESSENGER. You have no grandson any longer, Peleus.
    So many bloody blows from swords has he received
    At the hands of Delphoians and a man from Mycenae.
CHORUS. What's this, old man? Don't fall down.
    Lift yourself up.
PELEUS.   I'm nothing. I'm destroyed.
    My voice is gone, my limbs below are loosed.
MESSENGER. Listen to the deed, if you intend to defend your loved
    ones.
    Take hold of yourself and straighten up your body.

PELEUS. Oh my destiny! At the extremity of life
  You've made me wretched.
  But how did he die—my only grandson of my only child?
  Tell me. I'll listen to what no ears should hear.
MESSENGER. When first we came to the famous land of Phoebus,
  Gazing at the wondrous sight for three bright days,
  We filled our eyes with the beauty of it all.
  This caused suspicion, and the people of the god
  Gathered into circles to mutter their complaints.
  While Agamemnon's son went all about the town
  Whispering venemous remarks in every ear:
      "See that man walking about the shrines of the gods,
      Shrines filled with gold and the riches of men?
      He comes for the same reason as before—
      To plunder the holy temple of the god!"
  This caused an ugly rumor to spread. And in reply
  The magistrates, jamming the meeting places,
  Warders of the holy treasure, on their own authority
  Stationed a guard about the porches of the shrine.
  But we, in innocence, took our sheep,
  Pastured on the grass of Parnassos, and stood beside the altars
  With our patrons and the seers of Delphoi.
  And one of them spoke out:
      "Young man, why have you come to Delphoi?
      What prayer shall we offer to the god for you?"
  And he replied:
      "I wish to make amends for my past crime against Apollo,
      For I demanded that he pay for my father's murder."
  Then did the hateful lies spread by Orestes prove strong;
  They stamped my master a liar who came for crime.
  Then in he goes beyond the temple door
  To pray before the holy oracle of Phoebus.
  He's at the very act of sacrifice,
  While there in ambush lay a troop of men,
      camouflaged with laurel.
  Among them was the child of Clytemnestra, Orestes
  The filthy schemer who thought up all of this.

While Achilles' son prayed to the god before the eyes of all,
They stabbed him, standing there unarmed and unawares.
But their weapons failed at first and he retreated.
He took armor that was hanging from the doorpost
And stood upon the altar, looking like a gorgon.
From there he shouted to the people of Delphoi:
       "My purpose in coming here was holy.
       Why murder me? For what reason am I destroyed?"
Of the countless bystanders not one said a word;
They replied instead by stoning him.
He was pounded by a storm on every side.
He stretched forth his armor to ward off the blows,
Extending his shield now here, now there.
But it was useless; missiles fell at his feet—
Arrows, spears, javelins, spite sharp enough to kill a bull.
Terrible was the dance he did, as he guarded against the blows.
Then, as the whole mad crowd encircled him,
       not giving him a moment's rest,
He jumped from the sacrificial platform,
And with the dreadful leap that Trojans knew so well
He rushed upon his frightened tormentors,
Who, just like doves in terror of a hawk,
Turned their coward backs in flight.
In the confusion many fell, some wounded,
Others crushed in the scramble at the narrow exits.
In the holy temple an unholy cry rang out
And echoed off the rocks. For a sudden moment of calm
He stood there gleaming with his bright arms
Till someone from the inmost shrine sent forth
A terrible, chilling cry, urging on the mob to battle.
Then fell Achilles' son, stabbed through the side
By the sharp sword of a man from Delphoi,
Who killed him with the aid of many others.
As he fell to earth, every man ran up
To add another wound, to cast another stone,
His whole body and its beauty was torn by savage wounds.
They dragged his corpse from the sacred altar
And cast it outside the incense-scented temple.

We snatched him up as quickly as possible
And now carry him to you, old man.
Yours now for pity, tears, and lamentation;
Yours now to bury and to ornament his grave.
Thus the god who grants oracles to the world,
The judge of justice for all men,
Exacted cruel punishment from Achilles' son.
And so the god, like a hateful man, remembered
The bitter feuds of long ago.
How, then, could he be wise?
CHORUS. But look! Our lord is carried in
From the Delphoian land and reaches home—
The wretched sufferer. And you are wretched too,
Old man, for you receive Achilles' son
Home at last, but not as you would have him.
You too have chanced upon evil sufferings
And have hit upon the selfsame fate.

1st Strophe

PELEUS. Oh no! What an evil I am forced to look upon
And now must carry into the house.

Oh city of Thessaly, we are ruined.
I'm finished. My family is gone.
No children are left in the house.
I'm wretched in my suffering.
To whom, whom, can I turn my longing eyes?

[*turning to the corpse of* NEOPTOLEMOS]

Oh lovely mouth and cheek and hands,
Would that death had taken you at Ilion
Beside the banks of the Simois.
CHORUS. He would have won honor by such a death
And your lot, old man, would have been far happier

1st Antistrophe

PELEUS. Oh marriage, marriage, which ruined my house
And brought my city low.

Would that the hated sharer of your bed, Hermione,
Had never cast death upon you, my child.
She should have been blasted by lightning first.
Nor should a mortal man have
Ever rebuked the god Apollo for the
Murder of his father.

2ND STROPHE

CHORUS [*keening*]. I lament my dead master.
I begin my song
For the dead.
PELEUS.   And I lament in turn,
A wretched old man,
Unhappy I weep.
CHORUS. It's fate from god; god brought about catastrophe.
PELEUS. Loved one,
You've left an empty home
And a suffering old man.
You've left me childless.
CHORUS. Old man, you should have died before your children.
PELEUS. I'll tear my hair
And smash my wretched head. O city,
Phoebus has torn
Both my sons from me.

2ND ANTISTROPHE

CHORUS. Poor old man, you have seen and suffered much.
What sort of life
Is left for you?
PELEUS. Without a child, all alone, no end to troubles,
I'll drain
My bitter sorrows down to death.
CHORUS. In vain the gods have blessed your marriage.
PELEUS.   All gone,
Completely lost.
Far different from my lofty boasts.
CHORUS. All alone you'll roam an empty house.

PELEUS.   City, my city, you're no longer mine.
     Let this scepter fall from my hands.
And you, daughter of Nereus in your gloomy caves,
          You see me fallen,
          Completely ruined.

CHORUS. Look! Look!
     What moved? What divine act do I sense:
     Girls, look—behold the sight.
     Some god travels through the gleaming air.
          She is coming over the fertile
          Fields of Phthia.

[*Enter* THETIS.]

THETIS. Peleus, because of our former marriage
     I, Thetis, have come, leaving the home of Nereus.
     And first of all in these present problems
     I bid you to avoid excessive grief.
     For even I, who should have borne children
     Without a touch of grief, have lost my only child by you,
     The swift Achilles, foremost among the Greeks.
     Pay attention and I'll tell you why I've come.
     Take dead Achilles' son. Go to the altar
     At Pytho and bury him on the spot.
     His tomb will be a constant reproach to the Delphoians,
     As it declares his bloody death at Orestes' hand.
     As for the captive woman, I mean Andromache,
     She's fated to inhabit the Molossian land
     And share her life in marriage with Helenos.
     Her son goes with her; he's all that's left of the line
     Of Aiakos. The kingship will descend
     From him to others and will prosper greatly.
     Your race and mine is not completely overthrown.
     Troy lives on, for the gods watch over her too,
     Although she fell a victim to the eager zeal of Pallas.
     And you, old man, that you may be grateful for
     Our marriage, I release you from all mortal cares.

And shall make you a deathless, everlasting god.
And then in Nereus' shining house with me
You shall pass the time to come—god with goddess.
And lifting your dry foot from the sea
You'll see Achilles, your dear son and mine,
Dwelling on his island home beside
The shore of Leukē within the Euxine strait.
Come now. Go to the god-built city of Delphoi
Carrying this corpse along. And when you have buried
The body, come to the hollow haunt of the Sepian rock.
Remain there until with a band of fifty Nereids
I appear from the sea to lead you away.
Now you must carry out Fate's decree—Zeus' wish.
And cease your mourning for the dead.
For every mortal the gods have cast this lot,
And every man must die.

PELEUS. Revered lady, most noble sharer of my bed,
Welcome daughter of Nereus, what you will do
Is worthy of you and of your children.
I'll end my sorrow at your request, goddess,
And after I have buried him, I will go to the folds at Pelion—
The spot where I held your lovely body in my arms.
Shouldn't one marry from noble families?
And give away women to noble men,
If one has any sense?
And cast away desire for base marriages,
Even though they bring a handsome dowry to the house?

[*Exit* PELEUS.]

CHORUS. Many are the shapes of the gods,
And much they bring to pass against our expectation.
And that which was expected fails.
God finds a way where there was none.
    Such has happened here today.

EURIPIDES
The Trojan Women
TRANSLATED BY
CHARLES DORIA

INTRODUCTORY NOTE

The Trojan Women, a searing antiwar play, was produced in 415 at the height of Athens' power. The Athenians well knew what happened when cities were defeated. They had conquered many. It would be hard to dispute the interpretation which sees in this play Euripides' direct warning to his countrymen about the dangers of ambition and conquest. The sufferings of the defeated are shown most immediately, but the coming fate of the conquerors, well-known to the audience, is dwelt on repeatedly.

The action is arranged around the central consciousness of Hecuba and the arrivals and departures of her family and enemies. The arrival of Helen begins as another of these incidents, but turns into an elaborate trial between Hecuba and Helen in the presence of Menelaus, her cuckolded husband, who will succumb to her attractions again. The mixture in this scene of grief, sexuality, wit and outrage constitutes a dramatic masterpiece.

The play was part of a trilogy which won only second prize. The other tragedies were the *Alexander* and *Palamedes;* the name of the satyr play was *Sisyphus.* The titles of the other two tragedies show that the trilogy was conceived of as connected by the theme of Troy. "Alexander" is an alternate name for Paris and "Palamedes" is the name of a Greek leader unjustly murdered by his own comrades during the war.

CHARACTERS

POSEIDON, god of the sea
ATHENA, a goddess
HECUBA, queen of Troy
TALTHYBIUS, herald of the Greeks
CASSANDRA, a daughter of HECUBA
ANDROMACHE, widow of Hector
MENELAUS, king of Sparta
HELEN, wife of MENELAUS
CHORUS of captive Trojan women
(silent) Astyanax, infant son of Hector
and ANDROMACHE; soldiers; guards;
male and female attendants

The Trojan Women

THE SCENE. *A plain just outside the city of Troy; in the background are some tents and shacks that house the surviving population of the city, the women and children.* HECUBA *is discovered lying in front of one of the larger hovels, and she remains in this prone position until her first speech. The sky is dark and gives evidence of being about to storm; the sea is heard coming in relentlessly and with an uncertain beat.* POSEIDON *should appear to stride forward as if from the sea, off to one side yet facing the tents and the city obliquely.*

POSEIDON. I have come here, leaving behind the salty bottom
of the Aegean where choruses of Nereids unroll
in their dancing the loveliest of steps to my waves' song,
because of the time Phoebus and I, Poseidon, made the towers
    here
upon this Trojan earth with our masons' tools:
yes, I have never lost kindliness towards the Phrygians' city
which now has turned to ash and smoke, and plundered,
has been cast down by Argive spears—when
that carpenter from Parnassus, Epeus of Phocis,
assembled the designs of Pallas, and made the horse
pregnant of arms, and sent it inside the city's towers,
a weight of destruction (and that is why it will be called
by men in later time "the wooden horse," for it
gave shelter to a band of secret men). Now the temples
are lonely, and the groves of the gods wet with slaughter;
by the steps of the temple of Zeus, Protector of the House,
Priam the king fell dead. His gold and spoil they send
to their ships that wait for a sternwards breeze,

so that in this, the tenth year of war, they may see their wives
and children again, these Hellenes who marched against the city.

But as for myself, beaten by Hera, the Argive god,
and by Athena, who together helped destroy Phrygia,
I leave famous Ilium, and my altars, for whenever evil
desolation grips a city, there the business of the gods
is blighted, and they are not honored . . .
                           The river Scamander roars
with the shrieks of many captives allotted to the lords:
some the Arcadians, and other the Thessalians have,
and the sons of Theseus, the chiefs of the Athenians.
All the women of Troy who remain without an owner
lie beneath these tents, picked for the leaders of the army:
and with them is the Spartan Helen, Tyndareus's daughter,
rightly considered a captive. But if you want to see the one
truly miserable, look on Hecuba, lying in front of the gates,
weeping large tears for her many children, while her daughter,
Polyxena, unknown to her, has died a wretched death on the
     mound
of Achilles' tomb. Gone is Priam and his sons. The girl,
Cassandra, whom king Apollo turned to a virgin frantic with
     prophecy,
Agamemnon, passing over the god's will and common decency,
will marry by force to a secret bed.
                         But, city, prosperous once,
farewell. Farewell to your towers of stone. If Pallas,
Zeus's daughter, had not ruined you,
you would be firmly standing yet.
ATHENA. May I, putting an end to our old enmity,
address you, the nearest of my father's kin,
a great god, one honored even among other gods?
POSEIDON. You may, if you like, queen Athena—
for you know family ties certainly
are not the least of all love's charms.
ATHENA. Well, I'm honored. But I have something to say,
king, that will be important for both of us.

POSEIDON. So . . . you have some news from the gods?
from Zeus, perhaps, or some other god?
ATHENA. No, but it's about Troy, upon whose soil we stand:
I came here because of your godhead, to have it as ally.
POSEIDON. Hmm . . . you mean you've put away your anger,
and you come in pity of her the fire's turned to ash?
ATHENA. First, go back to what I asked before. Will you be my
partner,
and give your consent to what I'm going to do?
POSEIDON. Yes, of course . . . but what's your plan?
Are you here because of the Greeks or Trojans?
ATHENA. The Trojans, my former enemies: now I'd like to cheer
them up
by throwing a bitter homecoming for the Achaean army.
POSEIDON. But why do you jump about, now one way, now another:
now hating, now loving, in excess, whoever you light upon?
ATHENA. Ah . . . don't you know I was the victim of men's rage,
and my altars, too?
POSEIDON. Yes, I know: wasn't that because Ajax dragged Cassandra
out of the temple by force?
ATHENA. And the Greeks neither punished him, nor said anything
about it.
POSEIDON. Although thanks to you they destroyed Ilium.
ATHENA. So with your help I'm going to hit them back.
POSEIDON. I'm ready. What are you going to do?
ATHENA. I'm going to give them a bitter homecoming.
POSEIDON. While they're on land or the open sea?
ATHENA. Whenever they decide to leave for their homes,
Zeus is going to send them thunderstorms and hailstones,
for the like of which there are no words: there will be
a black blowing in the heavens down from the clouds,
and he will give me, he says, his thunderbolts
to smack their ships and set them ablaze with fire.
Now as for your part, make their path over the Aegean
boil with waves of unpassable size and with whirlpools of brine,
fill the hollow Euboean gulf with their bodies,
so that afterwards the Greeks may learn to have

some respect for temples and to fear the other gods.
POSEIDON. That's how it'll be:
  you don't need many words for a favor like that.
  I will rouse up the high seas; the headlands of Myconos
  and the Delian rocks, Scyros and Lemnos, and the cliffs at
    Caphareus,
  will take in the bodies of their many dead.
  But go now to Olympus, take the thunderbolts
  from your father's hands, and wait until
  the Argive army goes forth in lovely array.

  Of mortal men he is the fool, who is a sacker of cities,
  spoiler of temples and robber of tombs, shrines of men passed
    away:
  for giving them to desolation he is cut down in the end.

[POSEIDON *and* ATHENA *depart together.*]

HECUBA. Up.
  Lift up your head from earth,
  lift up your neck. What you see about you here—
  these things, pieces—they are Troy no longer,
  we are Troy's kings no longer.
  When your luck is changing, accept, endure:
  sail with the channel, sail with your fortune:
  do not set boat against the waves' path,
  for now you move at the whims of chance.
  aiai   aiai
  Still may I not, last remnant,
  groan melodiously when my land is gone,
  my children, husband?
  O the much weight of my ancestors
  how you have been reduced, until now you are nothing.
  Why be silent? why not be silent?
  why should I sing a funeral song?
  Pressed by a heavy fate I stretch out my limbs here
  in a mockery of sleep, I laid my back on this hard bed.
  My head aches, my temples ache,

my ribs ache:
how great is my desire to thrash about,
to hurl back, no, body,
against both walls, weeping always
for sorrow and pain:
This is the muse of those whom fortune's left,
she who celebrates a ruin without joy.
The ships' prows
with swift oars
cut the purple salt-sea of Hellas,
leaving her harbors, their safe moorings, behind,
while the hated war song of the flutes,
and the pert voice of panpipes,
echoes in time to their rowing,
but with the rope, Egypt's art,
made fast in the Troad gulf,
pursuing the wife of Menelaus,
Castor's harm,
Eurota's shame,
she who killed King Priam,
plower of fifty sons,
and I, unhappy Hecuba,
driven headlong to this ruin.
Aiai—on what kind of chair do I sit,
sitting near the camp of Agamemnon?
Both slave and old woman, who was carried out of my house
my hair plundered in grief for the dead.
O wretched wives of the bronze-speared Trojans,
o wretched maidens betrothed in an evil time,
slowly Ilium burns: let us cry aiai,
raise the cry,
aiai   aiai
just as a bird utters cries
for her feathered young, so I began my song
in measured movement,
but not, oh god,
not the one that once,

leaning upon the scepter of Priam
I began for the gods, my foot
leading the chorus, my people keeping the beat
in sharp strokes.

[*Enter* CHORUS.]

1ST STROPHE

HALF-CHORUS. Hecuba, why do you call out? Why do you cry?
What do your words portend?
Throughout the tents they heard your tears,
and in our hearts fear moves
with a quick daring motion—
in the hearts of Troy's women
who behind these walls of cloth
weep that they are slaves.
HECUBA. O child, already beside their ships
Argive hands keep oars at the ready.
HALF-CHORUS. What do they want from me, who have suffered
much?
Will they carry me off to the sea, away from my homeland?
HECUBA. I do not know, but in my heart I hold pictures of our
doom.
HALF-CHORUS. io
soon we shall hear,
"Women of Troy, come out of the tents.
The Greeks prepare to go home."
HECUBA. But let no one send for my maenad,
the bacchic-prophet, Cassandra,
to be shamed by the Greeks,
for me to suffer more by her suffering.
O Troy, Troy, unhappy city,
they have cut you down and burned you.
And we, we are unhappy
that, leaving you behind, both live,
and living are subject to another's will.

1ST ANTISTROPHE

HALF-CHORUS. Trembling I left the tents of Agamemnon
   to hear from you, queen,
   if it was their decision to kill me outright,
   or if they stand by their ships,
   making ready the oar.
HECUBA. Child, I came here shuddering,
   panic-stricken in my sleepless soul.
HALF-CHORUS. Has a Danaan herald been here already?
   To whom do I belong, whose long-suffering slave?
HECUBA. I think you are close to your fate already.
HALF-CHORUS. io   io
   which Argive, which Phthian,
   which islander, will lead me
   far from Troy, city without luck?
HECUBA. Where?
   In what part of the world?
   Shall I be a slave,
   I, an old woman?
   Like a drone I will serve,
   a paltry shape of woman,
   feeble picture of the dead,
   keeping watch before palace gates,
   or looking after children,
   I, who held ancestral honors of Troy.

2ND STROPHE

CHORUS. aiai
   With what songs of lament
   do you grieve for your ruin?
   I will not rock the shuttle back and forth again,
   spinning thread on the looms;
   for the last time I look upon the bodies of my children,
   for the last time: I shall have worse sorrows
   when I draw near the bed of a Greek:

may that night, that fate, be lost, perish;
or, fetching water from Pirene's spring,
I shall be the bedel of her holy well:
o to god I might go to the famous land,
the happy city Theseus rules—
Athens, it is of you I speak;
but no, not to the eddies of Eurotas,
not to that hated house of Helen
let me go, where I shall meet face to face
the ravager of Troy, Menelaus, Sparta's king.

2ND ANTISTROPHE

The holy land of Peneus
the exceedingly lovely valley of Olympus
I have heard men say are heavy with wealth
and rich fruitfulness:
it is there I would go, if the pleasant city
of Theseus is not my new home.
And the land of Aetna, Hephaestus' house,
facing the Phoenician sea, mother
of the Sicilian mountains, I have heard you
heralded to the world by the garlands of your excellence.
Perhaps I will go to live in the country
that lies near the Ionian sea,
to the land the river Krathis waters,
Krathis, loveliest of rivers,
she who turns blond hair red,
who feeds with her holy fountains
this land of heroes, and blesses it with men.

[*Enter* TALTHYBIUS.]

Look now: a herald is coming from the Danaan army,
a dispenser and dealer in words,
no, a diplomat, hastening swiftly.
What news does he bring?
that from now on we are slaves
in the land of Doris, home of Menelaus and Helen.

TALTHYBIUS. Hecuba, you know that I've come here many times
   as a herald from the Greeks to the Trojans—
   I am Talthybius, and I bring you news.
HECUBA. What we've feared for a long time, friends, has finally
   come.
TALTHYBIUS. Your lots have been cast—if that was your fear.
HECUBA. aiai
   What city in Thessaly, Phthia;
   where in Cadmus' land do you say I will go?
TALTHYBIUS. Each of you has been given separately to a different
   master.
HECUBA. But who has been awarded to whom?
   To which of Troy's women does a pleasant life await?
TALTHYBIUS. I know: but ask me one by one, not all together.
HECUBA. Tell me, my daughter Cassandra—
   who gets her?
TALTHYBIUS. King Agamemnon, not by lot, but because he chose
   her.
HECUBA. So she goes as a slave for his Spartan wife.
TALTHYBIUS. No, but into his bed in secret marriage.
HECUBA. Can that be? Apollo's girl, she who was to live
   a virgin all her life because of the god's gift?
TALTHYBIUS. Lust pierced him for this girl possessed by the god.
HECUBA. Throw away, daughter, the holy temple keys;
   rip off the sacred dress and the garlands about your neck!
TALTHYBIUS. But isn't it a piece of luck, to sleep in a king's bed?
HECUBA. What news do you have of that girl
   you took from me just recently?
TALTHYBIUS. Do you speak of Polyxena, or some other one?
HECUBA. Yes, her. To whom has the lot joined her?
TALTHYBIUS. She has been appointed to watch over Achilles' tomb.
HECUBA. I have given birth to a caretaker of the dead,
   a custodian of graves.
   But tell me, by what right, friend, what law,
   do they do this?
TALTHYBIUS. Say your child is lucky—she is happy.
HECUBA. What did you say? Does she see the sun?

TALTHYBIUS. Her fate is to be released from trouble.

HECUBA. What about Hector's wife, Andromache?
What do they plan to do with her?

TALTHYBIUS. The son of Achilles has selected her as his prize.

HECUBA. And whose handmaid am I? whose parasite?
whom will I trail after, leaning on this cane,
my third foot?

TALTHYBIUS. The king of Ithaca, Odysseus, won you as his slave.

HECUBA. eh!   eh!
Strike my cropped head
Scratch my face with nails

My lot has handed me over to a filthy deceiver,
to the enemy of justice, a lawless beast,
who twists and turns with forked tongue,
and decides the undecided
by making what was pleasant before
hateful to all.

Women of Troy,
weep for me.
I am ill-fated and as if dead.
By the unluckiest lot of all
I fall.

CHORUS. You know your disposition, queen—
but which Greek, which Achaean controls my fate?

TALTHYBIUS. Go! Right now it is your business to bring Cassandra
here—
as quickly as possible, so that I may give her to the army's
commander,
to deliver her into his hands. Only then will I take
those of you who've been allotted to their lords.

Eah! What's that light inside the tent?
Are they burning it? What are they doing?
Because they're going to be led away from this land

do they want to kill themselves? Certainly
the free spirit in them cannot bear troubles
with the patience and forbearance
due their present condition.

Open up! Open up!
If you do something to yourselves
the Greeks won't like,
I'll have to take the blame for it.

HECUBA. No, they are not setting fire to the tent,
    but my child, the maenad Cassandra, comes running out.

[CASSANDRA *comes out dancing with a torch in her hand.*]

CASSANDRA [*intoning*]. Lift up! Hold up! Bear up the torch!
    I worship! I burn!
You see, you see,
the temple burns with light;
Hymen io Hymenai io king
the king is happy;
I am happy to marry the bed,
the bed of the king,
in Argos, in Argos.
Hymen io Hymenai io the king

But you, mother, lament for father, fatherland;
both are dead;
you keep on weeping, sob.
I light up the light of fire,
mother, for marriage;
it dazzles, blinds;
o Hymenai, they give to you,
Hecate, give that torch,
the torch you give to the bride's bed.

Bring the chorus;
lift our feet in aerial dance;

evan!   evoi!
I cry for my fate, happiest of fates
in my father's time.
Holy is the chorus
Phoebus, lead the chorus
into the temple ringed with leaves,
where I used to sacrifice.
Hymen io Hymenai io Hymen.

Mother,
be of the chorus and dance.
Weave your feet with mine
in the dearest of dances.
Shout the hymenal song. Call it.
Call o Hymenai. Call the Hymenal.
O with happy song
sing the bride and bridegroom.
Go, lovely robed Phrygian girls,
be the chorus for my wedding,
the husband destined for my bed.

CHORUS. You will not forget your daughter although she rages
     like a Bacchant?
Do not, do not, allow her to go her nimble way to the Greeks.
HECUBA. Hephaestus, although it is true you carry the torch
     at the marriages of mortal men, now you are kindling a bitter
       flame,
     one far removed from any prospects of greatness. O, my child,
     I never imagined that you would be married at spear-point
     at the promptings of the Greeks. Give me that torch—
     it is not safe to carry one while you rage and dance
     like a worshipper of Bacchus. Your misfortunes, child,
     do not show soundness of mind, but you continue distraught.

Women of Troy, carry in the torch, and trade her marriage song
     for tears.

CASSANDRA. Mother, crown my head with garlands as you would a
     victor's,

and find pleasure in my royal wedding:
come with me to him—if I am unwilling,
push me along. If there really is an Apollo,
the god of words, Agamemnon, this great and famous king,
ruler of the Achaeans, forces me to a wedlock
more unmanageable than Helen's,
for I will kill him and ruin his home
in return for the sufferings of brothers and father.
But let that go, let us not sing of the axe-blade
pressed against my neck, and against others',
nor of the matricidal struggles which my marriage
will bring about, and the fall of the house of Atreus.
Instead I will reveal to you how much happier our city is
than the Achaeans—yes, the god is in me, but still
for as long as it takes to tell this, I won't rage like a Bacchant:
the Greeks because of one woman, of one man's lust for her,
became the ruin of many thousands in their quest for her,
and their general, the wise Agamemnon, because of what he
     hated
destroyed the things he loved most: the pleasures of home and
     children,
resigning them instead to his brother, because of a woman
not carried off by force, not raped, but one who came here
     willingly;
but when they reached the banks of the Scamander
they died, neither defending the boundary-stones of their land
nor the windy towers of their home country: those who died in
     the war
did not see their children again,
were not wrapped in funeral cloth by their wives' hands,
but in an alien land they were laid to rest;
while in their homes the same things came to pass:
widows died, fathers went to the grave, childless
though they had in fact raised up children and heirs,
and there was no one left who would give them
the gift of blood poured over the graves—
yes, in this fashion the army is well-praised:
I will not recount their villainies, my Muse cannot adorn

that song, whatever it is, that sings of evil.
But as for the Trojans—first of all, and greatest glory,
they died for their country; friends carried home the bodies
of those the spear slew, and gave them proper burial:
in the soil of our ancestors they enjoy the embraces of earth
because of the hands of those bound in duty to them alive or
     dead,
but before they died, they lived every day, they lived it
with their wives and children behind the walls, and under the
     roofs,
of Troy: but such pleasures did the Greeks enjoy?

Now hear for yourselves the tragic story of Hector—
how it really was:
when he died men thought him the best of fighters,
and the coming of the Greeks brought this about:
for had they stayed at home he would have gone unnoticed
although he was so brave.
But Paris married a daughter of Zeus: if he had not
he would have married some girl no one ever mentioned.
The man of sense, then, should avoid war as best he can,
but if it comes to that, it is a garland far from shameful
for a city if it perishes in glory, but disgraceful if it go down in
     cowardice.
Because of this, mother, there is no need to pity our land
or my new bed, for in this marriage I will destroy our enemies.
CHORUS. How sweetly, Cassandra, you laugh at your troubles
     and sing of what maybe you will not make true, for all your
          singing.
TALTHYBIUS. If Apollo had not given you a prophet's soul
     you would not dismiss the generals so lightly
     without giving them some reward from your talent.
     However, it is quite evident that people who seem great and wise
     in reality are no better than those worth nothing,
     for the mightiest king of all the Greeks,
     the beloved son of Atreus, has consented
     to marry this maenad girl: although I am a poor man
     and cannot afford her, yet I'd never buy her bed.

But, Cassandra, since you're not completely sane,
I'll take no notice of your insulting remarks;
let the winds, as it were, scatter them if they care to:
follow me to the ships, you are now the general's bride.
But in regard to you, Hecuba,
whenever Odysseus wants you, go along with him:
you will be the servant of a sensible woman—
at least that's what all the Greeks say about Penelope.

CASSANDRA. You're an ass, Talthybius—
Why do they call people like you "heralds?"
All men hate you—
you are the lackeys of tyrants and cities.
Are you sure my mother will go to Odysseus's palace?
Where are Apollo's words then?
They say (at least as I see them)
that she will die here:
I refuse to tell her about the rest,
it is better she does not know;
and Odysseus, that unhappy man,
he can't see what evils wait for him:
soon my misfortunes, and those of the Trojans,
will seem like precious gold to him: ten years of wandering
will be added to his ten years here,
before he returns home alone . . .
he will see where the mad Charybdis makes her home
in a narrow gorge between the rocks,
and the Cyclops, eater of raw flesh, living in the mountains,
and Ligurian Circe, who changes men to pigs, their true form;
he will know shipwreck many times in the salt sea
and the lust for the lotus flower,
the guilt for the cattle of the sun, whose flesh gives up
a bitter voice when slain;
to make a long story short, he shall go alive to the House of
    Hades,
and, escaping from the sea, return home to more evil:
but why do I feather the troubles of Odysseus, and shoot them
    forth?
My own approach—as soon as possible let me go to my marriage,

my husband, you will be buried at night, in an evil hour,
not in the daylight when no harm comes,
but while you dream of doing something great, O great Danaan
    prince;
and my naked body, thrown in a ditch, river on river
swollen with rain and melted snow, will hurry along,
past the nuptial tomb, past my husband's grave,
and give me, Apollo's girl, for the beasts to eat.

O wreath of the gods, dearest to me, emblem of enraptured
    prophecy—
good-by. Good-by,
I have left the banquets in the temple
where I found pleasures formerly.
Go away from the spasms of my flesh while my flesh is yet chaste;
I give them for the swift winds to carry away,
o prophet king.

The general's ship: where is she? How do I board her?
Let us go. Quickly. And wait for a breeze filling the sails:
I am one of the three furies you bring from Troy.

Good-by, mother, you weep over nothing.
Good-by, city, brothers beneath your earth, father who gave
    us life,
you will receive me soon.
I GO TO THE CONQUERING DEAD, TO THE
    RUINED PALACE OF ATREUS,
TO THE MAN WHO HAS TAKEN OUR LIVES.

[TALTHYBIUS *and* CASSANDRA *go off to the Greek camp.* HECUBA
starts to fall slowly to the ground, there to remain for some time.]

CHORUS. Watchers of the old Hecuba:
    don't you see how our old queen falls
    speechless to the ground? Help her up!
    Are you going to let her lie there?
    Help her to stand up straight!

HECUBA. Leave me: it would be kindness on your part
   to let me lie here, where I have fallen
   as if I were a corpse and one of the dead—
   I know suffering,
   I have known suffering,
   I shall know suffering.
   O gods! I do summon them though they've been poor allies—
   all the same, there's something to be said for calling on them—
   whenever one of us has fallen on evil days;
   for most of all I want to sing of happier times
   and stir up more pity for my woes:
   I was a tyrant, I was married to a king.
   I gave birth to the best children in the city
   not by reason of their number, but because of their virtue;
   no Trojan, no Greek, no barbarian woman would ever boast
   that she has given birth to such as they;
   when I saw them cut down fighting in the front ranks,
   I had my hair cut off in front of their graves;
   and Priam, their planter—I did not hear this
   but with my own eyes I saw him murdered
   in front of the household altar, and the city sacked;
   my girls, brought up for honorable marriage,
   snatched out of my hands, made the concubines of others,
   and now there is no hope we shall see them again
   or that they will come back to look at me, their mother;
   and the last thing, capstone of misfortune,
   is that I arrive in Greece an old woman and slave,
   where they will have me doing that which is most unsuited
   to old age: guarding the palace keys like a hired lackey,
   not like one who gave birth to a Hector,
   or making bread, and going to sleep on the ground—
   with my shrivelled body born in a royal bed—
   when I have clothed my ragged flesh in rags,
   the tatters of my royal robes: but O how unfit
   for the wearing of rich and happy folk;
   god, because of the marriage of one woman
   through what have I gone? through what shall I go?

Cassandra, my child, maenad, companion of the gods,
amid what misfortunes do you find an end to your maidenhood?
Polyxena, my other wretched daughter,
who knows where in the world you are?
Since not son or daughter, out of all those I mothered,
remains now to help me when I am made to suffer,
tell me why to stand up,
tell me upon what to stand?

Lead me, once your gracious queen,
now a slave, to some low bed
upon the city's battlements
where I will die
wasted away in tears:
count no one happy
until he is dead.

[HECUBA *is made comfortable while the* CHORUS *sings.*]

STROPHE

CHORUS. Sing to me of Ilium, Muse,
    amid our tears, find her funeral song
    and make it of new strange tones;
    for now I will cry out a melody for Troy,
    of how I was undone by the Greeks' hollow horse
    and made captive by their spears
    when they left it at our gates, embossed in gold,
    roaring to the skies with its cargo of arms,
    and the people raised up a cry, a victory shout,
    standing on the citadel of the city:
    "Go, you that have found rest from troubles,
    bring in this holy image
    for the Zeus-born Athena, the maiden of Troy."
    Which one of the young men was not there,
    which one of the old men?
    Rejoicing in their hymns
    they embraced a crafty ruin.

ANTISTROPHE

All the children of Phrygia
ran eagerly to the gates,
and gave to the goddess
this ambuscade, this Atē,
smoothly wrought in mountain pine
as a graceful gift for the virgin Pallas,
driver of immortal horses,
and like a ship's black hull
they dragged it through their city
with linen ropes, into the marble hall,
the stone floor, of Athena's temple
soon wet with my homeland's blood;
over them, amid their labor and their joy,
black night came,
while the Libyan flute, of tough jocander,
echoed Phrygian tunes, and maidens,
to the light beating of dancing feet,
sang a joyful song;
in our halls the radiant torch of fire
gave off a black gleaming,
the remedy for sleep.

Then was I singing in my halls
amid the choruses
Artemis, the mountain-dwelling goddess,
Zeus's child,
when up and down the city
a war cry of murder gripped the homes of Pergamon
and newborn children threw their hands fluttering
about their mothers' robes:
war had burst forth from his place of ambush,
the work of the war-maid Pallas,
we were murdered about the altars,
our throats cut like sheep and cows:
in their beds the young men were axed,

leaving our women alone,
to win a crown of valor for Hellas,
the good nurse of heroes,
and sorrow for the fatherland of Troy.

[ANDROMACHE *enters on a wagon drawn by horses. The wagon
is loaded with loot and* HECTOR's *arms.*]

CHORUS. See, Hecuba: Andromache is coming,
   drawn by a team of Greek horses;
   dear Astyanax, Hector's son, accompanies her,
   and waits upon the rocking of her breasts.
HECUBA. Where are you going, poor woman,
   on that wagon, with Hector's arms
   beside you, and the Trojans' spoil
      won by the spear?
   Is it with them that Achilles' son
   will build the shrines of Phthia?

1ST STROPHE

ANDROMACHE. The Greeks, our masters, lead me forth.
HECUBA. oimoi
ANDROMACHE.   Why do you bewail the paean
HECUBA. aiai
ANDROMACHE.   of my sorrows
HECUBA. O Zeus
ANDROMACHE.   and misfortunes?
HECUBA. My children
ANDROMACHE.   We are no more.

1ST ANTISTROPHE

HECUBA. Wealth has come and gone, and Troy
ANDROMACHE. that suffers,
HECUBA.   and my children's noble race.
ANDROMACHE. woe woe,
HECUBA.   yes, woe for my
ANDROMACHE. sorrows:
HECUBA.   pitiable the end

ANDROMACHE. of our city
HECUBA. which smolders and burns.

2ND STROPHE

ANDROMACHE. Come to me, my husband,
HECUBA. You are calling, my child,
  on one who is in hell.
ANDROMACHE. defender of your wife.

2ND ANTISTROPHE

HECUBA. O killer of the Greeks,
  oldest of all the sons
  I gave to Priam, let me sleep
  I pray, in hell's house.

3RD STROPHE

ANDROMACHE. Our losses are great, queen, we have suffered
    countless pains
  since our city died, and new pains come to rest upon the old,
  melancholia from the gods: all because your Paris fled from
    death
  and for a marriage brought destruction down on Troy's
    citadel—
  bleeding, the bodies of our dead lie here beside Pallas Athena
  for the vultures to pick: now Troy finishes her course.

3RD ANTISTROPHE

HECUBA. I weep for you, my fatherland,
  now you see your pitiable conclusion, my house
  where I bore children
  and all abandoned, left to the dogs and sackers;
  children, children, your mother leaves you forever
  when she leaves the city;
  with what wailing, what sadness,
  does tear fall after tear in an endless sequence?
  the dead in our houses lose thought of the body's pain
  and forget to weep.

CHORUS. For us how sweet are tears,
  threnodies, the music of sorrow.
ANDROMACHE. Mother, do you understand these things,
  you who have given birth to Hector,
  killer of the Greeks, their nightly fear?
HECUBA. Child, I see the gods in this, they make a city
  from nothing, then ruins from a fair appearance.
ANDROMACHE. My child and I are taken as plunder—
  high birth goes to slavery—
  these are the changes life takes.
HECUBA. Ananke's strange power: just now Cassandra
  was torn from me by force and dragged away.
ANDROMACHE. heu! heu!
  Another Ajax, it seems, is born
  another violator of your child,
  and still you suffer—
HECUBA. What I do I neither count nor measure:
  one pain competes with another.
ANDROMACHE. Polyxena died in front of Achilles' tomb,
  her throat cut in sacrifice for a corpse.
HECUBA. oimoi
  that enigma, that riddle, the herald set for me,
  is clear now, and the manner of its execution.
ANDROMACHE. I saw her myself, stepping down from the wagon,
  I hid her in my robes and beat my breasts for grief.
HECUBA. aiai—my child, for your unholy sacrifice.
  aiai—how wrongly they put you to death.
ANDROMACHE. She died as she died; by a kindlier death,
  more fortunate than my life, she died.
HECUBA. Child, death differs from the daylight in this—
  for the one is nothing, but hope lives in the other.
ANDROMACHE. Mother, listen—I will explain something
  to you, so you will be happy.
  I want to give you some words of comfort, if I can,
  and to lighten your heart, already too heavy:
  I tell you this—not to have been born
  is the same as death: but to die,

that is better than living in sadness;
but the lucky man, sometimes called "the happy,"
when his luck changes and goes bad,
wanders in mind far from his former state;
your child, Polyxena, died as if she had
never seen the light, had never known troubles:
but I, who aimed for everyone's approval,
got it, though I was still the loser;
those good qualities men find in women
I won by constant struggle in Hector's house:
first, whether real blame attaches to women
for this, still it automatically ruins their reputation—
I mean for a woman not to stay at home—
so I gave up all desire to go out.
I kept out the womenfolk with their pretty words,
I refused them gossipings and small talk,
being content to have mind as my schoolmaster
and to live virtuously at my husband's side,
for my husband I had a quiet tongue and gentle eye,
if ever we quarrelled about anything,
I knew when I should be the stronger,
and when the victory was his, rightfully. . . .
This, mother, when the Greeks heard of it,
that there was a woman and a wife like me,
destroyed me and laid me open: Pyrrhus,
Achilles' son, wanted me to wife,
to make me a slave in a murderer's home:
for if by rejecting Hector and his ghost,
I offer my heart to my new husband,
I will appear unfaithful to a dead man,
but on the other hand, if I spurn Pyrrhus
I shall win my master's hate.
Yet they say one night melts
a woman's hate for a man's bed.
I spit out the woman, whoever she is,
that, throwing off a former husband
for a new bed, loves another: yet

it is equally true that a young mare,
divorced from the companion of her youth,
does not take easily to a new yoke, a new friend:
and yet animals are born mute and dumb,
lacking reason they are inferior by nature.
You, Hector, by birth, intelligence, wealth,
were the fit mate for me,
great in your manliness and excellence,
you took me from my father's halls,
a girl pure of heart and unbroken spirit,
you were the first and only to bring me to bed:
now you have been cut down, and I leave my home,
my family, my city, a prisoner of the spear,
to set sail for Greece, to a slave's yoke:
now do you think that Polyxena's death,
for whom you were mourning just now,
is a greater thing than my misfortunes?
That which is left over for all men
is denied me: hope is no comfort in my life,
and I do not delude myself, thinking
I will attempt something useful—
but it is sweet to dream, and nothing more.

CHORUS. You have come to the limits of tragedy, even to my own
condition;
in your laments I seem to meet myself, my sorrow and
instruction.

HECUBA. I have never in my life been aboard a ship,
yet by looking at pictures and listening to stories,
I think I have come to understand them:
now if the sailors believe they can ride out a storm,
they are eager to find some safety by their own efforts;
one of them attends to the rudder, another to the sails,
while the rest are busy pumping out the bilge;
but when the sea, raging in confusion and uproar,
swamps their vessel, they give up that hope
and commit themselves to the waves' running:
and so, because I have suffered much

and seem at times to have lost the power of my voice,
the god's storm, falling on me as if from the stars,
defeats me . . . my child, listen to me—
give up your Hector. Tears cannot bring him back.
Instead honor your new husband, offer him your body's sweet
    trap:
do this, and you will delight your friends;
as for your boy, my son's son, bring him up for Troy's sake,
so that any children born out of you will
rebuild our city, and so make a Troy again.

But one story steps out of another:
what servant of the Greeks is this?
a messenger bringing news our way?

[*Enter* TALTHYBIUS.]

TALTHYBIUS. O wife of him once the best
    of the Trojans, Andromache, I mean:
    learn not to hate me: unwillingly
    must I announce the commands of the Greeks
    and Pelops' sons, Agamemnon, Menelaus.
ANDROMACHE. What are their desires? Do they mark
    a rebirth of evils for us?
TALTHYBIUS. It has been decided that this boy . . .
    [*aside*] now what's the best way to put it?
ANDROMACHE. Not that we're not to have the same master?
TALTHYBIUS. No Greek will ever be his master.
ANDROMACHE. That they will leave him here without me,
    one more ruin upon this empty plain?
TALTHYBIUS. I don't know how to tell you.
ANDROMACHE. I commend your modesty: now speak up.
TALTHYBIUS. They will kill your son, if you must know—
ANDROMACHE. Oh, I hear a tragedy worse than my marriage.
TALTHYBIUS. Odysseus, addressing the assembly, put the motion
    through,
ANDROMACHE. What we suffer is not to be measured by any man.
TALTHYBIUS. affirming that it was not in our best interests

to permit a Trojan hero's son to live in Greece.
ANDROMACHE. May that same sentence strike his own children.

[As the guards advance to seize ASTYANAX, ANDROMACHE *moves
to protect him and resist the soldiers.]*

TALTHYBIUS. Your son must be thrown down from that tower:
   let it be so, and show yourself the wiser for it;
   give him to me, and, like a woman of rank,
   suffer, if you must, but in silence, with dignity:
   hold back your tears and remember who you are,
   that you can do nothing against us, and from no place
   again may you draw strength. Think for a moment:
   we have put an end to your city, your husband;
   we hold you in our power: how can one woman
   think to fight us? therefore it is my wish
   that you give up this desire to fight about it,
   and to do what would be disgraceful for you
   and shame for you; and above all, to stop hurling curses
   at the Greeks.
   If you turn the army against you because of these insults,
   your child will rot unburied, no one will pay him
   the customary funeral rites: keep quiet and hope for the best,
   give in to the pressure of events: in this way you will at least
   insure your son a ritual death, and perhaps because of your
      decorum
   at this critical moment the Greeks will become your better
      friends.
ANDROMACHE. Dear, dear child, whom I prize in no ordinary way,
   you must die at the hands of our enemies,
   and leave behind you a ruined mother.

   Your father's courage that meant safety and shelter
   for others is the weapon of your destruction;
   his bravery proves your misfortune:
   unlucky that bed, that wedding,
   whereby I went into Hector's house
   to bring up my son as a sacrifice, an offering

to the Greeks, as if we never said that our boy
would grow up to be master of Asia, this fruitful land.
Do you weep, my son?
Do you understand your misfortune?
Why do you hold on to me, and pull at my clothing,
like a little chick seeking my wings' protection?
Famous Hector will not come out of the earth,
shaking a spear, to give you sanctuary;
no friend or kinsman of his breaks in upon us
and offers you an avenue of escape: the might
of Troy lies broken in these ruins behind us:
no, you are to fall and break your neck;
pitilessly will they force life's breath from you,
my child, whom I love to hold so close,
whose breath I find so sweet: to no purpose,
then, this breast that gave you milk
while you were bound in swaddling clothes,
the pangs of your birth, the mingled joys
and sorrows I felt on your behalf,
now reduced to petty griefs, helpless tears . . .
now, and never again, give your mother a kiss,
give yourself over to her who gave you birth,
come, give me your hands, let us embrace,
though it is for the last time, the last time.

[*They embrace and kiss,* ANDROMACHE *presents him to the
guards and the herald, and addresses them.*]

O Greeks, inventors of barbarian pain,
why do you kill this innocent boy?
Helen, daughter of Tyndareus, I say
you were not born of Zeus, but from many fathers:
Alastor was the first, vendetta's herald,
then Phthonos, hatred, Phonos, murder,
Thanatos, death: all these the earth rears up
to plague us, and Zeus had no part in their creating,
the common curse of Greek and non-Greek alike:
may you die and go over to nothing;

for from your lovely dashing eyes ruin fell
as envy's blight on Phrygia's still more lovely fields:
take him, lead him away, throw him down the wall,
if that is your plan, and eat his flesh,
for because of the gods we are dying
and cannot protect one small child from death.

Hide my body, throw it on the ship;
let me set sail for lovely bridal
now that I have lost my son.
CHORUS. Unhappy Troy, you have lost countless sons
because of one woman and her hated bed.
TALTHYBIUS. Come on, lad, let go of your mother;
she has her own sorrows: you must come
with me to that embrasured ancestral tower
where it has been decreed you shall die.
Take him: matters such as this
should have the services of a herald
who pitiless and shameless understands
the king's wisdom more than I.

[TALTHYBIUS *and attendants leave with* ASTYANAX; ANDROMACHE *retires.*]

HECUBA. Child, son of my son, without the least semblance
of right are we robbed of your life, your mother
and I: now what will become of me? What can I
do for you, but give you this—
blows on the head, blows on the heart?
That is what we command: we weep for you now
as we wept for the city: does anything hold us back
rushing down into complete destruction?

1ST STROPHE

CHORUS. O Telamon, king, ruler of Salamis, the land the bees
make honey from,
you who have made your home that island the sea waves
encircle,

a country that lies over and against those holy Attic cliffs
where for the first time Athena planted the root
of the shining olive tree, now a heavenly crown and adornment
of fruitful Athens:
was it from there once
you sailed with Alcmene's son, the archer Heracles
to lay Ilium, our Ilium, waste?
When you came from Hellas in those olden days,

1st Antistrophe

when that great hero, your comrade, was the first
who, gathering the flower of Greek youth,
led them to the banks of the lovely flowing Simois,
because our old king had denied him those immortal horses,
his rightful due, and
he anchored his ships there
lashing their cables firmly,
then, taking up his bow, brought murder to Laomedon's people;
the measured walls that Phoebus built to shelter us—
with the fire's red blast he cast them down and made a ruin,
subjecting the Trojan's lands to the horrors of a sack;
yes, twice the towers of Dardanus' city have fallen;
twice have the Greeks attacked
and covered this land with the blood of our people.

2nd Strophe

In vain, o delicate child, o Ganymede,
walking luxuriously amid the golden wine-pourers—
for us it does not matter you are Laomedon's heir
and have the duty of keeping Zeus's cup forever full,
a most honorable service, now that the land that has brought
    you forth
is to be consumed with fire, and the beaches where the waves
    roll in
send the shrieks of your people, women and children,
up like eagles wailing for their lost little ones,
some for their husbands and children,

the rest for their grey-haired mothers,
while your baths fed by the soft rain and the mountain springs,
the gymnasia, the race courses,
now are gone for good, but you, the gods' cupbearer,
your face always young and lovely, rejoicing in the graces' calm,
stand beside the throne of Zeus with a pitcher full of wine,
as Hellas destroys the race of Priam.

2ND ANTISTROPHE

Eros, Eros, you who visited, coming down from the gods,
the houses of Dardanus in days gone by,
how greatly then you did exalt our city when we were bound
   to them
by the glory of Ganymede's marriage: but now no longer
shall I insult Zeus or his dealings with us.
White-winged Eos, so dear to men,
looked down upon our land as it died,
looked down and saw our towers fall,
though she held in her bridal bower a son of our people,
and children by him
whom the golden chariot caught up, and made a home for
amid the stars, a great hope for his fatherland:
the gods' love for us, as all may see, has come to an end.

[MENELAUS *and his attendants appear.*]

MENELAUS. I am cheered by the brightness of today's sun
by whose grace I plan to master Helen, my wife,
for I am her husband, Menelaus, who together
with the army has worked long and hard for this moment:
I did not come to Troy, as many think,
because of the woman, but to take vengeance
on that man who, as my guest, deceived me;
now that he has with the help of the gods
paid the penalty, and his land has fallen
to our soldiers, I have come to fetch the woman,
as the name of wife I can no longer speak with pleasure
though she was once mine: in these huts

where the captive women wait our pleasures
she has been quartered along with the others;
when they captured her in the last battle
she was given to me to dispose of as I saw fit:
either to kill on the spot, or bring back to Argos,
and it was my plan to save her from death
in Troy, only to ship her back to Greece
where she will be executed to avenge
all my comrades who have died in this war.

[*to his attendants*]

Come on, go into the tents, bring her out,
drag her by the hair that still holds, I think,
some scent of the murders she caused;
as soon as we catch a favorable breeze,
we'll escort her home in the proper manner.

HECUBA [*in an attitude of prayer*].
   O great supporter of the earth,
   you who sit on her as if she were your chair of state,
   O whoever you are,
   as it is hard for us to know
   whether you are nature's law, or but exist in our minds,
   Zeus, I pray to you,
   I send up my thanks,
   for you settle the affairs of men with justice,
   walking a path that betrays your presence
   not by the least sound.

MENELAUS. What's this? How strangely she prays!

HECUBA. Menelaus, if you kill your wife
   I'll thank you for it: but take care
   when you see her, lest she slay you
   with desire, for she has caught
   the eyes of many men and destroyed
   their cities, burnt their homes,
   such is the power of her fascination.
   You and I, I think, know her, as indeed
   all do, who have suffered in this war.

[HELEN *is brought out by the attendants, and made to stand in front of* MENELAUS.]

HELEN. Menelaus, this is a beginning
  that could make me quake with fear;
  your servants dragged me out of the tent
  by force, and pushed me here in front of you;
  now, although you've reason to hate me
  well enough, tell me, please, what have you
  and the Greeks decided to do with me?
MENELAUS. You are mine to kill, the army
  gave me that right unanimously;
  I am the man you sinned against.
HELEN. Then may I discuss it with you for a little while,
  since, if I die without that, I die unjustly?
MENELAUS. I did not come for talk, but to kill.
HECUBA. Listen to her, so that she may die
  lacking nothing, not even this;
  let me be her prosecutor, for you have
  no knowledge of what she did in Troy,
  and when I've finished with her story,
  she will die with no defense left her.
MENELAUS. A chance to lecture us? If she wants to speak
  she may. But mark you, I grant her
  this favor for your words' sake, not her own.

[*The actors arrange themselves for a trial in the Athenian manner,* HELEN *and* HECUBA *to speak for defense and prosecution respectively.* MENELAUS *and his retinue stand between.*]

HELEN. Perhaps, your honor, it will happen that,
  whether I argue my case well or not,
  you will refuse to answer, laboring under
  the false assumption I am one of your enemies.
  Yet I shall answer what I suppose you will say
  in accusing me, opposing my charges for yours.
  To begin at the beginning: this Hecuba here
  is herself the prime cause of Troy's misfortunes

and our own, if only because she brought forth
her son Paris, and standing as her accomplice
in this I name her husband, old Priam,
not because he was the father, but for
the simple reason he refused to heed the oracle
which most clearly said that this son of his,
if he did not kill him while still a baby,
would prove the spark to burn Troy down.
Now as for the rest, the famous beauty contest, I mean,
held on the slopes of Mount Ida among the three goddesses,
I will dispose of briefly, as follows—
Athena promised him the command of the Trojan armies
to make war on and defeat those of Greece,
thereby dispelling and destroying the whole Hellenic people,
and Hera the joint throne of Asia and Europe, for Paris alone
      to enjoy,
but Aphrodite, amazed at how beautiful I was,
whispered to him sweetly of my surpassing beauty:
if she won out over the other goddesses, I would be his.
Thus it was that love and the Love Goddess carried the day.
My new marriage became the salvation of Greece,
for because of it you Greeks do not live today
under a foreign occupation or are forced
to minister to its needs. I was sold
for my sex to satisfy a prodigy's accursed desire
for happiness in order to save our homeland from ruin.
Under other circumstances, this would have earned me a crown.
Or do you say that I do not answer to the charge
of desertion, of abandoning you, my husband,
my child, and my home? He came, this avenging angel
of Hecuba's, whether you call him Paris
or Alexander, with no small goddess by his side,
whom you, churl, left me alone with in the palace,
when you sailed off from Sparta to Crete.
Well, let that be as it may . . .
I shall examine myself now, not you,
What idea drove me from home and family?

It was Aphrodite put this motion in my heart,
she who is stronger than all the progeny of Zeus,
for though he is accounted their father and holder
of supreme power, yet he is still her slave.
Therefore, forgive me. Yet perhaps in what follows
you will find some specious charge against me:
when Alexander died, departing the crease of this world,
it became my duty to leave the city and return
to the Greek ships, although by now the gods
had grown careless of who enjoyed my bed.
But against my will Deiphobus, who lies dead
over there, married me: even when I tried to escape
by means of sheets tied together, the sentries
captured me (Let them be called forth as witnesses!)
and brought me back despite the Trojans' reluctance.
How is it then right, husband, that I should die
justly by your hand, since he married me by force
and in his home I lived no life of triumph,
rather that of bitter slavery. If you think
to overcome the gods, your wish is stupid.

CHORUS. Speak for your children, your fatherland, queen:
  although there is some sense in what she says,
  yet it was a filthy whore who spoke.

HECUBA. I shall defend first of all the goddesses she dragged into
    her story
  in a fruitless attempt to absolve herself of guilt:
  does it seem at all likely that either Hera or Athena
  could so have lost their reason, for the one to sell Argos,
  homeland, to a barbarian, or for the other to enslave
  her own Athens to the Phrygians? In fact they came
  to Mount Ida for sport, simply to amuse themselves.
  Is there any reason why Hera should be so enamored
  of beauty as to show off before strangers, unless
  she really does want a better husband than Zeus?
  Or Athena—did she not demand perpetual virginity
  from her father at birth? Is she now pursuing
  some god or hero for marriage? Do not accuse then,
  blasphemer, the gods of folly, your own folly;

don't make them an adornment or accessory to your evil ways.
Now you also maintained that Aphrodite (oh, I can hear her
laughing right now) came with my son to Menelaus's house—
tell me, was it not in her power to take you,
together with your whole city of Amyclae, to Troy
while remaining peacefully in her heaven?
No, it was the beauty of my son,
which, when you had seen it, caught your fancy
and now call your Cyprian deity: all men's folly
is their *Aphrodite,* or rather, their *Aphrosyne.*[1]
For when you saw him in his barbarian clothes,
and gleaming with gold, madness visited you,
madness for the pomp and finery you had not in Greece,
but once having put Sparta far behind you,
you hoped to sink Troy, running over at that time
with wealth, in a flood of female extravagances.
You felt that Menelaus's fortune
had never been sufficient for you,
his palaces, cities, acreages, when you desired
to revel in luxury, and yet you still say
my son carried you off by force of love.
None of the Spartiates was aware
of what was taking place, you did not
scream and shout, although you lived with your brothers,
the heroes Castor and Pollux,
at the time not yet translated to the stars.
When you came to Troy, with the Greeks hot after you,
and there ensued that war, what did you do then?
You used to praise your old husband,
whenever he did well in the field of battle,
only to harass my son, casting it into his teeth,
as it were, how great a rival he had for your favors,
but whenever the fortunes of the Trojans prospered,
Menelaus was nothing to you—
so you passed the time, attending on the vagaries of chance,
but in no case did you ever appear to us,

1. pun on Aphrodite (love) and Aphrosyne (thoughtlessness).

or were you in fact, a lover of virtue.
You say you tried to steal your body away
by means of homemade ladders because you were being held
against your will: but whoever saw you
attempting to fasten a halter about your neck
or whetting a knife to slash your wrists,
as many a good and genuine wife did, after her husband's death.
Many times I gave you good advice: namely,
to leave Troy for good, and let my son marry again,
that, if you would do this, I would make arrangements
to send you back secretly to the ships and so stop the war
with the Greeks. But you took this in bad part;
you preferred a life of ease and comfort in Alexander's palace.
You wished the worship of barbarians:
that was your bounty. And you used to go abroad to take the air,
dressed in all the finery our condition afforded,
and gaze composedly at the sky, the same sky
your husband saw—just as you do now, beast, doxy, whore.
Far better were you to have shown yourself in rags,
trembling in fear of his just sentence,
your head shaved after the manner of a prostitute,
humiliating herself in front of her betters.
Menelaus, to put a quick end to argument,
give to Hellas one more crown of victory achieved:
slay her in a way worthy of yourself.
Establish this law for other women too:
whoever betrays her husband shall die at his hands.

CHORUS. Punish her, Menelaus, in a manner befitting your fathers
and your house. Show yourself a man to your friends
and a nobleman to your foes.

MENELAUS. I agree with you, gracious lady, in every point,
both of law and inclination, that of her accord
she left our house to grace a stranger's bed,
and that Cypris, to please her vanity,
is brought into the argument.
Therefore my sentence is:
you shall be stoned to death.
The long sufferings of the Greeks require this,

though it is small atonement, to teach you
you cannot bring me to shame.

HELEN. Do not, I beg you, do not accuse me
even now of a foul disease the gods sent me.
Pardon me, do not slay me.

HECUBA. King, you must not betray the memory of all those she slew
who were your allies: in the name of the dead and of their
children
I beseech you.

MENELAUS. Cease, old woman, I pay her no mind.
Attendants, convey her to our ship
until it sets forth.

HECUBA. Be careful: let her not walk the same deck with you!

MENELAUS. Now why is that? Is she so much heavier than I
remember
that she might sink the ship?

HECUBA. No lover but loves forever.

MENELAUS. No, not so. We are of that disposition
only while those we love are true.
Yet your point is well taken;
it shall be as you suggest.
We will not live together even on the same ship
for a few days, and when we land in Argos,
she will die as foully as she lived,
and by that teach her sisters in sin
a long-delayed lesson in chastity.
This is no easy way, yet thus will whores
though more depraved than she, learn fear.

[HELEN *is escorted off to the ships by the attendants;* MENELAUS
confers privately with HECUBA *for a moment, then follows them;
the* CHORUS *prepares to sing.*]

1ST STROPHE

CHORUS. So now, O Zeus, you have betrayed
to the Greeks your temples in Troy,
your altars heavy with incense—

with the flame of sacrifice rising—
the myrrh drifting—into the sky:
Pergamon—Ida's brook and woodland
dense with ivy climbing the slopes
watered by mountain streams,
cold-running, ice-clear:
the gleaming, the god-haunted hill,
mornings of all the world
struck first by the sun's light.

1st Antistrophe

Rites ruined! O Zeus
The well-omened cries of the dancers
far into the dark of night,
nightlong fetes to the gods,
images of their images,
polished, of silver,
held aloft by fluttering fingers,
holy moon festivals,
twelve in number—
I wonder, king of the sky, I wonder,
if, seated upon your throne in air,
you think of my city,
ruined city, consumed by the fire's bright rage.

2nd Strophe

O beloved, o husband,
dead you indeed wander,
unwashed, unburied;
though me the sea-burnt ship,
moved upon the wings of its oars,
will carry to Argos, nurser of horses,
where the walls of Cyclopean height
rise into the regions of air.
Our children crowd by the gates,
climbing, weeping, on their mothers' necks,
wail, wail,

"Mama, oimoi, they carry me off,
far from your eyes,
alone,
upon a sea-black ship,
oars cutting the sea,
to holy Salamis
to the hills of Isthmus,
bridging two seas, fundament
of the gates of Pelops."

2ND ANTISTROPHE

Would to god that Menelaus
in the midst of his ship
speeding upon the high sea
the thunderbolt might strike,
in mid-oar stroke fall
the Aegean's thunder-flash,
since from Ilium to Greece,—
from my land he banishes me—
wailing, weeping,
while she, received as Zeus's child,
fingers that delight of maidens,
a mirror beat of gold:
o may he never return to his homeland,
his fathers' bed,
never gain Pitane,
or the goddess' temple
with its gates of bronze,
for he holds her prize,
Helen, dishonor
got through wedlock
to great Hellas
and black woe
to the waters of Simois.

io   io
one anguish walks the earth

hard upon the other; see,
women of Troy, the body
of Astyanax whom they killed—
to them but a thing thrown—
from the towers of our town.

[*Enter* TALTHYBIUS *and soldiers bearing* ASTYANAX's *body upon*
HECTOR's *shield.*]

TALTHYBIUS. Hecuba, one ship remains still on the beach
to transfer Neoptolemus's spoil to Phthia,
although he himself has gone, having heard
bad news of Peleus, his grandfather—
that Acastus has exiled the old man
from the kingdom, and because of this,
too eager to delay, departed suddenly,
Andromache with him, drawing tears from me
as she sailed, groaning aloud for her homeland
and calling to Hector's tomb. She even begged
her lord to bury this body, Hector's child,
who died falling from your walls,
and this brass-backed shield, the Achaeans' dread,
which his father used to cast about his ribs—
she asked him not to carry it to Peleus's
ancestral halls or her new bride chamber,
though she is mother of this corpse,
widow of the shield (sadness came over me
then as I watched her), but, instead
of cedar chest or stone, to bury the boy
upon this shield, and give him into your arms
to wrap in garland shrouds as well as you can.
For since she sailed, her lord's swift flight
removed all chance of her giving him to tomb herself.
When you have arrayed the body, I will cover
him with earth and set sail:
your job is, now, to do what we command
and that, as quickly as possible.
I have already freed you of one burden:

just now I washed him in the Scamander
and bathed his wounds in clear water;
now I go to dig a trench. Come, let us
act quickly, and to one purpose,
the sooner to set sail for home.

HECUBA [*to attendants*].
  On the ground set—for me
  a bitter sight—that shield.
  O you that pride yourselves in weapons
  more than sense: why have you done this?
  Greeks so fearing a child as to commit
  new murder lest he raise anew a fallen city:
  certainly you did not so think
  while Hector prospered in the fight
  and yet we died.
  But when we fell, our people taken,
  you grew afraid of such a boy as he,
  and your dread (hardly worth the word)
  increased though you could not tell me why.
  O my darling, how has death, harbinger's ill,
  come upon you? For had you died fighting
  before the walls, had known Hebē, marriage,
  all that godlike kingship had in store,
  you could have died a man of good fortune, if indeed
  in any of these a man does find his fortune;
  but now, though marking, observing in your soul,
  you never knew them, having nothing,
  you could make use of nothing.

  [*She proceeds to examine his hair, eyes, lips, etc.*]

  Poor boy, how pitifully our ancestral walls,
  Loxias' fenced towers, have torn from your head
  those curls your mother tended as she would
  a garden of young and tender plants,
  and kissed that head laughing aloud
  its murder through a grin of shattered bone
  and flesh, a dishonor I cannot speak of:

hands! how sweetly like your father's
they seem, though unstrung from their joints;
lips that boasted, undone utterly,
lying to me that day in bed:
"Mother, when you die I shall cut my hair,
and, paying the last homage of voice,
bring my comrades to your tomb."
Not you, but I, old and childless,
without a city, bury a wretched body,
and with it, our embraces, efforts,
nights you slept, and I watching.
What shall the poet write?
All epitaph shames you, Greece.
"Because they feared they killed.
Here lies the body of a child."
Still, although nothing
of your father's you may inherit,
yours is the shield
that protected his lovely arms,
to rest upon, now he has gone.
The handle—see how prettily
his fingers have smoothed the grip,
sweat staining the well-rounded edge,
pressing against it with his beard
as he fought. . . .

[*addresses her attendants again*]

Come, prepare the body;
from what we have
let us make it
lovely, for fortune
does not permit him
a costly array.
All that I have
is his. Whoever
rejoices in
prosperity, thinking

it secure, is a fool
among men; chance
in her turnings
like a dance-drunk
dervish now leaps
one way and then
another; no one
prospers forever.

CHORUS. And see, they bring you
from the spoils of Troy
adornment to lay his body by.

HECUBA. O child, not for winning the horse race
or beating your comrades in archery
(these customs we observed and honored,
though not to excess), your father's mother
places these gifts once yours upon you:
but now Helen the god-hated has reft them
from you as she did your life,
destroying all house and family.

CHORUS. Twisting, twisting,
my mind with sorrow;
alas for Hector
once our king.

HECUBA. In those clothes you would have donned,
marrying the noblest of Asia's daughters,
in robes of Phrygian splendor I wrap you.

[*to the shield*]

And you, once triumphant on the battlefield,
Hector's dear shield, I ring with garlands;
you shall die with the dead, though undead;
you have won more honor than those arms
the cunning Odysseus says he won.

CHORUS. Boy, let the earth
receive your piercing sorrow,
your mother lift up
her wailing voice.

HECUBA. aiai

CHORUS.   Lift up a dead wail.

HECUBA.   oimoi moi

CHORUS. Of a truth this evil time will not be forgotten.

HECUBA [*encasing* ASTYANAX *in shroudlike windings*].
    Some of your wounds I heal with broad linen,
    a poor doctor, possessing that name without substance:
    the rest let your father avenge among the dead.

CHORUS. Beat, beat my head.
    Slap me again, again.

HECUBA. O women of Troy, deeply loved . . .

CHORUS. Speak what you dare to think!

HECUBA. So: I see it now—
    there was nothing in god's plan
    save trouble for me and the city,
    plagued beyond measure by them.
    In vain we offered up the best
    that we had; still if god had not cast
    us down, sunk beneath earth,
    we would have lived
    without being seen, none singing
    our tale, poets giving us life
    generation upon generation.
    Let us go, and lay his body to rest,
    for now death's shrouds cover him;
    but little, I think, profit the dead,
    from such petty magnificencies,
    which only are the living's hollow boast.

    [*Attendants exit with the body.*]

CHORUS. io   io
    mother of sorrow;
    what great hopes
    she buries in you,
    born of heroes' line,
    deemed unsurpassably
    happy, but now passed
    away in dreadful death.

Look. Look,
upon the walls,
I see what hands
gleaming with torches,
a new strange evil
about to fall?

[TALTHYBIUS *appears on the wall, with soldiers carrying torches.*]

TALTHYBIUS. I tell you since you have been ordered to burn
the city, no longer hold off with your torches,
but hurl them into the towers we toppled lately
into dust, so that contented we may depart for home.
And you, women of Troy, since my coming here
is for two-fold purpose: when the bugle echoes
the chieftains' desires, go forth to the ships;
you have been banished from this land.
                              Hecuba, fallen
from your former estate, follow these men who have come
from Odysseus, for as his slave the lot casts you forth.

[TALTHYBIUS *and attendants descend and approach* HECUBA *while
she speaks; the city begins to burn with evermore intensity until
the end of the play.*]

HECUBA. O woe. Last is this,
term of all my evils.
My land I must leave;
my city is afire. But,
ancient feet, hurry—
though it is hard,
so that I may take leave
of my sorrowing city.
Troy, great once amid Asia,
your glorious name you will
soon lose: you they burn;
us they lead away.
O gods. But why call?
Called on, they came not.
Come let us run into fire;

gloriously I would burn
with our burning city.

[*As* HECUBA *attempts to run behind the wall, the attendants,
urged on by* TALTHYBIUS, *subdue her.*]

TALTHYBIUS. She's lost her mind with grief.
Grab her! Don't just stand around.
Give her, as you were ordered, to Odysseus.
Don't let his prize escape.

HECUBA. otototototoi
Son of Cronus,
Phrygian lord,
Begetter,
Father,
how evils of
Dardanus' line
we suffer without
just cause
you see?

CHORUS. He sees:
that the city,
great city,
is no longer, that
there is a Troy
no more.

HECUBA. ototototototoi
Ilium
is a gleam
of fire;
the towers
crumple
in the blaze
of fire.

CHORUS. Smoke takes wing;
it is like the land
dying from the spears
rising skywards.
The roofs glow;

flame runs over them;
their blazing spears
point skywards.

STROPHE

HECUBA. Hail earth, nourisher of my children.
CHORUS. eh   eh
HECUBA. Hear me, my children;
catch your mother's voice.
CHORUS. To those who have died
you cry out in your keening.
HECUBA. Lying on the ground,
I stretch out my limbs
and strike it with my fists.
CHORUS. Our turn: bend knees
and call upon our men
beneath earth.
HECUBA. We are carried away;
we are driven away—
CHORUS. Pain, pain,
calls us to it.
HECUBA. To the slaves' house
far from our fatherland.
io   io
Priam, friendless:
Priam, tombless:
you are ignorant
of our doom.
CHORUS. For death made pure
by the blood
it impurely took
came black,
shrouded your two eyes.

ANTISTROPHE

HECUBA. Alas for the gods' halls,
alas for my city.
CHORUS. eh   eh

HECUBA. Receive the spear of death,
   the fire of death.
CHORUS. Earthwards swiftly falling,
   you shall pass away without a name.
HECUBA. Dust takes wing like the smoke in air,
   casts me senseless far from home.
CHORUS. We leave this land, nameless, invisible,
   scattered every which way.
   There is no more a Troy.
HECUBA. Did you feel it?
   Did you hear it?
CHORUS. The towers crash.
HECUBA. Their tremor shall engulf
CHORUS. all our city.
HECUBA. io
   Limbs that tremble with fear,
   support my steps;
   go, wretch,
   to a slave's life.
CHORUS. Alas for our city, unhappy city.
   But even so, wend your way
   to the ships of the Greeks.

EURIPIDES

The Bacchae

TRANSLATED BY
CHARLES BOER

INTRODUCTORY NOTE

The Bacchae is the only play about Dionysus and his worship which has survived, although we know the names of several others. As a consequence of this uniqueness, its interest for the history of religion occasionally obscures its appeal as drama, which is immediate and powerful. The young king Pentheus changes before our eyes from stern upholder of conventional decorum and masculine control into pliant mimic of Dionysian excess and femininity. While Pentheus' destruction at the hands of his mother and the other maenads is only reported, not shown, Euripides does not avoid the final dramatic logic of presenting Pentheus' ecstatic mother carrying her son's head and her slow realization of what has happened. The choral odes are masterful. So intimate is their connection with the plot that they appear to deny what was the case at this period, the chorus's gradual loss of importance and relevance.

As a document in the history of Greek religion, *The Bacchae* is hard to match. It describes the maenad ritual of *oreibasia*, "going into the mountains," *sparagmos*, "tearing apart," and *omophagia*, "eating raw." The extent to which this ritual was actually carried out by Greek women in historical times is disputed, but some aspects certainly existed. *Sparagmos* and *omophagia* represent one facet of Dionysus. The other appears in the release from care offered by wine drinking and festivals like the Spring Dionysia with its music, dance, and processions. That both the awesome personality changes of religious trance and the welcome renewal of fertility were seen as two sides of one god can remind us of how different our culture is from that of ancient Greece.

The Bacchae was produced posthumously; the exact year is not known. It won first prize together with its companion plays.

CHARACTERS

DIONYSUS, the god; son of Zeus and Semele

CHORUS of Asian Bacchae

TEIRESIAS, Theban prophet

CADMUS, former king of Thebes, father of Semele

PENTHEUS, king of Thebes, grandson of CADMUS

GUARD

HERDSMAN-MESSENGER

MESSENGER-SERVANT

AGAVE, daughter of CADMUS and mother of PENTHEUS

The Bacchae

THE SCENE. *In front of the royal palace at Thebes. In the fore-ground is the tomb of Semele. It is still smoking as* DIONYSUS *enters. He is wearing a fawnskin and carries a* thyrsus *or wand of ivy leaves. His appearance is somewhat effeminate. He wears a smiling mask.*

DIONYSUS. I've come—the son of Zeus—to this land of Thebes—
  Dionysus—whom Semele, the daughter of Cadmus, once
    produced,
  dropping me from her womb when the lightning came,
  and now, changed from a god into human shape,
  I'm here at Dirce's streams, the water of Ismenus,
  looking at the grave of my mother whom the lightning
    touched,
  near the house here, and the wreck of the house itself
  smoldering from the fire of Zeus that lives on and on,
  a perpetual insult to my mother from Hera.
  But I congratulate Cadmus, who put this sacred ground here
  for his daughter's grave, which I've covered
  with a vine's green cluster of grapes.
  I left the very golden fields of Lydia
  and Phrygia, and the sunburned flats of Persia,
  and the forts of Bactria, and the land of the Medes
  with its terrible winters. I passed through marvelous Arabia
  and all Asia, which lies along salt waters
  with Greeks and foreigners integrated
  in cities packed with beautiful towers,
  though this is the first Greek city I've come to,
  after getting my dances started elsewhere, my dances
  and ceremonies, so that I would be without doubt a god to men.

[1–22]   355

And the first in the Greek world I've excited
is Thebes, putting a fawnskin over its flesh
and a wand in its hand, a stick of ivy—
all because my mother's sisters, who should have been the last
　　ones
to speak, said Dionysus was not fathered by Zeus,
and that Semele, having done it with some man,
blamed her pregnancy on Zeus, "a scheme of Cadmus,"
they snickered, and said Zeus killed her,
because she lied about him as her lover—
so for all this I've pricked them out of their homes
with a craziness, and they now live in the hills, their minds
　　shot,
forced to go around in my orgy costumes—
everyone in fact who was a woman, all the female side
of Cadmus' people, I drove out of their homes,
so that they sit around now on open rocks, under pine trees,
together with the daughters of Cadmus.
For want to or not this city has got to learn
that it doesn't yet know my Bacchic program,
and that my mother's name will be cleared by me
when people see me as the god she produced with Zeus.
And Pentheus too, whom Cadmus gave the country and his
　　power to,
who was born from a different daughter,
Pentheus too, who fights the god in me, who pushes me away
from drink offerings, who never mentions me in his prayers,
I'll show Pentheus and every Theban that I am god,
and when I've set up everything here
I'll head for some other place,
exposing myself there—and if Thebes becomes mad
and tries to drive my Bacchae out of the hills by force,
I'll get maenads and take command myself.
This is why I have a human form, why I changed my shape,
why I turned my nature into a man's—
but hey, you women who left Fort Tmolus in Lydia,

my gang, whom I brought from foreign towns,
my helpers, my traveling companions,
lift up your native drums from Phrygia,
the ones I contrived, and Mother Rhea's,
and go around the royal house of Pentheus
banging them, so that the city of Cadmus will see it,
while I take off for the forests of Cithaeron,
where my Bacchae are, and where I will join their dancing.

[*Exit* DIONYSUS *as the* CHORUS *of Asian Bacchae enters.*]

CHORUS. We're Asians,
     we come from holy Tmolus,
     we came as fast as we could, working
     for Bromius, hard work but sweet too,
     we have sweet jobs, we say:
     "Bacchus, evoi!"

Who's on the street? Who's on the street? Who?
If anyone's still at home come on out,
but be quiet, and act holy,
I'm going to sing now
The Hymn to Dionysus:

1ST STROPHE

Oh how lucky you are, how really lucky you are,
if you know the gods from within,
if you're for clean living,
if you get the feel of Bacchus
and you do it in the hills
pure in your soul,
and to sit in on the orgies
of Great Mother Cybele,
to shake a wand in the air,
to wear ivy on your head,
to serve Dionysus, how lucky you are!
Go Bacchae! oh go Bacchae!

Bring home Bromius, the god Bromius, son of a god,
who? Dionysus! bring him from the Phrygian hills
through the highways of Greece! who? Bromius!

1st Antistrophe

He was born
when the wings of Zeus' thunder
forced his mother
to deliver, and how it hurt,
that being the end of her life
when the lightning struck,
and then the baby changed its womb
into father Zeus,
who tied him up inside his thigh
with golden pins
and hid the child from his wife,
and when the Fates were finally ready,
Zeus produced a god, bull-horned,
crowned him with a garland of snakes,
and that's why his maenads, holding their wands,
do up their hair that way.

2nd Strophe

Come on, Thebes, you nursed Semele,
put some ivy in your hair and
teem, I said teem with the green
of the beautiful smilax flower,
and do our Bacchic dance
with oak shoots and pine shoots,
and put a fringe on your spotted fawnskins,
a fringe of white-haired wool,
and be pious when you wave our lusty wands,
for every bit of this land will be dancing
when Bromius leads his gang
from hill to hill, where
his pack of females wait

crazed by Dionysus,
away from their shuttles and looms.

2ND ANTISTROPHE

O cave of the Curetes,
O sacred tenements of Crete
where Zeus was born,
where the Corybants dance
in their three-cornered hats
with the skin-stretched drum they found,
where they mixed up the Bacchic roar
with an intense sweet cry blasted
from Phrygian flutes, and with Bacchic screams
put this banging thing in Mother Rhea's hand,
after whom it ended up
in the hands of crazy satyrs,
and then our choral dance used it,
the one we have every year
in honor of Dionysus.

EPODE

Oh how tremendous it is, when someone is in the hills
and getting dizzy from all the fun
and he falls on the ground and the fawnskin
falls over him while he was chasing the goat for its blood,
and because he likes raw meat,
all the way to the hills of Phrygia, or Lydia,
and Bromius is leading you, Evoi!

The ground is flowing with milk, it's flowing with wine,
it's flowing with the nectar of bees, and a smoke
like Syrian incense, it's the Bacchant
who's holding the firelike pine torch
for a wand, and it spurts as he runs and dances
and as he pricks the slowpokes
screaming as if he'll throw it,

throwing his gorgeously curly hair to the wind,
and on top of everyone's screaming, he yells
"Go Bacchae!
Go Bacchae!
You glamorous girls of gold-flowing Tmolus,
demonstrate for Dionysus
with a strong beat on your drums
and enjoy your enjoyable god
with Phrygian shouts and songs,
when the holy flute blasts beautifully
the holy songs held in your feet
as you go from hill to hill." Then, thrilled,
like a colt jumping around its mother,
every Bacchant, one foot after the other, leaps.

[*Enter* TEIRESIAS, *who knocks on the gates of the palace.*]

TEIRESIAS. Is there anybody here at these gates, call Cadmus out
    for me,
Agenor's son, the man who left the town of Sidon
and put the towers on this city of Thebes,
oh please will somebody go and tell him Teiresias wants him,
he'll know why I'm here,
what we agreed on, as one old man to another—
to decorate wands and put on the skins of fawns
and crown our heads with pieces of ivy!

[*Enter* CADMUS *from the palace.*]

CADMUS. Why my dear friend, I heard your voice in my house
and I knew it was you, the wise voice of a wise man,
and I'm all set, I came wearing the costume of the god,
who is, after all, the son of my own daughter,
this Dionysus, who's shown everybody he's a god,
so that it's only right we honor him as much as we can, but
where should we dance, and where should we place our feet,
and where should we shake our grey heads, Teiresias,
tell me, as one old-timer to another, you who are the wise one,
and all night and all day I won't get tired

banging my wand on the ground, for how sweetly,
how sweetly we'll forget we're old men!
TEIRESIAS. You feel the same way I do then,
   as I feel young myself, and I'll certainly try these dances!
CADMUS. Do you want to go to the hills in our chariots?
TEIRESIAS. No, there wouldn't be much honor for the god in that.
CADMUS. Then as one old man leading the other, I'll show you
   the way.
TEIRESIAS. The god will guide us there with no trouble at all.
CADMUS. Are we going to be the only ones in town dancing for
   Bacchus?
TEIRESIAS. We're the only ones who know what we're doing, not
   those others.
CADMUS. We're taking too long. Take my hand and come on.
TEIRESIAS. Careful, hold my hand tight and lock it in yours.
CADMUS. I'm only a man, so I don't say anything against gods.
TEIRESIAS. No, we don't have much to do with theology, not we
   who've got our fathers' traditions, things old
   as time itself, which no argument's going to knock down,
   since no mind is sharp enough for that,
   and people will say I ought to be ashamed of myself,
   dancing at my age, putting ivy on my head,
   but the god didn't say anything about only the young
   ought to dance or only the old,
   he wants everybody to honor him,
   and what he doesn't want is segregation!
CADMUS. Since you can't even see this torch, Teiresias,
   I'll be your interpreter for you, and tell you that
   Pentheus is coming this way, in a hurry for the palace,
   Echion's son, the one I gave the government to,
   and he looks excited. He's got something to tell.

   [*Enter* PENTHEUS, *first addressing the audience.*]

PENTHEUS. It just so happens that while I'm out of town
   I hear about some new trouble in this city,
   how our women are leaving home
   pretending they're Bacchae or something, jumping in and out

of the hill trees, dancing, all for this Dionysus god,
who's the latest, whoever he is,
and right in the middle of all this ruckus are their wine jugs,
and each one sneaking off into a corner
where she takes care of some man's lust
on the excuse that they're maenad priestesses no less,
while it's really Aphrodite they take care of before Bacchus,
　　so that
I've arrested some of them, and my deputies have them
　　handcuffed
for safe keeping in the prison,
and those who got away I'll hunt down out of the hills,
those like Ino, and even Agave, who's my mother through
　　Echion,
and Actaeon's mother too, Autonoë,
all of whom I'll fit into iron nets
and stop this Bacchic trouble-making right away,
and as for this stranger they tell me has also come to town,
this trickster magician from the land of Lydia,
this curly-haired goldilocks who perfumes his hair,
who goes around with a sexy look in his eye,
who gets together with girls, daytime and nighttime,
proposing some secret pleasures to them,
well if I ever get him inside,
I'll put a stop to his wand-banging, I'll stop his hair
from tossing, why I'll cut his head right off his neck,
he's the one who says Dionysus is a god,
he's the one who says he was sewn up in Zeus' thigh,
when actually he and his mother both burned up
in the flames of lightning, when she lied about Zeus loving
　　her—
(To be so lewd, so insolent, doesn't it call for a hanging,
no matter who this stranger is?)
but isn't that Teiresias
I see in the spots of a fawnskin
and my grandfather too, laughing it up,
waving the wand of a Bacchant—Grandfather,

I can't stand seeing you without a brain in your old head,
won't you shake off that ivy stuff—
Grandfather, won't you please take that wand out of your
  hand—
it's you who got him into this, Teiresias,
you who just want to read bird omens and make more money
  on sacrifices,
so you thought you'd bring people this new god,
you who the only thing that's saving from sitting in prison
locked up with the rest of that Bacchic bunch is old age,
bringing here such sneaky rites, when in my opinion,
whenever an intoxicating beverage is served women at a party
it's the end of any good clean fun!

CHORUS. Such blasphemy! Stranger, where's your respect for gods,
  or even for Cadmus, who, after all, first propagated the race,
  you who are the son of Echion, are you speaking against your
    own family?

TEIRESIAS. When a wise man finds a good opening for a speech
  it's no great accomplishment to be eloquent,
  and you talk like a man with some sense in him, your tongue
    rolls on,
  but there's no sense in any of your words,
  and even if you're bold, powerful, and always ready to speak,
  you're still a bad citizen if you're stupid,
  for this new god whom you go around ridiculing
  will have so much greatness in Greece that even I
  can't say it, and yet there are two prime elements in human
    affairs,
  young man, and the goddess Demeter is one of them—
  she's earth—call her by whatever name you want—
  she's what feeds people with solid food,
  and right after her came the son of Semele, Dionysus,
  who invented wine from grape juice and presented it to men,
  wine which puts a stop to the misery of a weary man
  once he fills up on what flows from the vine,
  wine that is sleep-inducing and makes you forget your daily
    worries,

the only medicine there is for anxiety,
pouring like the god it is in libations,
so that through it men get good things,
and if you are mocking him because he was sewn into Zeus'
thigh,
I'll show you how beautiful this really is,
for when Zeus grabbed him out of the flame of the lightning
and brought the fetus up to Olympus,
Hera wanted to throw the divine little thing out of heaven,
but Zeus, like the god he is, counteracted,
breaking off a part of the gases which encircle the world
and making a copy of Dionysus, *to hide him* from Hera's
anger,
but, in time, people twisted the expression,
and said that Zeus *thighed him* from Hera's anger,
and so they made a legend out of it,
because Zeus copied the real Dionysus, *to hide him* from Hera,
and this god is a prophet, there's a lot of prophecy
in these Bacchic doings and in their hysteria,
and when that god gets deep in a man's body, why
he can make you tell the future, if you're really "gone,"
being a little like Ares, doing a little of Ares' job,
as when an army's all set up, all equipped and in line
and it panics even before it touches a spear,
another madness that you get from Dionysus,
whom you'll see on the rocks at Delphi yet,
jumping with his torches over the double peaks up there,
and he'll be leaping and he'll be shaking his Bacchic wand
and he'll be great throughout Greece, so listen to me, Pentheus,
and don't go boasting that force is the important thing with
men,
and don't think you're smart just because that sick mind of
yours
tells you so, but welcome the god into your land,
pouring libations, living it up, putting a crown on your head!
And Dionysus is not going to *force* women to be chaste—
certainly not—it's always in the character of a woman

whether or not she'll be chaste,
which you'd better take into consideration, and even in Bacchic
   ceremonies
if a woman's really chaste, she won't get hurt,
and you know how happy *you* get when mobs crowd the gates
and the whole city cheers the name Pentheus—
well it's like that with Dionysus, who likes to be honored too,
which is why Cadmus and I, whom you sneer at,
will ivy our heads and dance,
two old crackpots maybe, but we have to dance,
we won't fight the god just on your say-so.
You're the one who's really sick, and there's no medicine
you can take for it, because it's the medicine that made you sick!
CHORUS. Hey, old-timer, you certainly didn't knock Apollo with
    your speech,
   and you honored the great god Bromius very nicely!
CADMUS. Listen, son, Teiresias has given you good advice,
to live with our customs, not outside them,
you who fly off without knowing a thing you're talking about,
and even if this god isn't a god, as you say,
say he is anyway, for it's a beautiful lie to say he is,
and our Semele will then be a god's mother,
and think of the honor for our whole family.
You know how horribly Actaeon died,
how those vicious dogs he raised himself
tore him apart savagely because he bragged
he was better than Artemis in hunting,
well don't you go through something like that—here,
I'll cover your head with ivy, now honor the god with us.
PENTHEUS. Don't put your hands on me, go, play your Bacchus
but don't try to wipe off your nonsense on *me,*
though I'll get even with your teacher here in this foolishness—
quick, somebody go right away
to the place where this man does his birdwatching.
Use crowbars to heave it and turn it all upside down,
throw things all over the place,
toss his ribbons into the wind and into the storm,

that's the way to really hurt him,
and some of you go into the city and track down
the effeminate newcomer who's carrying this strange disease
to our women and spoiling our beds,
and when you catch him, bring him here
in chains—the punishment he gets is stoning,
so that he'll die feeling how sharply we appreciate revelry in
    Thebes!

[*Exit* PENTHEUS.]

TEIRESIAS. Why you cruel thing you, you don't really know what
    you're saying,
you're insane now, where before you were only out of your
    mind—
let's go, Cadmus, let's pray for this one,
wild as he is, let's pray for the city too,
so the god won't do anything strange,
come on, follow me with your ivy wand,
and try to hold my body up while I try to hold up yours,
for it's a shame if two old men like us fall. But we must go,
as Bacchus, the son of Zeus, must be served,
though watch out, Cadmus, that your house doesn't echo with
    repentance
for Pentheus! And I'm not talking prophet talk either,
these are facts—a fool like that is asking for it!

[*Exit* TEIRESIAS *and* CADMUS.]

1ST STROPHE

CHORUS. Did you hear what Pentheus said,
    did you, Holiness, did you, queen of gods, did you,
    Holiness that brings that golden wing of yours
    right down to earth,
    did you hear his outrageous stuff against Bromius,
    it wasn't very holy! against the son of Semele!
    against the top god at festivals
    where the beautiful garlands are!

The god who does these things: who
makes us riot in dances,
makes us chuckle to the flute,
makes us put an end to our worries
when the glory of the grape comes
to a party for the gods
and the wine jug snuggles us asleep
in our ivy, at feasts.

1st Antistrophe

When a man's tongue just won't stay tied
and his nonsense gets out of hand,
what comes is disaster!
And it's a life of peace and quiet,
of common sense,
that lasts without sagging,
that keeps your house together, without sagging,
and the gods up there living in that sky
are a long way off
but they see what's going on with people,
and a wise-guy isn't wisdom,
and if you won't think about human limits
you won't live very long,
and if you start chasing after the hardest prizes
you won't even end up with the easy ones—
it's crazy people do such stuff,
if you ask me, and people who like being mean!

2nd Strophe

I wish I could go to Cyprus,
Aphrodite's island,
where those lovely spirits live
who make men love-crazy,
and I wish I could go to Paphos
where the hundred mouths of that foreign river
saturate you with food though it never rains,
and I'd like to go to Pieria, which is just lovely,

where the Muses all sit around,
and I wish I could go to the sacred hill of Olympus,
oh take me there, Bromius, Bromius,
you're boss of Bacchae, you're our god,
take me where the Graces are and where Desire is
and where there's no law against living it up for Bacchants!

2ND ANTISTROPHE

It's our god, Zeus' son
who gets fun out of feasting,
it's he loves Peace, who brings good things,
a goddess who nurses youth,
and to the man on top
and the man on the bottom too
he brings the careless pleasure of wine,
but he hates the man who isn't interested,
who doesn't want to have the time of his life
by day and by beautiful night,
and he wisely shuns intellectualism
and he stays away from *superior* people,
and it's what the little man believes and does,
what the masses believe and do, that I'm for.

[*Enter* GUARD *with* DIONYSUS. PENTHEUS *enters from the palace.*]

GUARD. We're back, Pentheus, and we didn't go in vain,
  since we've caught that animal you sent us for,
  this wild one, though, was actually tame, not darting away
    from us
  trying to escape on foot, but holding out his hands of his own
    free will,
  and not turning pale, his cheeks weren't even flushed,
  but he laughed and told me to go ahead and tie him up
  and lead him away, and he waited, making my job a snap,
  though I was ashamed of myself, and I said: "I'm not taking
    you, mister,
  because I want to, but because I got orders from Pentheus. He
    sent me."

And remember those women you locked up, Pentheus, the ones
   you arrested
and put in chains in prison,
well, they're gone, they got free, they're out in the hill country
   somewhere
jumping up and down calling on "Bromius" their "god,"
their chains having come off their feet all by themselves,
the doors unbolted by themselves without anyone's hand on
   them—
this one came to Thebes with a lot of miracles in him,
and you take it from there!

PENTHEUS. Untie him—now that I've got him in my net
he's not so quick that he'll get away from me—
well, stranger, you aren't unattractive looking after all,
for women anyway—which is why you're in Thebes,
and judging by your long hair, I'd say you're no wrestler,
since it hangs all the way down to your cheeks—very sexy!
And you have white skin, what care that takes,
you must keep out of sunshine—it's in darkness
you go hunting for Aphrodite with your beauty—
well, first of all, tell me what country you're from.

DIONYSUS. That's an easy one, it's nothing to brag of,
I'm sure you've heard of Tmolus, and its flowers?

PENTHEUS. Yes, I've heard of it, it circles the town of Sardis.

DIONYSUS. That's where I'm from, Lydia's my native land.

PENTHEUS. Why did you bring these ceremonies into Greece?

DIONYSUS. Dionysus, the son of Zeus, consecrated me.

PENTHEUS. You mean there's some Zeus there who's manufacturing
   new gods?

DIONYSUS. Oh no, it's the same Zeus who put the yoke of marriage
   on Semele here.

PENTHEUS. Tell me, did he force you into this when you were
   asleep, or with eyes open?

DIONYSUS. Oh we saw eye to eye on the matter of orgies.

PENTHEUS. What exactly are these orgies that you've got?

DIONYSUS. That's a secret, and if you're not a Bacchant, you can't
   find out.

PENTHEUS. Well what does it do for you, to be in on this?

DIONYSUS. You're not allowed to hear about it, but it would be worth your while to know.

PENTHEUS. You're trying to fake me out, just so I'll want to hear it!

DIONYSUS. A man who does unholy things would loathe the god's orgies.

PENTHEUS. You mean you actually saw the god—what was he like?

DIONYSUS. He was like what he wanted to be like—I didn't compose him you know.

PENTHEUS. You got around that question too without saying anything.

DIONYSUS. Say something clever to a fool and he'll always think it's silly.

PENTHEUS. Is this the first place you've come to, bringing this god?

DIONYSUS. No, every foreign country is dancing to these orgies.

PENTHEUS. They aren't as bright then in their thinking as Greeks are.

DIONYSUS. No, they're smarter—they do have different customs you know.

PENTHEUS. Do you go through these ceremonies in daytime or at night?

DIONYSUS. Mostly at night, since darkness makes it all the more solemn.

PENTHEUS. Yes and more effective in tricking and corrupting the women!

DIONYSUS. You can find lewdness in the daytime too.

PENTHEUS. You'll pay for your wise little answers!

DIONYSUS. And you for your stupidity and your irreverence to the god.

PENTHEUS. How bold our Bacchant is, and by no means unskilled in words.

DIONYSUS. Alright, what am I going to suffer—what terrible thing are you going to do?

PENTHEUS. First of all, I'm going to cut off your pretty little hairdo.

DIONYSUS. My hair is sacred property, and I grow it for the god.

PENTHEUS. Next, hand over that wand of yours!

DIONYSUS. Take it yourself, I carry Dionysus' very own!

PENTHEUS. We'll keep your body under guard in prison.

DIONYSUS. The god himself will release me whenever I want.

PENTHEUS. Sure, sure, and you'll be calling him with the Bacchants
too!

DIONYSUS. Even now he's near, watching what I have to take
from you.

PENTHEUS. Well where is he, he isn't registering on my eyes!

DIONYSUS. Right by me, you can't see him yourself because you're
not holy.

PENTHEUS. Seize him, he's mocking me and Thebes too!

DIONYSUS. I'm warning you—don't chain me—I know better than
you do.

PENTHEUS. I'm the king around here, not you—and I said chain
him!

DIONYSUS. You don't even know your limits, or what you're doing,
or who you are!

PENTHEUS. I'm Pentheus, Agave's my mother, Echion's my father.

DIONYSUS. Your name is quite appropriate—it sounds like
repentance!

PENTHEUS. Get out of here—lock him up in the horse barn
so that he can only see darkness and gloom—
dance in *there,* and as for these ladies you've brought here,
your co-workers in crime, I'll sell them for slaves
or use them for laborers at my looms,
but I'll stop their thumbs from strumming on drums!

DIONYSUS. I'm going, but since I never have to suffer, I'm not
going to,
and Dionysus will get even with you for these insults,
the same Dionysus you say doesn't exist,
it's him you lead away in chains when you think you're
hurting me!

[GUARD *leads* DIONYSUS *away to the stables with* PENTHEUS.]

STROPHE

CHORUS. Dirce, you're the daughter of Achelous,
blessed virgin Dirce,
it was you who received the fetus of Zeus once

in your streams
when Zeus, who made him, scooped him up into his thigh
out of that continuing fire,
and screamed as follows:
"Come on, Dithyrambus,
get into this male womb of mine,
I'm naming you 'Dithyrambus'
and that's how I'm proclaiming you to Thebes."
And yet you drive me away, Dirce, you blessed stream, you,
when I come to you
wearing garlands and living it up, oh
why do you refuse me, why do you avoid me,
for I swear by the grapes
on the vines of Dionysus:
Bromius will interest you yet!

ANTISTROPHE

How outrageously
Pentheus gives away his own very earthly origin,
a product of the dragon
that Echion himself produced,
Echion the earthly, yes,
making Pentheus a wild-eyed monster
and not a human being,
a sanguinary giant that stands against the gods,
and he wants to put his ropes on me,
one of Bromius' own,
he already has our leader
inside his place, hidden away,
in the darkness of his dungeon, and oh,
do you see all this, Dionysus, son of Zeus,
do you see how we, your agents,
are forced into chains—
come on down from Olympus
and shake your golden wand
and cool off his murderer's rage.

Where are you, Dionysus, are you on Mount Nysa,

the mother of animals, waving
to your friends with your wand,
or are you on the tops of Corycia
or are you in some spot on Olympus
where all those trees are
and where Orpheus playing on his lyre
draws all those trees together with his songs
and draws all those wild animals together too,
but oh what a happy place you are, Pieria,
even Evius likes you,
he will come dancing with his Bacchae
when he has crossed the quick Axius river,
bringing his maenads as they gyrate
over Lydias too the Father of Waters,
the one that gives all good things to us all,
its beautiful waves fattening a land
famed for its horses.

DIONYSUS. LISTEN TO ME BACCHAE
LISTEN TO MY VOICE BACCHAE

CHORUS. What was that, that noise that sounded like Evius
calling me?

DIONYSUS. THIS IS THE SON OF SEMELE
THIS IS THE SON OF ZEUS CALLING YOU AGAIN

CHORUS. Oh master, master
come on out here to our activities,
oh Bromius, it's Bromius!

DIONYSUS. NOW BREAK, EARTH, LET THE FLOOR OF
THE EARTH BREAK OPEN!

CHORUS. Suddenly the palace of Pentheus is shaking and
it's going to fall!
and Dionysus is inside the palace,
let us all adore Dionysus—
we bow before him—
look everyone, those blocks over the door
are slipping from their pillars
and Bromius is shouting "Victory" in the palace!

DIONYSUS. BLAST THE LIGHTNING NOW, BLAST THE
BRIGHT LIGHTNING!

SPREAD THE FIRE AROUND PENTHEUS' PALACE!

[*The flame on Semele's tomb increases.*]

CHORUS. Do you see where the fire is! don't you see it
around the sacred tomb of Semele,
the same fire that Semele left us once before
when she was electrocuted by lightning from Zeus!
Throw yourselves down on the ground, maenads,
throw your trembling bodies down on the ground,
for here comes the one who destroyed this palace,
our king, the son of Zeus!

DIONYSUS. Ladies of Asia, were you so scared
that you had to fall on the ground, when you saw
Bacchus shaking up the palace of Pentheus—stand up, please,
and cheer up, get that trembling out of your systems!

CHORUS. Oh you are the brightest light in all our Bacchic activity,
and how happy I am to see you, for I was so lonely, so alone.

DIONYSUS. Were you all depressed when I was taken in,
as if I were really falling into Pentheus' dark dungeon?

CHORUS. How could we help it, for where was our protection if
something happened to you?
And how did you ever get away from that heathen?

DIONYSUS. I saved myself, and it was easy, no trouble at all.

CHORUS. But didn't he have you in handcuffs?

DIONYSUS. That's where I really insulted him—he thought he was
chaining me up
but he never touched me, never laid a finger on me, only his
hopes feeding him,
and in the stable he found a bull where he thought he was
getting me,
a bull which he tried to rope around its hooves and knees,
all the time panting away, sweating from every pore in his body,
biting his lips with his teeth, and I was right beside him
watching him from where I sat very calmly, and it was at this
time
that Bacchus came and shook the palace, and set fire to his
mother's tomb,

which, when Pentheus saw it, thinking his palace was on fire,
he rushed back and forth yelling to his slaves: Bring water,
  bring water,
and every slave he had was on the job—a waste of energy,
but then he put this work aside, afraid I was getting away,
and grabbing his black sword he ran into the palace,
where in the courtyard Bromius had made a kind of phantom
  of me,
or at least that's my opinion, a phantom, or how it appeared
  to me,
and going right for this thing, Pentheus slashed and stabbed at it,
the blazing air! as if he were cutting me up!
in addition to which, Bacchus, humiliating him some more,
knocked down his whole palace, it's all in shambles,
and how bitter he must have felt then for locking me up,
but anyway, out of sheer exhaustion, he dropped his sword,
only a man after all, though he dared to fight it out with a god,
and I walked away quietly and came out here to you, not caring
  about Pentheus,
although I think that sound from heavy shoes in there
means he'll be out front here right away—but what will he say
  after all this?
Even if he comes out with a big snort, though, I think I can
  handle him.
A wise man keeps his temper under control.
[*Enter* PENTHEUS.]
PENTHEUS. Oh, what I've been through! and the stranger got away
  from me,
  he was just a minute ago locked up as a prisoner—
  but there he is—what's going on here, what are you doing
  standing out front of my house here, how did you get out?
DIONYSUS. Calm down, and don't walk so heavily even if you *are*
  angry.
PENTHEUS. Tell me how you got out of my prison and got here?
DIONYSUS. Didn't I tell you, or didn't you hear me, that someone
  would set me free?
PENTHEUS. Who? You always say such strange things!

DIONYSUS. It was the one who grows vines for people—
    you scoff at this beautiful thing Dionysus does?
PENTHEUS. I'm ordering all the towers in this area to be locked up.
DIONYSUS. What for, don't you think gods can walk over walls?
PENTHEUS. You're a wise-guy, a real wise-guy, except where you
    ought to be wise.
DIONYSUS. Where I really ought to be wise I'm wise, don't worry,
    but listen first to what that man there has to say,
    he's come all the way from the hills just to tell you something,
    and I'll wait for you, don't worry, I'm not going anywhere.

[*Enter the* HERDSMAN-MESSENGER.]

MESSENGER. Oh Pentheus, you who rule over this land of Thebes,
    I have come from Mount Cithaeron, whereon never fail to fall
    the bright white arrows of the snow—
PENTHEUS. Alright, what's so important, what's the message?
MESSENGER. I have seen Bacchants raging, who, stung with frenzy,
    shot forth their feet of white, like darts, from this land,
    and I have come to tell you and the city
    what strange things they do—fantastic things!
    But first I have to know if I can talk freely,
    or if I have to cut my speech,
    for the swiftness of your moods, O king, I fear,
    and your anger that is so quick, so over-kingly.
PENTHEUS. Feel free to speak, you won't have any trouble from me,
    for with honest men like you I know better than to get angry,
    and the more you say about how bad these Bacchants are,
    the more I'll punish *this* man,
    who taught all these tricks to our women.
MESSENGER. Our cattle that were at pasture
    were even now on the hillside, climbing,
    when the sun sent up its rays to warm the earth,
    and I see these three bands of Bacchic women
    dancing, the first led by Autonoë,
    the second by your mother, Agave, the third by Ino,
    and all asleep they were, their bodies at rest,
    and some would lean their backs on pines

and some on leaves of oak thrown careless on the ground
would lean their heads, modest—not as you might think,
stoned from drinking and wandering after desire
through the wild wood with a noising of the flute—
and then your mother, standing up, cried out
to the Bacchae: "Wake up, everybody, don't sleep!"
when she heard the mooing of our herd.
And they stood upright, thrusting soft sleep
from their eyes, and it was marvelous, so orderly,
the young women, the old women, the virgins,
and first they dropped their hair down to their shoulders,
then they hitched up their fawnskins, whose bands
had loosened, and then they tied the dappled skins
with serpents that would lick upon their cheeks,
and some, holding wild fawns or wolf cubs
in their arms, gave them their own milk to drink—
they were new mothers who had left their babies
and their breasts were bursting, and they put ivy wreaths on
and wreaths of oak and the flowery smilax,
and one took her wand and beat upon the rock,
and a splash of dewlike water washed up,
and another cast her wand on the floor of the earth
where the god shot out a spring of wine,
and for anyone wanting milk
she sliced the earth with her fingertips
and milk was released, sweet streams of honey
dripping from their wands of ivy.
If you had been there, seeing all this,
you would have approached with prayer the god you now revile.
And then we herdsmen and shepherds came together,
to get each other's view
of what terrible things they were doing, terrible and marvelous,
when a man from the city, one quick with words,
said to us all: "You hill people,
what do you say we hunt for Pentheus' mother, Agave,
get her out of all this horsing around
and get ourselves in good with the king?"

And this seemed like a good idea to us, hiding ourselves in the
    leaves
for ambush, until at their appointed time
the Bacchae moved their wands in revelry, calling
"Iacchus, the son of Zeus," all together,
calling for Bromius, and then all the hillside
and all the beasts reveled too, and nothing was unmoved as
    they moved.
Then quite by chance Agave leaped near me,
and I ran out to try to grab her,
leaving behind the leaves where I was hid,
and she cried: "You bitches running with me:
MEN ARE AFTER US! Follow me,
use your wands as weapons!"
We immediately ran away, escaping
a Bacchic slaughter, while they, unarmed,
swooped down on our cattle grazing there,
and then you could have seen a heifer, deep-uddered,
mooing, cut in two by a woman's hands,
and others chopped up the calves into pieces
and ribs and cloven hooves
were thrown here and there, scraps of flesh
dabbled with blood dripping from the fir trees,
and bulls raging, angry in their horns,
stumbled their bodies onto the earth,
dragged down by the hands of masses of girls,
and they stripped the flesh
faster than you could blink your royal eyes,
and they went along like birds lifted soaring
over the on-lying plains which bear rich harvests
to the Theban people by the streams of Asopus,
on Hysiae, on Erythrae, towns beneath the hills of Cithaeron,
they swooped down like an enemy
turning over everything, up and down
they turned over everything, and they grabbed up
babies from their homes and all these
they put on their shoulders, and though they tied up nothing

with bonds, nothing fell down to the black earth,
nothing of bronze, nothing of iron, and they carried fire
in their hair, though it did not burn them,
till in anger people came out bearing arms against the Bacchae.
Then this terrible thing happened, O king,
sharp spears drew no blood from them,
but instead, the Bacchae, firing their wands from their hands
wounded *men,* and they, *women,* drove away *men*
in flight, some god being on their side,
and back they went to where they first moved their feet,
to those same founts sprung for them by the god
where they washed off the blood, and serpents from their cheeks
licked with their tongues the drops of gore.
Whoever, then, this god is, my lord,
welcome him to this city, for in addition to all this,
they say of him, I hear,
that he gave wine to man, an end to anxiety.
And when man shall be no longer wined,
there shall be no love, no further joy for humankind.

CHORUS. I'm scared to speak freely to this tyrant of ours,
but now I'll say it anyway:
No god is better than Dionysus!

PENTHEUS. What these Bacchae are stirring up is getting too hot
for us,
it's spreading like wildfire, it's disgracing us all over Greece,
so we'll waste no time—you, go to the Electra Gate,
order every soldier that's got a shield,
every rider than can handle a fast horse,
every man who can bend a bow with his hand,
everyone who can carry anything,
we're going to attack the Bacchae—this is going too far
to put up with all we've had to take from our women!

DIONYSUS. So you're still not convinced, Pentheus, after all I've said,
but though you've made me suffer terribly
I'll tell you again: don't lift a finger against a god
and hold your peace, for Bromius will not stand by
while you blast his Bacchae out of the hills they love.

PENTHEUS. Don't tell *me* what to do, you who got out of prison once,
do you want me to punish you again?

DIONYSUS. I'd rather offer a sacrifice than get angry
and have to kick against the pricks all the time, when it's man versus god!

PENTHEUS. Oh I'll sacrifice alright, and what's a worthy victim? His women!
There'll be a hot time in the woods of Cithaeron tonight!

DIONYSUS. You'll all end up running away from it, and what a disgrace then,
shields of bronze retreating from the wands of Bacchae!

PENTHEUS. It's no use getting all tangled up with this stranger,
for even when it hurts him he doesn't shut up.

DIONYSUS. My friend, I tell you this business can still turn out well.

PENTHEUS. What do I have to do, bow down to my own slaves?

DIONYSUS. I'll bring the women back here, and without an army.

PENTHEUS. Oh my, now you're trying to put me in a trap!

DIONYSUS. Where's the trap—can't I just want to save you with my own methods?

PENTHEUS. You're in cahoots with them, you just want this rabble-rousing to go on and on!

DIONYSUS. I'm in cahoots alright, but it's with a *god!*

PENTHEUS. Bring me my weapons, and will you please
SHUT UP!

DIONYSUS. Hold on—
How would you like to see what they're doing up in the hills?

PENTHEUS. Would I! I'd give anything to see it!

DIONYSUS. But why so anxious?

PENTHEUS. Well, uh, seeing them drunk, would be, uh, pretty ghastly . . .

DIONYSUS. Ghastly or not, you'd still like to see it, is that it?

PENTHEUS. Of course that's it! quietly, under the pines, lying still . . .

DIONYSUS. You know they'll track you down though, even if you do come secretly!

PENTHEUS. Yes, you're right, what you say is right, I'll go openly!

DIONYSUS. Shall I take you then, will you really give it a try?

PENTHEUS. Let's go right now, don't take any more time!

DIONYSUS. Put on some women's clothes then.

PENTHEUS. What *is* this, am I supposed to change from a man into a woman?

DIONYSUS. They'd kill you if you were seen there as a man.

PENTHEUS. Yes, you're right again, you're really very clever.

DIONYSUS. It's something I picked up from Dionysus.

PENTHEUS. Tell me what to do then, you're the one who's good at this.

DIONYSUS. I'll go in your palace and dress you, come on.

PENTHEUS. But in what dress, in a woman's dress? I'd be humiliated!

DIONYSUS. Then you're not very anxious after all to see the maenads, are you?

PENTHEUS. What dress do you want me to put on?

DIONYSUS. First I'll put a long wig on your head.

PENTHEUS. Then what, what's the rest of my outfit?

DIONYSUS. A dress that's down to your ankles, and a nice hat for your head!

PENTHEUS. And is there anything else you will give me?

DIONYSUS. A wand for your hand and a spotted fawnskin.

PENTHEUS. I JUST CAN'T PUT A WOMAN'S DRESS ON!

DIONYSUS. Then fight the Bacchae, spill blood.

PENTHEUS. Yes, you're right, first we've got to go spy on them.

DIONYSUS. That's at least wiser than trying to catch evil with evil.

PENTHEUS. But how can I get through the city of Cadmus without being seen?

DIONYSUS. The streets we take will be deserted, and I'll lead you.

PENTHEUS. Anything's better than having these Bacchae laugh at me,
   but I'm going inside now, I want to think over your advice.

DIONYSUS. That's fair enough, and in any case, I'm always ready to help.

PENTHEUS. I'm going in, and I'll either march out, armed to the teeth,
   or take your advice.

[*Exit* PENTHEUS.]

DIONYSUS. Well ladies, we've got our man in the net,
  and he'll find the Bacchae, but it will cost him his life.
  Dionysus, it's up to you now. You're close now.
  Now we'll get our revenge. First, put him out of his mind,
  then pour a little insanity in, since in his right mind
  he'd never be able to put a woman's dress on,
  but once he goes out of his mind he'll put it on,
  and after those threats of his before, which were just terrible,
  I'll make him the laughingstock of Thebes,
  led through the city looking like a woman.
  I'm going, I'll deck him out in the clothes
  he'll be wearing to Hades, slaughtered by his mother's hands,
  and he'll recognize Dionysus, the son of Zeus,
  who's out at last, the most terrible god of all,
  and yet the kindest too, for humankind.

[*Exit* DIONYSUS.]

STROPHE

CHORUS. Do you mean I'll be putting down my white foot again
  in those dances of ours that go all night
  living it up, and in the dew of the air
  I'll be tossing my neck,
  like a fawn playing again
  in the green pleasures of a meadow,
  when she gets away
  from the frightening hunt
  and jumps woven nets
  while the hunters speed up their dogs
  with all that screaming,
  when the running is so hard,
  when she has to leap like the wind
  over a river-plain,
  who loves the darkness of the forest,
  among the lonely tree shoots
  where there are no men?

What's wisdom or glory
next to this gift the gods give men:
to hold your winning hand
over the heads of your enemies,
for glory is something we'll always love.

ANTISTROPHE

Divine power doesn't come on strong
at first, but it sure is there,
knocking down the man
who exalts his own arrogance,
who keeps it up, all for some crazy notion,
and never thinks of the gods,
the gods who hide very slyly
but time's long foot marches on
and they hunt down the heathen,
and it's wrong to think you're better than the law,
and it's wrong to act as if you were,
and it doesn't cost you much
to believe in this:
what's divine is strong,
what we've had for a long time,
based on nature,
is to be believed.

What's wisdom or glory
next to this gift the gods give men:
to hold your winning hand
over the heads of your enemies,
for glory is something we'll always love.

It's a lucky man who escapes a storm at sea
and gets to where he's going,
a lucky man who can chuck his troubles
and one man always gets more than another
in money and power,
and for every million people

there are a million dreams,
and some people end up rich,
others bankrupt,
but it's the man who has a good life day by day
who's the happy one, bless him.

[*Enter* DIONYSUS *from the palace, calling* PENTHEUS *out.*]

DIONYSUS. Come on out here, you eager beaver for things you're
    not supposed to see,
always chasing after the wrong thing, yes I mean you, Pentheus,
come on out here in front of your palace, let's see you
now that you've got on your woman's dress, you mad Bacchant
    you,
spying on your own mother and her bunch—
oh my, if it isn't one of the daughters of Cadmus!

[*Enter* PENTHEUS, *dressed as a Bacchant.*]

PENTHEUS. Why—
    I think I see two suns
    and two cities of Thebes, each with seven gates,
    and you mister, you look like a bull going in front of me
    and you seem to have grown horns on your head.
    Were you an animal before too? You're certainly a bull now!
DIONYSUS. It's a god that's walking with you, one who wasn't
        gentle with you before
    but he's friends with us now, and what you see now you're
        supposed to see.
PENTHEUS. What do I look like, don't I look like Ino,
    don't I seem to stand like my own mother Agave?
DIONYSUS. Yes, as I look at you I do seem to see them,
    but wait, one of your curls has come out of place here,
    it's not how I fixed it under your hat.
PENTHEUS. I guess I knocked it out of place
    when I was throwing myself back and forth in my Bacchic
        frenzy.

DIONYSUS. I'll fix it again for you, I'll be your maid,
    just hold your head back.
PENTHEUS. There—now you take care of it, I'm leaving everything
    up to you.
DIONYSUS. Now your girdle's come loose
    and the pleats of your dress aren't hanging even at your ankles.
PENTHEUS. Oh, you're right, my right foot's not even
    but it's hanging right on the left side.
DIONYSUS. You know, you'll think I'm your best friend
    after the surprise of seeing how good the Bacchae really are.
PENTHEUS. Which way should I hold my wand, in the right hand
    like this,
    or like this, which way seems more professional?
DIONYSUS. You hold it in your right hand and at the same time
    you lift your right foot, and good for you for changing your
        mind.
PENTHEUS. Do you think I could lift up the whole of Mount
    Cithaeron
    on my shoulders, with all the Bacchae on it too?
DIONYSUS. You could if you want to, and though you were crazy
    before,
    you're now thinking like a sane man!
PENTHEUS. Will I heave up the cliffs with my arm or shoulders,
    or should we bring crowbars?
DIONYSUS. You don't want to destroy the nymphs' shrines, do you,
    and where Pan hangs out playing his pipe?
PENTHEUS. Oh no, you're right, women mustn't be beaten by force,
    I'll hide myself under the pines.
DIONYSUS. Hide? You'll have to hide
    if you come to the maenads spying and tricking them.
PENTHEUS. Yes, it's as if I can see them now, like birds in the
    bushes
    all tangled up in their loving.
DIONYSUS. That's why you're going—to watch them,
    and maybe you'll catch a glimpse of them, maybe they'll catch
        you!

PENTHEUS. Take me right through the center of Thebes,
  me, the only man in this whole city who'd dare this!
DIONYSUS. Yes, you're the only one whom the city wears out, the
    only one,
  and there's a hard job ahead of you,
  so follow me, I'll guide you there very safely,
  though somebody else will bring you back.
PENTHEUS. My mother, I'll bet you!
DIONYSUS. You will be noticed by everyone.
PENTHEUS. That's what I'm coming for!
DIONYSUS. You will be carried when you come back—
PENTHEUS. My usual luxury of course!
DIONYSUS. —in the arms of your mother.
PENTHEUS. Oh, you'll make me go soft!
DIONYSUS. Yes, you'll be very soft.
PENTHEUS. It's only what I deserve.
DIONYSUS. You're a strange man, a strange man, and it's a strange
    experience ahead of you,
  but the glory you will get from it will rise up to the sky.

[*Exit* PENTHEUS.]

Hold out your hands, Agave, and you other daughters of
  Cadmus,
for I'm bringing this youngster to a great contest,
where I will be the winner and Bromius will be the winner,
and everything else will be shown in due course.

[*Exit* DIONYSUS.]

STROPHE

CHORUS. Go you dogs of madness, quick, quick, go to the hills
  where the daughters of Cadmus are having their riot, quick,
  bite them rabid
  against this madman who spies on maenads
  in a woman's dress!

He'll be peeking from a smooth rock or from a tree
and his mother will be the first to see

and she'll yell to the maenads, she'll yell:
"Hey Bacchae, who's that Peeping Tom
that's come all the way up these hills
to see the women of Thebes running around,
who, who was *his* mother?
He wasn't born from the blood of a woman,
maybe from some lady lion
or from one of the Gorgons of Libya!"

Come on, Justice, show yourself, come on and bring your sword,
killing him clean through his throat
that godless lawless unjust earthborn son
of Echion.

ANTISTROPHE

He's got the mind of a criminal, he's got a criminal's rage
over your orgies, Bacchus, and your mother's,
he has the heart of a lunatic,
he has the gall of a true crackpot to come
thinking he'll beat with force those who are unbeatable!

There is no sorrow in life
for the wise mind, for the honest man concerned with the gods,
for the man who knows his limit,
and in the wisdom I am hunting for so happily
there is no envy, there are other things,
great things, and they have always been known,

the beautiful things in life
from day to night, and to be pure in my reverence,
honoring gods and keeping away
from outlaws.

Come on, Justice, show yourself, come on and bring your sword,
killing him clean through his throat
that godless lawless unjust earthborn son
of Echion.

EPODE

Let's see you as a bull, Dionysus,
let's see you as a dragon with lots of heads,
let's see you as a lion burning fire,
and hey, Bacchus, come on, put a smile on your face
and throw your net over this Bacchae-hunter,
as he falls
under the herd of your murdering maenads!

[*Enter* MESSENGER-SERVANT.]

MESSENGER. Oh to think this house was once so well-off in Greece
and that it was the old man from Sidon
who put the seed of the dragon in this land of the snake,
well how I weep for you, only a slave and yet
good slaves share the misfortunes of their masters.
CHORUS. What's the matter, do you have any news of the Bacchae?
MESSENGER. Pentheus is dead, the son of Echion is dead.
CHORUS. Oh Bromius, you *are* a king, now we see what a great
god you are!
MESSENGER. What are you saying, what is this, are you women glad
at this terrible thing for my master?
CHORUS. I'm a foreigner, and this is the way we rejoice abroad, and
hurray, I don't have to be afraid of going to prison anymore!
MESSENGER. Do you think Thebes is so out of men that—
CHORUS. It's Dionysus, it's Dionysus who rules me,
not Thebes!
MESSENGER. Well, you might be forgiven, except that it isn't nice,
ladies—
to rejoice when disaster has struck!
CHORUS. Tell me how he died, how an unjust man
who lived an unjust life died? Come on, tell us!
MESSENGER. Well, when we got past the last houses of this land of
ours, Thebes,
and we crossed the river of Asopus,
we started up the huge rock of Cithaeron,
Pentheus and I—I was working for my master,

and that stranger, who was to be our guide for the spectacle,
and first we sat down in a grassland,
keeping our feet still and our tongues from moving
so that we'd see them but they wouldn't see us,
and there was a valley, with cliffs all around it and broken by
    streams
and shaded very well by pines, and here the maenads sat
with their hands at work on things they enjoy,
some topping their shabby wands
with fresh leaves of ivy,
others like fillies that have just had their bridles removed,
chanting back and forth to each other some Bacchic music,
but poor old Pentheus, he couldn't see these women at all
so he said: "Hey, stranger, from where I'm standing
I can't see these phony maenads at all—
if I climb that hill, though, or that large pine over there
I could see the lewdness of these maenads a lot better,"
and then I saw the stranger do something very strange,
for then reaching the top branch of a towering pine tree
he pulled it and pulled it and pulled it down to the dark ground,
so that it was curved like a bow or like the curve of a wheel
after you turn it on a lathe to round off its edge,
and the stranger bent that mountain tree down to the ground
just like that with his own bare hands, which no man could do,
and then he set Pentheus down on those pine branches
and let the trunk slide up through his hands
very softly, making sure that it didn't throw him off,
and the tree straightened itself up into the sky
with my master sitting on top of it,
but the maenads saw him a lot better than he saw them,
and no sooner was he spotted up there
when BANG, the stranger was no longer anywhere around,
and a voice from out of the sky—it sounded like the voice of
    Dionysus—
cried out: "Well, girls, I've brought him to you, our orgy-mocker,
he mocks you and he mocks me and he mocks our orgies too,
    go get him!"

and just as he was speaking he fired a blast of terrible flames
up into the sky and down onto the earth,
and the air itself was soundless, and that whole shaded valley
held every leaf silent, and you couldn't hear a peep from any of
    the animals,
but the Bacchae didn't quite catch what the voice had said,
and they shot up bobbing their heads all over the place,
so that he sounded off again, and this time the daughters of
    Cadmus
knew very well it was an order from their Bacchus,
and they soared out and I tell you their feet were as fast as doves
that keep gaining on each other as they race,
Pentheus' mother, Agave, and her sisters
and all the Bacchae, and they went through a torrent even
and over boulders and the god was breathing madness into
    their feet,
and when they saw my master just sitting up there on top of
    his tree,
they climbed up a huge rock opposite his position
and fired boulders at him and then they launched spears made
    of pine
and others shot their wands through the air at Pentheus,
but their aim was poor, and they didn't get anywhere,
and poor old Pentheus just sat up there, way out of reach
knowing that things were now hopeless,
and as a last resort they banged down oak branches that fell
    like thunder,
and then with wooden crowbars they pried at the roots of the
    tree itself,
and when all this work got them nowhere,
Agave said: "Come on, girls, everybody grab part of the trunk,
we've got to catch this little animal we've treed
or he'll blab all the secrets of our god!"
And then a thousand little hands went around that pine tree
and they tore it right out of the ground,
and from his lofty perch Pentheus fell all the way down to the
    ground

with all kinds of screams and cries,
knowing now he was near the end,
and his mother was the first one to drop on him,
beginning the slaughter like a true priestess,
but he tore off the hat he had over his hair
so she'd recognize him and wouldn't kill him—
poor Agave—and he touched her cheeks and he said:
"It's me, mother, it's your son, Pentheus!
You and Echion are my own parents!
Have pity on me, mother! Don't kill your own son
just because he did something wrong!"
But she was foaming at the mouth and her eyes were rolling around
in her head like a crazy woman, and she was completely out of her mind,
a woman possessed by Bacchus, not thinking of her son,
and she grabbed his left arm at the wrist
and placed her foot against his ribs, the poor thing,
and then she tore his shoulder off, not by her own strength, of course,
the god put that power in her hands,
and Ino was working on the other side of him,
pulling off his flesh, and Autonoë was at it, and all the Bacchae
were hard at it, though there was only one screaming sound,
they yelling for joy, Pentheus yelling with what breath he had left,
and one of the Bacchae had taken off an arm, another
a shoe with the foot still in it,
his ribs being stripped to the bone in little shreds,
and they were playing ball with parts of his body, their hands all blood,
and his body is now lying all over the place, part of it next to some rocks,
some of it deep inside the forest in some leaves—
it would be a hard job to find it—and his pitiful head
which his mother happened to find, she picked up
and stuck on the top of her wand, and she's carrying it

all over Mount Cithaeron as if it were the head of a mountain
    lion,
having left her sisters behind doing their maenad dances,
and she's coming inside these walls gloating over her horrible
    catch,
calling to Bacchus, her "fellow hunter," her "helper in the chase,"
"the triumphant one," though for all her triumph she wins only
    tears,
but I'm getting out of this miserable place
before Agave gets back,
yes, the best thing for a man is to restrain himself, and be
    reverent to the gods,
I think this is the wisest thing any man can do.
It's his best possession. [*Exit.*]

ASTROPHA

CHORUS. Let's all do a dance for Bacchus,
    let's all shout about the death of Pentheus,
    the man who was born from a dragon is dead,
    the man who put on a woman's dress is dead,
    the man who took one of our beautiful wands
    has taken it down to Hades,
    letting a bull lead him to disaster,
    Bacchae, ladies of Thebes,
    you have a tremendous victory, a beautiful victory,
    in your tears and in your weeping,
    for it's a beautiful game, oh yes, when a mother dips her hands
    in the dripping blood of her son,

    but now I see the mother of Pentheus, I see you Agave,
    crazy-eyes, I see you running home,
    welcome to the party for our god!

[*Enter* AGAVE, *holding* PENTHEUS' *head on her wand. A few of her
followers wait by the entrance.*]

STROPHE

AGAVE. Bacchae! Asians!

CHORUS. What's all the excitement, speak up!
AGAVE. Look at this new hunk of ivy
    we've brought home from the mountain,
    a good catch!
CHORUS. I see it, welcome to our party!
AGAVE. I trapped him myself without any equipment,
    see, it's the cub of a mountain lion,
    that's obvious, isn't it?
CHORUS. How far out of your way did you go?
AGAVE. Cithaeron—
CHORUS. Cithaeron what?
AGAVE. Cithaeron killed him.
CHORUS. Who hit him first?
AGAVE. I did, he's my prize,
    "Lucky Agave" they call me at our assemblies.
CHORUS. What happened next?
AGAVE. The, uh, Cadmus', uh—
CHORUS. The what? Cadmus' what?
AGAVE. Daughters—
    they touched the beast only after me, after me, after me,
    oh what a great hunt,

ANTISTROPHE

    but you get your share of the feast: here!
CHORUS. You poor dear, what are you talking about, my share?
AGAVE. This is a young one:
    under the part of its head where the hair is
    there's a soft fuzz blooming on his cheeks.
CHORUS. Yes, with all that hair it does look like a beast.
AGAVE. Bacchus whipped up the maenads
    when they were hunting this one,
    Bacchus is great!
CHORUS. That's our king, Bacchus, a real hunter!
AGAVE. NOW do you praise me?
CHORUS. Why not, I praise you.
AGAVE. And soon the men of Thebes—
CHORUS. And of course your own son, Pentheus—
AGAVE. Yes, he too will praise his mother,

she caught this lion, she bagged it.

CHORUS. A very unusual catch!

AGAVE. Very unusually caught!

CHORUS. Are you proud of yourself?

AGAVE. I'm so happy—
    I did something big on this hunt, something great!
    It's so obvious!

CHORUS. Well then, you miserable woman, show everyone in
        town now
    your prize, show them what you've brought back.

AGAVE. Thebans! You who live in the land
    of the beautiful towers, Thebes, look what I've caught,
    not with any of those special spears you get in Thessaly,
    not with nets, we used our own lily white hands
    to catch this animal, we ladies of Thebes,
    so what good is all your bragging now,
    and all that silly gear you get from armorers,
    we caught this thing here with our bare hands,
    and we tore its limbs apart with our bare hands—
    but where's my father at—let him get a close look,
    and where's that son of mine, Pentheus?
    Have him set a ladder against the wall of the palace
    so he can nail up on the beam up there this head
    I brought home from some lion.

[*Enter* CADMUS *and attendants carrying the remains of* PENTHEUS.]

CADMUS. Follow me, men, bring that horrible pile of Pentheus
    and follow me out front of the palace.
    That's the body, after hard work and endless searching,
    or what I found of it scattered all over the valley
    of Mount Cithaeron, not one bit of it in the same place
    as the rest, and those woods just impossible,
    for I heard all about what my daughters were doing
    when I got back into town
    away from the Bacchae, with old Teiresias,
    and I turned right around for the mountain again
    to get my son those maenads killed,

and I saw the mother of Actaeon there, Aristaeus' wife,
and I saw Ino up there too in those oak trees
and both of those poor demented creatures were still excited,
one of them telling me that Agave was coming here,
raving—well at least that was the truth,
I see her now, not a very pretty sight.

AGAVE. Daddy, can you ever be proud of us,
you who produced the best daughters any man ever did
by a long shot—I say daughters, but I mean really me,
me, who left my shuttle by the loom
and took off for better things, hunting big game with my
    hands now,
and see this here, I brought it home in my own arms,
it's my trophy, we'll hang it up at home—
come on, father, you take it once in your hands,
and call all your friends for a party and enjoy my trophy,
for now that we've done this, father,
we'll have to call you blessed.

CADMUS. Oh, what agony, it's beyond my power to grasp, there's
    no end to it,
you did this murder with your own hands,
a fine sacrifice to be tossing to the gods,
a great feast to be inviting me and the rest of Thebes to,
I pity you, what you've done, and I pity myself too,
and the god was right to do it to us, it was Bromius, King
    Bromius
who ruined us, one of our own family!

AGAVE. How grouchy old men are, how creepy when they look
    at you,
I hope my son is more like his mother, a good hunter,
when he goes hunting with other Theban boys,
though all that one ever does is quarrel with the gods,
and if he deserves a talking-to, father,
it's your job to give it to him,
and will somebody please call him out here where I can see him
and where he can see what a happy mother he's got!

CADMUS. Stop it! Stop it! When you find out what you've really
    done, all of you,

your pain will be terrible, and only if you keep up this craziness
until the day you die
could you ever be well off—
AGAVE. What's wrong here? Why are you so miserable?
CADMUS. First lift your head up and look at the sky.
AGAVE. So—why do you want me to look up there though?
CADMUS. Does it look the same, or does it seem any different?
AGAVE. Why, it's brighter, it's clearer than before.
CADMUS. Do you still feel all shaken up inside?
AGAVE. I don't know what you mean by that, my head feels a little
    clearer though,
    it doesn't feel the same as it did before.
CADMUS. Can you hear me, can you give me a straight answer now?
AGAVE. I forgot what we were talking about before father.
CADMUS. Whose house did you marry into when you were married?
AGAVE. Why you gave me away to Echion, father.
CADMUS. And who was the son that you and Echion had?
AGAVE. Pentheus, Echion and I gave birth to Pentheus.
CADMUS. And whose head are you holding in your hands?
AGAVE. A lion's—that's what the hunters told me it was.
CADMUS. Look right at it, that's not much trouble, is it, to look
    right at it?
AGAVE [screams]. What am I looking at, what have I got in my
    hands?
CADMUS. Take a good look, make sure!
AGAVE. This is the worst thing I've ever seen!
CADMUS. Do you think it looks like a lion's head now?
AGAVE. It's Pentheus' head, I'm holding Pentheus' head!
CADMUS. I was crying long before you ever recognized him.
AGAVE. Who killed him, what is he doing in my hands?
CADMUS. What a horrible time to have to learn the truth!
AGAVE. Tell me, my heart's pounding at what you're going to say!
CADMUS. You did it, you killed him, you and those sisters of yours.
AGAVE. Where was he killed, at home, where?
CADMUS. Remember where those dogs once tore apart Actaeon?
AGAVE. Cithaeron, but why did my poor son ever go up there?
CADMUS. He went to mock god and to sneer at your orgies.

AGAVE. *Our* orgies? what were we doing up there?

CADMUS. You were crazy, everybody in town went crazy over
    Bacchus.

AGAVE. Dionysus destroyed us all, only now do I understand it.

CADMUS. In a way, you insulted him, you didn't think he was
    a god.

AGAVE. Father, where's the body of this son I loved so much?

CADMUS. I brought it here, after laboriously locating the pieces.

AGAVE. Is the body fixed properly?
    What did Pentheus ever do that he had to suffer for my
    foolishness?

CADMUS. He was just like you, he didn't have any respect for
    the god,
    and that's why we were all taken care of with one blast,
    you and your sisters, and him, the whole family gone to pieces
    now,
    myself included, never having had any sons of my own,
    and now I see this boy that came out of your womb,
    you poor creature, murdered in such a vicious way.
    Child, you were someone our house looked up to,
    you held it together, and you were the son of one of my own,
    you meant terror to the city, nobody insulted your grandfather
    once they looked you in the eyes or you'd make him pay for it,
    and now I have to clear out of here, in shame,
    me—the great Cadmus! who planted the seed of the Theban
    people
    and reaped such a grand harvest,
    oh, my son, I loved you more than anyone else,
    and even though you are dead now I still count you my most
    loved friend,
    your hand that will never touch my chin anymore,
    and you'll never grab me and say: "Grandfather,
    who's bothering you? Is anyone insulting you, old man?
    Who's getting on your nerves that you're so sad?
    Tell me, Grandfather, and I'll fix the troublemaker for you!"
    Well now I am really sad, and you're wretched,
    your mother and her sisters pitiful,

and if there is still anyone around who snubs the gods
he can look at the death of this one, and start believing!
CHORUS. I'm sorry for you, Cadmus, though your grandson got
    only what he deserved,
but I'm sorry that his death hurts you.
AGAVE. Father, you see how changed I am now,[1]
    [I see now that what I was carrying in my own hands
was a curse, but how can I hold this body in my arms now,
or press him to my breast in some tender way,
or cry over him?
Is there some cloth we can wrap him in?
Are my hands the ones that should take care of him?
But come, let's put his head back with his body
and lay out the body as best we can—
there is the face I once loved, how young it is,
I'm covering over your head now with this cloth,
I'm covering over these blood-soaked limbs of yours.

[DIONYSUS *appears above the wall of the palace.*]

DIONYSUS. Everything that this man suffered he deserved to suffer,
he deserved to be torn up on those rocks,
trying to chain me, insulting me,
that's why he was killed by the last person in the world
who should have killed him, but as for the rest of you,
I won't hide from you what this country has in store:
some day you will all be driven into other lands, away from here,
because of what you have done,
and you, Agave, and your sisters, must leave this city: get out,
you must pay for this murder of yours, leaving Thebes for good,
for murderers have no place beside the graves of their victims,]
and as for you, Cadmus, you will be changed into a snake,
and your wife, Harmonia, the daughter of Ares, becomes a
    snake too,
an animal, and the oracle of Zeus says that you and your wife
will drive a chariot of oxen, leading a pack of foreigners

---

1. The lines in brackets have been added by the translator to fill a lacuna
in the Greek text.

and with such an innumerable army you will destroy many
    cities,
but when they pillage the shrine of Apollo,
they will find their trip home a very bitter one,
but Ares will save you, and he will save Harmonia
and he will give both of you life among the blessed,
and I, Dionysus, tell this to you all—I who was not born of a
    mortal father,
but from Zeus—if you had only been wise before,
when you refused to be, you would be blessed now
and you would have the son of Zeus on your side.

AGAVE. Dionysus, we're begging you, we've sinned!

DIONYSUS. It's too late to know me now, you didn't when you had
    time to.

AGAVE. We know that now, but you're being too hard on us.

DIONYSUS. I am a god, I was deeply offended by you.

AGAVE. It isn't right that gods should get as angry as men.

DIONYSUS. My father, Zeus, arranged this a long time ago.

AGAVE. Father, it is all Fate, we are wretched exiles.

DIONYSUS. Why do you delay then, all these things have to be.

[*Exit* DIONYSUS.]

CADMUS. Oh my daughter, what terrible trouble we're in now,
all of us, you and your sisters and myself,
for I'm an old man and I have to go be an immigrant
and live among foreigners, doomed
to lead some mixed-up foreign army against Greece,
and my wife, Harmonia, the daughter of Ares,
I have to bring her against Greek altars and tombs
along with armed men, and both of us in the form of snakes
and my troubles will never stop, I won't even have the peace
of sailing down the stream of Death.

AGAVE. Oh father, I'll be an exile, I'll be taken away from you!

CADMUS. Why are you throwing your arms around me, you poor
    thing,
you're like a white swan with its tired old father.

AGAVE. Where can I go, I'm banished from my own country!

CADMUS. I don't know, child, your father's not much help anymore.

AGAVE. Then good-bye, my house, good-bye my city and land,
    I leave you, feeling miserable, an exile from the bed of my
        marriage!
CADMUS. Go on, child, try the house of Aristaeus.
AGAVE. Father, I just pity you.
CADMUS. I pity you, child,
    and I cry because of your sisters too.
AGAVE. Terribly, terribly
    Dionysus did this outrage
    to your house.
CADMUS. But he suffered some awful things from you, and the
      others.
    Remember, his name wasn't honored in Thebes.
AGAVE. Good-bye, father.
CADMUS. Good-bye, my daughter,
    if there's some good you can find—
AGAVE [*turning to attendants waiting at entrance to the stage*].
    Those of you who are going to guide me,
    take me to my sisters, we're fellow-exiles in our misery.
    I want to go
    where that filthy Cithaeron can't see me
    and where I can't see it with my own eyes,
    and where there's nothing to remind me of the wand.
    I leave all that to other Bacchae.

    [*Exit, followed by* CADMUS.]

CHORUS. The gods have many forms,
    the gods can bring many surprises,
    and they don't do what you usually expect,
    as this god who found a way for the unexpected.
    And that's how this whole thing happened.

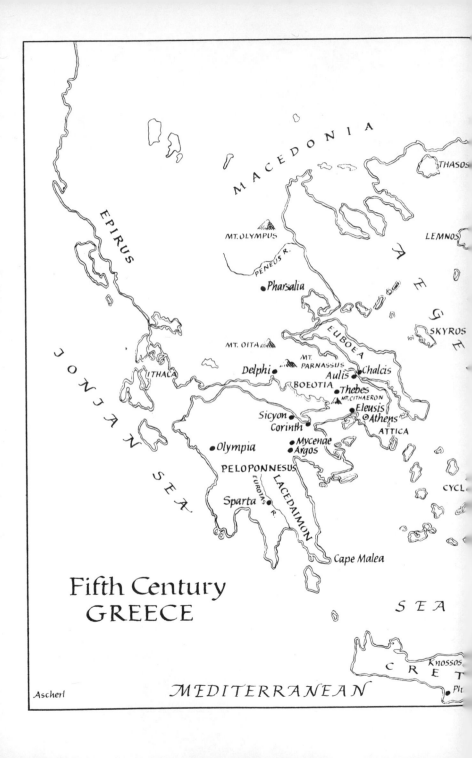

Fifth Century
GREECE

MEDITERRANEAN

EUXINE SEA
(BLACK SEA)

THRACE

PROPONTIS

HELLESPONT
Troy

PHRYGIA

LESBOS

IONIA

LYDIA

SAMOS

Miletus

CARIA

RHODES

CRETE

SEA

Paphos →
on CYPRUS

0   25   50   75   100
MILES

Eleusis

Salamis

SALAMIS

Colonus
Athens
Piraeus

SARONIC GULF

0   3   6   9
MILES